Mazes for the Mind:

Computers and the Unexpected

Mazes for the Mind:
Computers and the Unexpected

Clifford A. Pickover

St. Martin's Press New York

© Clifford A. Pickover, 1992

All rights reserved. For information, write:
Scholarly and Reference Division,
St. Martin's Press, Inc., 175 Fifth Avenue, New York, N.Y. 10010

First published in the United States of America in 1992

Printed in the United States of America

Library of Congress Cataloging-in-Publication Data

Pickover, Clifford A.
    Mazes for the mind : computers and the unexpected /
Clifford A. Pickover.
        p.   cm.
    Includes bibliographical references and index.
    ISBN 0-312-08165-0
    1. Computer games.   2. Puzzles.   I. Title.
GV1469.15.P53   1992
794.8—dc20   92-16668
                                                    CIP

To my parents

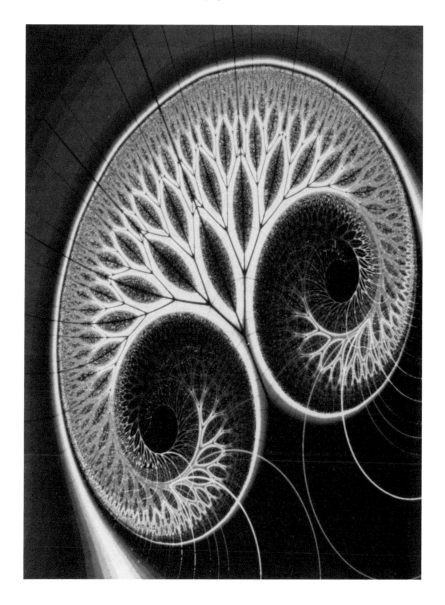

(Pictured here is a Glynn mapping for $z \to z^{1.5} - 0.2$.)

Preface

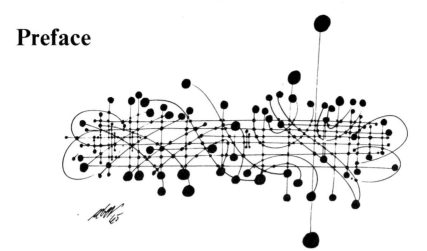

"The most beautiful thing we can experience is the mysterious. It is the source of all true art and science. He to whom this emotion is a stranger, who can no longer pause to wonder and stand wrapped in awe, is as good as dead."　　　　　　　　　　　　　　　　　　　　　　Albert Einstein

Welcome to my computer zoo. Think of this book's strange puzzles, problems, and artwork as exotic, sometimes beautiful, animals. The cages are the book chapters, computer programs, and your own thoughts. Sometimes the bars of a cage may bend a little, letting a weird animal escape. Don't run away. Keep it as a pet to stimulate your imagination.

You should get ready for a roller coaster ride through the unpredictable and exciting universe of computers, games, puzzles, mazes, and computer art. Topics include: fractal spiders, electronic kaleidoscopes, checkers-playing robots, and games which model the migration of early humans from Africa to the rest of the world. The emphasis is on creativity and fun. For many sections, no specialized knowledge is required. Even though there are a number of chapters with mathematical ideas and computer programming hints, almost all problems are of the "stop-and-think" variety that do not require programming or sophisticated mathematics to allow readers to explore and imagine.

For many years, I have been designing and collecting simple puzzles, games, and mazes – many of which can be explored either using a computer or with just a pencil and paper. A majority of the puzzles in my collection are entirely original; others are often extrapolated from, or inspired by, puzzles which date back several centuries and from various civilizations. Here I present a few favorites from my collection. Some of the puzzles are deceptively easy, while others are fiendishly difficult.

The book is organized into several parts:

1. **Pattern**. Computer graphics has become indispensable in countless areas of human activity. Presented here are experiments using graphics in mathematics and art. Topics include: fractal mazes, artificial kaleidoscopes, lava lamps in the 21st century, and number sequences from New Guinea.

2. **Games and Speculation**. Included in this section are discussions of board games from ancient civilizations, games played on a map of the human digestive system, and other speculative topics.

3. **Music Beyond Imagination**. Presented here are ways for creating "extraterrestrial melodies" and music from our genes.

4. **Space**. In this section are instructions on how to squeeze Einstein's brain into a 4-dimensional hypersphere, infinite cages for fleas, and related paradoxes concerning endless spaces.

5. **Time**. Throughout human civilization and experience, throughout the intricately synchronized biological rhythms of all living creatures, runs the elusive entity called time. In this section are several imaginative adventures examining the very fabric of time and eternity.

6. **Strange Technology**. This section describes several favorite and unusual technologies – from robot surgeons, to nomadology, to fractal optical pipes. Also presented are a few sections on strange chess machines, puzzles, miraculous chess solutions, and the difficult "Knights in Hell" problem.

7. **Weird Numbers**. Presented here are all kinds of strange numbers: parasite numbers, U-numbers, bicycle wheels from hell, pyramids of blood, and more.

In order to further stimulate your imagination, scattered throughout the book are **Interlude** sections which feature various professional artists using science and technology.

In the October 1991 issue of *OMNI*, Dave Jaffe (author of *Mathematical Games That Could Not be Solved by People Who Claim They Have High IQs*)

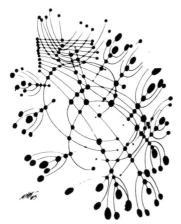

notes that "Math teasers break down into two categories, those that cannot be solved, and those that can be solved, but not by you." Most of the puzzles in my book do not fall in either category, and the concepts should be interesting for explorers of various ages and abilities.

Whereas my previous books *Computers and the Imagination* and *Computers, Pattern, Chaos and Beauty* were meant to *expand* your mind, this book is designed to shatter your mind. To this end, chapter sections such as "The Most Difficult Mazes Ever Imagined," "Caged Fleas in Hyperspace," "How to Stuff an Elephant in to a 24-Dimensional Sphere," and many others, attempt to tear the fabric of your ordinary thinking and to push your imagination to the breaking point.

The seemingly incongruous juxtaposition of mind-stretching exercises with sections on mazes, futuristic technology, and artists who use science and technology may bother some readers. I hope not. I think mental gymnastics and games go well with artistic stimulation and exploration. I add my voice to the chorus of others which are suggesting there is only a fine line between science and art. Sven G. Carlson in his letter to *Science News* says it well:

> "Art and science will eventually be seen to be as closely connected as arms to the body. Both are vital elements of order and its discovery. The word 'art' derives from the Indo-European base 'ar', meaning to join or fit together. In this sense, science, in the attempt to learn how and why things fit, becomes art. And when art is seen as the ability to do, make, apply or portray in a way that withstands the test of time, its connection with science becomes more clear."

Equations or No Equations?

In his preface to *A Brief History of Time* (Bantam), Stephen Hawking refers to an old saying of book publishing: "Someone told me that each equation I included in the book would halve the sales. In the end, however, I *did* put in one equation,

Einstein's $E = mc^2$. I hope this will not scare off half my potential readers." In the fall of 1989, Roger Penrose completed *The Emperor's New Mind*, which spent 14 weeks on the best-seller list. As *Publisher's Weekly* noted, the book was filled with "the kind of equations that make ordinary readers feel that they are 100 IQ points behind the times." Although my first inclination was to provide you with little or no mathematical formulas, I have backed away from this idea. For those readers who want to learn a little more, the equations will provide a useful path. Others will wish to pick and choose from the smorgasbord of topics and avoid those topics which rely on mathematical formulas. In order to encourage your involvement, computational hints and recipes for producing some of the computer-drawn figures are provided. Topics are often arranged randomly in each section to retain the playful spirit of the book, and to give you unexpected pleasures.[1]

In addition to my parents, this book is dedicated to other inspirers: Martin Gardner, Isaac Asimov, James Randi, and Arthur C. Clarke. Pictured here are Martin Gardner (top) and Arthur C. Clarke (bottom).

---

[1] There are a few places in this book where companies or products are mentioned. These are for illustrative purposes only, as I do not endorse any particular company, product, or technology. The artistic line and dot diagrams in this preface are by Robert Mueller and are described in "Interlude: Alien Musical Scores" on page 221. The "Appendix" contains solutions to several of the problems posed in this book, as well as a list of interesting products, software, and games.

"The seeker is a finder."

Ancient Persian Proverb

Contents

PART I

PATTERN

Chapter 1. Mazes for the Mind 3
1.1 Minotaurs, Mazes, and the Medieval Church 4
1.2 Movies and Mazes 5
1.3 Egyptian Labyrinth 6
1.4 The Largest Computer-Generated Maze in the World 7
1.5 Design Your Own Chinese Lattice Maze 9
1.6 Build Your Own Computer-Generated Mazes 9
1.7 Fractal Mazes: The Most Difficult Mazes Ever Imagined 10
1.8 The Fractal Dimension of a Maze 12
1.9 An Impossible Maze? 13
1.10 The Ultimate Maze Book 13
1.11 Truchet Mazes 14
1.12 Fact File: Tamil Women, Louis XIV, Etc. 15
1.13 Labyrinthodontia, Labyrinth Fish, and Labyrinth Parasites 17
1.14 Credits: Möbius and Stairway Mazes 21
1.15 The Diabolical Die 21
1.16 Cross References 21
1.17 For Further Reading 22

Chapter 2. Electronic Kaleidoscopes for the Mind 23
2.1 Teleidoscopes and Polyangular Kaleidoscopes 26
2.2 How to Create Kaleidoscopic Designs Without a Computer 27

Chapter 3. Interlude: I See Your Eyes at Night in Dreams 31

Chapter 4. Fantastic Feather Fractals 33
4.1 Cross References 34

Chapter 5. Smithson's Fractal Anabiotic Ana Sequences 35
5.1 Stop and Think 39
5.2 Cross References 39
5.3 For Further Reading 40

Chapter 6. Interlude: Fractals and Feminism 43

Chapter 7. Slugs Trapped in Jordan Curves 45

Chapter 8. Ghost Patterns and Puzzles 49
8.1 10,000 Dots 51
8.2 Fact File 52

Chapter 9. Is a Picture Worth 75 Words? 55
9.1 Comments from Colleagues 56
9.2 Stop and Think 57

Chapter 10. Siamese Fighting Fish Patterns 63
10.1 Amazing Latin Squares 64
10.2 Magic Squares, Emperor Yu, Chess Knights, Etc. 66
10.3 Cross References 67
10.4 For Further Reading 67

Chapter 11. Interlude: Pulsating Pumpkins, Helical Hedges, and Leaping Leaves 69

Chapter 12. The Drums of Ulupu 71
12.1 Cross References 76

Chapter 13. Beauty and the Bits 79
13.1 Cross References 82
13.2 For Further Reading 82

Chapter 14. Interlude: Animal Machines 85
14.1 For Further Reading 86

Chapter 15. Fractal Spiders and Frame-Robertson Bushes 87
15.1 Hairy Snowmen 87
15.2 Spider Fractals 89
15.3 Frame-Robertson Fractals 91
15.4 Pokorny Fractals 92
15.5 Cornfield Phantoms 93
15.6 Mandelbrot Set Comics 94
15.7 Shishikura's Extraordinary Boundary 94
15.8 Fractal Drums and Violence 95

15.9 Are Fractal Graphics Art? 95
15.10 Cross References and Credits 96
15.11 For Further Reading 96

Chapter 16. Mandalas, Screws, Pears, and Klein Bottles 97

Chapter 17. Labyrinthine Lundin Curves 103

Chapter 18. Interlude: Cemeteries of the Future, and Interstellar Art 107

Chapter 19. Lava Lamps in the 21st Century 109
19.1 Making Lava in a Checkerboard World 110
19.2 It's a Beautiful Day in the Neighborhood 112
19.3 Twisted 3-D Majority Rules, and Printer Dirt 113
19.4 For Further Reading 114

Chapter 20. Monster Contour Art 117

PART II
GAMES AND SPECULATION

Chapter 21. My Computer Esophagus 121
21.1 Computer Analysis and Play 126
21.2 Journal of Cancer Research 128
21.3 Liver Capture Scenario and Physiological Relevance 128
21.4 Party Version - Adjacent Esophagi Scenario 129
21.5 Anatomy Fact File 129
    21.5.1 The Visible Human Project 129
    21.5.2 Implantable Brain Pancakes 130
21.6 For Further Reading 130

Chapter 22. The Cro-Magnon Conquest Game 133
22.1 Genes and Languages 135
22.2 Stop and Think 136
22.3 The Bushmen 137
22.4 Fantastic Archeology 138
22.5 Valley of Life, and Kingdoms of Gold 138
22.6 The Greenland Mummies 139
22.7 For Further Reading 139

Chapter 23. Ghost Children in Our Genes 141
23.1 Fact File: Chinese Hamster Sperm, Bull Sperm, Etc. 142
23.2 Stop and Think 142
23.3 Cross References and Credits 142

Chapter 24. Pong Hau K'i 143
24.1 Stop and Think 143

**Chapter 25. The 10 Mathematical Formulas that Changed the Face of the
World** 145
25.1 The Top Ten 146
25.2 The Runners-Up 146
25.3 Nicaragua List 146
25.4 Solutions, Tsiolkovaskii's Rocket Equation, Etc. 147
25.5 Comments from Colleagues 148
25.6 Fact File 148

Chapter 26. Interlude: The Third Eye 149

Chapter 27. Aliens, and Pieces of Pi 151
27.1 Stop and Think 153
27.2 Fact File 153
27.3 Cross Reference 153

Chapter 28. Hyperdimensional Sz'kwa 155
28.1 Stop and Think 156

Chapter 29. Goddard, The Nile, and Claire de Lune 157
29.1 Stop and Think 159
29.2 Patents and Inventions 159

Chapter 30. Extraterrestrial Messages in Our Genes 161
30.1 Stop and Think 164
30.2 Fact File: Jurassic Park, SETI, Etc. 165
30.3 The Science Behind the Human Genome Project 166
30.4 Cross Reference 166

Chapter 31. Computers and Near-Death Experiences 167
31.1 Consciousness Explained 168
31.2 For Further Reading 168

Chapter 32. Is Computer Art Really Art? 169
32.1 Comments from Colleagues 170
32.2 Cross References 172

Chapter 33. Electronic and Fractal Ant Farms 173
33.1 Stop and Think 174
33.2 Fact File: Rats, Ants, and Mazes 176
33.3 Cross References 176
33.4 For Further Reading 176

Chapter 34. Toilet Paper and the Infinite 177
34.1 The Length of a Roll of Toilet Paper 177
34.2 Stop and Think 178
34.3 Strange Toilet Paper 179
34.4 Squashed Archimedean Model of a HyperToilet Paper 180
34.5 Stop and Think 181
34.6 Fact File: First Manufactured Toilet Paper 182
34.7 For Further Reading 182

Chapter 35. Bertrand Russell's Twenty Favorite Words 183
35.1 Batrachomyomachia 184
35.2 Stop and Think 185
35.3 For Further Reading 185

Chapter 36. Interlude: Stelarc's Third Hand 187

PART III
MUSIC BEYOND IMAGINATION

Chapter 37. Mutcer's Marvelous Music Machines 191
37.1 Music from Alpha Centuri 195
37.2 All the Melodies that Could Ever be Imagined 196
37.3 Merry Christmas 198
37.4 Pink Machines 200
37.5 A Simple Way to Produce Beautiful Music 201
37.6 Fact File 202
    37.6.1 Ink Splattered Scores 202
    37.6.2 Pigeon Music 203
    37.6.3 New York Skyline Music 203
    37.6.4 Hailstone Music 203
    37.6.5 Chess Music 204
    37.6.6 Latvian Folk Music 205
    37.6.7 Music Animation Machine 205
    37.6.8 Music in Paintings 205
    37.6.9 Mozart Numbers 206
    37.6.10 Music Notation Modernization Association 206
    37.6.11 Strange Musical Notation Patents 207
    37.6.12 Music of the Spheres 207
    37.6.13 Music of the Sumerian Tablets 207
37.7 For Further Reading 207

Chapter 38. Interlude: Computer Mouths 209

Chapter 39. There is Music in our Genes 211

39.1 Ohno's DNA Music 211
39.2 Munakata/Hayashi Gene Music 214
39.3 For Further Reading on Gene Music 216

Chapter 40. Bach's Impossible Violin 219

Chapter 41. Interlude: Alien Musical Scores 221
41.1 For Further Reading 222
41.2 Cross References 222

PART IV

SPACE

Chapter 42. How to Stuff An Elephant into a 24-Dimensional Sphere 225
42.1 Hyperspheres 227
42.2 Stop and Think 230
42.3 The Hypervolume of Temple Emanu-El and Related 231
42.4 Squeezing Einstein's Brain into a 4-Dimensional Sphere 232
42.5 Marbles and Worms 233
42.6 Student Exercises: Fractal Hyperspheres and More 233
42.7 Other Dimensions and Superstrings 234
42.8 Sparticles and 26-D Superstrings 235
42.9 Fact File 235
    42.9.1 Hyperbeings Look in Our Intestines 235
    42.9.2 Hyperdimensional Knights 236
    42.9.3 Where are Einstein's Children? 236
    42.9.4 Rubik's Tesseract! 236
42.10 For Further Reading 237
42.11 Credit 237

Chapter 43. Interlude: Tortured Surfaces 239
43.1 For Further Reading 239

Chapter 44. Caged Siphonaptera (Fleas) in Hyperspace 241
44.1 Various Zoos 243
44.2 4-Dimensional Cages 244
44.3 Stop and Think: Coney Island, The Ice Age, Etc. 245
44.4 The Ways of Coprophiles 246
44.5 For Further Reading 247

Chapter 45. Squashed Worlds That Pack Infinity into a Cube 249

Chapter 46. Bacon, the Mini-Oos 253
46.1 Intergenerational Incest 254
46.2 Intergenerational Oos Communication 255

46.3 A Memory from Bacon's Early Childhood 256
46.4 Love and War 257
46.5 The End of an Era, and Horseradish 259
46.6 Further Experimentation (with Purple Oos) 260
46.7 Destruction 261
46.8 Harsh Experiments with Beetle Oos and Purple Oos 261
46.9 What Transpired in the Oos Civilization Prior to the Snout 262
46.10 Contact 263
46.11 More on Roobles 263
46.12 What db said to Dr. Mutcer 264
46.13 Dr. Mutcer's Apartment 265
46.14 Oos-Lizards Battle the World 265
46.15 The Oos-Lizards Meet Tammy and Burt 266
46.16 A World Turns Purple 267
46.17 The Oos-King Reigns 267

PART V
TIME

Chapter 47. Time in a Bottle 271
47.1 Stop and Think: Old Wine and Cocky the Cockatoo 274
47.2 Hypertime and EternityGrams 275
47.3 Fact File: Chronons, Mastodon Feces, Etc. 275
47.4 For Further Reading 276

Chapter 48. Interlude: Art Beyond Space and Time 277
48.1 For Further Reading 278

**Chapter 49. Time-Skulls, Bouncing Bones, and Building Your own Time
Machine** 281
49.1 Build Your Own Time Machine 286
49.2 Stop and Think 287

Chapter 50. Interlude: Marking Time 289
50.1 Cross References 290

PART VI
STRANGE TECHNOLOGY

Chapter 51. Robot Checkers-Players, Surgeons, and Chefs 293
51.1 Checkers Enchiridion 293
    51.1.1 Fact File 295
51.2 Pizzabot 295
51.3 Robot Surgeons 296

Chapter 52. Bar Codes in the 21st Century 297

Chapter 53. Cyberspace and Nomadology 299
53.1 Sentient Trees in Multiperson Spaces 299
53.2 Nomadic Research Labs 299
53.3 Time Traveler 300
53.4 Virtual Reality, Al Gore, and Jerry Garcia 301
53.5 Fact File 302

Chapter 54. Practical Fractals 305

Chapter 55. Interlude: Embracing Euglenas with Invisible Pliers 309

Chapter 56. Miraculous Chess Solutions 311
56.1 Fact File 313
56.2 Superqueens, Amazons, and Pegasus Pieces 315
56.3 International Computer-Chess Championships 315
56.4 Relativistic Chess 315
56.5 Infinite Chess 316
56.6 Black Hole Chess 316
56.7 Gun Chess, Ghost Chess, Fairy Chess, and Other Variants 316
56.8 Madhouse Chess, and Martian Chess 317
56.9 Hexagonal Chess 317
56.10 5x5 Chess 318
56.11 Crushed Chess 318
56.12 Evolution Chess, Carnivore Chess, and Others 318
56.13 Fibonacci Chess 319
56.14 For Further Reading 319
56.15 Cross References 319

Chapter 57. Knights in Hell, And Other Chess Charivari 321
57.1 Knights in Hell 321
57.2 Fiendishly Difficult Eight Pawn Problem 321
57.3 Cross References 322
57.4 For Further Reading 322

Chapter 58. Interlude: Prehistoric Insect Sculptures 323

PART VII
WEIRD NUMBERS

Chapter 59. Bicycles from Hell 327
59.1 Solutions and Future Experiments 328
59.2 Bicycles Wheels From Purgatory 329

59.3 Fact File 329

Chapter 60. Shruludidi Spheres Between Uranus and Pluto 331
60.1 Stop and Think 333

Chapter 61. Interlude: Explosion Art (Detonography) 335

Chapter 62. Apocalypse Numbers 337
62.1 Stop and Think 338
62.2 Fact File: 666 in Beards and in Britain 338

Chapter 63. Interlude: Large-Scale Holosculptures 339

Chapter 64. 1597 Problem 341
64.1 Stop and Think 343

Chapter 65. Terrible Brahmagupta Numbers in the Seventh Century 345
65.1 Stop and Think 348
65.2 Wild India 348

Chapter 66. Incredibly Difficult Number Sequences 349
66.1 Crazy Sequences 350
  66.1.1 Schoenleber Number Sequence Problem 350
  66.1.2 Diep Number Sequence 350
  66.1.3 Somos Number Sequence Problem 350
  66.1.4 Chernoff Number Sequence 351
  66.1.5 Trice Number Sequence 351
  66.1.6 Balden Number Sequence 351
  66.1.7 Some Solutions 351

Chapter 67. Interlude: Catching Criminals 353

Chapter 68. The Arabian Nights Factorial 355

Chapter 69. U-Numbers and MU-Numbers 357
69.1 For Further Reading 359

Chapter 70. Phi in Four 4's 361
70.1 Closer and Closer 362

Chapter 71. Interlude: Microscapes 365
71.1 For Further Reading 365

Chapter 72. On Mountain Climbing and a Strange Series 367
72.1 Credit 369

Chapter 73. The Terrible Twos Problem 373
73.1 Hard Numbers 376
73.2 Unusual Solutions 377
73.3 References 377

Chapter 74. AIDS 379
74.1 Comments from Colleagues 381
74.2 Fact File 383
74.3 Mystery Dance 383
74.4 For Further Reading 384

Chapter 75. Musings on Large Robbins Numbers and Friden Calculators .. 385
75.1 Alternating Sign Matrices 387
75.2 Some Challenges 388
75.3 Stop and Think 388
75.4 What is a Friden Calculator? 389
75.5 Xi Xi Xi Xi 390
75.6 For Further Reading 390

Chapter 76. Interlude: Electric Sculptures with Swelled Heads 393

Chapter 77. Parasites on Parade 395
77.1 Behemoth Parasites 397
77.2 Fact File 398

Chapter 78. Pyramids of Blood 399

PART VIII
APPENDICES

Appendix A. Philobiblic Potpourri 405
A.1 Literature for Lacubration 405
A.2 Product Pavan 408
A.3 Curiosity Cavalcade 410
A.4 Descriptions of Color Plates 412
A.5 Acknowledgments and Credits 413
A.6 Additional Mental Machicolation 415

Appendix B. Solution Saraband 419

Index 421

About the Author 423

Part I

PATTERN

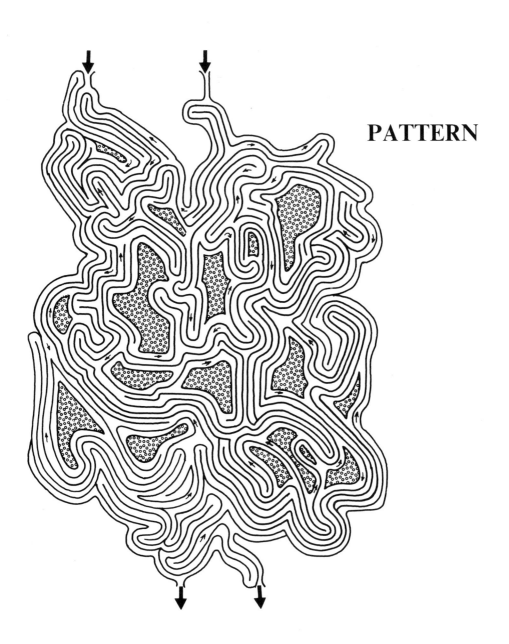

Chapter 1

Mazes for the Mind

"What is this mighty labyrinth – the earth – but a wild maze the moment of our birth? Still as we life pursue the maze extends, nor find we where each winding purlieu ends."   Unknown author (18th Century)

When I was a very little boy my father would often draw interesting mazes for me on the back of the cardboard inserts which came in his packages of new shirts. While growing up, I continued to be fascinated with mazes. In the fourth grade, I formed a "Maze Cooperative" where various friends would challenge each other with difficult mazes which had to be constructed in less than 15 minutes. Often our goal would be to make the maze aesthetically pleasing as well as interesting to solve.

Of the thousands of mazes I have studied both as a child and adult, my two favorite mazes are shown above and facing this page. To solve "The Möbius Maze," above, start at one worm and find the other by crawling along the pathways as they pass over and under. You must keep in mind which side of the path you are on, and you may not crawl over an edge. To solve the stairway maze, start at the star near the top, and travel the precarious pathways as they weave over and under themselves.

Figure 1.1. *Two depictions of a Minotaur.* According to ancient mythology, a Minotaur was a man-eating monster imprisoned in a maze. There drawings are from a Corinthian amphora (vase), 5th Century B.C.

I think that my father's early stimulation with mazes was an important influence in my life, and to this day I find that mazes provide an interesting boost for creativity. Wouldn't it be very useful for today's teachers to assign maze-drawing projects to their young students? Not only would this stimulate hand-eye coordination, but it would also encourage a wealth of useful traits such as patience, artistic skill, and an early fascination with solving problems.

1.1 Minotaurs, Mazes, and the Medieval Church

The world's most famous maze comes from ancient Minoan mythology. (The

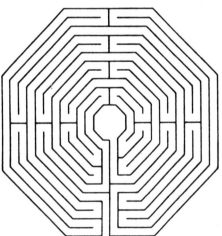

Minoans were people who lived during the Bronze age culture of ancient Crete, from 3000 B.C. to 1100 B.C.) The maze was built by Daedalus to imprison the Minotaur, a man-eating monster (Figure 1.1). Through the ages, many civilizations used mazes for amusement. They were used in the greenery at the Hampton Court palace near London, and in the pavements of medieval churches. The medieval Church actually used mazes to provide a compact path for pilgrims to follow on hands and knees by way of penance. These mazes usually consisted of a single, forced path to the center, with no choice of ways. The octagonal maze at St. Quentin, shown at the left, is an example. It measures 42 feet in diameter. A similar maze was found in Amiens Cathedral (1288), but most of it was destroyed in 1708.

Figure 1.2. *Computer-generated by Walter Pullen.* Pullen is famous for having created one of the world's largest mazes. His first gigantic computer maze covered 699 pages of paper and was over 23 feet long and 11 feet wide.

1.2 Movies and Mazes

Probably the first major movie featuring a maze was the 1953 horror movie *The Maze*. It had all the classic horror attributes: an ancestral Scottish castle, a frog-like creature, and an enormous hedge maze. *The Maze* was directed by William Cameron Menzies who was responsible for much of the look of *Gone With the Wind* and *Invaders from Mars*. Stanley Kubrik's *The Shining*, based on Steven King's novel, is a more current example of a movie maze. At the film's climax, Jack Nicholson, ax in hand, chases his son through the snow-covered maze. Luckily for the son, the deranged Nicholson gets lost in the maze. Yet another movie is *Labyrinth* where a young girl is given only 13 hours to traverse a maze. This movie starred rock music iconoclast David Bowie. Sarah, the girl, was forced to solve an enormous life-sized labyrinth, filled with dark passages, sneaky traps,

Figure 1.3. *Chinese lattice design experts.* Shown here are Daniel Sheete Dye (left) and Yang Chi-shang (right), who cataloged numerous Chinese lattice designs which are the basis for some of my own mazes in this book.

and fantastic creatures in order to rescue her baby brother who had been kidnapped by the Goblin King.

Although not yet made into a movie, *The Man in the Maze* by Robert Silverberg is a fascinating science fiction tale set in the future, in an age of frequent space travel and alien encounters. The maze is an abandoned city, filled with deadly traps to keep out intruders.

1.3 Egyptian Labyrinth

The term *labyrinth* is often used when referring to a maze. "Labyrinth" was the name given by the Greeks to buildings containing a number of chambers and intricate passages. Aside from the mythological Minotaur's maze mentioned in an earlier section, there may have existed an ancient Egyptian labyrinth situated somewhere to the east of Lake Moeris in northern Egypt. According to Greek historian Herodotus, who lived in the 5th Century B.C., the entire building contained 12 courts and 3,000 chambers (1,500 above and 1,500 below ground)! Herodotus himself went through the upper chambers but was not permitted to visit those underground, which he was told contained the tombs of ancient kings.

START   END

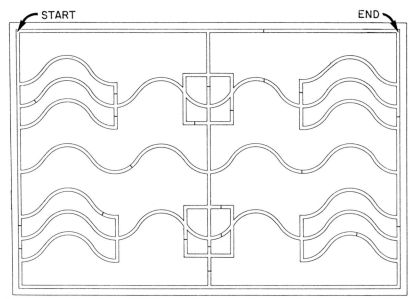

Figure 1.4. *Pickover Chinese lattice maze.*

1.4 The Largest Computer-Generated Maze in the World

Recently, one huge computer-generated maze stretched over 200 sheets of paper. Loren Buchanan, a visualization lab manager at the Naval Research Laboratory at Washington, D.C., once translated the program, which generated the maze, from BASIC to PL/I. The program could easily generate 1000-page mazes in less than 20 minutes. The largest maze Buchanan ever saw printed by the program was a little over 200 pages in length, computed on an IBM 4341. Larger mazes were avoided so as not to incur the wrath of the Computer Center employees. The 200-page maze took a little over 4 hours to solve by a team of 4 people.

   In 1987, one of the world's largest computer-generated mazes was produced by Walter Pullen of Kent, Washington. Pullen is currently 20 years old, and is a Senior in the Computer Science Department at the University of Washington in Seattle. His maze was over 23 feet long, 11 feet wide, and covered 688 pages. The intricate design took him 11 days just to print, with his computer running 8 hours a day. The maze is stored on eight floppy disks, and requires one megabyte of disk space (enough space to store about 1 million characters). The 688 pages were taped together using more than 20 rolls of transparent tape.

   For comparison with Pullen's maze, consider that one of the world's largest life-sized mazes is "Il Labirinto" in Italy, where Napoleon was lost in 1807. It has four miles of internal passages. Pullen estimates that his maze is two-tenths of a mile longer than Il Labirinto. The passageways of Pullen's maze are between one-eight and one-quarter inches wide, and it would take a human (with computer help) probably over a month to solve. Pullen has not attempted to work the maze manually with a pencil. Like myself, Pullen credits his father for getting him

START   END

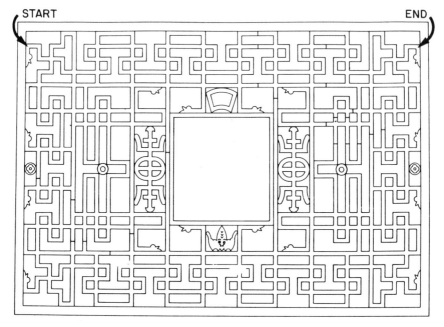

Figure 1.5. *Pickover Chinese lattice maze.*

started in mazes while he was in kindergarten. Today, Pullen hopes to use university computer science classes to help him create even better mazes. Pullen recently wrote to me:

> I notified the *Guiness Book of World Records* about my 688-page maze which had 100,000 dead ends and only one correct solution. My hope was to have it entered as a world record; however, Guiness wouldn't accept a *computer-generated* maze, because they only included mazes through which people can walk. I learned from Guiness that I wasn't the only person who had tried to make large computer mazes. Some students at a college in Massachusetts had created a computer maze which was printed on 2800 sheets of paper, measuring 7 inches wide and nearly half a mile in length! Not wishing to be outdone, I did create a new maze of the same elongated type, a few hundred feet longer than theirs! This maze had 22 miles of passages in it, stretched over 3031 pages, and required nine computer ribbons for printing. My memory efficient maze algorithm ran on a Radio Shack computer.

Pullen continues to design interesting mazes, although they are much smaller than his world-breaking masterpieces. Figure 1.2 is one of Pullen's recent designs. This "British Maze" was created by hand, with help from the computer in filling some of the area left in the maze after Pullen designed the solution and the main traps. To solve it you must start in the middle of Ireland, and then wind your way through the maze-map. Finally you must enter England and finish up at the location in London.

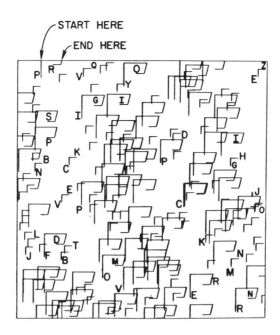

Figure 1.6. *Computer-generated maze.* Start at the region labeled "P."   Finish at the region labeled "R."   You may hop from one cluster of connected lines to another if they contain the same letters.

1.5 Design Your Own Chinese Lattice Maze

My own mazes (such as in Figure 1.4 and Figure 1.5) are based on the Chinese lattice designs of Dr. Daniel Dye and his assistant Yang Chi-shang (Figure 1.3). Dr. Dye's 1937 book *Chinese Lattice Designs* is a classic work, both in the West and in China, and it contains diagrams of the intricate geometric window grids of China.   Lattice windows were used in China for 3,000 years.   Many of the old windows were destroyed in the series of revolutions and local wars that took place from 1911 to 1949. The majority of my Chinese lattice mazes are based on patterns from the Szechwan Province in Western China.   Often I start with a design in Dye's book, and then block various "pathways" in order to create an interesting maze.

1.6 Build Your Own Computer-Generated Mazes

An intriguing computer-generated maze is shown in Figure 1.6. I constructed 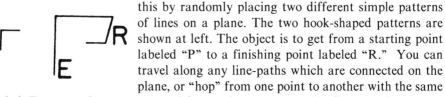 this by randomly placing two different simple patterns of lines on a plane. The two hook-shaped patterns are shown at left. The object is to get from a starting point labeled "P" to a finishing point labeled "R."   You can travel along any line-paths which are connected on the plane, or "hop" from one point to another with the same label. For example, you can travel from point *E* to *R* on this diagram. Once point

```
ALGORITHM: How to make a simple computer-generated maze.
DO i = 1 to 200
     x = Random
     y = Random
     PatternType = Random
     IF PatternType > .5 THEN DO
       MovePenTo(x,y)
       PlotLineTo(x + 0.03,y); PlotLineTo(x + 0.04, y + 0.04)
       PlotLineTo(x - 0.05,y + 0.04); PlotLineTo(x-.05, y-.05)
     END
     IF PatternType < .5 THEN DO
         MovePenTo(x, y); PlotLineTo(x, y + 0.03)
         PlotLineTo(x + 0.03, y + 0.03)
     END
END
```

Pseudocode 1.1. *How to make a simple computer-generated maze.* Random numbers are generated between 0 and 1. The lower left hand corner of the maze is at (0,0). The upper right is at (1,1). You can place labels on the intricate cluster of lines by hand. The two hooklike maze motifs are defined by the "PatternTypes" in the code.

R is reached, you then look for another point R labeling a line, or a connected cluster of lines, somewhere else on the plane. To draw the two simple maze motifs (hook patterns), use a random number generator to randomly position either of the two motifs. Draw the final intricate maze similar to the one in Figure 1.6 using the simple computer recipe in Pseudocode 1.1.

1.7 Fractal Mazes: The Most Difficult Mazes Ever Imagined

"I thought of a labyrinth of labyrinths, of one sinuous spreading labyrinth that would encompass the past and the future and in some way involve the stars."   J. L. Borgess, 1962, *The Garden of Forking Paths*

Mazes can be constructed from intricate geometrical shapes called fractals. Fractals are objects which continue to exhibit structural details no matter how much the edge of the object is magnified. These rough-edged objects or patterns often appear *self-similar* which means that no matter what scale is used to view the pattern, the magnified portion of the fractal shape looks just like the original pattern. Figure 1.7 shows a typical example derived from a simple mathematical formula of the form[2] $z' = f(z) + c$. B. Mandelbrot, the father of fractals, informally defines fractals as "shapes that are equally complex in their details as in their overall form. That is, if a piece of a fractal is suitably magnified to become of the same size as the whole, it should look like the whole, either exactly, or perhaps only after slight limited deformation."

---

[2] See Mandelbrot (1982), Pickover (1990), and Wegner and Peterson (1991) for more on this formula. See also "Fractal Spiders and Frame-Robertson Bushes" on page 87.

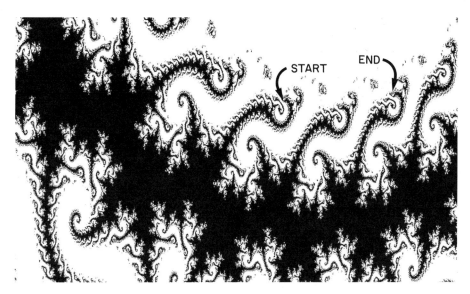

Figure 1.7. *An example of a fractal maze.* The path marked "end" is not actually the end of the maze; it is just the branch you have to travel on to reach the end of the maze which is too tiny to be seen without further magnification near this part of the figure.

Mazes constructed from fractals are probably the most difficult mazes that could ever be constructed. In order to solve a fractal maze, the viewer would have to magnify different regions of the maze to be explored. Connected regions of the maze necessary for the maze's solution would have to be magnified even to be seen. Like the ever-decreasing cats in Dr. Seuss's *The Cat in The Hat Comes Back*, certain aspects of the maze will never be seen unless one knows where to magnify the objects.

Consider the famous bush-shaped Mandelbrot set (M-set) for constructing mazes. This fractal object, pictured at left, is created using complex geometry and contains a myriad of minuscule tendrils. One could place the starting point of a  maze on one of the various tendrils, or stubs, and then place the finishing point somewhere else on the object at a different magnification. Extreme magnifications of the M-set maze are easy to display using a computer. Note that if you consider the width of a personal computer screen to be about a foot, and zoom into the M-set so that a piece of the M-set 1×10^{-12} units wide fills the screen, then the original M-set would extend to Jupiter. This naturally produces a pretty difficult maze to solve! The M-set contains so much detail, and is so extensive, that magnifications of the M-set will easily yield pictures never seen before by human eyes. The M-set structure consists of super thin spiral and crinkly paths connecting an infinite number of island shapes. The incredible vastness of the M-set with its infinite number of island shapes has lead Wegner and Peterson (1991) to remark: "You may have

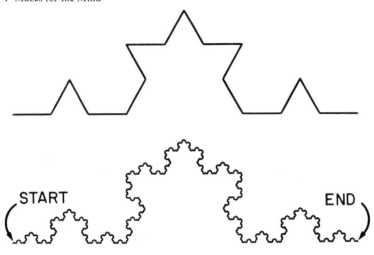

Figure 1.8. *Koch curve maze.* You can construct this maze by continually replacing the center third of every straight line segment with a V-shaped wedge. After a few million generations, the length of the curve has become so great that you could not trace the maze in your entire lifetime. Koch and Hilbert mazes are pretty boring since they consist of a single path with no choice of ways.

heard of a company that for a fee will name a star after you and record it in a book. Maybe the same thing will soon be done with the Mandelbrot set!"

Arthur C. Clarke recently published *The Ghost from the Grand Banks*, a book that describes a woman so enthralled with her computer-generated Mandelbrot picture that she spent virtually all her waking hours exploring the pictures intricacies. Eventually she went insane.

1.8 The Fractal Dimension of a Maze

A parameter called the *fractal dimension* can be used to describe the difficulty of some fractal mazes. Before continuing, let me explain more about this dimension parameter. The fractal dimension is a quantitative property of a set of points which measures the extent to which the points fill space. A line is one dimensional and a plane is two dimensional, but a bumpy curve with infinite length, such as a Koch snowflake curve (Figure 1.8), has a dimension between 1 and 2. This snowflake curve is obviously more crinkly – better at filling space – than a smooth curve which has dimension one. The closer the dimension is to 2, the more a curve fills the plane on which it is plotted. Mazes with a fractal dimension of 1.9 may be more "difficult," and more visually interesting, than mazes with a dimension of 1.1.

Consider a fractal maze based on the Koch curve or the Hilbert curve (Figure 1.9) which would take several lifetimes even to trace using pencil and paper. As you create a more and more complex maze by replacing straight line

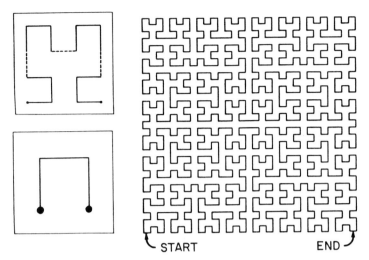

Figure 1.9. *Constructing a Hilbert curve maze.*

segments with the simple generating pattern, the length of the maze grows. After a few million generations, you could not trace the maze in your entire lifetime. Of course, this kind of maze is a little like the medieval Catholic church maze, discussed in "Minotaurs, Mazes, and the Medieval Church" on page 4, which provided a single, forced path for pilgrims to follow on hands and knees by way of penance. Koch and Hilbert mazes are also pretty boring since they consist of a single path with no choice of ways. Would the medieval Church have been interested in these 20th Century Hilbert mazes?

1.9 An Impossible Maze?

This section describes a maze that's sure to have you in a quandary. Start at any road in Figure 1.10 and see if you can spell out a complete English sentence by passing next to letters without travelling on the same road twice. That is, your path cannot cross itself. In 1991, I tested my maze on many people. Interestingly, everyone tested, even after many hours of deliberation, reported, "This is impossible." Yet it is a very simple puzzle. Here's a hint. The sentence starts on one of the four sides of the rectangular border and ends on another side. (See "Solution Saraband" on page 419 for the solution.)

1.10 The Ultimate Maze Book

David Anson Russo holds a black belt in jujitsu and is currently studying aikido. He is also author of some of the most visually interesting, and torturously difficult mazes dreamed of by humans (see Figure 1.11). His mazes often remind me of Celtic patterns, interwoven with ancient symbols and archetypes, with swirling knotlike structures. They also remind me of Leonardo da Vinci's drawing *Con-*

Figure 1.10. *Text maze.* Start at any road and see if you can spell out a complete English sentence by passing next to letters without travelling on the same road twice.

catenation which resembles both a mandala (a symmetrical Buddhist graphic symbol) and a maze. In da Vinci's pattern (shown in "Fact File: Tamil Women, Louis XIV, Etc." on page 15), a single line produces a complex pattern of knots that radiate and revolve outward from the center. In Russo's *The Ultimate Maze Book*, Russo tells a little bit about his philosophy concerning mazes:

> "My mazes have everything to do with my spiritual life. What drives me is to make the art and the viewer one. To challenge you, I build in quite a bit of psychological warfare as I design each maze. One of my favorite ploys is to overload your mind by suddenly giving it a multitude of possibilities from which to choose. Suddenly I'll bring you to an intersection of about six to eight trails and your first big decision."

Russo also makes three-dimensional maze sculptures on large wood turned bowls. They are carved in relief, with tunnels and bridges. See his book for more information.

1.11 Truchet Mazes

Tiles with simple designs can be used to create intricate mazes. The tiles I prefer to use are computer-generated "Truchet tiles" named after Dominican priest Sebastien Truchet, an engineer with an interest in mathematics and art. He also constructed interesting patterns using small tiles containing simple designs similar to these. To create Truchet mazes, use an orientable square tile with curved lines that join to produce continuous closures regardless of how the tiles are oriented. A generating tile is diagrammed at left. To produce a truchet maze (Figure 1.13) randomly orient the generating square and place it within the corner of a large checkerboard grid. Add successive adjacent tiles to the checkerboard for a partic-

Figure 1.11. *The Ultimate Maze Book.* Shown here is the *Open Access* maze from David Russo's *Ultimate Maze Book.* His mazes often consist of visually interesting, interweaving paths. Begin at the arrow at the upper left rim.   End in the swirling eddy at the maze's center. Beware of the many dead ends and "seductive paths" that could pull you far from your final goal. (See text for details. Figure © 1991 by D. Russo. Used with permission of Simon and Schuster. All rights reserved.)

ular row until it is filled, and start a new row. Continue until the entire checkerboard array is filled. Even nicer mazes can be created simply by randomly orientating a square tile with a single diagonal line through it (Figure 1.14).

1.12 Fact File: Tamil Women, Louis XIV, Etc.

"While I believe the computer will ultimately cause a minor revolution in all of the arts, the results to date are exceedingly poor and uninspiring."

Robert Mueller, 1972, *Art in America*

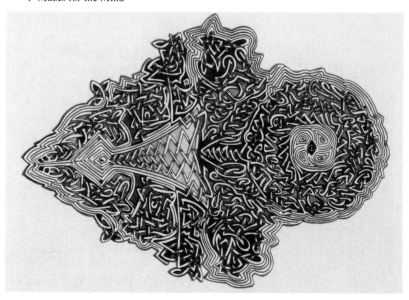

Figure 1.12. *Makai Maze.* Shown here is a sample maze from David Russo's *Ultimate Maze Book.* Begin at the black diamond region in the center of the white circle at the right. End at the arrow in the white arrowhead shape at left. The way to reach this maze's goal is through the linear zig-zag region left of the center. Here, be careful to choose the right road. (See text for details. Figure © 1991 by D. Russo. Used with permission of Simon and Schuster. All rights reserved.)

• The most elaborate hedge maze ever constructed was probably that of Louis XIV at Versailles. The maze contained 39 fountains and cost the equivalent of more than three million dollars to build.

• Even today, Tamil women in southern India draw labyrinthine patterns on the threshold of their homes for protection during the winter solstice period when the sun is considered to have "died."

• If you travel to the Midwestern United States, there is a beautiful labyrinth in New Harmony, Indiana. It is made with bushes, and in the center is a small circular building. Recently, the bushes have been cut back to rejuvenate the maze and get rid of all the shortcuts young folks have cut into the paths. The maze is large, and part of historic New Harmony which is managed by the University of Indiana.

• If you are in England, visit the Hampton Court Palace in East Mosely. It's just a 40 minute train ride from London. The

Figure 1.13. *Truchet maze.* Mazes can be constructed by computer using tiles with simple designs. See text for more information.

palace was occupied by King Henry VIII, among many other monarchs. In the garden is a tall hedge maze designed by Sir Christopher Wren, an architect of many of London's cathedrals including St. Paul's.

• There are many public domain, maze software packages available to personal computer users. For example, a "screensaver" program called *After Dark* for Macintosh computers (commercially available from Berkeley University) has a public domain shareware module which generates mazes and solves them.

1.13 Labyrinthodontia, Labyrinth Fish, and Labyrinth Parasites

As a child growing up with mazes all around me, I became interested in many words relating to, or sounding like, the word labyrinth. I'll spend a little time discussing them here for true labyrinth aficionados.

Let me start by telling you about carnivorous, fresh-water labyrinth fish of the order *Labyrinthi.* These are found in

southeast Asia (Figure 1.15) and Africa. Interestingly, they have a maze-like structure above each gill chamber which enables them to breath air while out of water. You can think of this as an auxiliary breathing apparatus which supplements the ordinary gills. It is called a labyrinth because the intricate structure has many fine capillaries to aid in oxygen absorption. To use the labyrinth, the fish goes to the surface of the water and forces a bubble of air through the labyrinth. It was once thought that these fishes

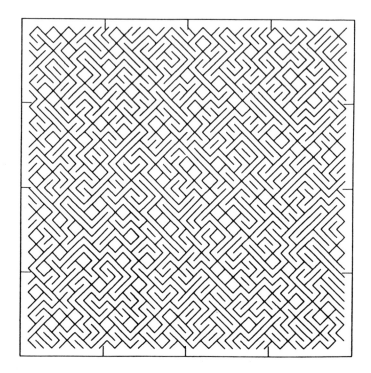

Figure 1.14. *Diagonal tile maze.* Mazes can be constructed by computer using tiles with straight lines. Each square of the lattice is cut along one diagonal at random. Is it possible to get from one side of the maze to an opposite side?

required direct contact with the air at the top of the water in order to survive, and could not rely on dissolved oxygen in the water alone. However, you can test this theory for yourself and prove it wrong! Buy a labyrinth fish, such as a Paradise fish, at your local pet shop. Place it in a bottle of water filled to the very top. Seal the jar so there is no air space. The fish will show discomfort, but, contrary to what might be expected, it will not suffocate for many hours. Of course, it is a great advantage to a fish to be equipped with both kinds of breathers in situations where the oxygen in the water is so deficient as to suffocate ordinary species. The labyrinth fish will be quite happy in oxygen poor environments. I raised quite a few labyrinth fishes as a boy, and here are some tips if you are interested in trying this yourself. For example, you will kill these fish if your aquaria are too small or too clean. The babies particularly require a considerable amount of microscopic food which can only be developed and maintained in old water. The presence of a few decaying aquarium plants is desirable. I would appreciate hearing from readers successful in maintaining these fish in their home aquaria.

Figure 1.15. *Where the labyrinth fish live.*

Figure 1.16. *Butterfly Maze.* Reproduced from *Maze Craze II* © 1973 with permission from Price Stern Sloan, Inc., Los Angeles, California. To order this maze book, dial (800) 421-0892. Start at the tiny word "BEGIN."

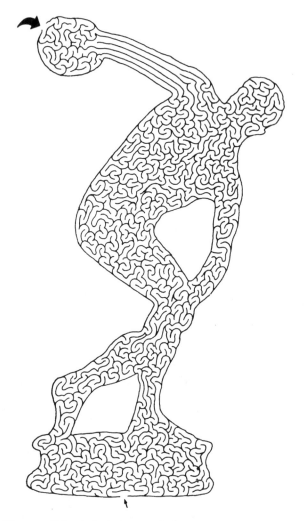

Figure 1.17. *The Discus Thrower (Discobolos), Rome, Italy.* Reproduced from *Tough Mazes III* © 1991 with permission from Price Stern Sloan, Inc., Los Angeles, California. To order this maze book, dial (800) 421-0892.

Aside from labyrinth fish, you may also be fascinated by the *Labyrinthodontia*, a major group of extinct amphibia, dominant in the late Paleozoic and Triassic. Some scientists think that the labyrinthodonts may have been the ancestors of all land vertebrates. These labyrinthodonts looked somewhat like today's newts – but some were as large as alligators. They had *labyrinthine teeth* where the dentin layer is enfolded into complex patterns and ridges. I am interested in hearing from readers with pictures of these teeth.

Laburnum is a genus of trees and shrubs with beautiful butterfly-like flowers.

Their roots taste like licorice, but please don't attempt to test my taste observation, since their seeds are highly poisonous. Cows which consume the plant will die, although rabbits remain totally unharmed. The wood of these weird laburnums has a striking greenish-brown or reddish-brown hue and is ideal for cabinet making. Laburnum wood was once of the most prized kinds of timber in all of Scotland.

Finally, *Labyrinthistis* is an inflammation of a mazelike structure in the internal ear, and *Labyrinthula* is a genus of an organism which is a parasite in aquatic plants.

1.14 Credits: Möbius and Stairway Mazes

The Möbius and stairway mazes at the beginning of this chapter are from master maze-maker Dave Phillips' book *Mind-Boggling Mazes* published by Dover (1979, NY). Some of his mazes have hundreds of possible solutions. Phillips remarks, "Do not expect to doodle your pencil leisurely through these mazes, for here you will find mazes which will intrigue you with their geometric trickery and will involve you in mystifying journeys."

1.15 The Diabolical Die

The following products all relate to mazes and should stimulate your imagination.

• Three-Dimensional Mazes: 1) *The Diabolical Die*. This wooden die contains a network of tunnels in which a metal ball is hopelessly lost. One of the holes is an exit. Ishi Press International, 76 Bonaventura Dr, San Jose, CA 95134. 2) *Miller's Maze*. 3-D marble maze. Creata International, Los Angeles, CA 90045. 3) *Snafooz*. Computer-designed jigsaw-like pieces which must be assembled to form a pretty, colorful cube. Idea Group, Box 12637, Palm Desert, CA 92260. 4) *Mighty Maze*. 3-D marble maze. Creata International, Crystal Lake, IL 60614.

• Two-Dimensional Mazes: 1) *Simply Amazing*. Mazes which contain a central rotating insert. Rotate the inner square by 90 degrees, and a new maze is created. Yiee Co., Newport Beach, CA 92660 ($2.00). 2) *Connections*. Fascinating strategy game for 2 players. Link opposite sides of the board with tiles. Connections North America, Box 49, Cardiff-by-the-Sea, CA 92007. 3) *Master Labyrinth*. A strategy game using 33 tiles to create a network of connected paths and dead ends. 2-4 players. The maze is made particularly difficult because the locations of the players, as well as the maze configuration, are constantly changing. Ravensburger/International Playthings.

1.16 Cross References

See "Knights in Hell" on page 321 for a chess maze. See "Slugs Trapped in Jordan Curves" on page 45 for Jordan curve mazes. For information on fractals, see: "Smithson's Fractal Anabiotic Ana Sequences" on page 35, "Fractal Spiders and Frame-Robertson Bushes" on page 87, and "Labyrinthine Lundin Curves" on page 103. For fractal integer sequences and patterns see "The Drums of Ulupu" on page 71 and "Beauty and the Bits" on page 79. For fractal attractors, see "Fantastic Feather Fractals" on page 33. For fractal ant farms, see "Electronic and Fractal Ant Farms" on page 173.

1.17 For Further Reading

1.   Abbott, R. (1990) *Mad Mazes*. Bob Adams: New York.

2.   Quinn, L. D. (1975) *Challenging Mazes*. Dover: New York.

3.   Hull, J. (1973) *Maze Craze 2*. Troubador Press: Los Angeles.

4.   Schroeder, M. (1991) *Fractals, Chaos, Power Laws*. Freeman: New York.

5.   Shepherd, W. (1973) *Big Book of Mazes and Labyrinths*. Dover: New York.

6.   Mandelbrot, B. (1982) *The Fractal Geometry of Nature*. Freeman: New York.

7.   Dye, D. S. (1981) *The New Book of Chinese Lattice Designs*. Dover: New York.

8.   Wegner, T., Peterson. M. (1991) *Fractal Creations*. Waite Group Press: California.

9.   Sullivan, S. (1990) *Tough Mazes III*. Troubador Press: Los Angeles. Also: Heimann, R. (1989) *Amazing Mazes*. Watermill Press: Mahwah, NJ.; Doob, P. R. (1990) *The Idea of the Labyrinth from Classical Antiquity through the Middle Ages*. Cornell: New York. (Describes labyrinths in literature and art.); Russo, D. A. (1991) *The Ultimate Maze Book*. Fireside (Simon & Schuster): NY.

10.   Pickover, C. (1990) *Computers, Pattern, Chaos, and Beauty*. St. Martin's Press: NY.

In the maze below, start at the tip of the man's finger and get to the soap without crossing any lines. (From Shepherd, 1973.)

Chapter 2

Electronic Kaleidoscopes for the Mind

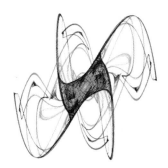

"The essences are each a separate glass, through which the sun of being's light is passed – each tinted fragment sparkles in the sun: a thousand colors, but the light is one."   Jami (15th Century)

For over a hundred years, kaleidoscopes have fascinated scientists, designers, artists, and children. In the late seventeenth century, small religious shrines began to take advantage of multiple mirror reflections characteristic of today's kaleidoscopes. Inside a wooden pavilion, tiny replicas of saints were placed in front of angled mirrors that gave added impact to the scene. Invented by Sir David Brewster, and patented by him in 1817, kaleidoscopes have since taken many forms.[3] Usually, they're simple tube instruments which produce a symmetrical image by the repeated reflections in a set of plane mirrors. Often the instrument consists of just two flat pieces of glass mirrors which meet; their planes are inclined to one another at some even submultiple of 360 degrees such as 30 degrees (360/12) or 22.5 degrees (360/16).

Here's a simple method used to create computer-generated kaleidoscopes, and the concept should be easy for most personal computer users. The kaleidoscopes are composed primarily of triangles, with a few circles also scattered about.[4] Start by randomly selecting 3 vertices of a triangle. I'll call the first three vertices (x_1, y_1), (x_2, y_2), and (x_3, y_3). Draw this triangle using any computer graphics package you have available to you (or if you have patience, draw it by hand!). This is the "parent" triangle. All the reflected versions are called "children." You can calculate the positions of the children points rather easily. Just take each of the three (x,y) coordinates, and negate them, or shuffle them in all

---

[3] An attempt was made to discount Brewster's kaleidoscope invention as being the same as the multiple mirror devices of Kircher, Harris, Bradley, Wood and others; however, none of these writers described the same arrangement of mirrors that produced Brewster's attractive symmetrical patterns.

[4] Rather than use triangles, you could easily apply these principles to a collection of points, if this is easier for you.

Figure 2.1. *Computer-generated kaleidoscope pattern.*

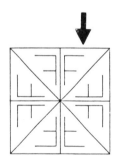

the possible ways: (x,y), $(-x,y)$, $(x,-y)$, $(-x,-y)$, (y,x), $(-y,x)$, $(y,-x)$, $(-y,-x)$. This produces a kaleidoscopic symmetry schematically illustrated at the left. To insure that the initially selected random points of the triangle fall within the triangular region of the plane marked by the arrow in the diagram, I actually swap x and y whenever a randomly selected x is greater than a y in an (x,y) pair. The pseudocode shows you how to do this. That's all there is to it. The same basic idea applies to the positioning of the small circles in the designs. You can choose colors randomly.

I have access to special purpose graphics hardware that can render many thousands of triangular facets in a second, but even with simpler computer systems, beautiful pictures can result fairly quickly. For additional beauty, translate the pattern described by the above (x,y) shufflings several times in a checkerboard pattern, as I have done for the figures here (Figure 2.1 and Figure 2.3). For additional beauty, I have also interpolated color across the facet of each triangle. This means that if one vertex is randomly chosen to be red, and the other two green, then various shades between red and green will show on the facets.

As I stare at the patterns moving and unfolding on the graphics screen I can only wonder what Sir David Brewster in 1817 would have thought. Would the

Figure 2.2. *Kaleidoscope pattern.* See "How to Create Kaleidoscopic Designs Without a Computer" on page 27 for information on how to create this pattern.

modern-day electronic kaleidoscopes discussed in this chapter, involving no physical mirrors, be infringements on his patent? No, but like the real thing, the electronic kaleidoscope's colored pieces make a fantastic "wallpaper for the mind." Why don't you try designing a similar system? Try applying different kinds of symmetries. You might even try to design a 3-D version, where the triangles and circles are scattered about in three dimensions, and not limited to a plane. Finally, you can introduce some asymmetry into your designs by choosing *not* to reflect certain triangles. Here's an interesting example where the computer allows you to design a non-physical kaleidoscope which could not be created using mirrors in the real world.

For those interested in learning more about traditional kaleidoscopes, consider *Through the Kaleidoscope and Beyond* by Cozy Baker (Beechcliff Books, 1987). The book describes handcrafted models, and contains beautiful color photographs. It also has a list of current kaleidoscope makers and shops. Another interesting book is *Computers in Art, Design and Animation* by Lansdown and Earnshaw (Springer, 1989). A chapter in this book discusses computer kaleidoscopes operating on digitized images of people and scenery. Another source for information on kaleidoscopes is *The Family Creative Workshop* series of books. This series published in 1974 by Plenary Publications in New York has a fasci-

Figure 2.3. *Computer-generated kaleidoscope pattern.*

nating chapter on how to create various kaleidoscopes using mirrors and acrylic strips.

2.1 Teleidoscopes and Polyangular Kaleidoscopes

"The computer is dangerously close to being our modern version of the kaleidoscope. The twists and turns of programs give unexpected variations of form that seem to be strikingly beautiful. But is it art? What is beauty?"
Robert Mueller, 1972, *Art in America*

A toy related to the kaleidoscope is the *teleidoscope*. Teleidoscopes have a lens so that the object or scene toward which you point the tube is reflected again and again. Artists often work with teleidoscopes, kaleidoscopes, and kaleidoscopic effects. Artist and educator Judith Karelitz, for example, has produced the Karelitz Kaleidoscope, a polarized-light sculpture in the Permanent Design Collection of the Museum of Modern Art in New York. Two of her kaleidoscopes are patented. Why not design your own kaleidoscopes and try to patent ones which have the most unusual principles of operation? Brewster himself and several later inventors created some advanced versions of the original instrument. These included: the *polyangular kaleidoscope*, which allows the user to vary the

Figure 2.4. *Kaleidoscope pattern.* See "How to Create Kaleidoscopic Designs Without a Computer" on page 27 for information on how to create this pattern.

angle between the mirrors, the *multimirror kaleidoscope*, where three or four mirrors are used instead of the usual two, and the *kaleidograph*, where the patterns are displayed on a screen.

2.2 How to Create Kaleidoscopic Designs Without a Computer

> *"Be sure that any eye which sees the light has seen it only by the light itself."*
> Shah Nematallah Wali (1st Century)

You may create your own kaleidoscopic designs, without a computer and without even any freehand drawing, simply by using sections from illustrations you find in

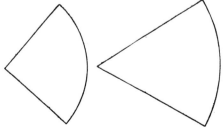

books and newspapers. Start by selecting an interesting design. Next use either of the wedged-shaped frames illustrated here. The frame on the left is used for creating a four-part circular design. The frame on the right is used for creating a six-part circular design. You can enlarge

three frames as needed. Cut out the wedge shape, thereby creating a window thor-

```
ALGORITHM: How to Create a Computer Kaleidoscope.
DO FOR i = 1 to 40
    x1 = random;    y1 = random
    x2 = random;    y2 = random
    x3 = random;    y3 = random
    /* Confine initial pattern to lower right quadrant */
    if ( x1 > y1 ) then (save=x1; x1=y1; y1=save;)
    if ( x2 > y2 ) then (save=x2; x2=y2; y2=save;)
    if ( x3 > y3 ) then (save=x3; x3=y3; y3=save;)
    DrawTriangleAt(x1,y1,x2,y2,x3,y3)
    /* Create 7 reflected images /
    DO FOR j = 1 to 7
        Flip (x,y) Points as Described in Text
        DrawTriangleAt (x1,y1,x2,y2,x3,y3)
    END
END
```

Pseudocode 2.1. *How to create a computer kaleidoscope.* Aside from using triangles, you can also use dots, lines, and circles.

ough which you can view sections of possible source illustrations. The most difficult part of this procedure is to make a mirror copy of the source illustration as shown at the end of the chapter. To create the mirror image, trace the original design using tracing paper. Turn the tracing paper over and retrace it onto another sheet of paper. Once you have created the mirror image you can assemble an amazing and endless number of kaleidoscopic designs by repeating (alternating) the two patterns in a circular fashion. Figure 2.2 and Figure 2.4 show two kaleidoscopic designs which were made using this approach. For more examples of this non-computer method, see Norma and Leslie Finkel's book *Kaleidoscopic Designs* (Dover, NY).

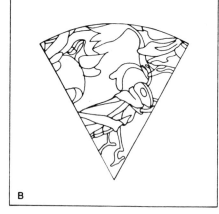

A   B

Halley map for the $Z^7 - 1 = 0$.

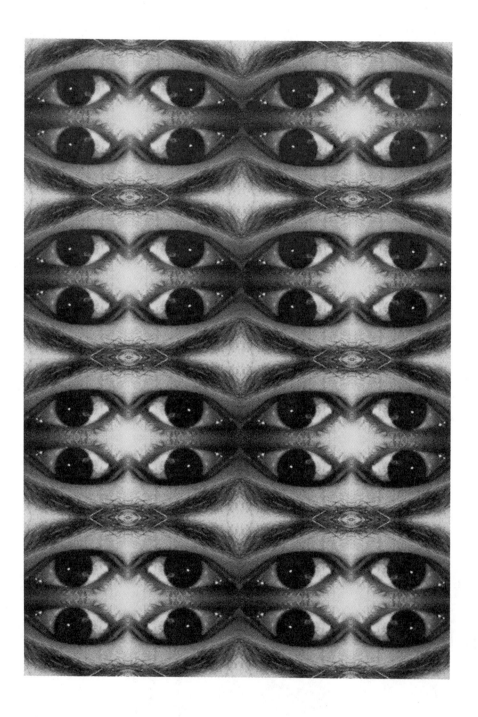

Chapter 3

Interlude: I See Your Eyes
At Night in Dreams

"The eyes have one language everywhere."   George Herbert

In order to stimulate your imagination, I have scattered various "Interlude" sections throughout the book which feature various professional artists using science and technology. This first Interlude shows some of my own work called "Eyescapes." These are symmetrical images created from a single human or animal eye. To create the image facing this page, I first digitized one of my own eyes using a video camera interfaced to a personal computer. Somewhat reminiscent of the ideas presented in the previous chapter on computer kaleidoscopes, I then applied various (software) mirror operations to create a larger composite image from the single eye. Below is an "Eyescape" created using a single animal eye. Can you guess what the animal is?

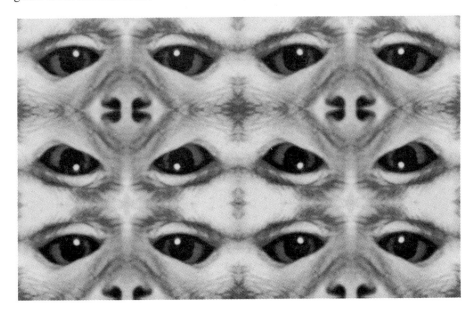

Chapter 4

Fantastic Feather Fractals

"Things in nature such as crystals or flowers, the human body, landscapes, and so on, can become a meaningful part of a work of art. But when nature is simply reflected – increasingly possible as computerized techniques advance – its value as art becomes problematical. The results may be impressive, but they lack the necessary human insight and intervention, remaining artlike rather than becoming art." Robert Mueller, 1972, *Art in America*

Among my favorite mathematical shapes are the *Fantastic Feather Fractals* which have an evanescent, wing-like appearance. With a computer, you can easily create them using *dynamical systems*. Dynamical systems are models comprised of rules describing the way some quantity undergoes a change through time. For example, the motion of planets about the sun can be modeled as a dynamical system in which the planets move according to Newton's laws. The frontispiece diagram for this chapter represents the behavior of mathematical expressions called *differential equations*. Think of a differential equation as a machine that takes in values for all the variables at an initial time and then generates the new values at some later time. Just as one can track the path of a jet by the smoke path it leaves behind, computer graphics provides a way to follow paths of particles whose motion is determined by simple differential equations. The practical side of dynamical systems is that they can be used to describe the behavior of real-world things such as planetary motion, fluid flow, the diffusion of drugs, the behavior of inter-industry relationships, and the vibration of airplane wings. Often the resulting graphic patterns resemble smoke, swirls, candle flames, and windy mists.

The *Feather Fractal* shown facing this page is an example of a strange attractor. As background, attractors represent the behavior to which a system settles down or is "attracted" (for example, a point or a looping closed cycle). An example of a *fixed point attractor* is a mass at the end of a spring, with friction. It eventually arrives at an equilibrium point and stops moving. A *limit cycle* is exemplified by a metronome. The metronome will tick-tock back and forth – its motion always periodic and regular. A *"strange attractor"* has an irregular,

```
ALGORITHM: How to Create Feather Fractals.
    aa = -0.48; b = 0.93; p = 9200000; c = 2.0 - 2.0*aa;
    x = 3.0; y = 0;
    w = aa*x + c*(x*x)/(1. + x*x);
    for(n = 0; n <= p; n++) {
        PlotDotAt (x,y);
        z = x; x = b*y + w; u = x*x;
        w = aa*x + c*u/(1. + u); y = w-z;
    }
```

Pseudocode 4.1. *How to create a Feather Fractal.* Examine the region between -10 and 10 in the *x* and *y* directions. (The program coded here is in the style of the C language.)

unpredictable behavior. Its behavior can still be graphed, but the graph is much more complicated. With "tame" attractors, initially close points stay together as they approach the attractor. With strange attractors, initially adjacent points eventually follow widely divergent trajectories. Like leaves in a turbulent stream, it is impossible to predict where the leaves will end up given their initial positions.

Pseudocode 4.1 shows you how to produce the feather pattern, a representation of a dynamical system. Simply plot a dot at positions determined by *x* and *y* through the iteration. Use double precision variables. This pattern is fractal; that is, as you continue to magnify any region of the feather, additional intricate structure is revealed. This class of fractal attractor has been described in greater detail in: Lauwerier, H. (1990) *Fractals.* Princeton University Press. (Section on Gumowski and Mira.)

4.1 Cross References

See the following sections for information on fractals: "Smithson's Fractal Anabiotic Ana Sequences" on page 35, "Fractal Spiders and Frame-Robertson Bushes" on page 87, and "Labyrinthine Lundin Curves" on page 103. For fractal mazes, see "Mazes for the Mind" on page 3. For fractal integer sequences and patterns, see "The Drums of Ulupu" on page 71 and "Beauty and the Bits" on page 79. For fractal ant farms, see "Electronic and Fractal Ant Farms" on page 173.

Chapter 5

Smithson's Fractal Anabiotic Ana Sequences

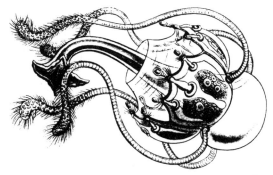

"He remembered exploring those other-worldly curves from one degree to the next, lemniscate to folium, progressing eventually to an ungraphable class of curve, no precise slope at any point, a tangent-defying mind marvel."
Don DeLillo, *Ratner's Star*

When Mike Smithson from James Cook University first told me about "Ana"  sequences, I first thought the name derived from the biological term "Anabiosis." Anabiosis is a state of suspended animation in organisms, such as rotifers, which can be induced simply by drying them. The minute one adds water, the creatures stir to life. A dry mud bed becomes a swarm of rapidly moving organisms in a short time. Like anabiotic animals, the Ana sequences described here also seem to come to life by suddenly growing and creating intricate patterns.

As background to the wonderful Ana sequences, in *Computers and the Imagination* I discussed a similar sequence, the *likeness sequence*, which yielded strange-looking designs when plotted as a sequence of connected lines. Because the sequence never seems to contain a number greater than 3, you don't need large computers to begin exploring.

The likeness sequence can be denoted by $u_{r,n}$, where r is the row number, and n the column number:

```
1
1  1
2  1
1  2  1  1
1  1  1  2  2  1
   . . .
```

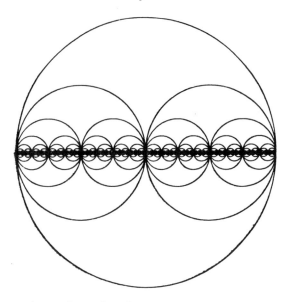

Figure 5.1. *Cantor cheese of nested circles.*

You probably can't guess the numerical entries for the next row. However, the answer is actually simple, when viewed in hindsight. To appreciate the answer, it helps to speak the entries in each row out loud. Note that row Two has two "ones," thereby giving the sequence 2 1 for the third row. Row Three has one "two" and one "one." Row Four has one "one," one "two," and two "ones." From this, an entire sequence $u_{r,n}$ can be generated. This interesting sequence was described in a German article, where M. Hilgemeier called the sequence "Die Gleichniszahlen-Reihe," which translates into English as "the likeness sequence." The sequence, also extensively studied by John H. Conway, grows rather rapidly. For example, row 15 is:

132113213221133112132113311121113122121321131211132
221123113112221131112311332111213211322211312113211

After reading about this likeness sequence in my book, Mike Smithson began studying a somewhat related sequence, the Ana sequence. The rule for generating Ana sequences is to begin with a letter of the alphabet and to then generate the next row by using the indefinite articles "a" or "an" as appropriate. (This will probably be best understood by English-speaking readers.) The most obvious letter to start with is "a":

```
a
ana
ana ann ana
ana ann ana ana ann ann ana ann ana
    . . .
```

Figure 5.2. *Cantor cheese-like drawing.* How many repeated levels do you see? ("Scruting the inscrutable," from Roger Shepard's *Mind Sights.* © 1990 by R. Shepard. Reprinted with permission of W.H. Freeman and Co.)

The first row contains an "a," giving us "ana" for the second row. How many different words can you generate with this method? It turns out that only the words "ann" and "ana" occur, but there is an interesting self-similarity cascade occurring here. Mike Smithson's following diagram will help you see this fractal structure. Here "a" is represented as a dark rectangle, and "n" is represented by a white space with no rectangle. The result is an *asymmetric Cantor dust* (Figure 5.3).

As background, a symmetrical Cantor set can be constructed by taking an interval of length 1 and removing its middle third (but leaving the end points of this middle third). The top two rows of Figure 5.3 show this removal. This leaves two smaller intervals, each one-third as long. In the symmetrical case, the middle thirds of these smaller segments are removed and the process is repeated. The symmetrical Cantor set has a "measure zero," which means that a randomly thrown dart would be very unlikely to hit a member. At the same time it has so many members that it is in fact uncountable, just like the set of all of the real numbers between 0 and 1. Many mathematicians, and even Cantor himself for a while, doubted that a crazy set with these properties could exist. As you have just

Figure 5.3. *Anabiotic Ana fractal.* The letter "A" is represented by a dark bar. The letter "N" is represented by a gap.

been shown, however, such a set is possible to formulate. The dimension D of this particular Cantor dust for an infinite number of iterations is less than one since $D = \log 2/ \log 3 = 0.63$. You can read more about the concept of fractional dimensions, and how 0.63 was derived, in Mandelbrot's *The Fractal Geometry of Nature*. Cantor dusts with other fractal dimensions can easily be created by removing different sizes (or numbers) of intervals from the starting interval of length 1. Cantor sets are highly useful mathematical models for many physical phenomena, from the distribution of galaxies in the universe to the fractal Cantor-like structure of the rings of Saturn.

A topologically similar set starts with a circular disc. Everything *except* for two smaller discs is removed. Here we use pairs of circles rather than pairs of lines, and the subdivisions are repeated as with the Cantor set described in the previous paragraph. We retain only those points inside the circles. Figure 5.1 is a picture of this Cantor cheese with each circle's radius slightly less than half of the previous generation's radius. (The term "generation" refers to the nesting level of the circles; see the program code). If we consider just the line along the diameter, the fractal dimension for the set of points is close to 1. Smaller fractal dimensions

```
ALGORITHM: How to Create Cantor Cheese.

m          - a 1-D array containing the midpoints of each circle.
gen        - the number of generations.
DrawCircleAt - draws a circle at (x,y) with a given radius.
The picture boundaries go from 0 to 100 in the x and y directions.

m(1)=50;    count=1;
radius=50; frac=1;
DrawCircleAt(m(count),50,radius);
do gen = 0 to 10;
    bot = 2**gen; top=(2**(gen+1))-1;
    radius=radius/2  ;  l=radius;
    do i = bot to top;
        m(count+1)= m(i) - frac*l;
        DrawCircleAt(m(count+1),50,radius);
        m(count+2) = m(i) + frac*l;
        DrawCircleAt(m(count+2),50,radius);
        count=count+2;
    end;
end;
```

Pseudocode 5.1. *Cantor Cheese construction.*

are obtained by using circles which are further shrunken and separated so that
they do not touch each other.

5.1 Stop and Think

1. What happens if you start the ana fractal sequence with a letter other than
    "a"? Is this new sequence fractal? (For more information on fractal
    sequences, see "The Drums of Ulupu" on page 71.)

2. Are there other verbal fractals waiting to be discovered using different rules?

3. How quickly do the rows of this ana sequence grow in size?

4. What is the ratio of the occurrence of "a's" to "n's" in each row as the
    sequence grows? Try other starting letters.

5. Draw a plot where "a" causes a line to be drawn in a vertical direction (up),
    and an "n" causes a line to be drawn in a vertical direction (down). As you
    proceed through the letters in a single row, move the pen one unit to the right
    for each letter encountered, creating a steplike function. What pattern do you
    get? What does this tell you about the distribution of letters in the row?

5.2 Cross References

See the following sections for information on fractals: "Smithson's Fractal Anabiotic Ana
Sequences" on page 35, "Fractal Spiders and Frame-Robertson Bushes" on page 87, and
"Labyrinthine Lundin Curves" on page 103. For fractal mazes, see "Mazes for the Mind"
on page 3. For fractal integer sequences and patterns, see "The Drums of Ulupu" on
page 71 and "Beauty and the Bits" on page 79. For feather fractals, see "Fantastic

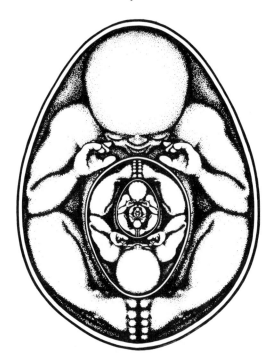

Figure 5.4. *Recursion in art.* How many repeated levels do you see? ("Eggspecting," from Roger Shepard's *Mind Sights.* © 1990 by R. Shepard. Reprinted with permission of W.H. Freeman and Co.)

Feather Fractals" on page 33. For fractal ant farms, see "Electronic and Fractal Ant Farms" on page 173.

5.3 For Further Reading

1. Hilgemeir, M. (1986) Die Gleichniszahlen-Reihe. *Bild der Wissenschaft.* 12: 194-195.

2. Pickover, C. (1987) DNA Vectorgrams: representation of cancer gene sequences as movements along a 2-D cellular lattice, *IBM Journal of Research and Development.* 31: 111-119.

3. Pickover, C., Khorasani, E. (1991) Visualization of the Gleichniszahlen-Reihe, an unusual number theory sequence, *Math. Spectrum.* 23(4): 113-115.

Computer-Generated Leaf Vein Pattern

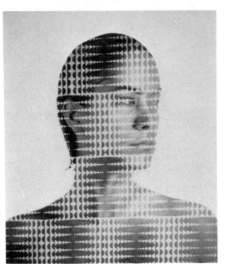

Chapter 6

Interlude: Fractals and Feminism

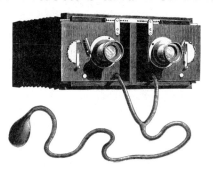

"Ellen Carey is an artist with a camera who manipulates images, making them larger than life. Her conversation leaps from feminist theory to fractal geometry." Anne Hamilton, 1991, *The Hartford Courant*

"Abstract photography is almost a contradiction in terms. Photographs, after all, always represent some trace of physical reality, even if it is not immediately recognizable." Andy Grundberg, 1990, *New York Times*

Many artists in the 1990's are intrigued with simple geometrical shapes and more complicated fractals forms. Ellen Carey, an Associate Professor of Photography at the University of Hartford in Connecticut, is just such an artist. Carey is a photographer who, in the 1980's, was chosen by the Polaroid Corporation to use its huge special camera that takes 20x24 one-of-a-kind pictures. The camera (initially located at the Cambridge, Massachusetts headquarters of the Polaroid Corporation but now in New York City) moves on wheels, and requires two assistants to operate!

Carey's use of the large format camera isn't for everyone, since there are only four such cameras in the world. Since Carey's work explores the proportional harmonies found in nature, science, and mathematics (especially fractal geometry), the Polaroid 20x24 complements her fascination with geometrical order by offering a contact (no negative) grain-free photograph with lush hues and a soft-edged brilliance specific to Polaroid film.

Although the process is expensive ($1,800 per day), Carey has enjoyed Polaroid's support since 1983, and has published and exhibited widely in museums, galleries, and corporate collections nationally and internationally.

Carey uses multiple exposures, with elaborate lighting set-ups and collaged patterns that find their visual sources in molecules, snowflakes, DNA, spirals, etc., which veil or camouflage her face. Primarily self-portraits, these images seem to speak of the self, as Carey says, "not only in existential terms (who am I?) but also on the complexity of 'selfness' in the larger context of the unknown and known complexities of nature, science, and mathematics."

Her technical breakthrough in 1984, in which designs simulate what a projector might do with pattern over a face, echo the legacy of the ancient ritual of body decoration taken into the 21st century while celebrating the kinship between art and science, chaos and order, symmetry and asymmetry, dark and light. Imagining photography as painting with light, her images are extraordinary and haunting, and the black and white examples shown here do not begin to do justice to the brilliant primary colors and intense hues of her original works. Carey writes:

> With the recent 150th anniversary of photography's invention, the once-familiar question "Can photography be art?" is hardly ever asked; most observers answered in the affirmative some time ago. ... I view myself as a late 20th-century woman artist using photography as the artistic tool which best reflects my time and my nature; In fact, I have made a conscious decision to work in a medium in which a machine can combine with imagination to redefine notions of truth and beauty at 1/125 of a second.

For more information, contact: Ellen Carey, Hartford Art School, University of Hartford, 200 Bloomfield Ave., West Hartford, CT 06117. The photograph of Ellen Carey sitting in the chair is courtesy of Albert Dickson, *The Hartford Courant, Sunday Magazine, Northeast.*

Chapter 7

Slugs Trapped in Jordan Curves

"What does the universe look like? A balloon that's expanding? A funnel full of ball bearings? A double helix? A strip of paper twisted and connected in a one-sided ring?" Don DeLillo, *Ratner's Star*

A few years ago I wrote a short science fiction tale about a creeping, sluglike creature from a planet where the moist inhabitants had a peculiar fascination with mazes. The slug kings would often place political prisoners in maze-like structures. If the slug citizen succeeded in freeing itself from the maze, it would be allowed to live. If not, it would be forever trapped, with no food, and would slowly die. In order to gain its freedom, the prisoner had a second option. The slug could slither up the wall and look over the wall to see what was on the outside of the maze, but it could not climb over the top due to barbed wire. If, as a result of looking, the slug could correctly guess whether or not it were *possible* to escape, the slug would be set free.

The slug prison mazes were of a peculiar type. Topologically they were *Jordan curves*, such as the ones below, which are merely circles that have been twisted out of shape. A circle divides any flat surface into two areas – inside and outside. Like a circle, Jordan curves have an inside and outside – and to get from one to the other, at least one line (wall) must be crossed.

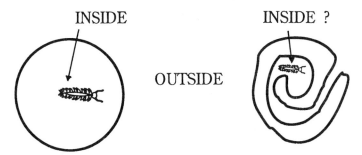

Let's return to the slug story. One day, a prisoner slug named Mr. Nadroj was able to accurately ascertain, simply by looking over the walls in one direction,

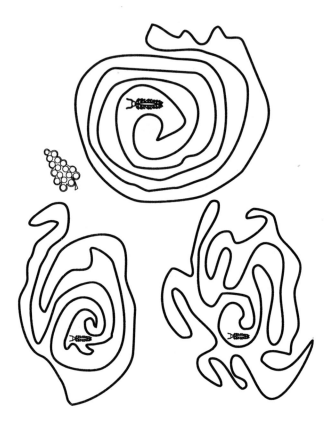

Figure 7.1. *Are the slugs inside or outside their curvy prisons?* To determine this, use the method described in the text whereby a straight line is drawn from the slug to the outside world, and count the number of times the line intersects a wall.

whether or not he was on the inside or the outside of the maze. The fact that such a prediction could be made took all of the sadistic fun away from the slug kings. Since that time, the penal system on slugworld has been thrown into chaos. Nadroj's quick way to tell whether he was inside or outside the Jordan curves was to count the number of times an imaginary line drawn from his body to the outside world crossed a wall. If the straight line crossed the curve an *even* number of times, the slug is outside the maze; if an *odd* number of times, the slug was inside.

Back on earth, Marie Ennemond Camille Jordan (1838-1922) offered a proof of the same rules for determining the inside and outside of these kinds of curves. (The proof was corrected in 1905 by Veblen.) Jordan was a French mathematician, originally trained as an engineer. It is doubtful that the slug from a distant planet heard of Jordan's work. Can you "solve" the Jordan curves in Figure 7.1? Are the slugs inside or outside of each maze? For other mazes, see "Mazes for the Mind" on page 3.

$Z \rightarrow Z^2 + (-0.74543 + 0.11301i)$

Chapter 8

Ghost Patterns and Puzzles

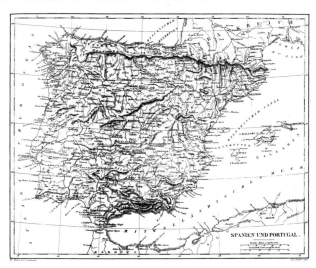

"I am half inclined to think we are all ghosts... They are not actually alive in us; but there they are dormant, all the same, and we can never be rid of them. Whenever I take up a newspaper and read it, I fancy I see ghosts creeping between the lines. There must be ghosts all over the world. They must be as countless as grains of sand it seems to me. And we are so miserably afraid of the light, all of us."
Henrick Ibsen

Place a piece of tracing paper, with equally spaced grid lines, over the map of any country in the world, or any state in any country. (Why don't you try this for Pennsylvania or the map of Spain pictured above.) Draw a large square on the tracing paper which surrounds a region containing around 100 towns. Next place a black dot over the largest cities or towns. If you do this for all the cities or

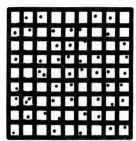

towns included in the large boundary square, you will have what looks like a random collection of hundreds of dots speckled on your graph paper. But are they truly randomly positioned? The human visual system is remarkable at detecting subtle patterns in near-random data, but in certain circumstances it is difficult for us to determine if a collection of dots is random by eye alone. It turns out that the collection of cities and towns in most regions of the world is not random. As an example, if you count the number of cities (dots) on your paper in each grid square, there will usually be fewer empty grid squares than you would measure for a truly random scattering of points. Also, there will be more squares containing just one town than you will measure for a truly random scattering of points. The late Polish mathematician Hugo Ste-

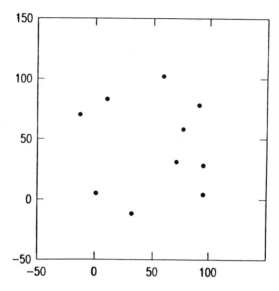

Figure 8.1. *Ghost pattern puzzle.* Is this a random collection of dots, or is there some structure present?

inhaus, in his book *Mathematical Snapshots,* believes that this effect is due to the trend of towns to keep apart from one another.

I've just described one example where the human eye finds difficulty in distinguishing random and non-random collections of dots. A few years ago I enjoyed creating what I call *ghost patterns*. Before explaining them and showing you how you can compute and draw these patterns, try the following exercise. Look at Figure 8.1 and Figure 8.2. Is there any pattern in the collection of dots in either of these two figures? It turns out that one of the two figures contains a random collection of 10 dots, while the other contains 5 dots superimposed on the same 5 dots which have been rotated by 60 degrees around the center of the plot. With this hint, can you determine which is the random one, and which is not? Unless you are more exceptional than most people I asked, you could not determine which is random and which is not. I like to think of this second copy of the same set of dots as "ghosts" or "doppelgangers." (Dictionaries define a "doppelganger" as a ghostly counterpart and companion of a person, or a ghostly double of a live person that haunts him through life and is usually visible only to himself.) In fact, the position of all the dots in Figure 8.2 was determined by a random number generator. In Figure 8.1 five dots were superimposed upon a rotated copy of the same five dots. Is this hard to see? Figure 8.3 will show you the position of the 5 dots before and after rotation. Try this puzzle on some friends. I have included a few additional ghost patterns for you to solve. Can you guess which of the remaining figures contain randomly positioned dots and which do not? I leave this as an exercise to you, and you may get better with practice. (See "Solution Saraband" on page 419 for the solutions.)

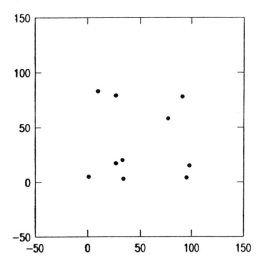

Figure 8.2. *Ghost pattern puzzle.* Is this a random collection of dots, or is there some structure present?

You could create your own *10-dot ghost patterns* simply by drawing 5 dots on a paper, making a copy of the paper on a transparency, and then rotating the transparency by 60 degrees about the center of the pattern. Alternatively, on a personal computer, you can make an endless variety of 10-dot ghost puzzles. Pseudocode 8.1 shows you how. In the computer program, if you make the variable *a* greater than 1, the new set of 5 dots will not only be rotated from the original dots, but the set will also undergo an expansion, as if the plane containing the dots were expanding like an inflating balloon. Setting *a* equal to 1, as I have done for the previous examples, makes the solution of the problems hard enough! Setting *a* somewhat greater than one makes the 10-dot puzzles impossible to solve by mere mortals. The computer makes experiments such as these quite easy to perform.

8.1 10,000 Dots

"Strip the veil from the eyes of world-sight. Look around thee, ahead, behind, up and down. Look and discover the nature of this whirling circle, and that which encompasses it, that which surrounds you."

Jami (15th Century)

Let me conclude by showing you an example of a gigantic random dot pattern created with 10,000 dots (Figure 8.6). Here is a pattern of 10,000 random dots which is superimposed on itself and rotated by a small angle and expanded. You can perceive spirals about the point of rotation. If the angle of rotation is

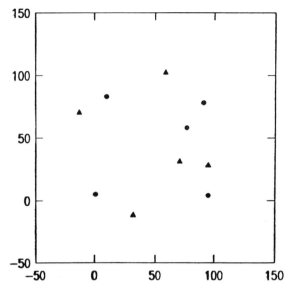

Figure 8.3. *Ghost pattern puzzle.* The 5 dots in Figure 8.1 before and after rotation.

increased, the perceived circles gradually disappear until a totally unstructured dot display is seen. This effect, studied by Leon Glass in the 1970's, demonstrates the ability of the human visual system to detect local autocorrelations and may suggest a physiological basis of form perception in higher animals. Though this pattern was produced by a computer, similar patterns can easily be generated using sprinkled ink and transparencies. Matisse, in 1908, aptly wrote in *Notes of a Painter*:

> If I put a black dot on a sheet of white paper, the dot will be visible no matter how far I stand away from it – it is clear notation; but beside this dot I place another one, and then a third. Already there is confusion.

8.2 Fact File

Twenty-five percent of American adults, 45,600,000 persons, believe in ghosts. There are an estimated 100 professional ghost investigators working in America. Of these individuals, three make more than $100,000 annually. (Source: Tom Heymann's *The Unofficial US Census*, Fawcett Columbine: NY (1991)).

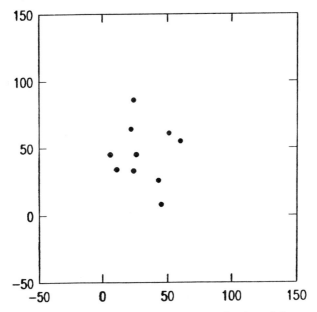

Figure 8.4. *Ghost pattern puzzle.* Is this a random collection of dots, or is there some structure present?

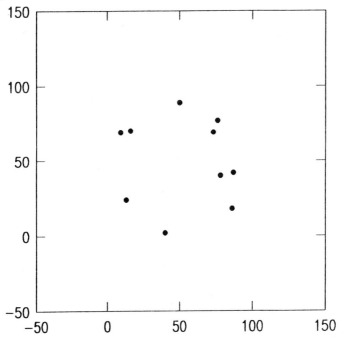

Figure 8.5. *Ghost pattern puzzle.* Is this a random collection of dots, or is there some structure present?

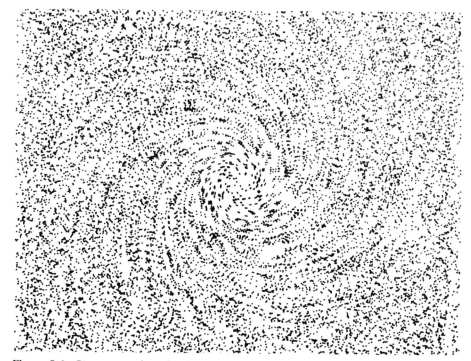

Figure 8.6. *Gigantic random dot-display.* This figure was produced by superimposing a figure containing 10,000 random dots upon itself and subsequent rotation by three degrees and uniform expansion by a factor of 1.1. Note: if the rotation is much larger, the eye looses the ability to perceive the spiral patterns.

```
ALGORITHM: How to Create Ghost Patterns
a= 1; /* scale factor */
DO FOR i = 1 to 5
   xr = random*100
   yr = random*100
   PrintDotAt(xr,yr)
   /* Rotate dot about center point 50,50 */
   xsave = a*((xr-50)*cos(angle)+(yr-50)*sin(angle)) + 50
   yr    = a*((yr-50)*cos(angle)-(xr-50)*sin(angle)) + 50
   xr=xsave
   PrintDotAt(xr,yr)
END
```

Pseudocode 8.1. *How to create Ghost Patterns.*

Chapter 9

Is a Picture Worth 75 Words?

"We cannot let ourselves be carried away with dazzling new scientific techniques, believing that they are automatically art just because they overwhelm our untrained artistic eyes. We must look at Leonardo before we can consider ourselves Leonardos." Robert Mueller, 1983, *Creative Computing*

The geometric designs of Russian artist Y. Chernikov never fail to entice the eye and titillate the imagination. Even though they were constructed well before computer graphics, Chernikov patterns often remind one of the computer-drawn "spirographic" art so popular in the 1970's and even today. Chernikov's original designs, published in Leningrad in his 1930 book *Ornament*, often contain motifs stemming from the combination of primitive Russian folklore, and the Byzantine style, with the Christian influence brought to Russia by the Tartars between 1237 and 1480. The first three figures in this chapter show a few of his designs. Chernikov's original Russian language book may be rather hard for you to obtain; however, you can easily obtain a reprint in the form of Gillon's 1969 book *Geometric Design and Ornament* (Dover: New York).

In August 1991 I conducted an experiment using one of Chernikov's simplest designs. My goal was to test the ability of words to describe a graphic diagram. I started by limiting myself to a 75-word description of a Chernikov pattern. Using only this description, I asked people to draw the target design. Here is my description of the target which is shown in Figure 9.4.

"There are four quarter-sized circles arranged so they touch. They are on top of one larger circle with a thick edge, and cover the circle slightly. Inside each of the four circles is a black dot which touches the edge of each of the circles. The four circles also contain six circles inside them. The six circles get smaller and smaller, but all of their edges touch the black dot."

Notice that I also limited myself to nonmathemtical terms when describing the target picture. The survey was conducted using the electronic mail networks, and participants included scientists, programmers, and administrators.

Figure 9.5 shows the several variations by Robert Guth, San Jose, California, whose "Variation 2" came incredibly close to the target image in Figure 9.4. The

Figure 9.1. *Chernikov patterns.*

remaining figures show the range of results I received, and just a few were almost as close as Guth's. (I reduced the respondents' original diagrams by a uniform amount to fit so many in these figures.) Each diagram represents a different respondent's attempt to draw the target according to my description.

9.1 Comments from Colleagues

A few respondents noted that my English language description was ambiguous. Some people asked me, "What is the diameter of the large circle?" "What does 'cover slightly' mean?" "How big is the black dot?" "Are the groups of circles nested or adjacent?" I could only respond to these critical people that the description was the best I could do with 75 words and without resorting to mathematical jargon. I received many suggestions on how to improve my English in the pattern description.

One Swiss respondent had difficulty with the expression "quarter-sized circles." He wrote, "First I translated it word by word into German and got *Viertel-Kreise*. My first sketch (not included) was obviously wrong. Later I received the advice that you probably meant a circle the size of a quarter US Dollar." One British respondent did not know how large a US quarter was so he assumed it to be "the size of a British 10 pence piece."

Figure 9.2. *Chernikov patterns.*

9.2 Stop and Think

This Chernikov target experiment provides an infinite number of possible future experiments. Here's just a few ideas, and I would be interested in hearing from any of you who have conducted the following tests with the Chernikov target figure.

1. How would *different* people describe, using no more than 75 words, the Chernikov target figure in Figure 9.4? Perhaps some of you could construct much more accurate descriptions which would therefore improve your respondents' diagrams.

2. Create a catalog of figures, such as in Figure 9.7 with different numbers of words allowed to describe the target figure. For example, what would pictures look like if only a 50-word description were allowed? What would respondents' pictures look like if only *25* words were allowed? What would pictures look like if 500 words were allowed?

3. Conduct an experiment where you take the worst representation (that is, the picture most different from the target), and use this as a *new* target for another experiment. Continue to propagate the error until the first target bears no resemblance to the new images. How many generations of selecting the least accurate representation would this require?

Figure 9.3. *Chernikov patterns.*

4. Just because a picture is simple does not mean 75 words could describe it in a way that allows respondents to accurately reproduce the picture, particularly if mathematical terms are not used. As an experiment, use the mathematical curve called the Witch of Agnesi as a target picture instead of the Chernikov target. For your interest, the equation of the curve is $4a^2(2a - y) = x^2y$. The distance of the curve's maxima from the origin is $2a$. The Witch of Agnesi is named

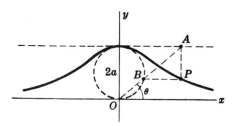

after Maria Agnesi (1718-1799) who in 1748 discussed the curve and referred to it as a versiera, which in Italian means versed sine or witch. (Maria Agnesi was a child prodigy, author, and mathematician who lived a life of extreme piety and charity.)

Figure 9.4. *The Chernikov target picture described using 75 words.*

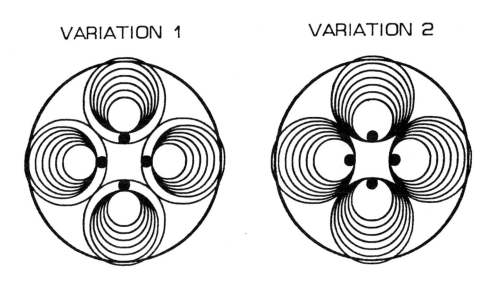

Figure 9.5. *Robert Guth's drawings of the target.* The drawings were based on his reading of the 75-word description. The rightmost figure is amazingly similar to the target Chernikov picture. Skeptical readers should not consider this as evidence for extrasensory perception.

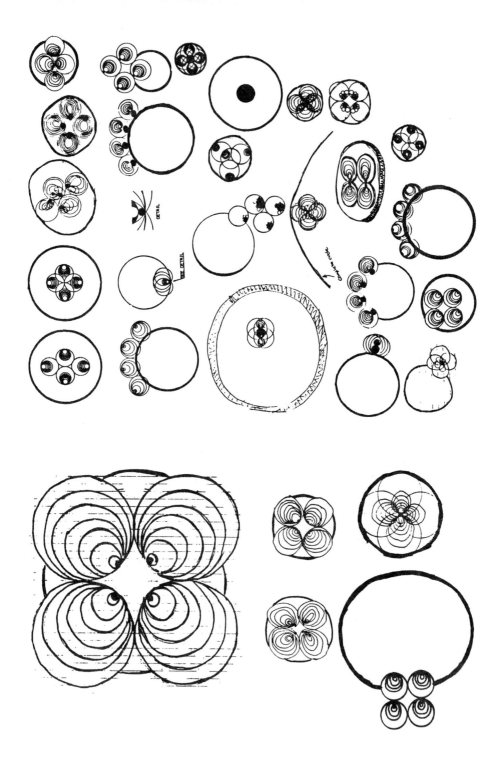

Figure 9.6. *A variety of drawings of the target from many different individuals.*

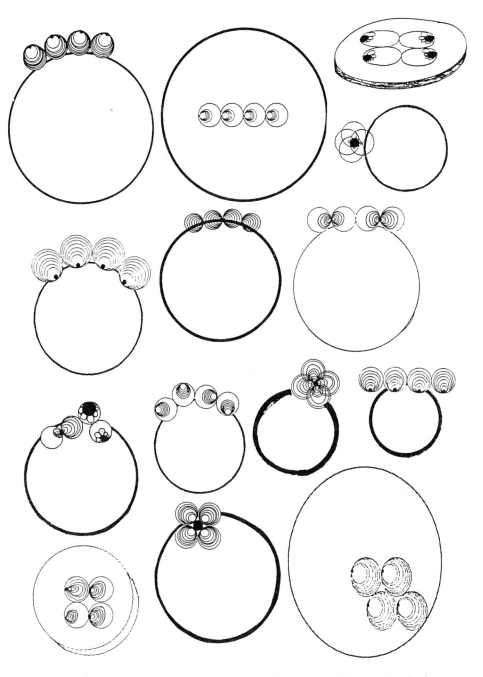

Figure 9.7. *A variety of drawings of the target from many different individuals.*

Chapter 10

Siamese Fighting Fish Patterns

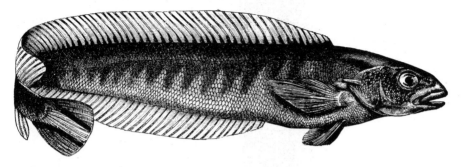

As most tropical fish hobbyists know, Siamese fighting fish have been bred by humans for decades in order to develop brilliant coloration, very long fins, and a belligerent, pugnacious disposition. In fact, it's best to keep the males of the species in separate enclosures so that they do not tear each other to shreds.[5] In 1927, a beautifully colored variety of fighting fish (*Betta splendens*) was first brought into San Francisco from Siam. The consignee, Mr. Locke, thought he had a new fish species, but his brilliantly colored variants of fighting fish, which we see often in pet stores today, were simply another race of their pre-1927 dull-colored cousins.

Fighting fish have been cultivated among the Siamese for many years, and just as some Americans enjoy watching wrestler Hulk Hogan batter a muscular opponent and gambling on the outcome, Siamese have often wagered large sums of money on the outcome of a fighting fish match. (There are 10 licensed places which permit public fighting fish combats and betting.)

Consider the following problem involving the arrangement of aggressive fish in different enclosures. It is the year 2000. Siamese fighting fish have been bred so that they will kill any other of their species with the same color, but they can comfortably live with members of different colors. Problem 1: You have 3 red, 3 green, and 3 amber fighting fish. To minimize fighting, they are to be placed in a 3x3 matrix of cells so that each row and column contains only 1 fish of a particular color. The matrix looks like a tic-tac-toe board in which you are not permitted to have two fish of the same color in any row or column. Is this possible? (Hint: it is possible.) Below is an arrangement prior to your attempt to minimize conflict:

```
Red     Red     Red
Green   Green   Green
Amber   Amber   Amber
```

---

[5] Male fish aggression is not limited to Siamese fish, but this is perhaps the most well known example. The frontispiece, and picture above, show other agressive species.

```
ALGORITHM: How to Scan for Latin Squares.
/* r is your Latin square array */
for (i = 0; i < n; i++) {
   for (j = 0; j < n; j++) {
      x = r(i)(j);
      /* check row */
      for (k=j+1; k<n;k++)
         if (r(i)(k) == x) goto nogood;
      /* check column */
      for (k=i+1; k<n;k++)
         if (r(k)(j) == x) goto nogood;
   }
}
prinft("You have a Latin square\n"); exit(0);
nogood:
prinft("This is not a Latin square\n");
```

Pseudocode 10.1. *How to scan for Latin squares.* (The program coded here is in the style of the C language.)

Problem 2: Next consider that you must place the fish so that each row and column contains exactly two colors. Is this possible?

You can design a computer program to solve Problem 1 by representing the fish as red, green, and amber squares in a 3x3 checkerboard. The program uses three squares of each color. Have the computer randomly pick combinations, and display them as fast as it can, until a solution is found. The rapidly changing random checkerboard is fascinating to watch. There are quite a lot of different possible arrangements. In fact, for a 3x3 checkerboard there are 1680 distinct patterns. If it took your computer 1 second to compute and display each 3x3 random pattern, how long would it take, on average, to solve the problem and display a winning solution? (There is more than one winning solution.)

In case you couldn't solve it, there is way to arrange the fish so that there are only two of the same color in each row and column:

Amber	Green	Amber
Green	Green	Red
Amber	Red	Red

Try this second problem on a few friends. I've found that most people have difficulty in solving this.

10.1 Amazing Latin Squares

The Siamese Fighting Fish problem can be though of as a special problem in the remarkably rich mathematical area concerned with *Latin squares*. Latin squares were first systematically developed by Swiss mathematical Leonhard Euler in 1779. (Euler's mental powers were so great that his capacity for concentrating on math problems did not decline even when he became totally blind.) He defined a

Latin square as a square matrix with n^2 entries of n different elements, none of them occurring twice or more within any row or column of the matrix. The integer n is called the *order* of the Latin square. Recently the subject of Latin squares has attracted the serious attention of mathematicians due to their relevance to the study of combinatorics and error correcting codes. Here's an example of the occurrence of a Latin square when considering the equation $z = (2x + y + 1)$ modulo 3:

```
   | 0   1   2
 --|---------
 0 | 1   2   0
 1 | 0   1   2
 2 | 2   0   1
```

To understand this table, consider the case of $x = 2$ and $y = 2$ which yields $2x + y + 1 = 7$. 7 mod 3 is 1 because 7/3 has a remainder of 1. This "1" entry is in the last row and column of this Latin square.

Here's an interesting example, from Denes and Keedwell (1974), of a Latin square of order 10 containing 2 subsquares of order 4 (consisting of elements 1, 2, 3, and 4) and also one of order 5 (with elements 3, 4, 5, 6, 7), the intersection of which is a subsquare of order 2 (with elements 3, 4):

```
                ------------
 1 9 2   8 0 |6 7   4 5 3|
 8 2 1   0 9 |7 5   3 4 6|
 2 1 0   9 8 |5 6   7 3 4|
         ----------       |
 0 8 9 |1 2 |3 4| 6 7 5|
 9 0 8 |2 1 |4 3| 5 6 7|
       |     ----|------
 5 6 7 |3 4   1 2| 0 8 9
 6 7 5 |4 3   2 1| 8 9 0
        ----------
 7 4 3   5 6   0   9 1 2 8
 3 5 4   6 7   8   0 9 1 2
 4 3 6   7 5   9   8 2 0 1
```

Can you create Latin squares with even greater numbers of internal subsquares than this? What is the world-record for the number of subsquares in an n x n Latin square?

A *traversal* of a Latin square of order n is a set of n cells, one in each row, one in each column, and such that no two of the cells contain the same symbol. Fascinatingly, even in cases when a Latin square has no traversals it is very often the case that partial traversals of $(n-1)$ elements occur in it. Do all Latin squares have a partial traversal of $n-1$ elements if the squares do not contain a true traversal? Here is an example of a Latin square with an $n-1$ traversal (I've marked the traversal path with a "*"):

```
1*  6   3   7   4   9   2   5   0   8
2   0*  4   6   5   8   3   1   9   7
3   9   5*  0   1   7   4   2   8   6
4   8   1   9*  2   6   5   3   7   0
5   7   2   8   3*  0   1   4   6   9
6   1   8   2   9   4*  7   0   5   3
7   5   9   1   0   3   8*  6   4   2
8   4   0   5   6   2   9   7*  3   1
9   3   6   4   7   1   0   8   2*  5
0   2   7   3   8   5   6   9   1   4
```

Let's conclude with an example of a Latin cube. You can think of it as a stack of file cards. Each card contains n rows, and n columns. Each number occurs exactly once in each row, once in each column, and once in each row and column in the third dimension:

```
0 1 2     1 2 0     2 0 1
1 2 0     2 0 1     0 1 2
2 0 1     0 1 2     1 2 0
```

Can you design a 4-dimensional Latin hypercube? Note that computers are much faster than humans in finding errors in Latin squares, cubes, and hypercubes. So, if you are not sure if the Latin square you've written down is correct, check each row and column with a computer program. (See Pseudocode 10.1.) Have your computer create 4x4 Latin squares by randomly selecting values for the squares and then checking if the results is a Latin square using the algorithm in the program code. How long does it take your computer to find a Latin square? Several minutes? Hours? My IBM RISC System/6000 took just seconds to find 3x3 Latin squares. For large squares, this random method is not very efficient.

10.2 Magic Squares, Emperor Yu, Chess Knights, Etc.

Another matrix of integers which has preoccupied both mathematicians and lay-people for centuries is the *magic square*. The first known example of a magic square is said to have been found on the back of a tortoise by Emperor Yu in 2200 B.C. A magic square is often defined as a matrix divided into N^2 cells in which the integers from 1 to N^2 are placed in such a manner that the sums of the rows, columns, and both diagonals are identical. My favorite magic square, invented by the same 18th century mathematician Leonhard Euler who studied Latin squares, is shown in the following diagram:

```
 1  48 31 50 33 16 63 18
30  51 46  3 62 19 14 35
47   2 49 32 15 34 17 64        Chess Knight
52  29  4 45 20 61 36 13        Magic Square
 5  44 25 56  9 40 21 60
28  53  8 41 24 57 12 37
43   6 55 26 39 10 59 22
54  27 42  7 58 23 38 11
```

Each horizontal or vertical row totals 260. Stopping halfway on each gives 130. Even more exciting is that a chess Knight, starting its L-shaped moves from the upper left box (marked "1") can hit all 64 boxes in numerical order. (You can locate the "2" to find the knight's first move.) Can you trace out the path of the knight through the board?

Another interesting magic square is the enigmatic π-square invented by T. E. Lobeck of Minneapolis. He starts with a conventional 5 by 5 magic square and then substitutes the nth digit of π for each number n in the square. This means that a 3 is substituted for a 1, a 1 is substituted for a 2, a 4 substituted for a 3, and so on. Amazingly, every column sum duplicates some row sum for the π-square. For example, the top row sums to 24 as does the 4th column.

5x5 Magic Square   Pi Square

```
17 24  1  8 15          2 4 3 6 9
23  5  7 14 16          6 5 2 7 3
 4  6 13 20 22          1 9 9 4 2
10 12 19 21  3          3 8 8 6 4
11 18 25  2  9          5 3 3 1 5
```

10.3 Cross References

For other references on chess, see "Miraculous Chess Solutions" on page 311, "Knights in Hell" on page 321 and "Fiendishly Difficult Eight Pawn Problem" on page 321. For specific information related to the movement of chess knights for the purpose of producing artistic patterns and music, see "Chess Music" on page 204.

10.4 For Further Reading

1. Denes, J, Keedwell, A. (1974) *Latin Squares and their Application.* Academic Press: New York.

2. Gardner, M. (1992) *Fractal Music, Hypercards, and More...* Freeman: NY.

Chapter 11

Interlude: Pulsating Pumpkins, Helical Hedges, and Leaping Leaves

"I would like to design forms which lift away from the pull of gravity, and are therefore graceful. I believe my ideas may help make computer-drawn images more organic in appearance."   Joan Rudd, *1991*

The title of this "Interlude" chapter lists three names of mathematically-inspired sculptures created by Joan Rudd. When I visited her home in Seattle, Washington, artist Rudd showed me how she applies plaster over recycled sytrofoam computer packing to create the forms. Sometimes she uses internal wire or welded armatures as needed for support. The final surfaces are painted and ultimately lacquered. Shown here is "Leaping Leaf" (12x5x6.5", facing page, turned 90 ° so as to enlarge the image as much as possible), and "Helical Hedge" (above, 24x14x14"). Some of her work is reminiscent of mathematical surfaces created using computer aided design (CAD) tools; however, Rudd cheerfully notes:

> What I did, of course, was to make sculpture *as if* I had access to a sophisticated CAD program, but I make real objects with handpainted "wire frame" surfaces! I am now back to making figurative work, in carved styrofoam (to be cast), at least until I can afford a math co-processor and Generic CAD.

Not only has Joan's work been featured in various newspapers, magazines, and juried exhibitions, but she also teaches numerous courses with titles such as "Outdoor Sculpture in Concrete." She is editor of the *Cast Stone, Concrete, Plaster Sculptor's Newsletter*, and is the advertising representative of the magazine *Sculpture* (see "Product Pavan" on page 408). Joan Rudd can be reached at: PO Box 25803, Seattle, WA 98125.

Chapter 12

The Drums of Ulupu

"I like that abstract image of life as something like an efficient factory machine, probably because actual life, up close and personal, seems so messy and strange. It's nice to be able to pull away every once in awhile and say, 'There's a pattern there after all! I'm not sure what it means, but by God, I see it!'" Stephen King, *Four Past Midnight*

Late last autumn, while enjoying the brisk New England air, I took a walk with Bijan, my octogenarian friend. In his usual, hushed voice, he told me about his

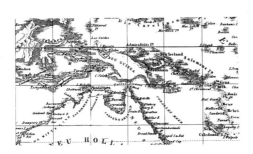

buddies who once explored Ulupu in the Northern Maprik district of New Guinea. I should tell you right up front that I can never be certain as to the accuracy of Bijan's tales. During the past ten years his stories have evolved into highly embellished tales, composed of myth and truth, perhaps more of the former than the latter, depending on his mood. Whatever the case, I recount his colorful story here and let you decide about the authenticity of Bijan's old recollections.

Apparently Bijan's New Guinea explorer friends were camping on a river bank when they heard strange drum beats. There was a certain rhythm to the drums, but the drums never quite repeated themselves. A few men explored the surrounding bush, but even after much searching never succeeded in locating the source of the sounds. Sometimes the sounds seemed to come from the North, at other times from the East.

The beats emanated from a two-tone drum or, perhaps, from two drums of different tones, one high and one low. At other times in the night, a single drum seemed to beat, and the sounds consisted of short-duration beats and long-dura-

```
0110100110010110100101100110100110010110
0110100101101001100101101001011001101001
0110100110010110011010011001011010010110
0110100110010110011010010110100110010110
0110100110010110100101100110100101101001
1001011010010110011010011001011001101001
0110100110010110100101100110100101101001
1001011001101001100101101001011001101001
0110100110010110011010011001011010010110
0110100101101001100101100110100110010110
1001011001101001100101100110100101101001
1001011010010110011010010110100110010110
0110100110010110100101100110100110010110
0110100101101001100101100110100110010110
1001011001101001100101100110100101101001
0110100110010110011010010110100110010110
0110100110010110100101100110100110010110
0110100101101001100101101001011001101001
0110100110010110011010011001011010010110
0110100101101001100101101001011001101001
1001011001101001100101101001011001101001
0110100101101001100101100110100110010110
1001011001101001100101101001011001101001
1001011001101001100101101001011001101001
0110100110010110100101100110100110010110
0110100101101001100101101001011001101001
0110100110010110011010011001011010010110
0110100101101001100101101001011001101001
1001011010010110011010011001011001101001
1001011010010110011010011001011001101001
0110100110010110100101100110100101101001
1001011010010110011010011001011001101001
0110100110010110100101100110100110010110
0110100101101001100101101001011001101001
0110100110010110011010011001011010010110
0110100110010110011010010110100110010110
0110100110010110100101100110100101101001
1001011010010110011010011001011001101001
0110100110010110011010011001011010010110
0110100110010110011010010110100110010110
1001011001101001011010011001011001101001
1001011010010110011010011001011001101001
0110100110010110011010011001011010010110
0110100101101001100101101001011001101001
1001011001101001011010011001011010010110
0110100101101001100101100110100110010110
1001011001101001011010011001011010010110
0110100110010110011010010110100110010110
0110100110010110100101100110100110010110
0110100101101001100101101001011001101001
0110100110010110011010011001011010010110
0110100110010110011010011001011010010110
0110100101101001100101101001011001101001
0110100110010110011010011001011010010110
01101001
```

Figure 12.1. *A Morse-Thue sequence for the 11th generation.*

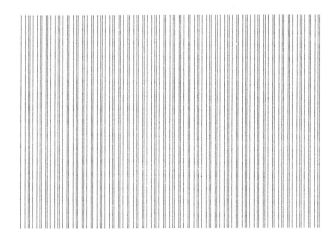

Figure 12.2. *Aperiodic Morse-Thue bar code.* Vertical lines are placed wherever a 1 occurs in the sequence. Spaces are skipped wherever a 0 occurs.

tion beats. One of the explorers was interested enough in this peculiar phenomena to record the beats in his tattered notebook. Later, Bijan had the opportunity to look at the notebook where the explorer used L and S to represent the long and short beats he heard. Luckily the drum beats were slow enough to allow the explorer to accurately record the rhythmic pattern. The first few entries were: SLLSLSSL. Then the drummer would pause for a minute and then start again. On the next line of the notebook were the letters: SLLSLSSLLSSLSLLS. The notebook contained several pages of these symbols. By midnight, the pages of the notebook were exhausted. The drum sounds were supposedly strange to hear.

Years later, Bijan came into possession of the notebook from the man who had originally recorded the drumbeats. The man who recorded the patterns croaked, "It's the strangest thing ye ever heard. It ain't exactly irregular and it ain't exactly regular, either." Bijan, who has some mathematical training, spent many days examining the pages of S and L symbols. His conclusion was startling.

We continued our walk in the cool night air. Suddenly, Bijan stopped dead in the middle of the sidewalk under an amber streetlight. He looked me in the eye. "You might not believe this, but that strange pattern of S and L symbols turned out to be a well-known but very exotic pattern of binary numbers called the *Morse-Thue* sequence – a interesting sequence generated with a string of 0's and 1's." Bijan went on to explain that the sequence is named in honor of the Norwegian mathematician Axel Thue (1863-1922) (pronounced "Tew") and Marston Morse of Princeton (1892-1977). Thue introduced the sequence as an example of an aperiodic, recursively computable string of symbols. Morse did further research on the sequence in the 1920's.

There are many ways to generate the Morse-Thue sequence. One way is to start with a zero and then repeatedly do the following replacements: 0 → 01 and 1 → 10. In other words, whenever you see a 0 you replace it with a 01. Whenever

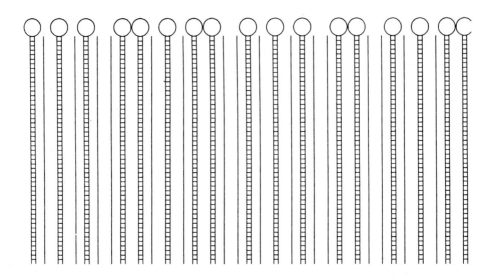

Figure 12.3. *Morse-Thue Lollipop forest*. To make the positions of "11" entries clear to the human eye, wherever two 1's appear consecutively, they are joined together by short horizontal steps.

you see a 1 you replace it with a 10. Starting with a single 0, we get the following successive "generations":

```
0
0 1
0 1 1 0
0 1 1 0 1 0 0 1
0 1 1 0 1 0 0 1 1 0 0 1 0 1 1 0
```

You begin with 0, and replace it by 01. Now you have a sequence of length two. Replace the 0 by 01 and the 1 by 10. This produces the sequence 0110. The next binary pattern is 01101001. Notice that 0110 is symmetrical, a palindrome, but the next pattern 01101001 is not. But hold on! The very next pattern 0110100110010110 is a palindrome again. Does this property continue to hold for alternate sequences? The mysteries of this remarkable sequence have only begun.

Notice that the fourth line of the sequence can translate into the SLLSLSSL drum beats in Bijan's story.

You can generate the drum sequence in another way: each generation is obtained from the preceding one by appending its complement. This means that if you see a 0 1 1 0 you append to it a 1 0 0 1. There is yet a third way to generate

```
ALGORITHM: How to Create Ulupu Drum Beats.
/* */
Number_of_Beats = 10
k = 0
DO i = 1 to Number_of_Beats
   count = 0
   num = k
   DO while num > 0
      IF ((num // 2) = 1) then do
            count = count + 1
            num = num - 1
      END
      num = num/2
   END    /* while */
   bit = count//2
   Print(bit)
   k = k + 1
END  /* do i */
```

Pseudocode 12.1. *How to create Ulupu drum beats.* The "//" denotes modular arithmetic. Print out the value for bit (1 or 0) to generate the sequence.

the sequence. Start with the numbers 0, 1, 2, 3, ... and write them in binary notation:

0, 1, 10, 11, 100, 101, 110, 111, ...

(Binary numbers are explained more fully in the next chapter.) Now calculate the sum of the digits modulo 2 for each binary number. That is, divide the number by 2 and use the remainder. For example, the binary number 11 becomes 2 when the digits are summed, which is represented as 0 in the final sequence. This yields the sequence

0, 1, 1, 0, 1, 0, 0, 1 ...

which is the same sequence as yielded by the other methods!

Let me tell you why this sequence is so fascinating. For one, it is *self-similar*. This means you can take pieces of the sequence and generate the entire infinite sequence! For example, retaining every other term of the infinite sequence reproduces the sequence. Try it. Similarly, retaining every other pair also reproduces the sequence. In other words, you take the first two numbers, skip the next two numbers, etc. Also, the sequence does not have any periodicities as would a sequence such as 0 0, 1 1, 0 0, 1 1. However, although aperiodic, the sequence is anything but random. It has strong short-range and long-range structures. For example, there can never be more than two adjacent terms that are identical. One method for finding patterns in a sequence, the Fourier spectrum, shows pronounced peaks when used to analyze the sequence.

The sequence grows very quickly. The following is the sequence for the 8th generation.

01101001100101101001011001101001100101100110100101101001100110010110100101100110100110010110011010010110100110010110100101101001100110010110
01101001100101100110100101101001100101100110100110010110100110010110
01101001100101101001011001101001100101100110100110010110011010010110
011010011001011010010110010110100101100110100110010110011010010110100110010110

Figure 12.1 shows the sequence for the 11th generation. Sometimes certain

patterns emerge when a sequence is stacked up on itself in this manner. Can you see any patterns here? Another way to represent the Morse-Thue sequence is to redraw it as a "bar code" of sorts, as in Figure 12.2. Vertical lines are placed wherever a 1 occurs in the sequence. Spaces are skipped wherever a 0 occurs. Figure 12.3 shows a Morse-Thue Lollipop forest. To make the positions of 11 entries clear to the human eye, wherever two 1's appear consecutively, they are joined together by short horizontal steps. What would it be like to walk through this strangely spaced forest?

Why would some obscure tribes in a remote New Guinea rain forest be beating this sequence upon their animal skin drums? I might have doubts as to the accuracy of Bijan's story, but the rhythm pattern is certainly strange to hear. You may wish to beat the sequence out on your desk, or have your computer-controlled musical instrument play the eerie rhythm. If you prefer, you can beat the sequence out on a table top with a finger to represent a low tone and a pencil to represent a high tone, rather than using short and long duration beats. Do you hear a pattern? It is strangely compelling, yet it never quite repeats itself in the way that most rhythms do. If the sequence is not random, what is it's structure?

Not only do binary numbers provide for musical possibilities, they also can yield artistic patterns. Graphic patterns produced by numbers represented in binary notation are so interesting that I'll devote the next section entirely to this subject. Interesting information on fractal number sequences can also be found in M. Schroeder's *Fractals, Chaos, Power Laws* (Freeman: NY). See "Curiosity Cavalcade" on page 410 for information on IBM PC programs allowing you to produce these strange rhythms on personal computers.

12.1 Cross References

For other examples of aperiodic bar codes in mathematics, see "U-Numbers and MU-Numbers" on page 357. For examples of unusual bar codes for product coding, see "Bar Codes in the 21st Century" on page 297.

Chapter 13

Beauty and the Bits

The humble bits that lie at the very foundation of computing have a special beauty all their own. It takes just a little logical coddling to bring the beauty out. Who would guess, for example, that intricate fractal patterns lurk within the OR operation applied to the bits of ordinary numbers?

Binary numbers consist of the digits 1 and 0. Some say they were invented by Leibniz while waiting to see the Pope in the Vatican with a proposal to reunify the Christian churches. Here are the first seven numbers represented in binary notation:

0, 1, 10, 11, 100, 101, 110, 111,...

The sum of the digits for each number form the sequence (in decimal notation):

0,1,1,2,1,2,2,3,1,2,2,3,2,3,3,4,...

Notice, just like the Morse-Thue sequence, (previous chapter) this sequence is *self-similar*: if you retain every other term you still have the same infinite sequence! The following few paragraphs will show you how wonderful graphic patterns can emerge when working with binary numbers. In fact, very complex patterns with scaling symmetry can arise from the simplest of arithmetic operations which use logical operators such as "AND" and "OR." Figure 13.1 was created using an "OR" operation. For this demonstration

$$c_{i,j} = i \ OR \ j \tag{13.1}$$

$(1 < i < 800) \ (1 < j < 800)$. For example, if $i = 6$ and $j = 1$, $c = 7$ because 111 = (110 OR 001). Just apply a logical operation one bit at a time. (For example: 1 OR 0 is 1; 0 OR 0 is 0; and 1 OR 1 is 1.) The variables i and j are the x and y axes of the figures in this chapter. The value of c is represented by shades of gray. Figure 13.1 illustrates c modulo 255. The brightest picture element is therefore 254 and this corresponds to bright white. 0 is represented by black. The black, triangular, gasket-like structure represents those ($c = 255$) pixels which are made

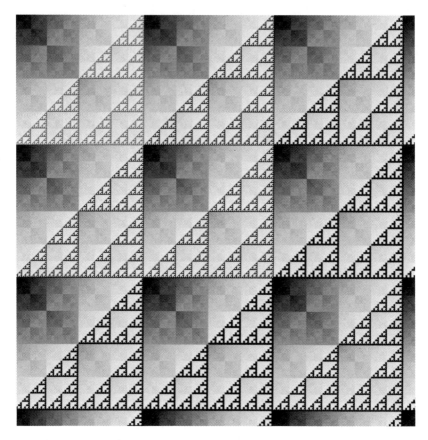

Figure 13.1. *Pattern of bits.* The pattern was produced by $c_{i,j} = i \ OR \ j$ for $(1 < i < 800)$ $(1 < j < 800)$. The values of c modulo 255 are represented by shades of gray.

black by the modular arithmetic. The fractal nature of the entire pattern is evident. The black pattern is called a Sierpinski gasket, commonly seen in cellular automata applications. In fact the same pattern is seen when the even entries of Pascal's triangle are colored black. Let us call the pattern a "Logical" Sierpinski gasket.

Figure 13.1 indicates self-similarity of the gaskets for several orders of dilational invariance, and they possess what is known as nonstandard scaling symmetry, also called dilation symmetry, i.e. invariance under changes of size scale. Dilation symmetry is sometimes expressed by the formula $(\vec{r} \rightarrow a\vec{r})$. Thus an expanded piece of the gasket can be moved in such away as to make it coincide with the entire gasket, and this operation can be performed in an infinite number of ways.

The following discussion considers the case for $(0 \le i \le 256)$ $(0 \le j \le 256)$. This is the upper left "block" of the 9 blocks shown in Figure 13.1. Let us consider the number of pixels in the image of a particular shade of gray in order to

Figure 13.2. *Another bit pattern.* Same as previous figure, except for $c_{i,j} = (i \, OR \, j)$ $OR \, (i \times j)$.

better understand the resulting patterns. For example, there are only three possible (i,j) pairs which form the Logical Sierpinski gasket for $c = 256$, since c is 100000000 in binary. The only three ways to make 256 with "OR" are (256,0), (0,256), and (256,256). However for 255, all 8 bits must be ones, and there are an amazing 6,561 possible values which satisfy Equation (13.1) for $c = 255$. These 6,561 values are colored black for the Logical Sierpinski gasket in Figure 12.1 To determine the number of equal-valued pixels there are for a particular value of c, you can use $N = 3^k$ where N is the number of different entries in the (i,j) array which satisfy $c = i \, OR \, j$, and k is the number of 1's in the binary representation of c. We can understand this equation by considering that for each 1 in the binary representation of c, there are three bit-pairs (1 OR 1, 0 OR 1, 1 OR 0) that produce a 1 under the OR operation. For each zero in the binary representation of c, the corresponding bits of i and j must be both zero.

Notice that if we define (1,6) and (6,1) as duplicate solutions to Equation (13.1), then we obviously have a smaller number of pairs for a particular value of c. Let $b(c)$ be the number of 1-bits in c. Then the number of unordered pairs whose OR'ed value is c can be written as

$$3^{b(c)} - \sum_{i=0}^{b(c)-1} 3^i. \tag{13.2}$$

For example, if $c = 17$, then $b(c) = 2$, so there are $3^2 - 3^1 - 3^0 = 9 - 3 - 1 = 5$ solutions. They are $(0,17),(1,16),(1,17),(16,17),(17,17)$. Alternatively, one can count the "duplicate" members by considering that there is only one pair of identical numbers, and all other combinations occur twice. Therefore there are $(3^{b(c)} - 1)/2 + 1 = (3^{b(c)} + 1)/2$ unique combinations.

Figure 13.2 is included in order to show that very complicated patterns can evolve for just slightly longer logical operations. Figure 13.2 is the same as Figure 13.1 except that $c_{i,j} = (i \; OR \; j) \; OR \; (i \times j)$. The multiplication is undoubtedly responsible for the attractive hyperbolic contours that emerge from this beauty.

Obviously, I have barely scratched the surface of the subject. There are endless combinations of logical (and arithmetic) operators to be tried on the humble binary numbers. In the process, some of you will discover worlds neither I nor anyone else has seen.

13.1 Cross References

See the following sections for information on fractals: "Smithson's Fractal Anabiotic Ana Sequences" on page 35, "Fractal Spiders and Frame-Robertson Bushes" on page 87, and "Labyrinthine Lundin Curves" on page 103. For fractal mazes, see "Mazes for the Mind" on page 3. For fractal integer sequences and patterns, see "The Drums of Ulupu" on page 71. For feather fractals, see "Fantastic Feather Fractals" on page 33. For fractal ant farms, see "Electronic and Fractal Ant Farms" on page 173.

13.2 For Further Reading

1. Schroeder, M. (1991) *Fractals, Chaos, Power Laws*. Freeman: New York.
2. Mandelbrot, B. (1982) *The Fractal Geometry of Nature*. Freeman: New York.
3. Pickover, C. and Lakhtakia, A. (1989) Diophantine equation graphs for $x^2y = c$. *Journal of Recreational Math.*, 21(3), 167-170; Szyszkowicz, M. (1991) Patterns generated by logical operators. *Computers and Graphics*, 15(2): 299-300.
4. Pickover, C. (1992) Intricate patterns from logical operators. *Theta.* (Spring) 6(1), in press; Pickover, C. (1991) *Computers and the Imagination*. St. Martin's Press: New York.

Could the patterns of bits in this chapter be converted to interesting sounding music?

Chapter 14

Interlude: Animal Machines

"In these animal machines, the combination of organic and technoid materials is in the foreground. Bones are combined with steel parts..."
Michael Schulze

"The self-concept of our society can be inferred from its garbage."
Edward Kienholz, *Werke aus den 80er Jahren*

Michael Schulze is one of my favorite modern sculptors. He is a German artist who, in his studio on Naumannstrasse in Berlin, creates unusual art works from an eerie fusion of objects from the organic and inorganic world. Often his sculptures contain pine cones, fur, stuffed animals, garden implements, small motors, wheels, axles, cranks, or pulleys, and his works are often electrically or manually powered. Schulze explains his early works as follows. "Starting with a store-window mannequin, artificial limbs, and other mechanical parts I took from a garbage container, I built my first series of mechanical-figure objects in 1979-1980."

The most interesting of his sculptures are the weird and wonderful "animal machines" which combine bones, heads, and fur, with machine parts from bikes and automobiles. In one of his sculptures, the speedometer of a VW is used as an eye. He uses polyurethane and polyester for binding different parts of the animals to the sculpture.

In 1984, as a contribution to a cultural magazine, Schulze prepared one thousand dead houseflies sealed in photographic slides. Schulze is inspired by these fly structures and forms:

"In the bodies of insects, function and technology are bound up in the biological determination of the respective species. Joints, arms and layering, as well as mechanical

processes, are visibly comprehensive. Fragility and stability complement each other....
Nature is still my best source of inspiration."

Schulze's thoughts echo those of biologist Loren Eisely who wrote in his book *The Immense Journey*:

> "I have come to suspect that this long descent down the ladder of life, beautiful and instructive though it may be, will not lead us to disclose the final secret... It is only that somewhere among seeds and beetle shells and abandoned grasshopper legs I find something is not accounted for in the dissections to the ultimate virus or crystal or protein particle."

Those of you who wish to see more of his surreal and wonderfully shocking work should consult Schulze's article in *Leonardo*. He can be reached at: Michael Schulze, Naumannstrasse 36, 1000 Berlin 62, Germany.

14.1 For Further Reading

Schulze, M. (1990) The forming process of assemblages and objects. *Leonardo*. 23(4): 371-375.

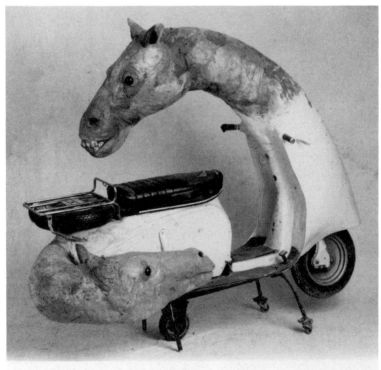

Chapter 15

Fractal Spiders and Frame-Robertson Bushes

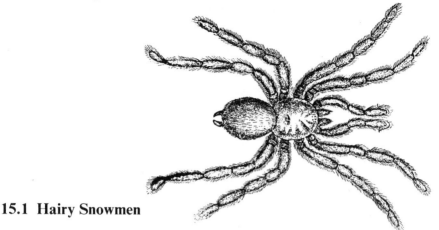

15.1 Hairy Snowmen

In principle ... [the Mandelbrot Set] could have been discovered as soon as men learned to count. But even if they never grew tired, and never made a mistake, all the human beings who have ever existed would not have sufficed to do the elementary arithmetic required to produce a Mandelbrot Set of quite modest magnification.

Arthur C. Clarke, *The Ghost from the Grand Banks*

Since its discovery around 1980, the Mandelbrot set has emerged as one of the most scintillating stars in the universe of popular mathematics and computer art.

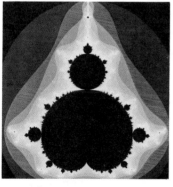

The set resembles a hairy snowman, and it serves as an important example of how simple mathematical operations can produce astonishingly complex geometrical forms. The more you magnify the figure's border, the more complicated it gets. When most people talk about the Mandelbrot set, however, they usually mean the bushy shape created by repeating the following two equations over and over again for complex numbers: $z' = z^2 + c$, $z = z'$. (Think of this as a mathematical feedback loop where the output returns to the input.) But there is also incredible beauty produced by other formulas, as some of the quick recipes in this chapter demonstrate. As has been reported in many books and papers, you can create your own Mandelbrot set diagram by starting with $z = 0$, and determining which values of c produce z values which explode to infinity. For some c values, such as (0.03, 0.03) the z values do not explode even if you repeat the operation $z' = z^2 + c$ hundreds of times. In these cases, we say that

Figure 15.1. *A spider fractal.* Black areas correspond to points which do not explode, even after repeated application of the mathematical feedback loop.

the orbits (or trajectories) of the starting point are bounded, and we color black the location on the screen which corresponds to c.[6]

Your computer program will look something like the program outlined in Pseudocode 15.1. In the code, the complex function combines the real and imaginary terms of C to form a complex number C. In other words, $C = C_{real} + C_{imag}i$. The magnitude is the length of the line drawn from the origin to the complex number, C.

In pursuing the strange equations which follow, I will not dwell on their connection with stability and chaos in dynamical systems. The connection lies in the closely-related Julia sets named after French mathematician Gaston Julia. You

---

[6] If you want a gradual programming tutorial on the Mandelbrot set, try: Pickover, C. (1989) Inside the Mandelbrot set. *Algorithm*, Nov/Dec 1(1): 9-12. (This issue can be ordered from Algorithm, P.O. Box 29237, Westmount Postal Outlet, 785 Wonderland Road S., London, Ontario Canada N6K 1M6.)

Figure 15.2. *A spider fractal.* Same as previous figure, except with contours indicating the rate of explosion of initial points.

may delve into such matters by consulting the bibliography at the end of this chapter.

15.2 Spider Fractals

I always shared in my parent's (surprised) awareness that some people lived by and for creating new mathematics.   Benoit Mandelbrot

Here my goal is to give you a simple recipe for producing the wonderful *Spider Fractals* generated by $z' = z^2 + c$ where $c' = c/2 + z'$. This means that the value of c changes through the iteration, even though the initial value for c controls where you plot your black or white dots on a computer graphics screen. The spider mapping yields graphically interesting dynamical behavior with beautiful symmetries (Figure 15.1 and Figure 15.2). Try starting the iteration with an initial value of $z = c$ instead of $z = 0$, and observe the differences between the

Figure 15.3. *Frame-Robertson multisegment fractal.* Contours indicate the rate of explosion of initial points.

plots. As indicated earlier, bounded orbits, which do not explode, correspond to the black regions (Figure 15.1). Around the set in Figure 15.2 are contours indicating the rate at which the iteration explodes (i.e., the number of iterations required for the magnitude of z to be exceed a threshold value). One of the hallmarks of fractal objects is that they continue to yield incredible detail and beauty as their edges are magnified. Try magnifying different regions of this fractal and viewing the resulting pictures.

The spider fractal in Figure 15.1 was computed for ($-2.0 < C_{real} < 0.24$) and ($-1.2 < C_{imag} < 1.2$). I learned about Spider Fractals from Wegner and Peterson's book *Fractal Creations,* where they attribute the function to a Lee Skinner. I created Figure 15.1 using a high-resolution postscript printer, and the resolution of the image is 4000x4000 dots.) The generating program was written in PL/I and ran on an IBM 3090 mainframe, but the program could easily be written using other languages and run on personal computers.

Figure 15.4. *Pokorny fractal.* Contours indicate the minimum value achieved by an initial point as it meanders around the complex plane.

15.3 Frame-Robertson Fractals

"Today you might say that, until fractal geometry became organized, my life had followed a fractal orbit."   Benoit Mandelbrot

Figure 15.3 shows a Frame-Robertson Fractal for the equation $z' = (1/5)z^3 + z^2 + c$. The picture boundaries are ($-4.95 < Z_{real} < 0.67$) and ($-1.34 < Z_{imag} < 1.26$). These fractals form very tall, multisegmented sets. You can read more about these fascinating bushy sets in (Frame and Robertson, 1992). To form the set, iterate the equation until the magnitude of z exceeds 10. The black interior region are those points which never exceed 10.

Figure 15.5. *Pokorny fractal.* The previous diagram is modified by plotting line-contours which indicate the minimum value achieved by an initial point as it meanders around the complex plane.

15.4 Pokorny Fractals

"I am distressed by how little geometry there is in American high schools."

Benoit Mandelbrot

Figure 15.4 shows a Pokorny fractal produced by iterating $z' = 1/(z^2 + 0.5 + 0.1i)$ for complex numbers z. In order to produce the attractive detail in the figure, I plotted contours of the minimum value an orbit achieved during the iteration. Picture boundaries are: $(-1.5 < Z_{real} < 1.5)$ and $(-1.5 < Z_{imag} < 1.5)$. Figure 15.5 shows a contour line plot of the same function.

```
ALGORITHM: How to Create fractals.
DO For Creal -2 to 2 by 0.1
   DO For Cimag -2 to 2 by 0.1
      C=Complex(Creal, Cimag)
      DO i = 1 to 100
         Z = Z ** 2 + C
         if (Magnitude of Z) > 2 then
         jump out of loop
      END
      If i = 101 then DrawDotAt(Creal, Cimag)
   END
END
```

Pseudocode 15.1. *How to create fractals.* "Z" and "C" are complex numbers.

15.5 Cornfield Phantoms

"Benoit Mandelbrot was very pleased to hear of the theory taking root."
John Glaskell, reporting on the cornfield Mandelbrot set

The August 25th, 1991 issue of the *Sunday Telegraph* (London) contained an article titled "Cornfield phantom has farmers foxed." Apparently the Mandelbrot set's fractal shape had appeared as a beautifully executed 180-foot design in a cornfield[7] south of Cambridge. Its massive and intricate structure was only recognizable by viewing it from above in an airplane. The main body and various buds were rendered very carefully. The heart shape tapered down to a *single* stalk of wheat, and every stalk in the main body of the set had been flattened to one quarter of an inch above the soil. The Cambridge mathematics department

---

[7] The cornfield picture is courtesy of Gregory Sams, owner of the shop *Strange Attractions*. His store is dedicated exclusively to computer art, chaos, and fractals. According to Gregory, this is Britain's first shop dedicated to chaos theory. The shop sells mugs, posters, greeting cards, badges, teeshirts, and puzzles. For more information, contact: *Strange Attractions*, 204 Kensington Park Road, London W11 1NR England. To order additional fractal images, you can also contact him by phone: (44) 71 229-9646, FAX (44) 71 229-4781. This crop circle image shown here is © 1991 by David Parker / Science Photo Library.

denied involvement in the construction of the fractal, although others have speculated that the cornfield shape might be an elaborate hoax perpetrated by the Cambridge University students. The article quotes Mandelbrot as saying, "I think it's extremely amusing. And it's certainly pleasing to be remembered in this way. But I can tell you, I plead not guilty. Was it a student's joke? I don't think it was the work of extra-terrestrials. I can't wait to see what the next one will look like."

15.6 Mandelbrot Set Comics

"Fractal geometry became organized. My way of life changed profoundly. You may say I have become the slave of my creation. "
Benoit B. Mandelbrot, 1985, *Mathematical People*

Comic strips are the dominant graphic mythology of the 20th century. Many people on earth don't have TVs, but they do have access to newspapers. Over 100 million Americans – virtually half the population – read one or more comic strips regularly. It was not until 1991 that a Mandelbrot set fractal pattern first  appeared in a comic book. The scene is one where a magic ritual is being performed. To symbolize that magic is beginning to have an effect, the background sky is patterned as a Mandelbrot set. (See: Chichester, D., and Johnson, P. (1991) *Hellraiser Nightbreed - Jihad*. (*Jihad* Book 2 of 2.) Published by Epic Comics, 387 Park Avenue South, New York NY, 10016. ISBN #0 - 87135 - 768 - 2.)

15.7 Shishikura's Extraordinary Boundary

"The Mandelbrot Set is more than a mathematical plaything. It offers one way of exploring the behavior of dynamical systems in which equations express how some quantity changes over time or varies from place to place. Such equations arise in calculations of the orbit of a planet, the flow of heat in a liquid, and countless other situations."
Ivars Peterson, 1991, *Science News*

The year 1991 was a year for "firsts" in the world of fractals (see previous section). Mathematician Mitsuhiro Shishikura of the Tokyo Institute of Technology proved that the Mandelbrot set's intricate boundary has a "fractal dimension" of 2. This means that the edge of the set is so convoluted that it appears to have the same dimension as a plane, even though it is still mathematically a curve with zero area!

Shishikura was born in 1960 – in Isesaki, Gumma, Japan. He received his Ph.D. from Kyoto University, in 1988, and the title of the thesis was *Trees Asso-*

ciated with the Configuration of Herman Rings. Pictured below is mathematician Mitsuhiro Shishikura.

15.8 Fractal Drums and Violence

In 1991, Bernard Sapoval and his colleagues at the Ecole Polytechnique in Paris found that fractally shaped drum heads are very quiet when struck. Instead of  being round like an ordinary drum head, these heads resemble a jagged snowflake. Sapoval cut his fractal shape out of a piece of metal and stretched a thin membrane over it to make a drum. When a drummer bangs on an ordinary drum, the vibration spreads out to affect the entire drum head. With fractal drums, some vibrational modes are trapped within a branch of the fractal pattern. Faye Flam in the December 13th, 1991 issue of *Science* (vol. 254, p. 1593) notes: "If fractals are better than other shapes at damping vibrations, as Sapoval's results suggest, they might also be more robust. And that special sturdiness could explain why in nature, the rule is survival of the fractal." Fractal shapes often occur in violent situations where powerful, turbulent forces need to be damped: the surf-pounded coastline, the blood vessels of the heart (a very violent pump), and the wind- and rain-buffeted mountain.

15.9 Are Fractal Graphics Art?

The general question of whether or not computer art is really art is discussed in "Is Computer Art Really Art?" on page 169. However, here are some specific remarks on fractal art.

Roger James is a fluid dynamics programmer at Pratt and Whitney. His programs are used to predict the behavior of jet engine combustor sections. He writes to me:

> Art is the creation of the mind, an idea. A painting, a piece of music, or a sculpture is only the embodiment of that idea. Turning an idea into a work of art is a skill. There must be a direct relationship between what the observer senses and the original idea.

You have to see exactly what the artist saw. Choosing coloration for a Mandelbrot set fractal pattern is not art because the "artist" saw an equation and a set of rules, while the observer sees a colorful rendering of the Mandelbrot set. It may be interesting to look at, but it is not art.

Tom McMillan, Editor of *Resolution*, writes:

Art affects the sense of beauty, and we all know that beauty is in the eye of the beholder. Try as he or she might, an artist is not an artist unless his or her work affects someone else's sense of beauty. The so-called art world tends to discredit art in the computer graphics medium, making it difficult for artists even to get an audience. While [computer art] may not rank up there with Monet's paintings, it nonetheless does affect my sense of beauty.

15.10 Cross References and Credits

The quotations of Benoit Mandelbrot come from: *Mathematical People* published by Birkhauser Boston (1985). In this book, Mandelbrot is interviewed by Anthony Barcellos.

See the following sections for information on fractals: "Smithson's Fractal Anabiotic Ana Sequences" on page 35 and "Labyrinthine Lundin Curves" on page 103. For fractal mazes, see "Mazes for the Mind" on page 3. For fractal integer sequences and patterns see "The Drums of Ulupu" on page 71 and "Beauty and the Bits" on page 79. For feather fractals, see "Fantastic Feather Fractals" on page 33. For fractal ant farms, see "Electronic and Fractal Ant Farms" on page 173.

The following sections are concerned with questions regarding whether or not computer-generated art is really good art: "Is Computer Art Really Art?" on page 169, "Interlude: Alien Musical Scores" on page 221, and "Interlude: Marking Time" on page 289.

15.11 For Further Reading

1.   Pickover, C. (1990) Inverted Mandelbrot sets. *Visual Computer*. 5: 377.

2.   Peitgen, H., Richter, P. (1986) *The Beauty of Fractals*. Springer: Berlin.

3.   Wegner, T., Peterson, M. (1991) *Fractal Creations*. Waite Group Press: California.

4.   Mandelbrot, B. (1983) *The Fractal Geometry of Nature*. Freeman: San Francisco.

5.   Stevens, R. (1989) *Fractal Programming in C*. M and T Books: Redwood City: California.

6.   Frame, M., Robertson, J. (1992) A generalized Mandelbrot set and the role of critical points. *Computers and Graphics*. 16(1), in press.

7.   Lakhtakia, A., Varadan, V.V., Messier, R., Varadan, V.K. (1987) On the symmetries of the Julia sets for the process $z \rightarrow z^p + c$. *Journal of Physics A: Math. General*. 20: 3533-3535.

8.   Pokorny, C., Gerald, C. (1989) *Computer Graphics*. Franklin, Beedle and Associates: California.

Chapter 16

Mandalas, Screws, Pears, and Klein Bottles

In the last decade, even serious mathematicians have begun to enjoy and present bizarre mathematical patterns in new ways — ways sometimes dictated as much by a sense of aesthetics as by the needs of logic. Moreover, computer graphics allows non-mathematicians to better appreciate the complicated and interesting graphical behavior of simple formulas.

Here are some recipes for producing a beautiful graphics gallery of mathematical surfaces. To produce these curves, I place spheres at locations determined by formulas which are implemented as computer algorithms. Many of you may find difficulty in drawing shaded spheres; however, quite attractive and informative figures can be drawn simply by placing colored dots at these same locations. Alternatively, just place black dots on a white background. As you implement the following descriptions, change the formulas slightly to see the graphic and artistic results. Don't let the complicated-looking formulas scare you. They're very easy to implement in the computer language of your choice by following the computer recipes and computational hints given in the program outlines.

As opposed to the curves which you may have seen in geometry books (such as bullet-shaped paraboloids, and saddle surfaces) which are simple functions of x and y, certain curves occupying three dimensions can be expressed by *parametric equations* of the form: $x = f(u,v)$, $y = g(u,v)$, $z = h(u,v)$. This means that the position of a point in 3-D is determined by three separate formulas. Because f, g, and h can be anything you like, the remarkable panoply of art forms made possible by plotting these curves is quite large! Some personal favorites are listed in the following. For simplicity, you can plot projections of these curves in the x-y plane simply by plotting (x,y) as you iterate u and v in a computer program. Alternatively, here's a handy formula for viewing the curves at any angle:

Figure 16.1. *Wiwianka surface.*

$$x_p = x \cos \theta + y \sin \theta$$
$$y_p = - x \sin \theta \sin \phi + y \cos \theta \sin \phi + z \cos \phi \qquad (16.1)$$

where (x,y,z) are the coordinates of the point on the curve prior to projection and (θ, ϕ) are the viewing angles in spherical coordinates.

Figure 16.1, which resembles a pear, can be computed using

$$x = f(u,v) = \left(1 + e^{-100u^2}\right) \sin(\pi u) \sin(\pi v)$$

$$y = g(u,v) = \left(1 + e^{-100u^2}\right) \sin(\pi u) \cos(\pi v) \qquad (16.2)$$

$$z = h(u,v) = \left(1 + e^{-100u^2}\right) \cos(\pi u)$$

I call this pear-like surface a *Wiwianka surface* in honor of Waldemar Wiwianka (IBM) who first drew this surface using more traditional representations. To produce the graphic representations, compute x, y, and z for many different

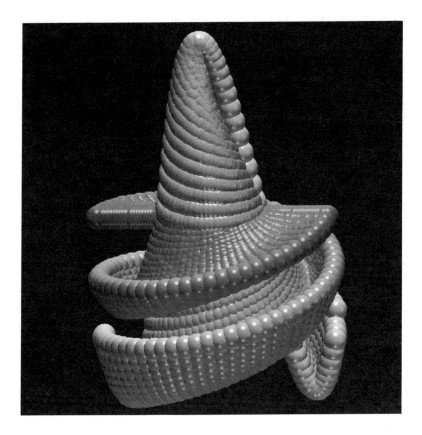

Figure 16.2. *Steinbach screw.*

values of *u* and *v*. My preference is to represent these formulas in new ways by "undersampling" the surfaces so that they produce wiry, see-through surfaces (as in Figure 16.1). In addition, I enjoy plotting the curves using spheres to give them an interesting, artistic texture. Pseudocode 16.1 indicates that the *u* sample points go from 0 to 1 in steps of 0.005, and that the *v* sample points go from 0 to 2 in steps of 0.1 in order to produce the see-through look.

The screw-like surface in Figure 16.2, or *Steinbach screw*, can be computed from

$$f(u,v) = u \cos(v)$$
$$g(u,v) = u \sin(v)$$
$$h(u,v) = v \cos(u)$$

(16.3)

With a few changes to the ranges of *u* and *v* (see the program examples), you can produce a very different mandala-like surface (Figure 16.3). (Mandalas are ornate, schematic, graphic depictions of the universe used chiefly by Buddhists.)

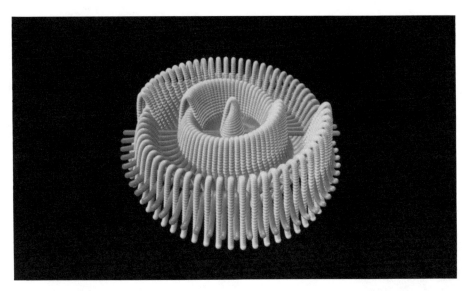

Figure 16.3. *Mandala.*

Figure 16.4, which shows a wiry, artistic version of a Banchoff Klein bottle, can be computed from:

$$f(x,y) = \cos(x)(\cos(x/2)(s + \cos(y)) + (\sin(x/2)\sin(y)\cos(y)))$$
$$g(x,y) = \sin(x)(\cos(x/2)(s + \cos(y)) + (\sin(x/2)\sin(y)\cos(y))) \quad (16.4)$$
$$h(x,y) = -\sin(x/2)(s + \cos(y)) + \cos(x/2)\sin(y)\cos(y)$$

Here $s = \sqrt{2}$. The Banchoff Klein bottle is based on the Möbius band, a surface with only one edge. The Möbius band is an example of a nonorientable space, which means that it is not possible to distinguish an object on the surface from its reflected image in a mirror. This Klein bottle contains Möbius bands and can be built in 4-D space. Powerful graphics computers allow us to design unusual objects such as these and then investigate them by projecting them in a 2-D image. Some physicists and astronomers have postulated that the large-scale structure of our universe may resemble a huge nonorientable space with Klein bottle-like properties, permitting right-handed objects to be transformed into left-handed objects.

If you are a teacher, have your students design and program their own patterns by modifying the parameters in these equations, and make a large mural of all the student designs labeled with the relevant generating formulas.

```
ALGORITHM: How to Create a Wiwianka pear Surface
for(u = 0; u < 1; u = u + 0.005){
   for(v = 0; v < 2; v = v + 0.1){
      x = (1. + exp(-100.*u*u))*sin(pi*u)*sin(pi*v);
      y = (1. + exp(-100.*u*u))*sin(pi*u)*cos(pi*v);
      z = (1. + exp(-100.*u*u))*cos(pi*u);
      DrawSphereCenteredAt(x,y,z);
   }
}
```

Pseudocode 16.1. *How to create a Wiwianka pear surface.* (The program code here is in the style of the C language.)

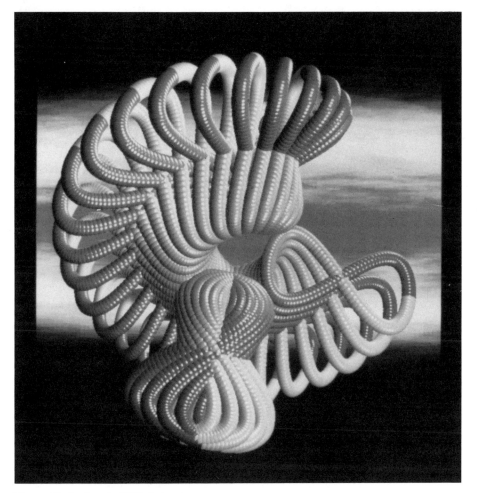

Figure 16.4. *Banchoff Klein bottle.*

```
ALGORITHM: How to Create a Banchoff Klein Bottle
 for(u= 0; u < 9.56; u = u + .2){
  for(v= 0; v < 6.28; v = v + .05){
    x= cos(u)*(cos(u/2)*(sqrt(2)+cos(v))+(sin(u/2)*sin(v)*cos(v)))
    y= sin(u)*(cos(u/2)*(sqrt(2)+cos(v))+(sin(u/2)*sin(v)*cos(v)))
    z= -sin(u/2)*(sqrt(2)+cos(v))+cos(u/2)*sin(v)*cos(v);
    DrawSphereCenteredAt(x,y,x)
  }
 }
```

Pseudocode 16.2. *How to create a Banchoff Klein Bottle.* (The program code here is in the style of the C language.)

```
ALGORITHM: How to Create Mandala and Screw Surfaces
 for(u= -8; u < 16; u = u + 0.15){
    for(v= 0; v < 12.56; v = v + 0.1){
      x = u*cos(v);
      y = u*sin(v);
      z = v*cos(u);
      DrawSphereCenteredAt(x,y,z);
    }
 }
```

Pseudocode 16.3. *How to create Mandala and Screw surfaces.* (The program code here is in the style of the C language.) Note: play around with the bounds for *u* and *v* in the "for" loops. The screw is produced with bounds closer to $-4 < u < 4$ and $0 < v < 2\pi$.

Chapter 17

Labyrinthine Lundin Curves

"The dreamer, a soldier in repose, applied the methods of algebra to the structures of geometry, bone-setting the measure land, expressing his system in terms of constants, variables, and position coordinates, all arranged in due time on the scheme of crossed lines forming squares of equal size."

Don DeLillo, *Ratner's Star*

There are all kinds of crazy and exotic curves inhabiting the mathematical world of functions. Some are easy to graph, some are more difficult. My favorites contain an infinite number of bumps and wiggles. These infinitely bumpy curves come in two flavors: fractal and nonfractal. By now, many readers are probably aware of fractal curves (see "Fractal Spiders and Frame-Robertson Bushes" on page 87). These days computer-generated *fractal* patterns are everywhere. From squiggly designs on computer art posters, to illustrations in the most serious of physics journals, interest continues to grow among scientists and, rather surprisingly, artists and designers. Fractals are curves or patterns which exhibit increasing detail ("bumpiness") with increasing magnification. Many interesting fractals are self-similar. B. Mandelbrot informally defines fractals as "shapes that are equally complex in their details as in their overall form. That is, if a piece of a fractal is suitably magnified to become of the same size as the whole, it should look like the whole, either exactly, or perhaps only after slight limited deformation."

To get a better understanding of fractal structures, I find it helpful to consider some very bumpy-looking, *nonfractal* curves for comparison. First consider the following question. How can a fractal shape (like the Koch curve in Figure 1.8) with infinitely many bumps between bigger bumps, in a finite region in space, be continuous?

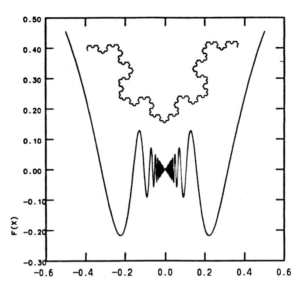

Figure 17.1. *x sin(1/x)*. This mathematical function has the property of being everywhere continuous, even though it has infinitely many oscillations in the neighborhood of $x = 0$, where the size of the oscillations becomes infinitely small. The frequency near $x = 0$ is infinite and the spacing between the maxima is zero! A Koch curve (top) is superimposed for comparison.

Intuitively one might imagine that this shape, which contains infinitely high frequency patterns in a finite space should "break up," i.e. become discontinuous. Continuity for a function, f, may be informally defined: points that are very close together are mapped by f into points that are very close together. This type of question is often difficult to deal with either on an intuitive level or by studying natural shapes. Instead, one may wish to study the following more simple mathematical function with startling properties. This prickly curve masquerades as a fractal until one takes a closer look.

Consider the function $x \sin(1/x)$. The graph of this function for $|x| < 1$ shows smaller yet more rapid oscillations the nearer it approaches zero. Its limit as x approaches zero can be expressed as:

$$\lim_{x \to 0} x \sin\left(\frac{1}{x}\right) = 0 \tag{17.1}$$

Let's now define a quite related function

$$\Psi(x) \equiv \begin{cases} x \sin\left(\dfrac{1}{x}\right) & \text{if } x \neq 0 \\ 0 & \text{if } x = 0 \end{cases} \tag{17.2}$$

Like a Koch curve, this curve has infinitely many bumps, decreasing in size, in a finite region of space. Is the curve generated by this formula continuous? Since

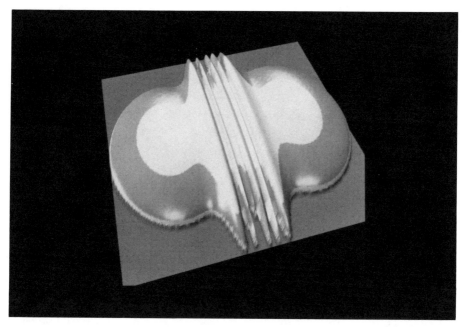

Figure 17.2. *Lundin surface.* I rendered this using custom software running on an IBM RISC System/6000 equipped with a high performance graphics card.

$\sin(x)$ is everywhere continuous, and $1/x$ is continuous for $x \neq 0$ it follows that the *composite* function $\sin(1/x)$ is continuous for $x \neq 0$. Therefore $\Psi(x)$ is a simple mathematical function (Figure 17.1) that is *everywhere continuous*, even though it has *infinitely* many oscillations in the neighborhood of $x = 0$, where the size of the oscillations becomes infinitely small. However, unlike fractals, $\Psi(x)$, for $x \neq 0$, is differentiable (i.e. smooth), even though the frequency near $x = 0$ is infinite and the spacing between the maxima is zero!

A more interesting curve, which I think many educators and graphics specialists will enjoy, is the Lundin function named after John Lundin of the University of Richmond who has explored this curve in detail. The 3-D shape can be described by:

$$x^2 + y^2 + (z^2 - 1) \times ((1 - d) + d\cos(1/z)) = 0 \qquad (17.3)$$

where $0 < d < 0.5$. Like the previous Ψ curve, this one has a wealth of structural details. The Lundin curve is really a surface of revolution of a pathological 2-D curve. (By "pathological" I mean a curve that has infinitely many bumps in a finite area.)

Figure 17.2 is a plot of half this surface. In order to create the 3-D graphics rendition, the surface was divided into thousands of tiny triangular facets which were lit and shaded. Coloration was also determined by the height of the function at a particular point. You can rotate the function

$$x = \sqrt{((1 - z^2) \times ((1 - d) + d \times \cos(1/z)))} \qquad (17.4)$$

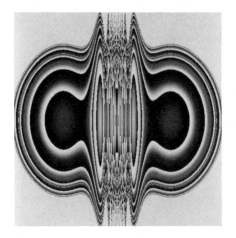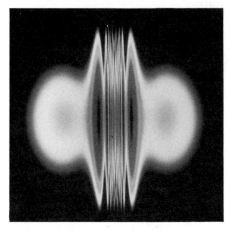

Figure 17.3. *2-D Lundin surface projection.* Height is mapped to color in two different representations.

around the z axis to arrive at the full Lundin surface. For graphic beauty I compressed the surface a bit along the x-axis, destroying rotational symmetry. Also many of the oscillations near $z = 0$ are missing since some points were lost in order to produce the 3-D rendition without resorting to an overwhelming number of facets. However, by representing the function as a 2-D image in Figure 17.3, these artifacts are reduced, and you can see more of the ripples.

You may wish to consider values of x as you vary z. The quantity $(1 - z^2)$ must be positive or there is no solution. Therefore z must lie between -1 and 1, and when $|z|$ is one, x must be zero (top and bottom points of the surface).

Lundin notices that if $d = 0$ the second term under the radical disappears, and one is left with a a sphere with a finite surface area and volume. On a globe, the $(|z| = 1, x = 0)$ points are the poles, and $(z = 0, x = 1)$ forms the equator. Next examine the second term when d is nonzero. This varies from $1 - 2d$ to 1 and shrinks the radius of the globe at that z value. In effect, we are cutting grooves around it parallel to the equator. Each groove adds an increment of area to the surface and drops the volume slightly. Closer to the equator, the grooves become slightly deeper and both narrower and closer together. At $z = 0$ there is no way to determine how deep to make the groove (the surface does not exist), there are infinitely many grooves, the area is infinitely large, and the volume has remained finite.

A Lundin curve with somewhat similar properties, as yet undrawn, is

$$(x - d \sin(k/z))^2 + (y - d \cos(k/z))^2 + z^2 = 1 \tag{17.5}$$

John Lundin notes that this curve "fits in a cylinder of radius $1 + d$ and height 2, and should be even prettier than the one shown in Figure 17.2."

Chapter 18

Interlude: Cemeteries of the Future, And Interstellar Art

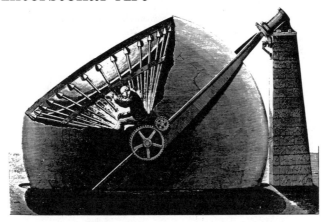

What will technology, life, and art be like in the future? This is a question continually on the mind of artist Stephen s'Soreff, editor and publisher of AGAR (Avant-Garde Art Review). AGAR is an art experience in itself, and it is free to all who write him, as long as the subscribers state their reasons for wanting AGAR. All of the artists and art works in AGAR, though quite realistic looking, are fictional. s'Soreff is interested in what art *might* look like a few decades in the future. His artwork has made such predictions as believable as possible, with collaged and retouched illustrations and feasible technology.

In the past, AGAR has covered fictional artists who have worked with genetically engineered art, cloud seeding, sculptures of silence, thought-activated paintings, poetry composed by the sea, sculptures produced by exponentially growing cells and brainwaves, and much more. Each AGAR issue is wonderfully illustrated with ultra-futuristic, surreal images which look so real that you want to reach out and touch them. Back copies of AGAR are available by writing to Stephen s'Soreff, 79 Mercer St. New York, NY 10012.

AGAR is just one of many interesting ideas that s'Soreff dreams about. A few years ago he conceived the notion of establishing an interstellar art gallery via videotape that would picture art for sale on earth and then would beam it to other stars. Two years later, he became acquainted with a Texas millionaire who was interested in experimental art and who owned four television stations. As a result, the tape was broadcast into space in 1983.

s'Soreff also envisions future tombstones set with computerized video simulations of the deceased talking and moving in response to visitors. A person who wished to have this kind of tombstone would, while still alive, visit a group of psychiatrists and sociologists, and he or she would be taped uttering various words. This data would then used by a computer program to simulate the person's replies to greetings or questions after his or her demise.

Chapter 19

Lava Lamps in the 21st Century

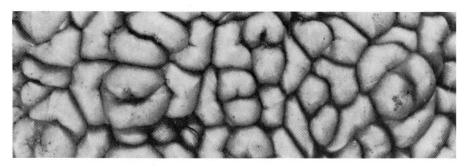

"Consider the true picture. Think of myriads of tiny bubbles, very sparsely scattered, rising through a vast black sea. We rule some of the bubbles. Of the waters we know nothing..." Niven and Pournelle *The Mote in God's Eye*

The preceding quotation from Niven and Pournelle's futuristic science-fiction novel describes both the vast mystery of our universe and the strangely shaped

objects we might one day encounter in outer space. In the 1990's, however, we don't need a space ship to explore strange new worlds consisting of bubble-like forms. Rather, all that is required is a small set of mathematical algorithms running on a good graphics computer. In fact, the blob-like shapes which illustrate this chapter move and coalesce in ways which resemble the mixing of oil and water. From a visual standpoint, the moving shapes on the computer screen remind one of lava lamps – those decorative lights, popular in the 1960's, which contain illuminated, moving, colored globules in a liquid-filled glass globe. The lava lamp (properly known as the "Lava Lite") was invented in the early 60's by an Englishman named Craven Walker. The lava in the lamp is made of a wax substance, and the wax and surrounding liquid are composed of 11 secret ingredients. The specific gravities of each batch of wax and liquid must be individually matched, or the wax will break up into tiny bubbles, crawl up the side of the glass, or just float on top of the liquid.[8]

---

[8] The photographs of Lava Lites are courtesy of Gregory Sams, owner of *Strange Attractions*, the first store in the world devoted to chaos and fractals (Greg Sams, 204 Kensington Park Rd, Lonon W11 1NR UK.) Lava Lites are manufactured today by Lava-Simplex Internationale, Chicago, Illinois.

Figure 19.1. *Two-dimensional lava.* A single time frame from a time-evolving (2000x2000 cell) 2-D lava created by the *M46789* rule described in the text.

19.1 Making Lava in a Checkerboard World

"The city of the future is a city of light. A realm of constantly shifting, ebbing and flowing colors and forms. A world that will constantly hold the eye and mind in a calm and meaningful movement on a level between rest and alertness." Alex Gross, 1969, *East Village Other*

Lava Lites decorating living rooms of the future will include computerized versions where the waxy globules are simply mathematical/computer graphical entities displayed on a computer screen. In order to create the undulating lava, you may first wish to construct a 2-dimensional model where the forms move, coalesce, and break up in the infinitely thin space between two glass plates (Figure 19.1). The simulation involves the use of "cellular automata." Cellular automata (CA) are a class of simple mathematical systems which are becoming important as models for a variety of physical processes. CA are mathematical idealizations of physical systems in which space and time are discrete. Usually cellular automata consist of a grid of cells which can exist in two states, occupied

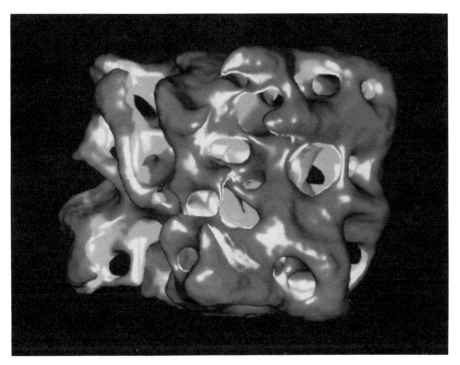

Figure 19.2. *M14 lava on a 50x50x50 grid after 10 iterations.* As with all of the 3-D figures, three "artificial" light sources are positioned and computed using a computer graphics program.

or unoccupied. The occupancy of one cell is determined from a simple mathematical analysis of the occupancy of neighbor cells. One popular set or rules is set forth in what has become known as the game of "LIFE." Though the rules governing the creation of cellular automata are simple, the patterns they produce are very complicated and sometimes seem almost random, like a turbulent fluid flow or the output of a cryptographic system.

To create a CA, each cell of the array must be in one of the allowed states. The rules that determine how the states of its cells change with time are what determine the cellular automata's behavior. There are an infinite number of possible cellular automata, each like a checkerboard world. All the shapes in this chapter were produced by initially filling the CA array with random 1's and 0's. The rules of growth which determine the states of the cells in subsequent generations are discussed in the next section.

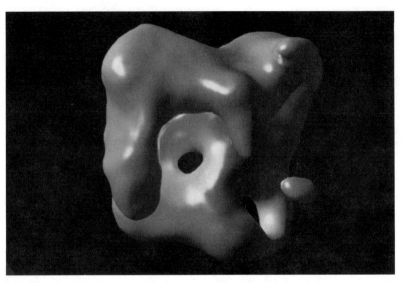

Figure 19.3. *Same as previous figure, after more iterations.*

19.2 It's a Beautiful Day in the Neighborhood

> *"It moved through the otherwise dark wall in scores of separate amoeba-like forms that constantly flowed together and separated into new shapes; it was like a one-dimensional representation of the kaleidoscopic display in one of those old Lava lamps. The ever-changing patterns evolved on all sides of them..."*
>   Dean Koontz, 1991, *Cold Fire*

The systems in this chapter evolve in discrete time according to a local law. As with most cellular automata, the value taken by a cell at time $t + 1$ is determined by the values assumed at time t by the neighboring sites and by the considered site itself:

$$c_{i,j}^{t+1} = f(a,b) \tag{19.1}$$

where

$$a = c_{(i,j)}^{t},\, c_{(i+1,j+1)}^{t},\, c_{(i-1,j-1)}^{t},\, c_{(i-1,j+1)}^{t}, \tag{19.2}$$

$$b = c_{(i+1,j-1)}^{t},\, c_{(i+1,j)}^{t},\, c_{(i-1,j)}^{t},\, c_{(i,j+1)}^{t},\, c_{(i,j-1)}^{t} \tag{19.3}$$

(The division of sites between a and b is artificial and used only for ease of typesetting.) In this equation, $c_{i,j}^{t}$ denotes the state occupied at time t by the site (i,j). The nine-cell template used in this chapter is referred to as the *Moore* neighborhood (as opposed to the *von Neumann* neighborhood consisting only of orthogo-

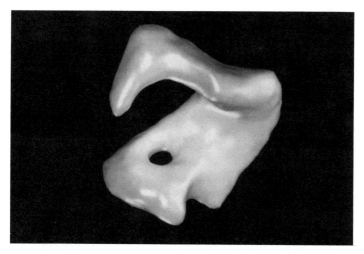

Figure 19.4. *Same as previous figure, after more iterations.*

nally adjacent neighbors). One interesting simulation simply examines the neighbor sites to determine if the majority of neighbors are in state one. If so, then the center site also becomes one. We can represent those cells in the on (one) state as black dots on a graphics screen. In other words, this rule is a *voting rule* which assigns 0 or 1 according to the "popularity of these states in the neighborhood," and interestingly it generates behavior found in real physical systems. This simple *majority rule automata* produces hundreds of coalesced, convex-shaped black areas but does not lead to interesting graphical forms. A way to destabilize the interface between one and zero areas is to modify the rules slightly so that a cell is on if the sum of the one-sites in the Moore neighborhood is either 4, 6, 7, 8, or 9, otherwise the site is turned off. This rule has been studied previously (in lower resolution), and, since it uses a Moore neighborhood, it has been termed *M46789* by Vichniac in 1986. Such simulations have relevance to percolation and surface-tension studies of liquids.

19.3 Twisted 3-D Majority Rules, and Printer Dirt

Figure 19.1 shows an *M46789* 2-D lava which has evolved after several hundred time steps from random initial conditions on a 2000x2000 square lattice. The tiny dust specks sparsely scattered between the coalescing blobs are not dirt left by the graphics printer, but rather they are stable structures such as
```
**
**
```
where each site has exactly 4 "on" members (out of 9) in its neighborhood, and thus stays on. The surrounding sites that are off have at most 1 or 2 neighbors that are on, and thus they stay off. There are probably quite a few other stable structures like this, though this rule does not seem to give rise to the zoo of stable objects allowed by, say, the game of Life.

The twisted majority rule for 2-D Moore neighborhoods just described naturally leads to curiosity about how 3-D lava forms evolve when displayed using high-resolution graphics on graphics supercomputers. I have recently created 3-D lava simulations by extending the 2-D simulation to an $M(13,15,16,17,18, 19,20,21,22,23,24,25,26,27)$ simulation on 50x50x50 and 100x100x100 3-D lattices. For the remainder of this chapter I will call this rule $M14$ to indicate where the twist, or skip, in the majority rule takes place. To create the remaining figures in this chapter, $M14$ lava is allowed to evolve for 10 to several hundred generations starting from randomly filled arrays of 0's and 1's. In order to visually decrease grid artifacts, the final site values for the cellular automata are determined by replacing the center site value with the mean value of its 27-cell Moore neighborhood prior to display. This effectively turns the discrete on/off collection of sites into a slightly smoother continuum. The final graphic form is created by computing an equal-valued surface, or "isosurface," at a particular value in the 3-D data set. These equi-valued surfaces, which represent the smooth boundary between the 1's and 0's, are the final form the viewer actually sees. The equi-valued surface sculptures in this chapter were rendered using a program which computes and represents surfaces as a collection of small triangular facets. The triangles which make up the surface are smoothed, shaded, rotated, and lighted using a general purpose display program, running on a powerful graphics workstation such as a Stellar GS2000. All numerical simulations were computed on an IBM RISC System/6000, using an optimized C program.

Like a submarine pilot exploring coral formations in the Sargasso sea, modern graphics supercomputers, such as the Stellar GS2000, allow one to explore the strange and colorful $M14$ lava caverns using a mouse. As the simulation progresses, starting from randomly mixed zeros and ones, those cells in the lava (that are in the one state) move around randomly until they meet and join by cohesion — forming visually interesting aggregates due to the $M14$ rule.

Unlike a real Lava Lite, the globules in this simulation eventually disappear as time progresses. That is, the globules' mass is not conserved! In order to produce an interesting lava lamp one needs to repeatedly execute the simulation, each time starting with new random seeds. Alternatively, one can inject random new on-sites periodically.

19.4 For Further Reading

1. Adams, C. (1988) *More of the Straight Dope* Ballentine: New York

2. Pickover, C. (1991) Virtual voltage sculptures. *Leonardo.* 24(5), 622-624.

3. Toffoli, T. (1984) The CAM Celluar Automata Machine. *Physica* 10D: 195-204.

4. Pickover, C. (1991) *Computers and the Imagination.* St Martin's Press: New York.

5. Poundstone, W. (1985) *The Recursive Universe.* William Morrow and Company, New York.

6. Vichniac, G. (1986) Cellular automata models of disorder and organization. In *Disordered Systems and Biological Organization* Bienenstock., E., Soulie, F., and Weisbuch, G., eds. Springer: New York.

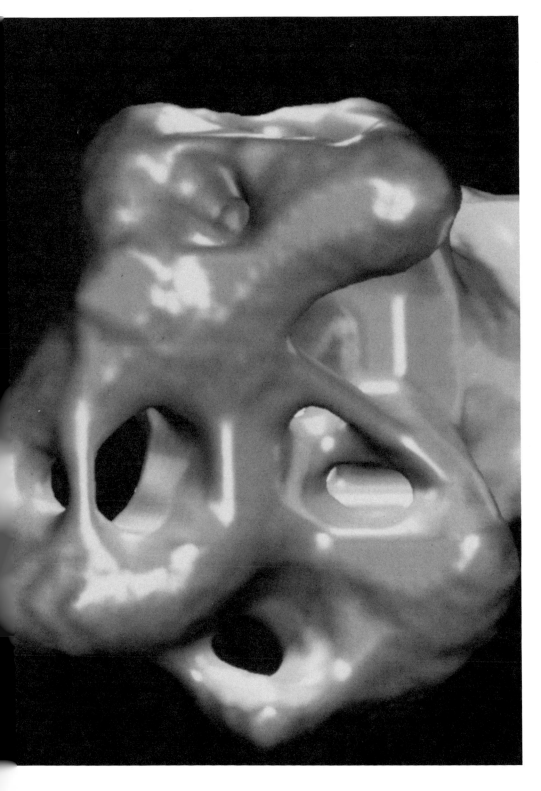

Chapter 20

Monster Contour Art

Contour lines have been used for decades to show bands of equal elevations in maps of geographic terrain. Contour lines are also often used for producing minimalist computer art. Instead of indicating elevation, the lines may indicate regions of equal intensity in a photograph. Shown here is a photograph of a clay sculpture (facing page) and its contour map (below). You may wish to show the contour line drawing to some friends as a test of the ability of the human visual system to see the original pattern using the minimalist representation. Do your friends recognize a face in the complicated mixture of lines, or is the contour map too abstract to permit recognition? (I computed the contour lines using software running on an IBM RISC System/6000. The original photograph is of a sculpture which I constructed with clay.)[9]

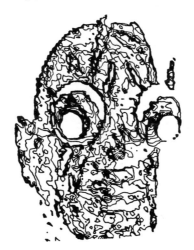

---

[9] For computer scientists: to compute the contours, I first triangulate the original image represented as a square arrays of intensities. Next I consider the contour value S_0 and compare it to the intensity of each pair of points S_2 and S_1 in the triangle. If the intensities of the three points on the triangle are all greater than or all less than the contour value, then no line segment is drawn. Otherwise, the intersection of the line segment with the triangle is computed using $x = x_1 + [(S_0 - S_1)/(S_2 - S_1)] (x_2 - x_1)$. ($x$ is a 3-D vector locating a point in 3-space.)

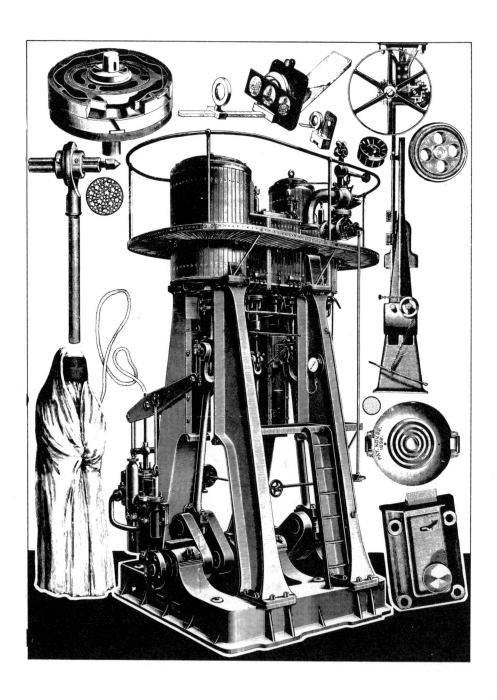

Part II

GAMES AND SPECULATION

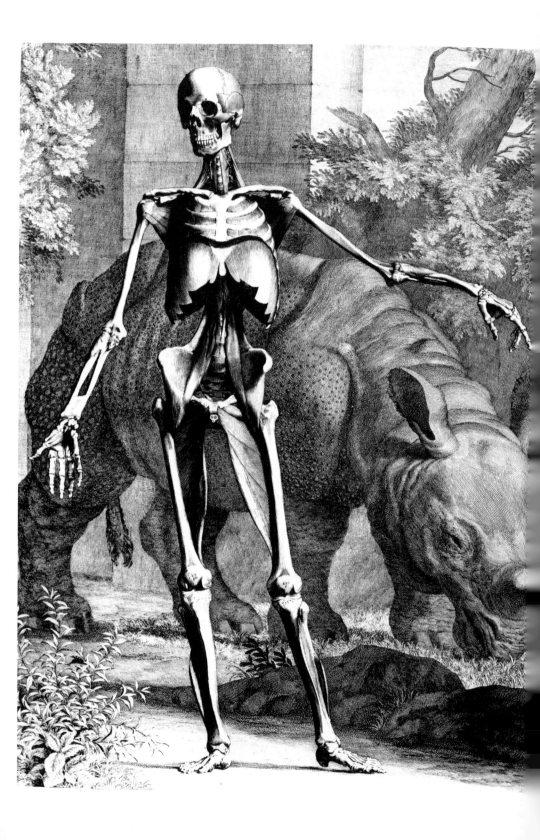

Chapter 21

My Computer Esophagus

My interest in human anatomy began in early childhood. I remember going into my father's study and gazing at the anatomical works of Bernard Siegfried

Albinus, the greatest descriptive anatomist of the eighteenth century. In 1725, after Albinus found a fresh skeleton of a fully grown male "with all the tendons, ligaments, and cartilage attached," he became determined to make careful drawings of the body and skeleton for use by both artists and anatomists. He preserved the soft parts by soaking them in vinegar. One of his first drawings is shown facing this page. It is from my early fascination with human anatomy that the Computer Esophagus game grew.

The Computer Esophagus is a simple but unusual game I designed several years ago. Hopefully you will not find the game morbid but rather an interesting exercise in strategy and computer simulation. The game is played on a simplified 2-D representation of the human body, and the object of the game is to occupy every

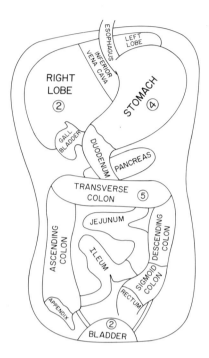

Figure 21.1. *The playing board for the Computer Esophagus.*

organ system on the playing board (Figure 21.1).[10] To increase the visual appeal of the game, you might consider designing a board using a figure from *The Illustrations of the Works of Andreas Vesalius of Brussels* (Dover, 1973) (Figure 21.2). If you like, you can think of the game as a battle between antibodies and infectious agents such as viruses or cancer cells. Alternatively, some of my friends like to think of the game as a contest between two or three hostile governments that have used futuristic technology to miniaturize submarine crews which have been placed inside the body of some important governmental official.

The game is designed for two or three players. To play the non-computer version, you may want to enlarge the playing board shown here. You'll also need playing pieces to place on the organs systems of the board. Each player's pieces must be distinguishable from the others' pieces (e.g. red and black checkers, pennies and dimes, different colored seeds, or playing pieces from games such as Parker Brother's *RISK*). Let's call these playing pieces "cells." The board shows four major organ systems, or regions, each of which is subdivided into a number of *territories*. The *Stomach Region* consists of the esophagus, duodenum, gall

---

[10] After giving the game to my brother (who at the time was a medical student at New York University and now is a prominent gastroenterologist in Boston), I'm told the game was played late at night by several students in the little spare time they had.

Figure 21.2. *A diagram from Andreas Vesalius (1514-1564).*

bladder, and pancreas. The *Liver Region* consists of the right lobe, inferior vena cava, and left lobe. The *Intestine Region* consists of the appendix, ascending colon, transverse colon, descending colon, sigmoid colon, rectum, ileum, and jejunum. The *Bladder Region* is one large territory on its own and does not consist of separate, individual territories. It helps to color the outlines of these regions using different colors to help remember which territories comprise a particular organ region. In my personal game version, I color the Stomach Region yellow, the Liver Region red, the Colon Region blue, and the Bladder Region green. Before the game starts, each player counts out a number of cells for initial occupation of the organ systems. The number of cells is determined by the number of competing players. If there are two players, each player gets 19 cells. If there are more than two players, each player gets 8 cells. At this point, it's time to fill the board with cells. Roll a die, or use a computer random number generator, to select who goes first. The person with the higher number goes first.

Let's assume there are two players. The first player takes one of his 19 allotted cells and places it on any one of the 17 organ territories of his choice. The second player then places one of his cells on any one of the remaining unoccupied territories. Players alternate until the body has one cell on each organ territory. Each player then continues to add cells to any territories he owns. He can place them all on one territory or scatter them over several territories he controls. Once each player has 19 cells on the board, the actual play begins. At the beginning of each turn, a player gets one "free" extra cell to place on any territory he owns.

At each turn, a player's objective is to attack a bordering organ territory. For example, cells positioned on the right lobe can only attack the gall bladder, stomach, duodenum, and inferior vena cava – because these territories are adja-

```
ALGORITHM: How to Play the Computer Esophagus.
 1 Player(1) = 1
 2 Player(2) = 2
 3 Do for each attack
 4    Organ_Number = (a number designating attacking organ)
 5    n = Organ(Player(2),Organ_Number) - 2)
 6    if (n < 0 ) Say 'Cannot attack with fewer than 2 cells'
 7    r = random
 8    f = (6-n)*(7-n) / 72
 9    Organ_Number = (a number designating defending organ)
10    if r > f  then Organ(Player(1),Organ_Number) =
11                     Organ(Player(1),Organ_Number) - 1
12    if Organ(Player(1),Organ_Number) = 0 then
                      (Attacker occupies organ)
13    Organ_Number = (a number designating attacking organ)
14    if r <= f then Organ(Player(2),Organ_Number) =
15                     Organ(Player(2),Organ_Number) - 1
16    end
```

Pseudocode 21.1. *How to play The Computer Esophagus, using a computer program.* (If a computer is not available, you can use dice to determine the outcome of cancer/antibody engagements.)

cent. The bladder is considered adjacent to the ascending colon and sigmoid colon via the two thin connecting strands of mesentery. The probability of winning an attack is determined by the number of cells in the attacking organ. In order to attack, a player must have at least two cells on his organ territory.

First I'll describe how the results of a "cancer-antibody engagement" are determined if you are using dice, rather than a computer program. Only two dice are needed for play – one for the attacker and one for the defender. First, the attacker declares which organ territory he is attacking. Then the players each rolls a die. The player with the greater number wins. However, the attacker can add to his die roll a number which depends on how many cells are in the attacking territory. Here are the three cases that can arise. *Case 1:* As just stated, if the attacker has 2 cells, and the attacker's die number is *greater* than the defender's number, he wins. *Case 2:* However, if the attacker has 3 cells, the attacker adds a *one* to his die result. For example, if he rolls a 3, he actually has a 4. Again, if the attacker's number is higher than the defender's number, he wins. *Case 3:* If the attacker has 4 or more cells, the attacker adds a *two* to his die result. For example, if he rolls a 3, he actually has a 5. If the attacker's number is higher than the defender's number, he wins. The defender always wins ties. Unlike the attacker, the defender does not receive any extra special "credit" for having a large number of cells on an organ. However, the defender does have a better chance of defending an organ territory if he has many cells on it because the chances of an attacker winning many separate battles is less than for winning just a single battle, for example. This is described in the next paragraph.

A player may continue to attack an adjacent organ territory so long as he has 2 or more cells. When the attacker wins, a cell is removed from the defender's

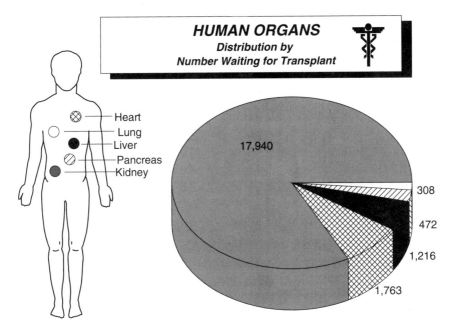

Figure 21.3. *Organ Waiting Lists.* In 1991, more than 21,000 Americans were on waiting lists to receive organ transplants. Here is a list of the number of people waiting for an organ for five major organs. (Source: Tom Heymann's *The Unofficial US Census*, Fawcett Columbine: NY (1991)).

territory. When the attacker loses he removes a cell from his own territory. If there are no longer any cells on the defender's territory, then the attacker moves at least one cell of his into the new territory. He may not move all of his cells into the new territory, because at no time during play may an organ territory be empty of cells. He must leave at least one cell behind on the attacking organ. The attacker may continue his turn for as long as he likes, or until he has run out of cells, at which point he passes the turn to the other player, who then becomes the attacker.

At the beginning of every turn that all the territories in an organ system are occupied by a player, the player is entitled to extra cells in accordance with the following table:

```
Liver Region, 2 cells; Stomach Region, 4 cells;
Intestine Region, 5 cells; Bladder, 2 cells.
```

(These values are printed beneath large territories within each of the four regions on the board.) He may place these extra cells on any organ territory he controls before the attacking begins. Therefore it is advantageous to capture and maintain control over entire organ systems. The cancer or antibody wins when either occupies every organ territory of the body, thereby eliminating the opponent's playing pieces.

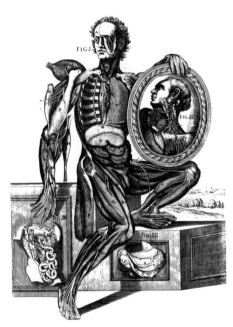

Figure 21.4. *The Visible Human Project.* In 1991, researchers at the University of Colorado Health Science Center in Denver, Colorado are excited about their new project to create "the ultimate digital model" of the human anatomy. This complete, 3-D model will contain high-resolution images and information concerning every cubic millimeter of a male and female corpse. (See text for details.)

21.1 Computer Analysis and Play

Those of you who wish to play the board game, and not concern yourselves with a computer implementation and mathematical analysis, may skip this section. For those with access to color computer graphics, it is relatively easy to draw a playing board. For simplicity, the organ territories can be shaped like rectangles, and computer-drawn text can be placed in the rectangles. Playing pieces, in the form of colored X's or O's, can be also be drawn on the organ territories. Instead of rolling dice, it is a fairly simple matter to use a random number generator to simulate the win/lose rules discussed previously for cancer-antibody engagements. One can show that for Case 1, where the attacker has only 2 cells, the probability of winning an engagement is $15/36 = 42\%$. For Case 2, with 3 cells, the probability of winning is $21/36 = 58\%$. For Case 3, with 4 or more cells, the probability of winning is $26/36 = 72\%$.

In fact, Kevin McCarty of the Rolm Corporation has computed probabilities for the 3 cases I outlined by counting squares in a 6x6 grid. You can best understand this by listing the results of the defender's die roll down the side of a square array, and the attacker's roll across the top (see following diagram). Enter A in the cell when the attacker wins, otherwise enter a D.

```
        CASE 1                  CASE 2                  CASE 3
    A                       A                       A
    1 2 3 4 5 6             1 2 3 4 5 6             1 2 3 4 5 6
D 1 D A A A A A         D 1 A A A A A A         D 1 A A A A A A
  2 D D A A A A           2 D A A A A A           2 A A A A A A
  3 D D D A A A           3 D D A A A A           3 D A A A A A
  4 D D D D A A           4 D D D A A A           4 D D A A A A
  5 D D D D D A           5 D D D D A A           5 D D D A A A
  6 D D D D D D           6 D D D D D A           6 D D D D A A

A wins 15/36           A wins 21/36           A wins 26/36
```

In general, when the attacker adds n $(0 < n < 6)$ to his die roll, the defender has $(6 - n)(7 - n)/72$ chances of winning. (You may wish to draw a curve of this second degree polynomial function to see how it behaves.) Incidentally, if the attacker were to subtract n $(0 < n < 5)$ from his die roll, the attacker has $(5 - n)(6 - n)/72$ chances of winning.

Using a computer, the 42% probability of the attacker's winning for Case 1, for example, can be programmed as follows:

```
IF Number_Attack_Cells = 2 then do;
   r = random
   IF r > .42 then attacker wins,
              else defender wins
END
```

The random number generator produces numbers between 0 and 1. A more general simulation would use the polynomial equation which determins the winner of an engagement. In Pseudocode 21.1, the variable "Player," for the two-player version, is either 1 or 2. In the example in Pseudocode 21.1 Player 2 is attacking Player 1.

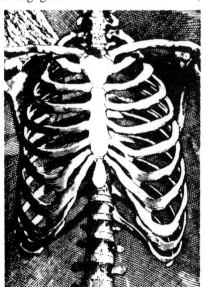

The variable "Organ" is a 2-D array which contains the number of cells in a particular organ territory for a particular player. (Remember that since only one player can occupy any organ territory at a time, the value of "Organ" is zero for all players but one). In line 5 of Pseudocode 21.1 "OrganNumber" is simply a number from 1 to 17 which designates which of the 17 organ territories is under consideration in an engagement. For example, you might designate the esophagus as 1, the left lobe as 2, etc. Statement 5 simply subtracts 2 from the number of cells in an attacking organ. This is used to determine the attacker's probabilistic advantage in an engagement in statement 8. Statements 9 to 12 subtract a cell from the defender if he loses. Statements 13 to 15 subtract a cell from the attacker if he loses. Of course, in any program you write, you should check that an attacking organ is adjacent to the defending organ, since only territories which touch can attack one another. You can do this by making a connectivity table based on which organs touch. Here is just a portion of such a table as an example:

	Stomach	Duodenum	Pancreas	Gall Bladder
Stomach	-	1	0	0
Duodenum	1	-	1	1
Pancreas	0	1	-	0
Gall Bladder	0	1	0	-

1 and 0 differentiate adjacent from non-adjacent areas. Are territories with a high connectivity more strategic to capture than isolated territories?

21.2 Journal of Cancer Research

The Computer Esophagus game can provide endless hours of challenging fun and mental stimulation. Of course, there have been many contemporary and ancient war games which, like the Computer Esophagus game, involve the movements of pieces on a playing board. Similarly, the Computer Esophagus is interesting because of its simple rules of engagement which provide for an exciting and simple-to-implement game with or without a computer. You may also be intrigued to know that there have been recent computer programs which model the growth of tumor cells using a game-like simulation on a 3-D checker-board of points. These have been described in journals such as *Journal of Cancer Research and Clinical Oncology* and *BioSystems*. Although not very similar to the Computer Esophagus, these are examples of simple games which yield clinically relevant results (see refs.).

21.3 Liver Capture Scenario and Physiological Relevance

It is possible to play special versions of the game that more closely resemble physiological happenings within the human body. These games also have educational value for young students. For example, one version of the game I have played gives added importance to organ systems essential for human survival. In the "Liver-Capture" game, the object of the game is to gain control of the liver territory. The liver, because of its secretory and metabolic functions, is more important for human survival than, say, the bladder or large intestine. Another version of the game allows cancer cells to metastasize to non-adjacent organs via the blood stream and lymphatic systems. In this version of the game two dice are rolled at the beginning of each turn of an attacker. If two sixes are rolled, one organ territory, for this turn, is permitted to attack another organ territory which is not adjacent to the attacking territory. You might also like to add the following rule to confer additional defensive advantage on an organ which has many cells: If an attacking organ territory loses 2 consecutive engagements with the same defending territory during a turn, the attacking cells are "weakened" and may not attack the same organ territory again during the same turn. The attacking cells may, however, attack another adjacent organ territory during the turn.

What strategies do you find useful in order to win the Esophagus game? Is capturing and retaining control of the easy-to-defend Bladder Region (which yields 2 extra cells at the beginning of each term) a better strategy than trying to capture the entire Intestine Region? How could you make the game a more realistic simulation of the disease processes in the human body? How might you simulate auto-immune diseases? My board is primarily concerned with the digestive system. Perhaps you can design a 3-D board which also includes the heart, lungs, and kidneys. Or you might concentrate your board on just a single organ such as the heart or brain.

You might also have the computer start with an initial random configuration of cells and play itself while you watch the simulation results on the display.

21.4 Party Version - Adjacent Esophagi Scenario

Finally, you may want to try a "party version" of the game where several game boards are used, and infectious cells spread to adjacent boards, from one adjacent esophagus to another. I've tried this with interesting results. For a more educational game, include the endocrine system and the brain, and then model the effect of hormones on the survival of your enemy. You may be able to kill your opponent's cells from a distant organ or vessel simply by shutting down blood flow or appropriate hormone secretions.

21.5 Anatomy Fact File

21.5.1 The Visible Human Project

Imagine pungent smelling male and female corpses being scanned for hours by the most modern, medical computer devices. This is not a scene from a Dean

Koontz novel, but rather the basis for a scientific study taking place in Denver, Colorado. Researchers at the University of Colorado Health Science Center in Denver are excited about their new project (started in 1991) to create "the ultimate digital model" of the human anatomy. This complete, 3-D model will contain high-resolution images and information concerning every cubic millimeter of a male and a female corpse. Medical students, for example, could use this data to precisely visualize the locations of blood vessels within the brain or nerves within the spine. Powerful graphics computers can then use this data to draw realistic 3-D renderings, animations, and magnifications from any angle, of any part of the body. This *Visible Human Project*, as it is called, involves the capturing of image data from medical image scans (CT and MRI) of human cadavers, as well as digitization of cryosection photographic data. No doubt, in a few years, you'll be able to take a simulated submarine ride through the heart and aortic arch, much like the scientists did in the famous science fiction tale *Fantastic Voyage*.

21.5.2 Implantable Brain Pancakes

Surgeons at the Johns Hopkins School of Medicine in Baltimore, Maryland are implanting small, drug-filled, pancake-shaped wafers in the brain. After

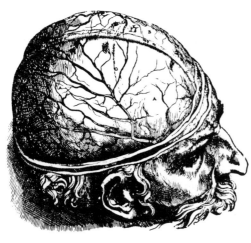

removing a tumor, they leave behind several wafers in the skull which release drugs over four weeks as the wafers dissolve. The surgeons hope to prevent tumor recurrence. Robert Langer, a professor of biomedical engineering at the Massachusetts Institute of Technology, created the wafers, and he notes that it is easy to control the drug dose if you know how fast the wafers dissolve. Another of Langer's wafers makes use of a maze of tiny tunnels within the wafer to allow drug molecules to slowly escape over months of time. Experiments are underway to determine how effective the "brain pancakes" are in preventing tumor recurrence.

21.6 For Further Reading

1.   Duchting, W. and Vogelsaenger, T. (1983) Aspects of modelling and simulating tumor growth and treatment. *J. Cancer Research and Clinical Oncology*. 105: 1-12.

2.   Duchting, W. and Vogelsaenger, T. (1985) Recent progress in modelling and simulation of three-dimensional tumor growth and treatment. *BioSystems*. 18: 79-91.

3.   Saunders, J. and O'Malley, C. (1973) *The Illustrations from the Works of Andreas Vesalius of Brussels*. Dover: New York.

4.   Hale, R., Coyle T. (1979) *Albinus on Anatomy*. Dover: New York.

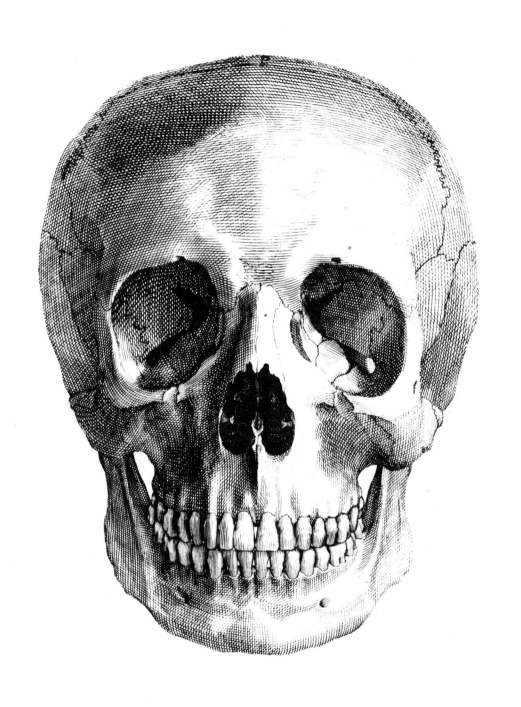

AFRIKA

Chapter 22

The Cro-Magnon Conquest Game

"Civilization begins where chaos and insecurity end."
Will Durant, *Our Oriental Heritage, 1954*

The spread and migration of humans from their primitive beginnings in Africa is a source for endless scientific study and debate. It is also the source for an interesting computer simulation which may be educational for history, geography, and science students. (It's also quite a fun game, as you shall see.)

Many scientists today believe that Africa was the cradle of humankind. Several million years ago the Ramapithecines began to run upright on their hind legs in the African savanna. By three million years ago, different tribes of Ramapiths had evolved into three different species of hominids, or human-like creatures: *Australopithecus robustus*, *Homo habilis*, and *Australopithecus africanus*.

Cro-Magnon people, with their high foreheads, first appeared some 40,000 years ago and quickly spread throughout the world. For instance, about 15,000 years ago, a tribe of Siberians or Mongolians crossed a land bridge that joined Asia to Alaska at the time. They then migrated downward through North America, through central America, to South America (Figure 22.1). By 11,000 years ago, people of modern type had filled every corner of the world.

An amusing computer game, which I call "Cro-Magnon Conquest," can provide hours of intrigue for students interested in modelling the spread of human civilizations. First have the computer draw a map of the world. If this is too difficult, you can represent each of the continents by square or rectangular regions. Next select a site for the origin of humans. One possible location is in East Africa. From this point on the map, have the computer use a random number generator to move your humans on the map of the world. To do this, the humans move in a random direction, for each increment of time. This is known to mathe-

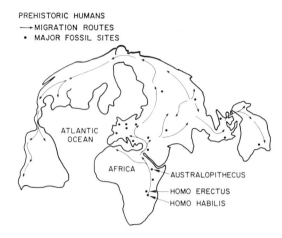

Figure 22.1. *Migration routes of prehistoric humans.* Dots represent major fossil sites. (Drawing adapted from the *Hammond History Atlas* (Hammond, 1987, New Jersey)).

maticians as a "random walk." For example, if your original screen coordinates are at (x_0, y_0), change them by adding ± 100 miles to x and y for each time step. The program outline should help you understand the process. If you don't have access to a computer, why not use dice to control the movement of your humans on graph paper?

As your humans, represented by a dot on the screen, move about, why not have the computer draw a line so that you can see the trail that they leave? By

doing this, you will gradually be drawing a crinkly line that soon meanders about all over Africa. Whenever it hits the edge of a continent, simply reflect it back (rather than have it wander off into an ocean.)

How many time increments, or "years," does it take for your human tribes to migrate to Egypt and then out of Africa into the Tigris-Euphrates valley? As mentioned earlier, about 15,000 years ago humans crossed a land bridge that joined Asia to Alaska at the time. How long does it take your humans to arrive in North America and South America, by randomly walking on the map of the world?

In human history, from 4000 B.C. to A.D. 400, there was a gradual migration of centers of civilizations from: (1) Egypt to (2) Babylonia, Chaldea, and Persia to (3) the Aegean Sea, to (4) Greece, to (5) Rome. Do your humans follow this pattern? Some historical texts include India and China in their list of the cradles of civilization from 3000-1000 B.C.: (1) Egyptian Civilization (3000 B.C.), (2) Indus Valley Civilization (3000 B.C.) (near the Indus River in India), (3) Sumerian Civilization (2800 B.C.), (4) Chinese Civilization (2200 B.C.) (near the

```
ALGORITHM: Migration Paths for Cro-Magnon Conquest
YEARS = 10,000
StepSize = 100 miles
x = x0
y = y0
MoveTo(x,y)
DO FOR i = 1 to YEARS
    r = Random
    if r > 0.5 THEN sign = 1
              ELSE sign = -1
    x = x + sign*StepSize
    r = Random
    if r > 0.5 THEN sign = 1
        .     ELSE sign = -1
    y = y + sign*StepSize
    IF (x,y) in ocean, reflect back.
    DrawTo(x,y)
END
```

Pseudocode 22.1. *Migration paths for Cro-Magnon Conquest.* (If a computer is not available, you can use dice to direct your humans on a sheet of graph paper.)

Huang or "Yellow" River), (5) Minoan Civilization (2000 B.C.), and (6) Hittite Civilization (1700 B.C.). Do your humans follow this pattern?

At this point, I have probably angered every historian and anthropologist reading my simplistic descriptions of the spread of humans through the world. Please consider this more of a game than a real simulation. However, in order to make your simulations more realistic, why not have the humans be attracted to rivers, which are often the sites of early civilizations. In other words, rather than having the humans walk in a totally random fashion, they can have a tendency to migrate to rivers. (If you like, you can use gravity-like equations from physics text books to attract the roving bands of humans.) Do you begin to see clumps along the Nile river or the Tigris and Euphrates Rivers? Instead of having a single point, or a single band of humans, wandering around the globe, you might send off several different tribes − all starting from the same location in East Africa − and see where they eventually end up. Have a contest with your friends to see whose humans arrive in North America first.

22.1 Genes and Languages

"The heat of the tropics, and the innumerable parasites that infest them, are hostile to civilization. Lethargy and disease, and a precocious maturity and decay, divert the energies from those inessentials of life that make civilization. Nothing is left for the play of the arts and mind."

Will Durant, *Our Oriental Heritage, 1954*

Luigi Luca Cavalli-Sforza, a professor of genetics at Stanford University, has studied the paths by which early humans may have spread through the world by examining both the genes of modern humans and the various languages of the world. Family trees created using linguistic and genetic methods are very similar and imply a series of human migrations. The biological evidence suggests a homeland in Africa. The genetic distances between Africans and non-Africans exceed those found in other intercontinental comparisons. This is what one would expect

if the African separation was the first and oldest in the family tree of humans. Archeological evidence also provides Cavalli-Sforza with data implying that Africa was the original homeland of hominids, and from there migrations proceeded from Africa to Asia via the isthmus of Suez, and later from Asia to Europe. The settlement of Australia and the Pacific Islands must have been accomplished only recently, after marine navigation was possible. It turns out that the distribution of genes in populations corresponds to the distribution of languages, so a language can serve to identify a genetic population and help to build models of the spread of early humans through the world. As an example, there are nearly 400 languages in the Bantu family of central and southern Africa. These are related to one another and correspond closely both to tribal boundaries and genetic affiliation among tribes. As the early Bantu farmers expanded into central and southern Africa around 3,000 years ago, their languages diverged, along with the genes of these populations. For more information, you may wish to read Cavalli-Sforza's paper in the November 1991 issue of *Scientific American*.

22.2 Stop and Think

1. Figure 22.1 shows a map of the world during the time of prehistoric man. How would the world be different today, geopolitically speaking, if the ancient land masses had never drifted apart and, therefore, today's world consisted of a single supercontinent?

2. What would today's world be like if the land mass which formed the Greek peninsula never existed?

3. What would today's world be like if the land bridge which joined Alaska to Asia never existed?

4. Why do all the major peninsulas on earth point south? See for example: Italy, Greece, Florida, and Baja, and the tips of Africa, South America, India, Norway, Sweden, Greenland, and many other landmasses.

5. Experiment with more sophisticated models of migration which also include mountains, ocean currents, and natural resources.[11]

6. How would the number of languages on earth today be different if the ancient landmasses never migrated apart and, therefore, today's world consisted of a single supercontinent?

7. If a magical being descended from outer space and offered you either of the following abilities, which would you prefer: a) instantaneous fluency in all the European languages, or b) instantaneous fluency in all the Asian languages? If the magical being also offered you either of the following abilities, achieved at the snap of its fingers, which would you prefer: 1) immediate skill of the 10th best piano player in the world, or 2) immediate fluency in 10 languages of your choice?

22.3 The Bushmen

"Ex Africa semper aliquid novi. (There is always something new out of Africa)"   Pliny

In the summer of 1991, Professor Luigi Luca Cavalli-Sforza and molecular anthropologist Allan Wilson made an urgent plea for help and money in order to collect DNA samples from aboriginals populations around the world before these

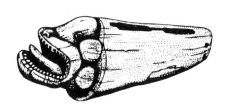

groups vanish. The basic plan is to collect blood samples from the Hill People of New Guinea, the Bushmen of southern Africa, and about 100 other populations. The October 25th, 1991 issue of *Science* noted that these populations, isolated for hundreds of thousands of years, "contain in their genes clues to human evolution, migration, and diversity."   As society encroaches upon these once-distinct populations, the opportunity to analyze their genes is rapidly vanishing.

---

[11] *Sim Earth* is a commercially available personal computer simulation enabling users to take charge of an entire planet from its birth until its death 10 billion years later. The detailed personal computer graphics enhance the rich variety of ecological parameters available to users. For more information, contact: MAXIS, Two Theatre Square, Suite 230, Orinda, CA 94563-3346. 510 254-9700. Fax 510 253-3736. Tel order: 800 33-MAXIS. Another personal computer game, *Sid Meier's Civilization* allows users to build an empire to "stand the test of time." Users control the technology available to their societies and view the results. Contact: Microprose, 180 Lakefront Dr., Hunt Valley, MD 21030. 301 771-1151.

22.4 Fantastic Archeology

Sharon Begley in the Columbus Special Issue of *Newsweek* asked the question,

"If humans crossed the Bering Strait 12,000 years ago, then who built the 40,000-year-old sites that are scattered from the hills of Pennsylvania to the tip of Chile?" These are exactly the kinds of archeological hoaxes that Stephen Williams loves to debunk in his book *Fantastic Archeology*. Williams, a former director of the Peabody Museum of Anthropology at Harvard, concentrates on North American prehistory. William Goetzmann in the December 6, 1991 *Science* says the following about *Fantastic Archeology*: "Williams' book is a wonderful ride through Never-Never Land where Vikings land in western Oklahoma and sail away into the sunsets of California deserts; where all over the continent are clues by way of ancient Hebrew inscriptions, Egyptian hieroglyphics, Phoenician villages, Ogam inscriptions, Kufic Arabic treatises, golden tablets of Moroni, Norse rune stones and rusted swords, and Barry Fell's sacrificial altars at North Salem, New Hampshire." Williams' book is listed in the "For Further Reading" section.

22.5 Valley of Life, and Kingdoms of Gold

For those of you interested in a breathtaking photographic tribute to the African Rift Valley, which stretches 3,500 miles along the east side of Africa, Chris Johns' *Valley of Life: Africa's Great Rift* (Thomasson-Grant, 1991, 143 p., color, $39.95) is essential reading. Johns is a *National Geographic* photographer, and he lived along the Rift for 18 months, photographing the people, wildlife, and land. As *Science News* exclaims, "His spectacular collection of photos and his brief, personal reflections capture the mystery and magnificence of humankind's possible birthplace."

Those of you interested in Africa's island neighbor Madagascar, should read Ken Preston-Mafham's *Madagascar: A Natural History* (Facts on File, 1991, 224 p., color, $45.00). Madagascar's separation from the African continent 65 million years ago allowed its animals to evolve in isolation into some of the world's most remarkable and unusual wildlife.

Brian Fagan's book *Kingdoms of Gold, Kingdoms of Jade: The Americas Before Columbus* (Thames Hudson, 1991, 240 p, color, $24.95) is a fascinating account of pre-Columbian civilizations that flourished in the Americas (Aztec, Inca, Olmec, Maya, Chavin, Nazca, and native North American). During this time there were spectacular and sophisticated cities as large as Constantinople, and powerful chiefs ruling in splendor in the Mississippi valley. The book contains many photographs and maps.

Jean Guilaine's *Prehistory: The World of Early Man* (Facts on File, 1991, 192 p., color, $39.95) describes prehistoric cultures from around the world. Topics: the spread of civilization, human evolution, the appearance of writing and art, the arise of symbolic thought, the development of early economies, and more.

Did you know that Amazonian tribes are disappearing at a rate of one tribe per year in Brazil alone? Mirella Ricciardi's *Vanishing Amazon* (Abrams, 1991, 240 p., $49.50) contains photographs and facts regarding the threatened Indian tribes in the Amazonian basin. Mirella lived among various tribes, and her stunning photographs reveal a beautiful and sad story about the end of a people.

22.6 The Greenland Mummies

In 1972, archeologists discovered eight mummified women and children in the frigid lands of Greenland. The bodies, which have been dated to 1475, were remarkably preserved by the intensely cold weather and dry air. If you would like to learn more about medieval Inuit culture and living conditions, read *The Greenland Mummies*, by Jens Peder Hart Hansen, Jorgen Meldgaard, and Jorgen Nordqvist (Smithsonian, 1991, 192 p., color, $39.95).

22.7 For Further Reading

1. Williams, S. (1991) *Fantastic Archeology: The Wild Side of North American Prehistory*. University of Pennsylvania Press: Philadelphia.

2. Goetzmann, W. (1991) The rage for antiquity. *Science*. 254(5037): 1528-1529.

3. Cavalli-Sforza, L.L. (1991) Genes, peoples and languages. *Scientific American*. 265: 104-110.

4. Rapacz, J. et al. (1991) Identification of the ancestral haplotype for apolipoprotein B suggests an African origin of Homo sapiens sapiens and traces their subsequent migration to Europe and the Pacific. *Proceedings of the National Academy of Science USA*. 88: 1403-1406.

5. Cann. R.L., Stoneking, M. and Wilson, A.C. (1987) Mitochondrial DNA and human evolution. *Nature*. 325: 31-36.

6. Vigilant, L. et al. (1989) Mitochondrial DNA sequences in single human hairs from a southern African population. *Proceedings of the National Academy of Science USA*. 86: 9350-9354.

7. Cavelli-Sforza, L.L. et al. (1988) Reconstruction of human evolution: bringing together genetic, archaeological, and linguistic data. *Proceedings of the National Academy of Science USA*. 85: 6002-6006.

8. Vigilant, L. et al. (1991) African populations and the evolution of human mitochondrial DNA. *Science*. 253: 1503-1507.

Chapter 23

Ghost Children in Our Genes

"Ethereal, transparent figures crossed the large central area: men in business suits toting briefcases, women in smart travelling dresses... . He saw a ghost father leading two small ghost-children... Then color dove into the shapes in a series of cometary flickers, solidifying them, and the echoing voices resolved themselves into the prosaic stereo swarm of real human voices."

Stephen King, *Four Past Midnight*

If you were given the opportunity of viewing a book containing millions of small photos of all the possible offspring you and your spouse could potentially produce,

would you view such a book? Assuming that you could squeeze 100 small photos on a page, how big would such a book be?

This is not too difficult to compute. Let's assume that a woman's ovaries contain about 500 eggs. Let's also assume that a man produces about 6 trillion (6.57×10^{12}) sperm in a lifetime. (This figure is computed using a figure of 300 million sperm per day multiplied by 60 years.) For every possible sperm there are 500 different eggs, giving us 500 multiplied by 6 trillion possible children's photos. This is about

3,280,000,000,000,000 (3.28×10^{15})

photos. At 100 photos per page, this would produce a book about 32 trillion pages in length.

Of the people I surveyed, only about 50 percent would choose to gaze into the book of photographs. Some respondents noted that many of the children would look so similar that they would prefer to look at a book which were reduced to a reasonable size by showing only one photo representing a *class* of similar appearances. Many others I surveyed indicated that they would be more interested in their genetic possibilities with regard to personality, temperament, and *talent.* One respondent noted, "What if you glimpsed a potential child so heartbreakingly beautiful, or so winning and delightful, that your real children suffered by comparison? What if you took your disappointment out on them?"

Others noted that they would like to peek at some amusing, impossible combinations such as John Lennon and Margaret Thatcher.

23.1 Fact File: Chinese Hamster Sperm, Bull Sperm, Etc.

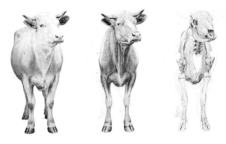

• The size of a sperm is not correlated with the size of the individual organism. The longest mammalian sperm, for example, is found in the Chinese hamster. The sperm measures 250 microns in length, quite easy to see with the naked eye.

• A bull produces 800,000 sperm per cubic centimeter of semen. For comparison, a horse produces 600,000, and a pig 100,000.

23.2 Stop and Think

1. Would you like to visit, for one hour, a ghost world, where you could watch and talk to your ghost children?

2. Compute the number of ghost children for simpler organisms by searching the scientific literature for the number of sperms and eggs produced for an insect or a fish.

3. The largest encyclopedia is *La Enciclopedia Universal Ilustrada Europeo-America* (J. Espasa & Sons, Madrid) totaling 105,000 pages. How much larger is the book of ghost children?

23.3 Cross References and Credits

The photo of the child with the geometrical shape is from Anton Bakker (Norfolk, VA) who built this sculpure based on the work of Professor Koos Verhoeff. "There is Music in our Genes" on page 211 describes the relationship between music and the heridtary information in our genes. "Extraterrestrial Messages in Our Genes" on page 161 describes the coding of messages in genetic sequences.

Chapter 24

Pong Hau K'i

I learned about a seemingly simple board game a few years ago when speaking to

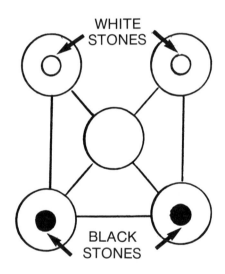

a friend's grandfather who had been born in Canton, China. In China the game is called Pong hau k'i, while in Korea it is called Ou-moul-ko-no. You can play it with pencil and paper, or by designing a computer program, or by moving stones on a game board. Looking at the playing board, you might be deceived into thinking that the game is easy. But such is not the case! You can play the game using two black stones and two white stones. The black stones are placed on the bottom two circles. The white stones are placed on the upper two circles. One player, the owner of either the white stones or the black stones, moves a stone along a line to an adjacent empty point. The other player then moves his stone. The players alternately move one stone at a time along any line to an adjacent empty space. The aim is to block the opponent's stones so that he or she cannot move.

24.1 Stop and Think

1. Is it better to be black than white?

2. How many different positions are there?

3. Write a computer program that plays a human opponent or plays itself. Can you write a program which learns strategies by playing hundreds of games and observing its mistakes?

4. If you are a teacher, why not have your students design related variants of this game by adding a few line segments to the Pong hau k'i board, or by adding additional stones.

5. Instead of starting from a set position, some players place their stones at the beginning of the game on any of the 5 points, or place their stones (at positions of their choice) in alternate turns of play, and then continue as described.

6. Develop a multidimensional Pong hau k'i game, such as illustrated in the following diagram, where the center board position connects center positions on adjacent boards:

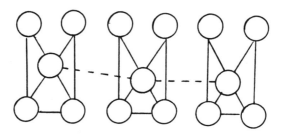

It turns out that there are 30 different possible positions in Pong hau k'i, if reflections are allowed, and that either player can always force a draw. Can you change this outcome by adding a few line segments to the Pong hau k'i board, or by adding additional stones? "Hyperdimensional Sz'kwa" on page 155 discusses another board game from China.

Chapter 25

The 10 Mathematical Formulas That Changed The Face of the World

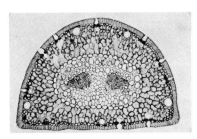

"Though we can say that mathematics is not art, some mathematicians think of themselves as artists of pure form. It seems clear, however, that their elegant and near-aesthetic forms fail as art, because they are secondary visual ideas, the product of an intellectual set of restraints, rather than the cause of a felt insight realized in and through visual form."

Robert Mueller, 1972, *Art in America*

A few years ago, Nicaragua issued ten postage stamps bearing "Las 10 Formulas Matematicas Que Cambiaron La Faz De La Terra" (The 10 mathematical formulas that changed the face of the world).[12] I'm not sure how the Nicaraguan government determined which particular formulas should be elevated to so high a status for placement on the stamps. Perhaps a survey was conducted among the mathematicians in the country. In addition to scientific merit, perhaps such practical issues as space limitations were considered so as to avoid long formulas on small stamps.

In October of 1991 I conducted my own informal survey as to which formulas scientists considered "The 10 Mathematical Formulas that Changed the Face of the World." The survey was conducted via electronic mail networks, and a majority of the respondents were mathematicians (professors, other professionals, and graduate students). Here's the answer to this question from approximately fifty interested individuals who gave me their opinions as to the most important and influential equations. The equations are ordered from most influential to least influential, based on the number of different people who listed the same formulas when they sent their lists to me. For example, $E = mc^2$ received the most votes.

How many of the following can you identify?

---

[12] Isn't it admirable that a country so respects mathematics that it devotes a postage stamp series to a set of abstract equations? Have other countries produced a similar series?

25.1 The Top Ten

Here are the ten most influential and important mathematical expressions, listed in order of importance:

1. $E = mc^2$
2. $a^2 + b^2 = c^2$
3. $\varepsilon_0 \int_{cs} \vec{E} \cdot d\vec{A} = \Sigma q$
4. $x = -b \pm \sqrt{b^2 - 4ac} / 2a$
5. $\vec{F} = m\vec{a}$
6. $1 + e^{i\pi} = 0$
7. $c = 2\pi r, a = \pi r^2$
8. $\vec{F} = Gm_1 m_2 / r^2$
9. $f(x) = \Sigma c_n e^{in\pi x/L}$
10. $e^{i\theta} = \cos \theta + i \sin \theta$
    tied with $a^n + b^n = c^n, n \geq 2$

25.2 The Runners-Up

Other mathematical expressions which did not score high enough to be included in the top 10 but which scored favorably were: 1) $f(x) = f(a) + f'(a)(x - a) + f''(a) \ (x - a)^2/2! \ldots$, 2) $s = vt + at^2/2$, 3) $V = IR$, 4) $z \rightarrow z^2 + \mu$, 5) $e = \lim(1 + 1/n)^n$, 6) $c^2 = a^2 + b^2 - 2ab \cos C$, 7) $\int K dA = 2\pi \times \gamma$, 8) $d/dx \int^x f(t)dt = f(x)$, 9) $1/(2\pi i) \int_{cs} f(z)/(z - a)dz = f(a)$, 10) $dy/dx = \lim \ (h \rightarrow 0) \ (f(x + h) - f(x))/h$, and 11) $\partial^2 \psi / \partial x^2 = -[8\pi^2 m/h^2(E - V)]\psi$.

These "runners-up" are listed in no particular order. To be eligible for the runners-up list, at least two mathematicians had to include the formula in their own top 10 list.

25.3 Nicaragua List

Here is a list of Nicaragua's postage stamp equations for "Las 10 Formulas Matematicas Que Cambiaron La Faz De La Terra." Note how many of these formulas agree with the "Top Ten" list based on my own informal survey.

1. $1 + 1 = 2$
2. $F = Gm_1 m_2 / r^2$
3. $E = mc^2$
4. $e^{\ln N} = N$
5. $a^2 + b^2 = c^2$

6. $S = k \log W$

7. $V = V_e \ln m_o/m_1$

8. $\lambda = h/mv$

9. $\nabla^2 E = (Ku/c^2) \ (\partial^2 E/\partial t^2)$

10. $F_1 x_1 = F_2 x_2$

25.4 Solutions, Tsiolkovaskii's Rocket Equation, Etc.

Here are the solutions for the Nicaragua stamp list: 1) Basic addition formula. 2) Isaac Newton's law of universal gravitation. If the two masses m_1 and m_2 are separated by a distance, r, the force exerted by one mass on the other is F, and G is a

constant of nature. 3) Einstein's formula for the conversion of matter to energy. 4) John Napier's logarithm formula. This allows us to do multiplication and division simply by adding or subtracting the logarithms of numbers. 5) Pythagorean theorem relating the lengths of sides of a right triangle. 6) Bolzmann's equation for the behavior of gases. 7) Konstantin Tsiolkovskii's rocket equation. It gives the speed of a rocket as it burns the weight of its fuel. 8) de Broglie's wave equation, relating the mass, velocity, and wavelength of a wave-particle. h is Planck's constant. de Broglie postulated that the electron has wave properties, and that material particles have associated with them a wavelength. 9) Equation relating electricity and magnetism, derived from Maxwell's equations which form the basis for all computations involving electromagnetic waves including radio, radar, light, ultraviolet waves, heat radiation and x-rays. 10) Archimedes' lever formula.

Here are explanations for some of the formulas in my own lists. No. 3 is one of Maxwell's equation for electromagnetism. No. 4 is the quadratic formula for solving equations of the form $ax^2 + bx + c = 0$. No. 5 is Newton's second law, relating force, mass and acceleration. No. 7 gives the circumference and area of a circle. No. 9 represents a Fourier series. Complicated wave disturbances may be represented as the sum of a group of sinusoidal-like waves. The first formula in No. 10 is Euler's identity relating exponential and trigonometric functions. The second formula represents Fermat's last theorem. No. 7 (Runners-Up) is the Gauss-Bonnet formula, where γ is the Euler characteristic. No. 9 (Runners-Up) is Cauchy's integral formula in complex analysis.

25.5 Comments from Colleagues

Clifford Beshers of Columbia University had some interesting remarks regarding equation No. 8 on my list, which was first on his list: "Gravity keeps our planet in orbit about the sun, keeps the moon in orbit about the Earth, makes the rain fall on our heads, and keeps  kids' marbles (and kids, for that matter) from becoming comets. Sunlight, tides and weather have made life on this planet flourish." He also suggested adding a fixed loan payment formula to the top 10 for the following reasons. "Equations that govern industrial economies have had a great impact on our world. The formula for a fixed payment loan is a simple, well known equation, and I would guess that it is among the formulas most widely used today. We have always been able to dream of changing the world, but investing has made it possible." The fixed loan payment formula involves variables such as the monthly interest rate, principal, and duration of the loan.

Roy Smith of the Public Health Research Institute in New York noted the following about $c^2 = a^2 + b^2$ (the Pythagorean formula for right triangles):

> This formula is vital to any vector problem, and hence vital to most of physics. Any field of study using complex numbers, such as electronics, involves the conversion between polar and rectangular forms, and this formula has application here. This formula is one of the first things the Scarecrow in "The Wizard of Oz" recited when he got his brain. If you consider the formula's logical extension, the law of cosines for non-right triangles ($C^2 = A^2 + B^2 - 2AB \cos(\theta)$), then you have the basic formula that surveyors use to measure land. The related formulas for solving spherical triangles were used for celestial navigation, which allowed people to explore the entire world by sea.

25.6 Fact File

• A few respondents suggested Fermat's last theorem be included on the list of the ten influential mathematical expressions because a siginficant amount of research and mathematics is a direct result of failed attempts to prove the theorem. This theorem by Pierre de Fermat (1601-1665) states that there are no whole numbers a, b and c such that $a^n + b^n = c^n$ for $n > 2$. In 1769, Leonard Euler stated that a related formula

$$a^4 + b^4 + c^4 = d^4 \tag{25.1}$$

had no possible integral solutions. Centuries later, Noam Elkies of Harvard University discovered the first solution to Equation (25.1): $a = 2,682,440$, $b = 15,365,639$, $c = 18,796,760$, and $d = 20,516,673$. (For more information, see: Elkies, N. (1988) On $a^4 + b^4 + c^4 = d^4$. *Mathematics of Computation*. Oct. 51(184): 825-835. For Noam Elkies' fractal musical artwork, see Figure 37.4.)

• Mathematicians Philip Davis and Reuben Hersh have suggested that in the year 1900 it would have been quite possible for an individual to know essentially the whole of mathematics as it existed then. Today, an individual mathematician can hardly know, in any deep sense, more than five percent of the mathematical corpus.

Chapter 26

Interlude: The Third Eye

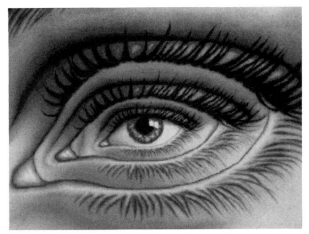

"To paraphrase the comedian, why is it that computer art 'don't get no res-pect?' Why are we feared – or at best misunderstood by the gallery world?"

Ilene Astrahan, 1990

Ilene Astrahan is an internationally known computer artist living in New York City. Her work has been featured in numerous shows and magazines, and it often includes mathematical concepts of fractals and recursion. My favorite piece of hers is titled "Third Eye," and it is shown here in a black and white reproduction of the color image. To create the artwork, Ilene first digitized a photograph of an eye and then enhanced the image using a paint program called Deluxe Paint running on her Amiga computer. Since the digital file produced a crude image, she spent several days in improving it so that it would look nice using just 32 dif-ferent colors. After creating the recursive eyelids, the slide was printed using a Polaroid Palette film recorder. The piece required two weeks to complete. Ilene remarks:

> I do not try to imitate the effects of traditional painting. After all, watercolorists don't imitate oil painting. The artifacts of computer graphics such as jaggies, dith-ering and scan-lines are a valid part of the medium, as are the paint strokes, impasto, canvas texture, etc. of traditional media. The strength of the computer is its ability to do infinite variations of color and image processing, plus being the ultimate collage machine. One could spend a lifetime exploring the variations possible in just one image, learning new software or doing animation.

For more information, contact: Ilene Astrahan, P.O. Box 660, Cooper Station, New York, NY 10276.

Chapter 27

Aliens, and Pieces of Pi

"A space flight to the moon could not take place with only 3-digit-precision knowledge of π. "
John Hesse

"I don't like nonrepeating decimals. Pi makes me furious."
Don DeLillo, *Ratner's Star*

In the October 1991 issue of *Omni* magazine, Dave Jaffe quoted from his upcoming anthology of brainteasers titled *Mathematical Games That Could Not be Solved by People Who Claim They Have High IQs*:

> Numbers have always played an important role in mathematics. Without them such fields as geometry never would have progressed beyond "Fun With Squares." Yet it's long been known that besides zero through nine there exists an extra digit wedged somewhere between six and seven. Mathematicians have avoided using the mystery number because it is tricky to spell and has an embarrassing shape.

As silly is this sounds, it's interesting to speculate what would happen today if an alien creature came down from the heavens and inserted a digit into the decimal expansion for π. Now instead of π being 3.1415926535..., it would have an extra digit, "1," making it: 3.11415926... What effect would this have on the world and the fabric of reality? As a result of this new value for π, would various previous engineering calculations be so much in error that skyscrapers would fall to the ground? Would satellites fly out of orbit? How accurate a value for π do engineers really need for architectural construction? Obviously you don't need to know the value of π at all to draw a circle and many other structures, but π does appear in many kinds of geometrical engineering calculations. Note that the ancient Greeks did just fine when the decimal value of π was only known to a few decimal places. They built perfectly stable and beautiful buildings. In 1579, Viete computed the value of π to a remarkable 10 figures.[13]

---

[13] In one of his greatest books *The Measurement of the Circle*, Greek mathematician Archimedes proved that the circumference of a circle is less than 3+1/2 and greater than 3+ 10/71 times its diameter. For more on Archimedes, see "Strange Toilet Paper"

Normally we think of π simply as the ratio of the circumference of a circle to its diameter. So did pre-17th Century humanity. However in the 17th century, π was freed from the circle. Many curves were invented and studied (various arches, hypocycloids, witches...), and it was found that their areas could be expressed in terms of π.

Finally π ruptured the confines of geometry altogether. For example, today π relates to unaccountably many areas in number theory, probability, complex numbers, and simple fractions, such as $\pi/4 = 1 - 1/3 + 1/5 - 1/7....$ As another example of how far π has drifted from its simple geometrical interpretation, consider the book *Budget of Paradoxes*, where Augustus De Morgan explains an equation to an insurance salesman. The formula, which gave the chances that a particular group of people would be alive after a certain number of days, involved the number π. The insurance salesman interrupted and exclaimed,

"My dear friend, that must be a delusion. What can a circle have to do with the number of people alive at the end of a given time?"

Let's return to the subject of aliens altering the decimal value of π. If the aliens were to change π, the problems we encounter will propagate since the value of other constants will also probably change due to simple relations such as

$e^{i\pi} = -1$. In addition, Planck's constant in modern physics is often used in connection with π in the form $(h/2\pi)$. This would probably cause a lot of trouble in our universe.

Here then is the main question for you to ponder. At what year in human civilization would this malicious, alien, decimal insertion in π have mattered to engineers for the sake of practical designs (bridge building, various construction, etc)? Note that thirty nine decimal places of π suffice for computing the circumference of a circle girdling the known universe with an error no greater than the radius of a hydrogen atom! However, John Hesse has suggested that a flight to the moon could not take place with only 3-digit precision knowledge of π because NASA makes a tremendous number of orbital mechanics calculations involving π. The iterative nature of these calculations demand the full precision provided by whatever processors are used.

---

on page 179. A refined value of π was obtained by the Chinese much earlier than in the West. Some scholars have suggested that at the time the Greeks knew π to three digits, the Chinese knew the value to two or three additional digits.

27.1 Stop and Think

• If you are a teacher, have the students make various computations involving π with this alien insertion. For example, how much does the circumference of a 12-foot radius sphere change as a result of the inserted digit? From a historical perspective, what was the first structure or machine for which a value of π was needed?

• These hypothetical aliens who altered π might have been more interested in interfering with the human ability to do mathematics rather than in altering mathematical constants. Dawn Friedman (Harvard University) asks the following:

> If it were possible to set a limit on the mathematical ability of humans by altering the physical structure of the brain, what would these aliens have to do, and what mathematical limit would they need to set, to prevent human beings from: building a cathedral, a potter's wheel, a race car, a computer, or a nuclear bomb? What mathematical limit would they need to set to prevent human beings from doing the spectroscopic experiments and the calculations needed to discover the double helix? How would a field like medicine be affected? At what date in the history of medicine would the divergence from current history begin? With the microscope, perhaps, if the math-level were set low enough? It might be interesting to determine which inventions depend on a particular level of math.

• There are a few physical constants which appear to govern the properties of our universe, for example: the speed of light, the gravitational constant, and Planck's constant. If an alien decided to tinker with just one of these three constants by changing a digit, which of the altered constants would cause the least havoc to your daily life?

• Do the measurements of the lengths and areas of *all* simple curved shapes involve π?

27.2 Fact File

• The first six digits of π (314159) appear at least 6 times among the first 10 million decimal places of π.

• In ancient China, Ch'ang Hong (125 A.D.) gave $\pi = \sqrt{10} = 3.162\ldots$.

27.3 Cross Reference

"Extraterrestrial Messages in Our Genes" on page 161 describes an alien tampering with the sequence of bases within DNA, and also messages contained within π.

Chapter 28

Hyperdimensional Sz'kwa

A few years ago, Bijan, my octogenarian friend, was exploring the Nen river in the valley of the Great Khingan mountain range in Northern China. There he learned about a fascinating children's game called Sz'kwa which was often played on a board sketched out in the dirt by a sharp stick (see diagram at left). One child holds 25 white stones in his or her hand; the other holds 25 black stones. At the start of the game, the circular board shown here would have no stones. Each player would take turns placing stones on the board, at the positions with black dots. If a player's stone were completely surrounded by the opponent's stones it was captured. The left diagram of Figure 28.1 shows the capture of a black piece, and the right diagram shows the capture of two white pieces. When a player would have no stones left to place on the circular board, or no empty sites on which to place a stone without it being captured, the game ended. The winner would be the player who held the greatest number of stones.

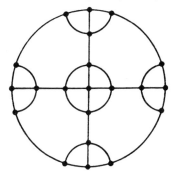

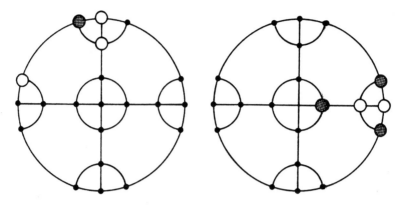

Figure 28.1. *The Chinese game Sz'wa.* A board configuration showing the capture of a black piece (left), and a board configuration showing the capture of two white pieces (right). (Figure adapted from the fascinating book: Bell, R., and Cornelius, M. (1988) *Board Games Round the World.* Cambridge University Press: NY.)

28.1 Stop and Think

1. How many different arrangements of stones on the playing board exist?

2. Is it better to be the first player?

3. Write a computer program that plays a human opponent or plays itself. Can you write a program which learns strategies by playing hundreds of games and observing its mistakes?

4. If you are a teacher, have your students design a related variant of the game by adding a few line segments to the Sz'kwa board, or by using additional stones.

5. Develop a multidimensional Sz'kwa game, such as illustrated in "Pong Hau K'i" on page 143, where the center site on the Sz'kwa board connects center sites on adjacent boards. First try a game using just two boards, and then three. Generalize your discoveries to *N* boards.

At the beginning of this chapter is a painting on a plate by the Chinese artist Kee Fung Ng showing Chinese children playing Sz'kwa. If you look closely, you can see the stones placed at the Sz'kwa positions on the dirt. "Pong Hau K'i" on page 143 describes another Chinese board game.

Chapter 29

Goddard, The Nile, and Claire de Lune

"Where there is an open mind, there will always be a frontier."
Charles F. Kettering

Imagine a future world where a computer program randomly assigns its inhabitants important goals that must be achieved in their lifetimes. When a person is born, the parents would be handed a computer printout with, let us say, one-hundred goals chosen at random from a huge list of goals in the computer's memory. Some would be difficult goals to achieve (pass a course on differential geometry and topology) while others would be simpler (play "Mary had a Little Lamb" on the piano.) As a stimulus to a nation's citizenry, if one were to achieve all 100 goals, there would be a reward of one million dollars. What would such a world be like? What are some goals that a computer should assign? What would a human faced with this list really achieve?

Such an idea is not preposterous; in fact, there is a human today who forced himself to achieve over 100 goals set down on paper in the early years of his life. The man's name is John Goddard. When John was only a teenager, he took out a pencil and paper and made a long list of all the things he wanted to achieve in life. He set down 127 goals. Here is a list of just some of his goals:

1. Explore the Nile river.
2. Play "Claire de Lune" on the piano.
3. Read the entire *Encyclopedia Britannica.*
4. Climb Mt. Everest.
5. Study primitive tribes in the Sudan.
6. Write a book.
7. Read the entire bible.
8. Dive in a submarine.
9. Run a five-minute mile.
10. Circumnavigate the globe.
11. Explore the Great Barrier Reef of Australia.

Device	Feature
Pen	LED Flasher
Clock	Bell
Key	Speech Synthesis
Mouse	Light Meter
Keyboard	Touch Activated Switch
Joystick	Timer Plus Relay
Graphics Puck	Missing Pulse Detector
Trackball	Voltage-Controlled Oscillator
Terminal Screen	Frequency Meter
Pencil	Light Dimmer
Terminal Keys	Infrared Security Alarm
On/Off Switch	Analog Lightwave Transmitter
Dial	Protection Circuit
Remote Control	Adjustable Siren
Compass	LED Regulator
Level	Wrist Band Attachment
Screw Driver	LED Transmitter/Receiver
Watch	Speech Recognition
Cursor	Volume Control
Menu Icon	1-Minute Timer
	Dual LED Flasher
	Neon Lamp Flasher
	Solar Cells
	Dark-activated LED Flasher
	Break-Beam Detection System
	Phone Activated
	Phone-Controlled
	Piezioelectric Buzzer
	Bargraph Voltmeter

Figure 29.1. *Patentable inventions.* Pick a device from the first column, add the word "with," and then chose a feature from the second column.

12. Climb to the very top of Cheop's Pyramid.

Impractical? Not at all. Today John Goddard is 66 years old, and he has accomplished at least 104 of his original 127 goals. He's become one of the most famous explorers in the world. Goddard was the first man in human history to explore the entire length of both the Nile and Congo rivers. His remaining goals are not so easy. He wants to visit the moon and explore the entire Yangtze River in China. He still has not visited all 141 countries, but this goal is almost achieved. He also wishes to live to see the 21st century.

29.1 Stop and Think

Several colleagues thought that the Goddard list approach should be modified. For example, one person remarked:

> *All* the things on Goddard's list are important. Accomplishing them has no doubt made him a happier person. Happy, satisfied, self-assured people are the ones we need. They are the ones who are able to provide all those great things you want humanity to attain.

Another colleague responded:

> I think people should be able to pick their 100 goals from a much longer list, and not have a computer do it for them. Even Goddard might not have gotten very far if he had been given the wrong list. For example, what if he were given the following: "Live in the same place for 40 years; successfully cultivate the Himalayan poppy; breed a high-producing, pest-resistant orange tree; raise 12 children...?" My officemates suggested that the prize money was absolutely necessary!

A final response from another scientist:

> This is exactly what we should not be doing. The goals which we know how to achieve have already been accomplished. The ones which we do not know how to achieve cannot reasonably be assigned. In addition, who should try to do what depends on the temperament and ability of the person. These goals may be important for personal satisfaction, but will not help humanity one bit. None of the goals listed involve even the acquisition of facts previously unknown to mankind. Is running a 5-minute mile (one of the goals on the list) important?

29.2 Patents and Inventions

Those of you who are interested in computers or who are creative engineers may like to use the "Goddard list approach" for inventing new products and patenting the results. One way to stimulate your imagination is to have a computer program

generate an invention title by randomly choosing from a list of devices and then also choosing from a list of features. If you can think of suitable applications for the invention, it is relatively easy to embellish the basic concept suggested by the random title and generate patentable ideas using this approach. The list in Figure 29.1 will help you understand this approach. Pick a device from the first column, add the word "with," and then chose a feature from the second column. For example, "Mouse with Infrared Security Alarm" might be the title of your invention. Think about all the ways this could be achieved and all the applications of the device. Have your friends add devices and features to your own lists for more interesting patent ideas.

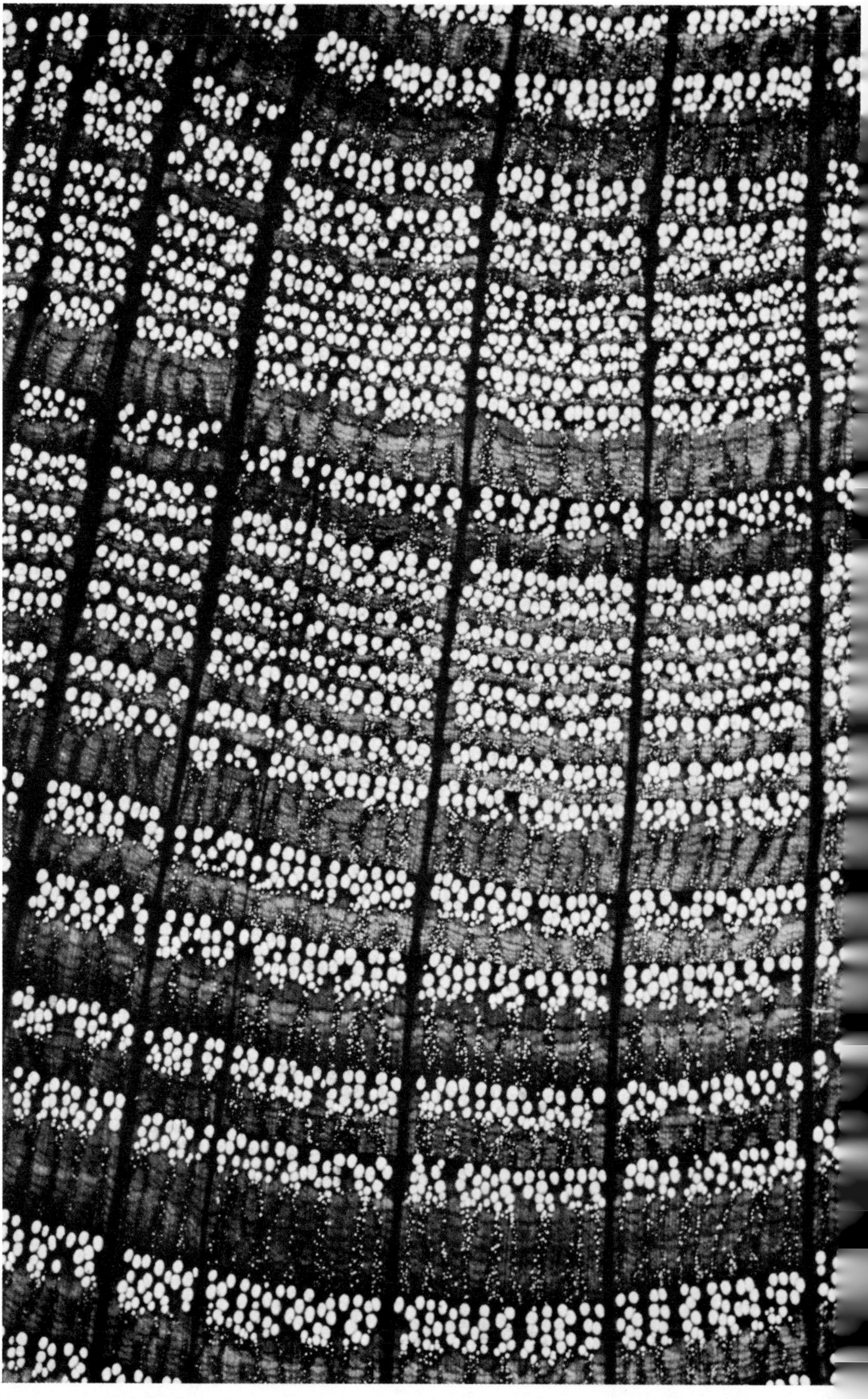

Chapter 30

Extraterrestrial Messages in Our Genes

"We feel certain that the [extraterresrial message] is a mathematical code of some kind. Probably a number code. Mathematics is the one language we might conceivably have in common with other forms of intelligent life in the universe. As I understand it, there is no reality more independent of our perception and more true to itself than mathematical reality."

Don DeLillo, *Ratner's Star*

"When asked why he doesn't believe in astrology, the logician Raymond Smullyan responds that he's a Gemini, and Geminis never believe in astrology."

John Paulos, *Innumeracy*

The year is 2050. Science has progressed to the point where geneticists can obtain a complete printout of the hereditary material of an organism simply by placing a corpse of the organism in a machine and flicking a switch. From out of the side of the machine comes a computer diskette listing the DNA sequence for the organism, expressed as the standard four letter code using the symbols G, C, A, and T. In the same machine exists sophisticated pattern matching software which automatically searches for all kinds of biologically relevant information contained within the DNA sequence.

On one cold December day in 2050, a researcher at the National Biomedical Research Foundation in Washington, DC places the corpse of a tarsier inside the sequencing box. A minute later a billion letters representing the animal's genetic sequence are in the computer's memory. (A tarsier, pictured above, is a tree-dwelling mammal from the East Indies. Tarsiers are about the size of a small squirrel and have large goggle eyes.) After the computer analyzes the DNA, it finds something peculiar, and notifies the researcher using its computerized voice. The researcher looks at his computer keyboard, and then he faints, because the computer has determined that a large portion of the tarsier's genetic material codes for the decimal digits of π (3.1415...).

A month later, there is a ban on all trade in tarsiers, because scientists, in their zeal to study the tarsier in greater detail, have depleted the world population of these mammals. There is also a mad rush to sequence and study other similar tree-dwellers such as the slender loris, a lemur from southern India. Various sci-

entific and philosophical meetings are convened to determine what the tarsier-π message could signify? Various questions are asked. What is special about the Tarsier? Could some outerspace civilization have placed this hidden message in the Tarsier's gene sequence?

It's easy to imagine a science-fiction plot, such as the one just outlined, where scientists find some odd patterns in the DNA code of certain organisms. The DNA sequence, expressed as a four letter code using the symbols G, C, A, and T, could code for practically anything. It could contain the value for π (3.1415...) or any other famous mathematical constant. But how many decimal digits of π encoded in the DNA would impress a scientist as something special? After all, just a few digits in sequence could occur simply by chance. A few hundred digits might make a scientist gasp in shock.

Astronomers for years have scanned the heavens for radio messages from alien creatures. If you were an alien creature trying to code a message using the four symbols (G, C, A, and T), how would you accomplish this, and what message would you encode?

The idea of placing messages in genetic sequences is not entirely fanciful. Joe Davis at MIT hopes to place encoded messages in the DNA of a bacterium which could duplicate and spread through the galaxy. His collaborator, Dana Boyd, a geneticist from Harvard, has synthesized a short sequence of DNA consisting of 47 base pairs with a brief coded message. When converted to a grid of binary digits, the message appears as a sketch of part of the human body. 100 million copies of this message have been stored in a vial. Of course Davis and his colleagues do not really plan to disperse these bacterial spores, but Davis has noted that this "may be the only practical way for humans to explore the cosmos."

Using just the 4 symbols G, C, A, and T, what are some ways you can think of for coding messages for transmission into outerspace? (Biochemists refer to these symbols as "bases.") One way to encode a message using just 4 bases is to

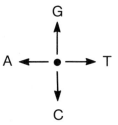

draw a picture using line segments, the direction of which are directed by the sequence. For example, G could cause a graphics pen to walk one unit up, C one unit down, A one unit left, T one unit right. Using this transformation, the genetic sequence can create detailed line drawings controlled by the sequence of letters. Another way to store and code information in the genetic sequence uses base 4 arithmetic and assigns values to the bases as follows. Set G = 0, C = 1, A = 2, and T = 3. The number 314159 (in base 10) would be represented as 1030230233 (in base 4, where no digit can be greater than 3). Therefore, CGTGATGATT would code for the first 6 digits of π. To understand numbers base 4, the presence of a "1" in a digit position of a number base 4 indicates that a corresponding power of 4 is used in determine the value of the number. A 0 in the number indicates that a corresponding power of 4 is absent from the number. The 1111, in base 4, represents $(1 \times 4^3) + (1 \times 4^2) + (1 \times 4^1) + (1 \times 4^0)$ in decimal notation. The number 1000 represents 1×4^3. The decimal number 4 is therefore represented as 10 (base 4). The decimal number 5 is represented as 11 (base 4).

I consulted with a number of experts in information theory or genetics for their opinions on the subject. Dr. John Garavelli at the National Biomedical Research Foundation in Washington DC suggests that a certain repeating sequence be used to clue the observer that something interesting and non-biolog-

ical was to follow. He suggests a 5-base segment repeat, such as TCAGTTCAGTT-CAGT. Garavelli notes that a biochemist might see the 5 base segment repeated, look for secondary structural indicators, and not seeing any assume that the repetition had some other significance. However, care should be taken to make sure that the sequence is neither self-complementary nor palindromic, since this often has biological significance. It's also important to avoid a repe-tition of a 3-base segment since the genetic code is expressed as a triplet code for producing proteins, and Garavelli believes that a triplet code is highly probable even for extraterrestrial life.

Phil Hanna (Poughkeepsie, NY) notes that any message we send to the stars must meet two criteria:

1. The sequence must indicate that it is the product of an intelligent and technically advanced civilization.

2. The sequence must be decipherable by totally alien, yet technically-advanced, civili-zations that we know nothing about, and with whom we have nothing in common.

If an alien culture were advanced enough to receive a DNA message and know how to examine it, we must assume that they have developed mathematics. Hanna believes elementary number theory is known to most advanced civiliza-tions. He therefore suggests either of two types of messages:

1. A list of the prime numbers (2, 3, 5, 7, 11, 13, 17, ...) up to some convenient limit. This is highly unlikely to occur in nature.

2. A list of primitive Pythagorean triples such as (3, 4, 5), (5, 12, 13), (7, 24, 25), and (8, 15, 17). (These give the integer lengths of sides for certain right right triangles.)

As I discussed previously, numbers such as these could be coded using base 4 arithmetic (G=0, C=1, A=2, T=3), but this would require that the decoding civili-zation understand a positional number system. Hanna suggests a simpler means. The civilization sending out spores should write a number n using a repeated string of *n* G's followed by CAT as a delimiter. In this notation, the prime number list would be:

```
GGCATGGGCATGGGGGCATGGGGGGGGCAT
GGGGGGGGGGGGCATGGGGGGGGGGGGGGGCAT
```

George Wilson has suggested the following way to encode information using the four bases:

```
G = 00 (binary)
C = 01 (binary)
A = 10 (binary)
T = 11 (binary)
```

Michael Somos thinks that looking for decimal digits of π is very futile. "Why any alien race would encode π using base ten is beyond me unless by some tremendous coincidence. You might as well expect the Gettysburg Address in English."

Amos Bairoch notes that any advanced civilization which launched spores a billion years ago for decoding by another civilization in the future would use a genetic message which will not change and evolve. The most stable genetic

sequences are those that also code for important life functions. These essential sequences cannot substantially change through time because changes would adversely effect a basic biological process. However, in reality, even the most biologically important messages in the genetic data (such as the codes for DNA replication proteins, ribosomes or other essential enzymes) change as species evolve. Therefore, if there ever were a coded message, it would probably be lost forever amidst the sands of time, or require significant archeological detective work to restore the original DNA.

30.1 Stop and Think

"One can precisely calculate the decimal expansion of π to any finite length, so in this sense the expansion is not random. Viewed as a sequence of digits, however, π is as ugly and disordered as any randomly generated list of numbers. No one has ever found a pattern..."   Martin Gardner, 1992

1. What message does the following piece of genetic material encode?

    AGTTTACTACCAACAAATGTCGAGCGAGCATAAAGGAGCTT

2. Is the following beautiful and compact arithmetic expression true or false?

$$\pi^4 + \pi^5 = e^6. \qquad (30.1)$$

Test this with a pocket calculator. ($\pi = 3.14159 \ldots$, $e = 2.71828 \ldots$.)

30.2 Fact File: Jurassic Park, SETI, Etc.

"McDonough and Carl Sagan seem to share the romantic view that a scientifically and technologically advanced civilization is likely to be a morally advanced civilization. If this is the case, then perhaps they can present some evidence from recent human history."

David Savignac, 1991, *Skeptical Inquirer*

• On Columbus Day 1992, after two decades of lobbying for funding, NASA scientists with the agency's SETI (search for extraterrestrial intelligence) project expect to activate a network of microwave receiving dishes for the most ambitious search for advanced life in outer space. NASA scientists still have some bothersome details to address: If they do detect a signal from an outerspace civilization, should the signal be answered, and what should they say? (Source: "Chatting with ETs," *Science* 254: 649, 1991.)

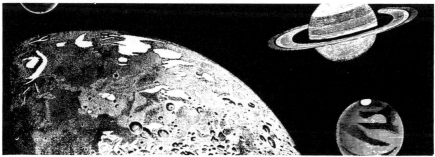

• It is estimated that around the year 2005, biologists will have obtained the exact sequence of all 3 billion nucleotides arrayed along the human chromosomes. How will they read the language of this long string of A's, G's, T's, and C's? How will they be able to find the genes, which account for only 5% of the genome, amidst the mass of extra "junk" DNA? Like an airplane searching for small, lost ships on an uncharted ocean, a new artificial intelligence program, called GRAIL, can pick out the coding regions of genes in the long stretches of DNA. The program first asks seven questions of each 100-base section of DNA sequence (including: what is the fractal dimension of the DNA?) and then feeds the answer into a neural network which learns to pick out the coding regions. When the reachers (Ed Uberbacher at the Oak Ridge National Laboratory and colleagues) tested GRAIL on 19 human genes, it located 90% of the coding regions. (Source: Roberts, L. (1991) GRAIL seeks out genes buried in DNA sequence. *Science*. Nov. 8, p 805. For electronic information: grailmail @ornl.gov.)

• Mark W. Ravera of the Department of Medical Biochemistry at the Rhone-Poulenc Rorer Central Research Center tells me that some institutions have suggested the use of plasmids (short pieces of extrachromosomal DNA) to carry some unique code that could be easily detected at a later date. This imprint would be a short DNA sequence that would code for a tiny protein which would name the originating institution. For example, plasmids made at the Merck company would all contain a short DNA stretch that would code for the small protein segment:

Met-Glu-Arg-Cys-Lys
 M   E   R   C   K

(The symbolic representation of amino acids as single letters uses a standard one-letter naming system commonly used by biochemists today.) This DNA stretch could always be detected by a simple genetic technique called DNA hybridization at any time.

• Carl Sagan, writing in his novel *Contact*, suggests that π contains a message from the stars. In the book, computer searches are conducted not only within decimal expansions of π but also in π represented in different bases. Blocks of 1's were 0's are interpreted as graphical dots (or lack of dots). In his novel, a graphical representation of the series of digits in the expansion of π base 11 produced a diagram of a circle. This circle diagram coded in π, Dr. Sagan argues, could be regarded as evidence of an intelligent creator of the universe.

• For trivia aficionados, the first published genetic sequence of a dinosaur occurred in Michael Crichton's novel *Jurassic Park* (1990). In his book, Crichton lists some 1000 bases starting with:

GCGTTGCTGG CGTTTTTCCA TAGGCTCCGC CCCCCTGACG

Do you think Crichton chose this sequence randomly, or is there some particular reason he selected this sequence of bases for use in his novel?

30.3 The Science Behind the Human Genome Project

For those readers interested in learning more about the multimillion-dollar international effort to map the human genome, Chris Wills' *Exons, Introns, and Talking Genes: The Science Behind the Human Genome Project* (Basic, 1991, 369 p., $23.00) is a must reading. Written for laypeople, the book covers the people and politics involved in this gigantic project, as well as the ethical questions raised. This intriguing introduction to the science behind the project also includes a useful glossary of technical terms.

30.4 Cross Reference

"Aliens, and Pieces of Pi" on page 151 describes an alien tampering with the sequence of digits within π. "Ghost Children in Our Genes" on page 141 describes the number of possible children which chance combinations of sperm and egg could produce. "There is Music in our Genes" on page 211 describes the relationship between music and genetic sequences.

Chapter 31

Computers and Near-Death Experiences

"Some say the tunnel is a symbolic representation of the gateway to another world. But then why always a tunnel and not, say, a gate, doorway, or even the great River Styx? Why the light at the end of the tunnel? And why always above the body, not below it?"

Susan Blackmore, 1991, *Skeptical Enquirer*

One of the most unusual applications of computer software in the 1990's has been to the study of visual experiences reported by people who have almost died. Many people, who have "come back" from states close to death, have reported pleasant experiences at death's door. Some have reported seeing lights at the end of a dark tunnel. Susan Blackmore, a researcher with the Department of Psychology at the University of Bristol, along with colleague Tom Troschianko, used a computer program to answer the question: Why do almost-dead people see tunnels?

Researchers in the past have shown that several patterns are likely to appear to people whose brains have been subject to drugs or abnormal electrical stimu-

lation as occurs in epilepsy. These patterns include the tunnel, the spiral, the lattice or grating, and the cobweb. Their origin has been thought to lie in the structure of the visual cortex, the part of the brain concerned with vision. Blackmore and Troscianko's computer program simulates what would happen when there is gradually increasing electrical noise in the visual cortex. The computer program starts with thinly spread dots of light, with more towards the middle and very few at the edges of the pattern. (Blackmore notes that in the cortex there are many more cells representing the center of the visual field but very few for the edges.) When the computer simulation is run, gradually the number of dots increases, and the center begins to look like a white blob. The researchers were shocked to see on their display a dark speckled tunnel with a white light at the end. The light grows bigger and bigger (giving the appearance that the observer is getting nearer and nearer) until it fills the whole screen. Is this the tunnel some see at the threshold of death? It may be too early to answer this with any certainty. Blackmore notes, "Our program and theory also make a prediction about near-death experiences in the blind. If they are blind because of problems in the eye but have a normal cortex, then they too should see tunnels."

If you wish to gaze at the eerie and crepuscular death-tunnels produced by their computer simulations, see Blackmore's 1991 *Skeptical Inquirer* article. (The issue containing the article is available from: *The Skeptical Inquirer*, Box 229, Buffalo, NY 14215-0229. Or call toll-free 800-634-1610. $6.25 plus $1.25 postage and handling.)

31.1 Consciousness Explained

For those readers interested in a provocative and entertaining treatise on human consciousness, see Daniel Dennett's *Consciousness Explained* (Little, 1991, 511 p., $27.95). His various discussions include unusual thought experiments and bitter attacks on the consciousness theories of Descartes. Other topics: biology, artificial intelligence, cognitive psychology.

31.2 For Further Reading

1. Blackmore, S. (1991) Near-death experiences: in or out of the body? *Skeptical Inquirer*. Fall 16: 34-45.

2. Blackmore, S., Troscianko, T. (1989) The physiology of the tunnel. *Near-Death Studies*. 8: 15-28.

3. Morse, J., Castillo, P., Venecia, D., Milstein, J., and Tyler, D. (1986) Childhood near-death experiences. *American Journal of Diseases of Children*. 140: 1110-1114.

Chapter 32

Is Computer Art Really Art?

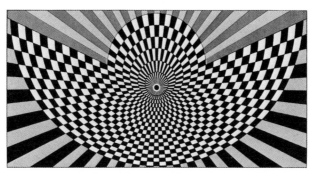

"There is more to art than the fun of putting together images and being amazed at the serendipitous results displayed on a color monitor."
Robert Mueller, 1983, *Creative Computing*

"I would choose the painting of a monkey over anything generated electronically, because I am more fascinated by the direct evidence of a mind at work (even if accidental or random) then I am by the output of machines."
Gary Glenn

"To secure the value of my purchase, I would have to demand that the artist's own digital copy be erased from his or her hard disk."
Morton Bartholdy

If Pablo Picasso (1881-1973) were alive today, would he give up his canvas, oil paints, and brush for a computer terminal? What about Lenoardo da Vinci (1452-1519)? Even if they could not obtain funding from the National Science Foundation or the National Endowment for the Arts, they could – with just a personal computer – create, manipulate, and store fairly sophisticated art works. Perhaps Leonardo would spend a large amount of his time inventing entirely new computer input devices to substitute for today's standard mouse. These devices would allow him to precisely emulate his own masterful brush strokes, the viscosity and drip of wet paint, or a chisel chipping away at an imaginary chunk of shiny marble.

In addition to these questions, which I posed in a survey to *Computer Graphics World*[14] readers, I also asked the following specific questions, all of which aimed to answer "Is computer art really art?" Given high-resolution computer prints of the following, which could you consider as art:

1. A table of numbers, generated at random?

2. A black and white fractal pattern derived from pure mathematics, with no human intervention?

---

[14] *Computer Graphics World*, One Technology Park Drive, PO 987, Westford, MA 01886.

3. A fractal derived from mathematics, with colors selected by a human?

4. A computer picture drawn by a human using a mouse?

5. A picture painted by a monkey using oils and paint brushes?

6. A photograph of a pretty mountain, photographed by a robot holding a camera? Both the robot and camera are positioned randomly.

Again, for the above six patterns, which could you consider spending over 500 US dollars for the purpose of displaying on your living room wall?

32.1 Comments from Colleagues

"The art of Picasso together with the collective formulations of da Vinci suggests that only the media has advanced – not the artist."   Donald Strauss

"I just don't get off on glossy intestines with eyeballs, and other wet, organic looking forms. Why do the mathematician-artists always insist upon a glossy sheen to their renderings?"   Keith Rogers

The following is a selection of intriguing responses to many of the questions I posed in the previous section. These responses were sent to me from artists, educators, writers, and technologists. Tom McMillan, Editor of *Resolution*:

My dictionary defines art as "the conscious production or arrangement of sounds, colors, forms, movements, or other elements in a manner that affects the sense of beauty; specifically, the production of the beautiful in a graphic or plastic medium." There's nothing there that disqualifies the computer as a tool for producing a work of art. Art is art, regardless of the medium.

Gary Glenn, an art school graduate and painter who currently works for a medical publisher, had the following to say:

I do not regard computer "art" as art. Of the choices you listed, I would choose the monkey's painting. To be considered as art, artists who use computers will have to recognize and place themselves within art history. Computer art is devoid of sensation; there is no direct encounter with materials. Traditional materials do not hide what has been done; there are brush strokes, chisel marks, etc. The viewer can linger in front of a painting and attempt to follow the logic and sequence of the brushstrokes, the strategy of the painter. There is a record of the artist's gesture and presence. There is an absolute lack of humaneness in computer-generated art. Is there an artist who works solely with computers and solely for esthetic or artistic reasons?

Richard Dube, Vice President of Celandine, Inc., noted:

An artistic intent is not necessary for a work to be art. Andrew Wyeth's father was a noted illustrator for books such as *Robinson Crusoe*. However, during his time, the work that he produced was not considered to be "art."

The primary criterion is not what created the art, but rather how much the piece appealed to me personally. I once photographed some shelf fungus on a decaying stump and entered it in a prestigious black and white photography show, and was elated when it was accepted. As I was very proud of this piece, I made a Christmas present of it to my mother. She looked at it with some puzzlement and thanked me for the nice picture of "hot dogs."

The tool and the artist make the art, the type of tool does not dictate whether something is art or not. Would Shakespeare have used a word processor if it were available? Absolutely.

Deborah Greh teaches Communications at St. John's University and has two degrees in Art. In her article "Is it Art Yet," published in the September 1991 issue of *inCider/A*, she stated:

Perhaps we can say that art is an attempt to arrive at some revelation. Of course, one common criterion of value is a piece's *timelessness* – whether it has withstood the criticism of the years, weathered the passing fancies and changing tastes. Witness the works of the masters of various eras – Michelangelo, van Gogh, Monet, Picasso, Dali. The newness of computer art precludes the test of time.

Keith Rogers is a hardware design engineer of flight simulators at the Evans & Sutherland Computer Corp. He wrote to me:

I ought to confess my great dislike for most computer art. First, lots of computer art pictures are very "cartoonish." The colors are too bold, too varied and too primary. The shapes are either utter chaos or simple graphic primitives. Second, many of them glitter like tinsel. Computer artists are too fond of reflections.

One whole genre of computer art that amuses me is the one that contains all the abstract 3-D glossy sculptures. You have a couple of photos of that type in your article.[15] While I find it amazing that many of them are the graphical manifestations of mathematical algorithms and formulae, I just don't get off on glossy intestines with eyeballs and other wet, organic looking forms. Why do the mathematician-artists still insist upon a glossy sheen to their renderings?

Anthropologists have a devil of a time trying to understand aesthetics in humans. However, one aspect of art they tend to agree on is that most of us prefer art which makes us feel comfortable. And what makes us feel comfortable is what was comforting to *Homo sapiens* tens and hundreds of thousands of years ago: images of food, abundant lakes and streams beside rich forests, cliffs which have caves for shelters, the cool pastel colors of nature, and so forth. I fall in this category.

Finally, Charles Ehlschlaeger noted:

Only the monkey's painting has a decent chance of making big bucks in the art industry (meaning people buying artworks for living rooms).

---

[15] Pickover, C. (1991) The ultimate survey. *Computer Graphics World*. November. 57-64. Pfitzer, G. (1991) Computer laboratory horrors. *Computer Graphics World*. October. 65-65.

The questions posed in this chapter are not easy to answer. Nor are the questions easy to define. Marcel Duchamp, the French Surrealist, once labeled as "art" a defaced poster of the Mona Lisa, a big battered bottle rack, and a mass produced urinal. I think most people would consider a beautifully rendered, carefully-colored fractal pattern more of an artwork than a urinal. On the other hand, computer art does have its limitations. Patrick Hanrahan of Princeton University once noted that 90 to 95 percent of the pictures you see as photographs can't even be simulated on a computer screen.

Finally, some of you may be curious to find out that a majority of those who answered "Is Computer Art Really Art?" by sending me electronic computer mail said "yes." A majority of those who wrote their answers to me using paper letters mailed through the conventional mail system, said "no."

32.2 Cross References

Those of you interested in the specific question of whether *fractal* patterns are art should see "Fractal Spiders and Frame-Robertson Bushes" on page 87. "Interlude: Marking Time" on page 289 and "Interlude: Alien Musical Scores" on page 221 also contain several interesting opinions on this subject by well-known computer artists.

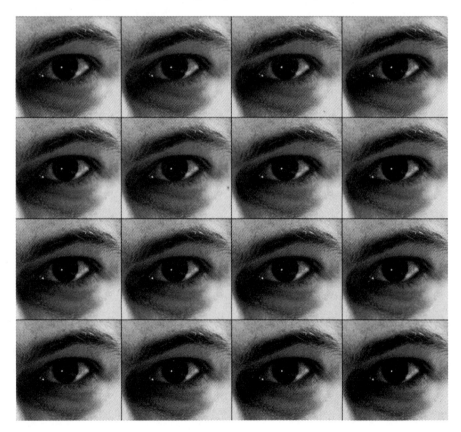

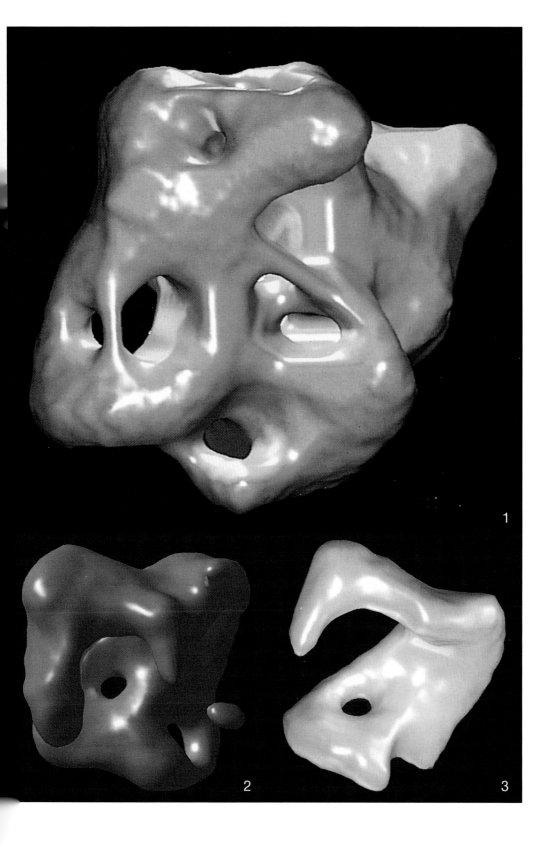

1

2   3

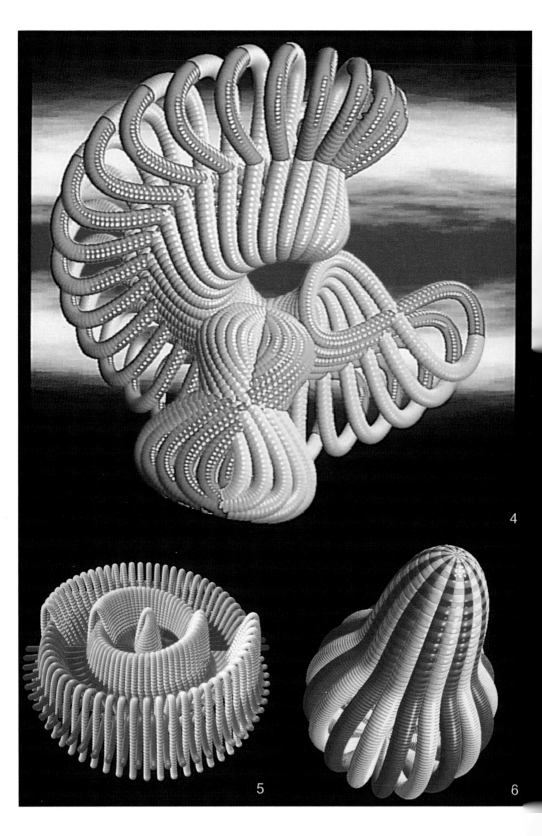

4

5   6

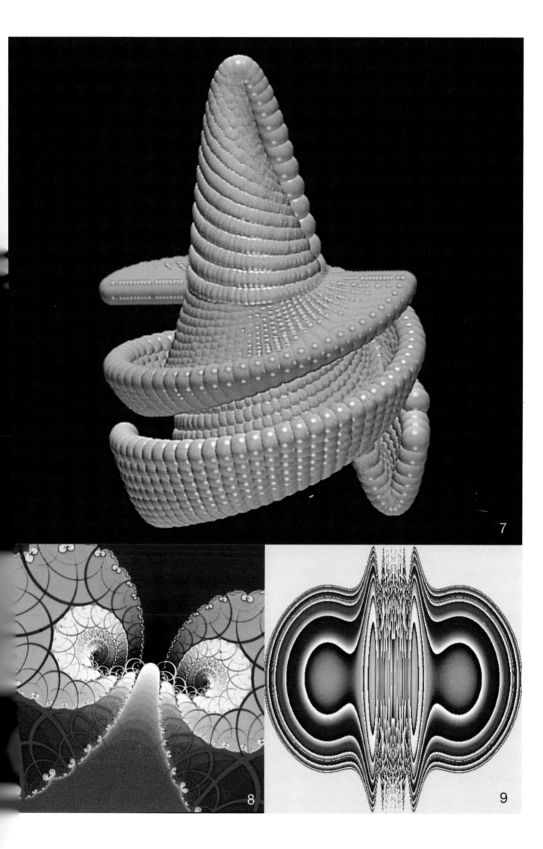

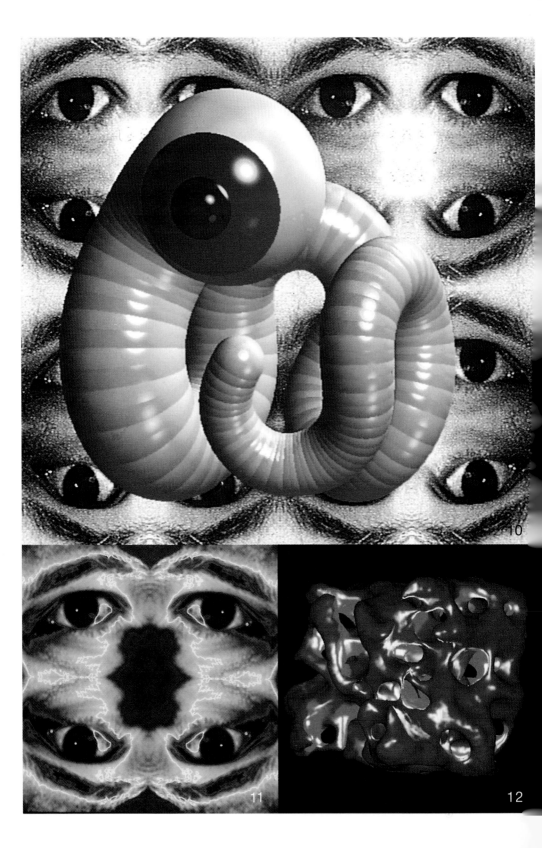

10

11

12

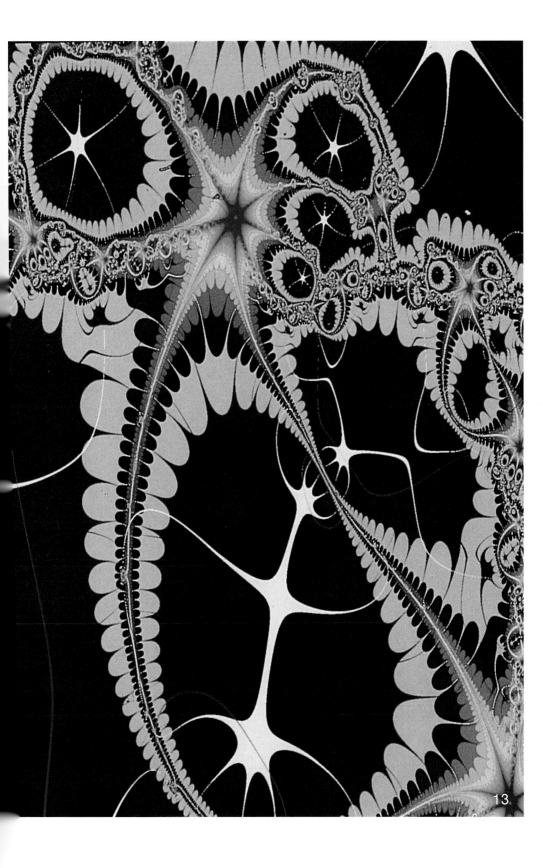

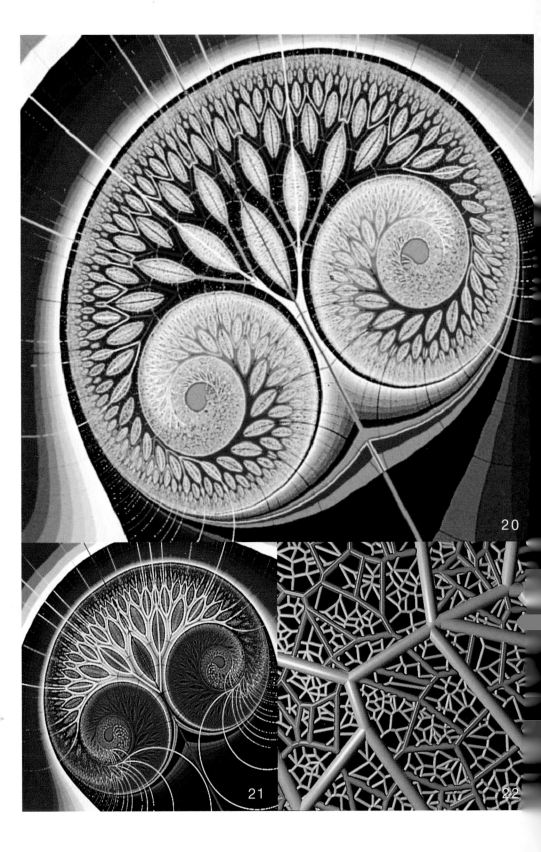

20

21

22

Chapter 33

Electronic and Fractal Ant Farms

"The ants and their semifluid secretions teach us that pattern, pattern, pattern is the foundational element by which the creatures of the physical world reveal a perfect working model of the divine ideal. "

Don DeLillo, *Ratner's Star*

As a child I once had an "Ant Farm" consisting of sand squeezed between two plates of glass which were separated by only a few millimeters. When ants were added to the enclosure they would soon tunnel into the sand creating a maze of intricate paths and chambers. Since the space between the glass plates was very thin, confining the ants to living essentially in a 2-D world, it was always easy to observe the ants and their constructions. Food and water could periodically be added to the enclosure.

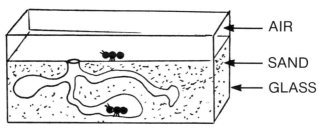

You can build your own computerized Ant Farm[16] through which ants can travel by defining a map of tunnels and chambers. Next have your simulated ants crawl through the tunnels using a random walk procedure. (Rather than describe and repeat the program outline necessary to accomplish this here, you can refer to "The Cro-Magnon Conquest Game" on page 133 for further information on

---

[16] I'm told that the following terms are trademarked by Uncle Milton Industries: "Ant Farm," "Ant Farmers," "Ant Farm Village," "Ant Way," and "Ant Port." You can purchase already assembled, low-cost ant farms from: Uncle Milton Industries, Culver City, CA 90232. The term "Ant City" is a trademarked term of another ant enclosure manufacturer: Ant City, Natural Science Industries, Far Rockaway, NY 11691.

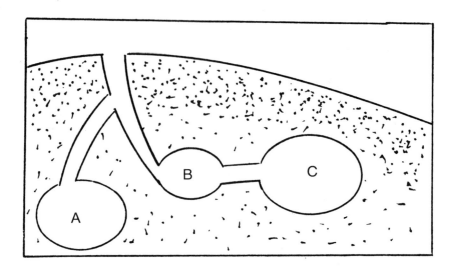

Figure 33.1. *An Ant Farm.* After following the randomly walking ants for a few hours, where do you expect the ants most likely to be: in chambers A, B, or C, or on the surface of the soil?

random walks). For example, start with 10 ants described by their (x,y) positions in the ant farm. Have the computer draw each ant as a little black circle, or as a triplet of circles to represent the head, thorax, and abdomen. For each increment in time, move the ants a random short distance. If an ant bumps into a wall, reflect it back into the tunnel or chamber. You can make the simulation easier to program on a computer by representing the chambers and tunnels as squares connected by straight, thin tubes. Those of you without computers can accomplish this simulation using dots on a graph paper, and by throwing dice to control the ants's movements.

33.1 Stop and Think

• In the ant farm in Figure 33.1, after following the randomly walking ants for a few hours, where do you expect the ants most likely to be: in chambers A, B, or C, or on the surface of the soil?

• Suppose you are given a fractal ant farm, where the chambers are recursively placed at different size scales. One can also ask the question as to where the ants are most likely to be, through time, during their random walks. (See "Labyrinthine Lundin Curves" on page 103 and "Fractal Mazes: The Most Difficult Mazes Ever Imagined" on page 10 for background information on fractals.) You can think of a fractal ant farm as an infinitely branching system of tunnels such as in the lung's bronchial trees where the tubes become smaller and smaller,

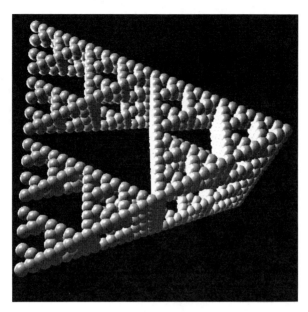

Figure 33.2. *A 3-D fractal Ant Farm.* (I computed this image using an IBM RISC System/6000.)

or like the trunk, branches, and twigs on a a tree. The figure at left is an example

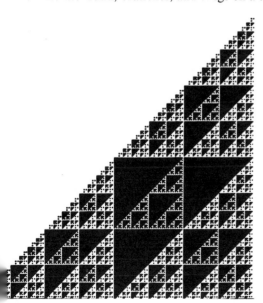

of a fractal ant farm[17] with triangular chambers. Figure 33.2 shows a 3-D representation of this fractal ant farm. Dan Platt, a physicist at IBM, notes that the distribution of ants in a fractal ant farm changes in an interesting way as one examines the chambers at higher and higher magnifications. The distribution of ants is called a *multifractal*, requiring an infinite number of dimensions to describe the distribution of ants as one increasingly magnifies the ant farm complex. Multifractal distributions are finding increasing application in areas such as the study of snowflakes, and the penetration of oil through porous rocks.

---

[17] This fractal triangular figure is called a *Sierpinski gasket*, and is discussed in detail in my first book *Computers, Pattern, Chaos, and Beauty* (St. Martin's Press).

33.2 Fact File: Rats, Ants, and Mazes

• Ants make up from 10 to 15 percent of the entire animal biomass in most terrestrial environments, and turn more soil than earthworms.

• When rats and ants learn to run the same maze, they do so in different ways. Rats seem to learn a "map" of the maze as a whole, whereas ants appear to learn the maze as a series of separate problems, one at each branch point of the maze. As *rats* master a maze, their performance improves when confronted with a *new* maze, but this same maze mastery actually hinders the performance of *ants* in new mazes. In other words, when an ant solves a maze, its behavior in new mazes becomes less flexible.[18]

33.3 Cross References

See the following sections for information on fractals: "Smithson's Fractal Anabiotic Ana Sequences" on page 35, "Fractal Spiders and Frame-Robertson Bushes" on page 87, and "Labyrinthine Lundin Curves" on page 103. For fractal mazes, see "Mazes for the Mind" on page 3. For fractal integer sequences and patterns, see "The Drums of Ulupu" on page 71 and "Beauty and the Bits" on page 79. For feather fractals, see "Fantastic Feather Fractals" on page 33.

33.4 For Further Reading

1. Keeton, W. (1973) *Elements of Biological Science*. Norton: NY. (Contains information on ants solving mazes.)

2. Schroeder, M. (1991) *Fractals, Chaos and Power Laws*. Freeman: NY. (Contains information on multifractals.)

3. Hölldobler, B., Wilson, E. (1990) *The Ants*. Harvard University Press: NY. 732 p. (Details of anatomy, social organization, ecology, and natural history of ants by the world's leading myrmecologists. Many photographs. 1991 Pulitzer Prize winner for general nonfiction.)

---

[18] *Sim Ant* is a commercially available electronic ant colony, for personal computers, based on the biology and behavior of ants. The detailed graphics enhance the rich variety of behavioral parameters available to users. For more information, contact: MAXIS, Two Theatre Square, Suite 230, Orinda, CA 94563-3041. 415 254-9700. Fax 415 253-3736. Tel order: 800 33-MAXIS.

Chapter 34

Toilet Paper and the Infinite

"We do not know now whether the man who drew the pictures on cave walls was the first scientist or the first artist. It may be that he was both, for science and art ... are alike, dedicated to exploring and questioning."

Helen Poltz, 1955, *Imagination's Other Place*

34.1 The Length of a Roll of Toilet Paper

In 1990, Don Thatcher of Leicester Polytechnic published a paper titled *The Length of a Roll of Toilet Paper* in a scientific book on mathematical modelling. In the paper he asks students the following: "Given a roll of paper find, without unwrapping it, the total length of paper on the roll." In the paper he discusses the necessary mathematics, which lead to the formulas:

$$n = \frac{r_2 - r_1}{t} \tag{34.1}$$

and

$$l = \pi \frac{r_2^2 - r_1^2}{t} \tag{34.2}$$

where n is the number of turns, l is the total length of paper, t is the thickness of a

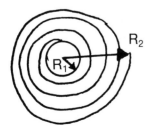

sheet of paper, r_1 is the distance from the center of the roll to the cardboard tube within the roll, and r_2 is the distance from the center of the roll to the outer edge of the toilet paper. For "Izal Medicated Toilet Roll," the relevant figures are: $r_1 = 18.8$ mm, $r_2 = 32.6$ mm, and $t = 0.0373$ mm, giving a total length of 59.4 meters (or 65 yards).

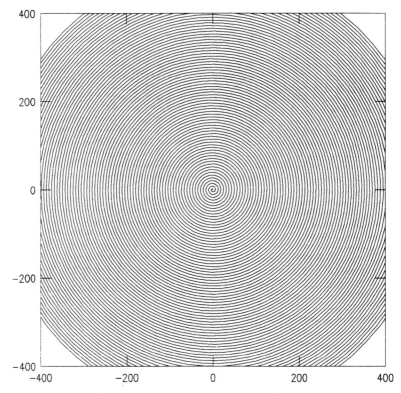

Figure 34.1. *Archimedean spiral model of a toilet roll of paper.* Can you guess how long this line is? (The line represents the edge of the roll of paper. See "Strange Toilet Paper" on page 179 for information.)

34.2 Stop and Think

1. How large a roll of paper would be required to contain a length of paper equivalent to the height of Mount Everest (2.9×10^4 feet)? Could such a roll fit inside your house?

2. How many turns would the paper undergo in creating a length of paper equal to the length of the Panama Canal (2.68×10^5 feet)?

3. Make a 3-D graph showing the relationship between the number of turns, the radius r_2, and the total length of paper.

4. Some of the methods mentioned here have practical applications, for example, in computing the length of a spiral groove in a record. See also Huntley (1981) for practical applications.

```
ALGORITHM: How to Create Archimedean Toilet Paper.
theta = 0; d = 0; xold = 0; yold = 0;
ttheta = 0; a= 1.0;
finc = 1;    /* crudest sampling */
finc = 0.1; /* finest sampling */
DO i = 1 to 5000;
   theta = theta +  finc;
   ttheta = ttheta +  finc;
   if (theta > 6.2831) then theta = theta - 6.2831;
   r = a*ttheta;
   x = r*cos(theta);
   y = r*sin(theta);
   if (ttheta = finc) then d = 0; else
   d = d + sqrt((x - xold)**2 + (y-yold)**2);
   xold = x; yold = y;
   MoveLineTo (x , y)
END;
Print ('Total Distance is', d);
```

Pseudocode 34.1. *How to create Archimedean toilet paper.*

34.3 Strange Toilet Paper

"I am not saying that computer graphics, when produced by extremely sophisticated software, is not art.   I am saying, however, that most of it appears very boring to an eye trained to recognize interesting visual images."
Robert Mueller, 1983, *Creative Computing*

Toilet paper geometry, discussed in the previous sections, can be modelled by an Archimedean spiral of the form

$$r = a \times \theta. \tag{34.3}$$

Here, r is the radial distance of a point on the toilet paper from the center of the spiral.   The scale factor a controls the size, and θ is the angle of the point as it revolves around the center of the roll. The Archimedean spiral was developed by Archimedes (287-212 B.C.), a Greek mathematician and inventor.   Archimedes was born in Syracuse, in Sicily.   He was on intimate terms with (or even related to) the great King of his day, Hiero II. Aside from playing with spirals, Archimedes also devised for Hiero II various killing machines, including burning instruments which terrified the Romans and lengthened a war with Rome for several years.   In 212 B.C., while Archimedes leisurely drew a mathematical figure in the moist sand, a sword from a Roman soldier was driven straight through his aging torso. Archimedes died immediately and was soon buried, and in accord with Archimedes' wishes, his tomb was marked by a sphere inscribed in a cylinder.   Archimedes considered his discovery of the relation between the surface and volume of a sphere and its circumscribing cylinder to be his most valuable achievement in life. (For more on Archimedes, see "Aliens, and Pieces of Pi" on page 151.)

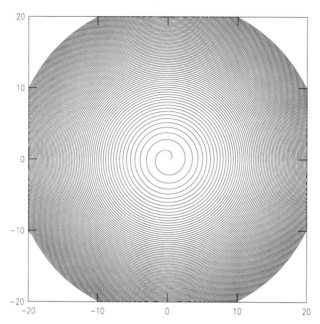

Figure 34.2. *Squashed Archimedean model of a hyper-toilet roll of paper.* This nonlinear toilet roll can hold an amazing length of paper. Can you guess how long this line is, which represents the (2-D) edge of the roll of paper?

As discussed in the previous sections, it is possible to compute the length of real toilet paper rolls using simple formulas. The spiral toilet paper geometry is also a compact way to store a surface area in a small volume. Figure 34.1 shows an Archimedean spiral I computed using Equation (34.3). Can you guess how long the line segment is? If you assume the scale in the figure to be in inches, then the line is an amazing 123,000 inches long. Pseudocode 34.1 shows you how to draw this and other figures, and to compute the total distance travelled by the line.

34.4 Squashed Archimedean Model of a HyperToilet Paper

> *"Most productive of the sciences in philosophical speculation, mathematics is as well most productive in humor."*
>
> Helen Poltz, 1955, *Imagination's Other Place*

My favorite toilet paper topologies are not the simple (but realistic) Archimedean kinds, but rather the squashed Archimedean variety, an example of which is shown in Figure 34.2. The reason they're my favorite is that they are pleasing to look at, and also because this nonlinear toilet roll can hold an amazing length of paper. Can you guess how long this line is in Figure 34.2 which represents the

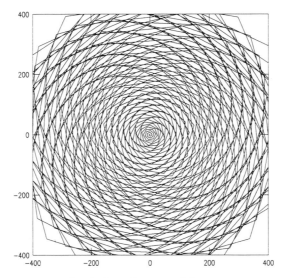

Figure 34.3. *A variation on the Archimedean spiral theme.*

(2-D) edge of the roll of hypertoilet paper? Here's the answer. If the scale in the figure represents inches, than the length of the line is 7,400 inches. I created the figure using

$$r = \sqrt{a\theta} \qquad\qquad (34.4)$$

Since the compression is nonlinear, your line segment can grow wildly in length while being constrained to a small area of the graph paper. Could an infinitely long toilet paper be contained in a finite, compressed hyperoll?

The remaining figures in this chapter show toilet rolls topologies created using Pseudocode 34.1 at different sampling rates. This means that the Archimedean spiral is drawn using fewer points (skipping ones normally plotted) to create these choppy, intricate designs.

34.5 Stop and Think

1. If one were to construct a real hypertoilet paper roll, of the kind shown in Figure 34.2, how much space would the roll require if it were to contain an amount of paper equal to the height of the tallest bridge in the world? (The tallest bridge in the world is the Golden Gate Bridge in California. The towers of the suspension bridge extend 745 feet above the water.)

2. If one were to construct a real hypertoilet paper roll, of the kind shown in Figure 34.2, how much space would the roll require if it were to contain an amount of paper equal to the length of the largest submarine river? (In 1952, a river beneath the surface of the Pacific ocean was discovered which flows

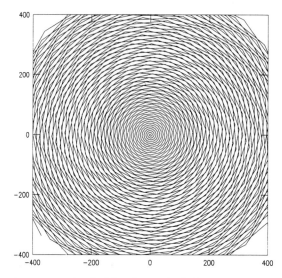

Figure 34.4. *A variation on the Archimedean spiral theme.*

for 3,500 miles along the equator. Its volume is 1,000 times that of the Mississippi river.)

3. Can you construct other ornate toilet paper spirals by altering the program in Pseudocode 34.1?

34.6 Fact File: First Manufactured Toilet Paper

The first toilet paper manufactured in the United States was a pearl-colored manilla hemp paper made in 1857 by a New Yorker named Joseph Gayetty. The paper sold for 50 cents (for 500 sheets).

34.7 For Further Reading

1. Thatcher, D. (1990) The length of a roll of toilet paper. In *Mathematical Modelling.* Oxford University Press: NY. (Teachers and students of mathematical modeling will find this book a rich source of examples ranging from insulating houses to basketball, and from modelling epidemics to studying the generation of windmill power.)

2. Huntley, I. (1981) Air gap coiling of steel strips. In *Case Studies in Mathematical Modelling*, James, D. and McDonald, J., eds. Stanley Thornes (Pub): Cheltenham, England.

Chapter 35

Bertrand Russell's Twenty Favorite Words

"This desire to communicate is basic both to science and to poetry. The scientist seeks to find the order of the universe through the discipline of experiment; the poet, through the discipline of language."

Helen Poltz, 1955, *Imagination's Other Place*

Language is the primary medium with which we think and communicate ideas to others. When one reads language in written form, one is really decoding symbols. It is through the interactions of such symbols that we create new worlds, new images, new thoughts. Readers of my book *Computers and the Imagination* will know that for a long time, I have held a fascination with colorful symbols and words. Words allow us to transcend space and time, and to inspire visions. In *Computers and the Imagination*, I gave a list of interesting words to be used in computer- and human-generated fiction. In this chapter, I list a few of my favorite words as well as the twenty favorite words of Bertand Russell.

Philosopher Bertrand Russell was many things: a mathematician, a logician, an atheist, a champion of peace, a controversial political figure, and a recipient of the Nobel Prize in literature. He was born on May 18, 1872. In 1958, Bertrand Russell was asked to list his twenty favorite words in the English language. His list is as follows:

wind, heath, golden, begrime, pilgrim, quagmire, diapason, alabaster, chrysoprase, astrolabe, apocalyptic, ineluctable, terraqueous, inspissated, incarnadine, sublunary, chorasmean, alembic, fulminate, ecstacy.

How many of these words do you like or comprehend?

35.1 Batrachomyomachia

"When the Cimetiere des Innocens at Paris was removed in 1786-1787, great masses of adipocere were found where the coffins containing the dead bodies had been placed very closely together."

Adipocere *Encyclopedia Britannica, 11 Ed.*

Friends familiar with my own fascination with words have asked me to list my own "Top Twenty" words in this book. Therefore, for the record, here are my twenty favorite words in the English language:

1. agapemone - a religious community founded in 1846, which flourished for years at a mansion called the "abode of love."
2. adipocere - the gruesome, soapy substance which a corpse buried in moist ground converts to after many days.
3. batrachomyomachia - struggle.
4. batrachophagous - feeding on frogs.
5. chryselephantine - gold and ivory.
6. demilune - a crescent.
7. eburnian - ivory.
8. empyreal - heavenly.
9. enchiridion - a handbook.
10. erubescent - reddening, reddish.
11. ferruginous - rust-colored, rusty.
12. gerontocracy - government by old men.
13. hyperborean - living in the extreme north.
14. kakistocracy - the dominance of the depraved.
15. mamelon - a breast shaped hill.
16. mundungus - foul-smelling tobacco
17. ochreous - yellowish.
18. scordatura - intentional detuning of musical instruments.
19. Xanthian marbles - a collection of marble sculptures brought to the British museum from Xanthus in 1838.
20. Yggdrasill - a mystical, mythological tree which embraces the entire universe.

35.2 Stop and Think

1. What makes certain words our favorite? Is it their sound, their look, their meaning, or something else entirely?

2. If you have access to a computer (on-line) dictionary, have the computer select twenty words at random. How many words do you know the meaning of? How many would be candidates for your own "Top Twenty" list? If you don't have an on-line dictionary, simply select twenty words at random from a paper dictionary. Gaze at your random list. Why are so few of the randomly selected words competitive candidates to the words on Russell's list in terms of beauty, meaning, and sound?

3. Could a best-selling author, such as Stephen King or Carl Sagan, succeed in creating a best-seller if forced to use 10 randomly selected words in the first ten pages of a novel?

4. How will this chapter appear when this book is translated into different languages such as German and Japanese? Will the foreign language translators retain the English words in the word list?

35.3 For Further Reading

1. Feinberg, B., Kasrils, R. (1969) *Dear Bertrand Russell.... (A Selection of His Correspondence with the General Public 1950-1968)*. Houghton Mifflin: Boston.

2. *Dictionary of Unusual Words, Part A*. (1946) The Thames Bank Publishing Company Limited, 1773 London Road, Leigh-On-Sea: Essex, UK.

"Losing the collected wisdom of the rain forest tribes would be like burning every library in the world without bothering to look at what was on the shelves." Anita Roddick, *Body and Soul*

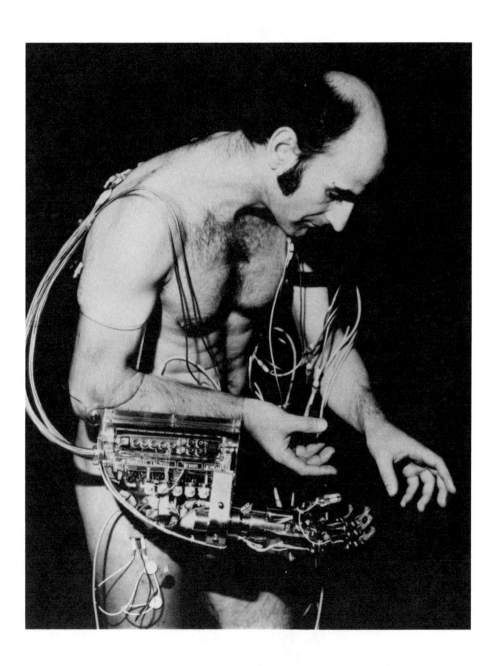

Chapter 36

Interlude: Stelarc's Third Hand

"Technology has greatly expanded our senses and made our natural abilities obsolete."   Stelarc

"When someone once asked Stelarc what he though of art, he plugged himself into an electro-encephalogram, pondered on the subject for a few moments and gave the questioner a printout of the reading." Tokyo Journal

Stelarc, pictured here, is an Australian performance artist who has worked in Japan for many years. He is interested in forming hybrid humans composed of both organic and synthetic parts, and in using his body to make art and music. The connection of technology to the body has always fascinated Stelarc. In past performances, he has used an artificial hand attached to his body and activated by EMG muscle signals.

In his event called "Amplified body, sound-responsive eyes, automatic arms, and third eye," he was connected to dozens of electronic wires that monitor his every move to create visual and acoustic effects. He uses equipment borrowed from medical companies to monitor brain waves, heartbeats, blood flows, and muscle contractions to create a visual and acoustic performance using gestures, posture, and internal control. Each time the third hand moves its fingers, there is a horrible metal shriek. Over his face, a steel structure supports fiber optic rods which end in front of his eyes so laser beams seem to come from his eyes. Random electronic signals send his left (real) arm twitching up and down, out of control. The artificial hand is actually quite sophisticated, having functions such as pinch-release, grasp-release, 270 degree wrist rotation, and a tactile feedback system for a "sense of touch."

Perhaps Stelarc is most famous for his naked mid-air suspensions using 18 four-inch fish hooks through his skin. Born Stelios Arcadious in Cyprus in 1946, he was raised in Melbourne. He studied painting and sculpture, and in 1970 he moved to Japan and changed his name to Stelarc. In 1990, with a grant from the Australian Council, he was artist-in-residence at Ballarat College of Advanced Education, where he conducted research and development of a whole artificial arm.

Part III

MUSIC BEYOND IMAGINATION

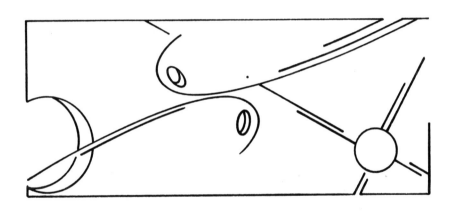

Voyager III

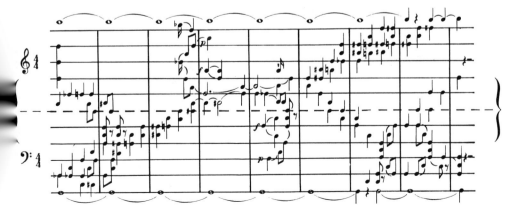

Can you identify these two famous musicians?
(For the solution, see the end of the Acknowledgment section.)

Chapter 37

Mutcer's Marvelous Music Machines

"There are exactly 1675458239173299266836297116378658809745485176287748187444105157677156615313228453018924254389862 4   imaginable melodies from which humans construct their songs."   Prof. David Mutcer

"Although we might regard musical compositions as the most abstract and therefore probably the most intellectual form of human artistic endeavor, melodies are clearly not human inventions; the songs of skylarks, canaries, and certain other songbirds are as pleasing to our ears as they must be to themselves, as well as to their prospective mates."
Susumu and Midori Ohno, *Immunogenetics*

Here's a story I wrote a few years ago describing a music generating machine with interesting properties. The machine is not some hypothetical or theoretical device beyond human construction. In fact, the machine can easily be constructed by anyone with some electrical engineering experience. I urge those of you with access to the necessary analog or digital equipment to attempt such a construction. Who knows, maybe it will make you rich...

In 1975, a Professor Mutcer of the Electrical Engineering Department at Harvard University decided to build a musical melody generator that would continuously produce different 50-note melodic progressions. The melody machine would generate one melody after another, selecting for each melody a different combination of notes from the piano keyboard. His machine consisted of 88 oscillators, each of which produced a single tone. A random number generator was used to select which of the 88 oscillators were playing at any particular moment. The machine played the 50 random notes, one at a time.

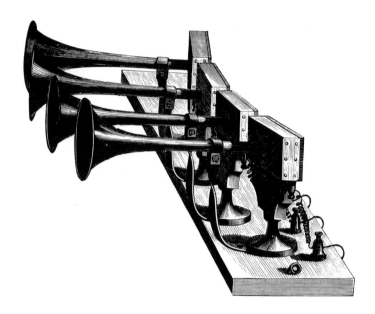

Figure 37.1. *An early version of Mutcer's Music machine.* 84 speaker horns were soon added to produce 88 different pitches corresponding to the 88 keys of a piano. Mutcer eventually abandoned this apparatus in favor of modern electronic music synthesizers.

Other versions of his music machine generated all possible 50-note melodies by sequentially trying all 88 tones for the first oscillator, while keeping all the others constant, and then stepping each oscillator sequentially (something like an odometer on your car's dash board). Here are the first few melodies this version of the machine produced for Professor Mutcer. First it stepped through all possible notes for the first position in the melody, starting with the lowest note on the piano (A = 27.5 Hertz):

```
A, B, C, D, E, F, G, ...    (First Melody)
B, B, C, D, E, F, G, ...    (Second Melody)
C, B, C, D, E, F, G, ...    (Third Melody)
D, B, C, D, E, F, G, ...    (Fourth Melody)
       . . .                (Etc.)
```

The first song that the machine produced using this approach (top line in the example) was simply a melody consisting of the first 50 white notes on a piano keyboard played in order from low to high pitch. In the second melody, the first A note has switched to B, and so on. Later black notes were also included. Either of these versions of the music machine (i.e., random or "odometer" versions), could be built without much difficulty. Figure 37.1 is a drawing of Mutcer's first machine, which he later abandoned in favor of modern electronic music synthesizers. The duration of each note (quarter note, half note, eighth note, etc.) could

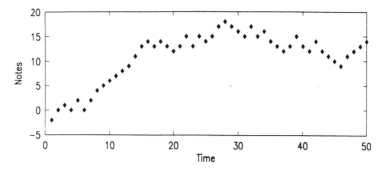

Figure 37.2. *Computer-generated melody using the simple algorithm described in the text.* This simple approach produces surprisingly nice melodies. (See Pseudocode 37.1.)

also be selected at random. Processor Mutcer set the machine in action and began to listen to the endless sequence of different melodies that came from the music machine. Most of the melodies made no sense at all to his Western ear. They looked like this:

But since the music machine played *all* possible combinations of musical notes, Mutcer began to find some nice tunes among the senseless, junk melodies:

Mutcer reasoned that a careful search would also reveal every melody written by Michael Jackson, Madonna, Beethoven, Bach, the Beetles, and Bananarama. It would also produce every melody that Madonna discarded in frustration in her plush and high-tech recording studios.

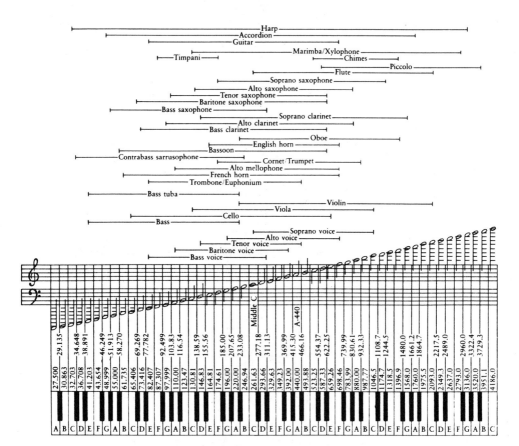

Figure 37.3. *Musical notes of various instruments.* The diagram relates the notes of the musical scale, the positions of the keys of the piano, and the frequency of the pitches in Hertz. If you play tones above and below the range of the piano keyboard, changes in frequencies don't correspond to clear musical intervals. Although the sensation of pitch does go up and down with frequency, these sounds don't have a useful *musical* pitch. (From John Pierce's *The Science of Musical Sound.* © 1983 by *Scientific American Books.* Reprinted with permission of W.H. Freeman and Co. Pierce's diagram is an adaptation of a drawing appearing in Donald Hall's book *Musical Acoustics.*)

Mutcer's music machine would even generate every melody ever played since ancient humans blew on wooden flutes or on the horns of goats. Moreover the machine would play every popular tune in the future, every musical hit from the year 2200. Musical publishers having Mutcer's machine would simply have to sit and listen, and select the good songs from the gibberish – which they do daily anyway.

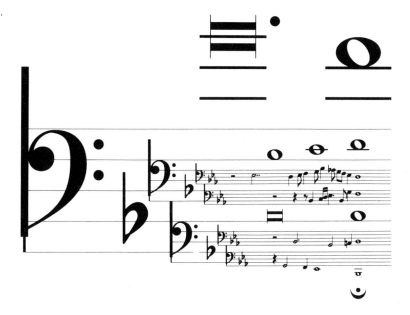

Figure 37.4. *Fractal Bass Clefs.* Noam Elkies, a number theorist at the Department of Mathematics at Harvard University, produces interesting musical designs reminiscent of Escher's engravings or perhaps Scott Kim's inversions. He recursively places bass clefs and other musical symbols on a musical staff at different size scales. © 1991 by N. Elkies. (Hardware used: a 300dþi PostSrcjpt printer. Software used: the muSCRIBE set of PostScript macros for printing musical notation. At one point in his life Elkies considered making music his career but decided against it because it would have required him to neglect mathematics. For more of Elkies' work, see "Fact File" on page 148.)

37.1 Music from Alpha Centuri

You may occasionally encounter natural scenes that remind you of a painting, or episodes in life that make you think of a novel or a play. You will never come on anything in nature that sounds like a symphony.

Martin Gardner, 1992

A day after he built the music machine, Professor Mutcer proudly showed the device to several of his graduate students. A week later, he instructed his students to plug themselves into the music machine every day and to press a button, to record a musical score, whenever they heard a particularly interesting melody. A few machines were built, and students took turns listening. No machine was ever idle for more than a few seconds as one student replaced another at this listening task. Interestingly, after about an hour of listening, one student was rumored to hear several phrases from the beautiful *Moonlight Sonata.* After two weeks, Mutcer himself heard both the *Cantata No. 96 Aria. Ach, ziehe die Seele mit Seilen der Liebe,* by Bach and *Havah Nagilah* (Israeli Hora). Another student fainted when she heard a particularly powerful and hypnotic tune. Although she

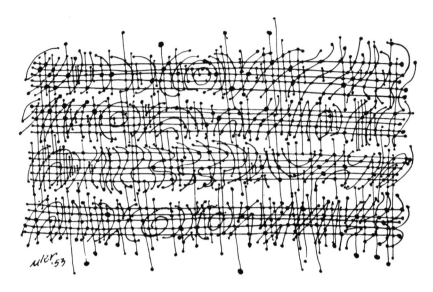

Figure 37.5. *Alien musical score.* See "Interlude: Alien Musical Scores" on page 221 for more information. (Drawing © 1992 by Robert Mueller.)

did not know it, the tune just happened to be a current best seller on a small red planet circling the star Alpha Centuri. Mutcer copyrighted the best of the new musical scores, which were soon bought by large music publishers in New York and Rio de Janeiro. Mutcer was a millionaire.

37.2 All the Melodies that Could Ever be Imagined

"We all are reluctant, with regard to music and art, to examine our sources of pleasure or strength. In part we fear success itself – we fear that understanding might spoil enjoyment. Rightly so: Art often loses power when its psychological roots are exposed."

Marvin Minsky, 1981, *Computer Music Journal*

You can construct your own music "machine" using dice to select random notes, or by using current MIDI (musical instrument digital interface) sequencers and synthesizers. However it turns out you'd have to listen for a long time if you were waiting for the music machine to produce a particular melody such as *Stairway to Heaven* by Led Zeppelin or the finale to *Let the Sun Shine In*, from the rock musical *Hair*. In fact, you can calculate how long it would actually take to listen

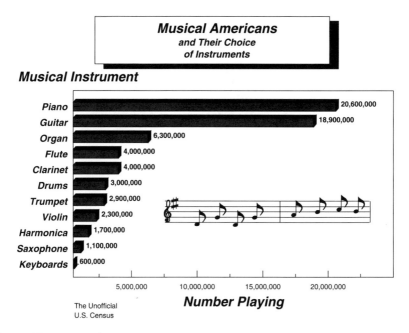

Figure 37.6. *Musical Americans.* More than 57,000,000 Americans play a musical instrument. Nearly half of these people play more than one instrument, and a majority play regularly. (Source: Tom Heymann's *The Unofficial US Census*, Fawcett Columbine: NY (1991)).

to all the melodies that could ever be imagined. There are 88 piano keys. Let us assume that, as stated for the Professor's machine, each melodic sequence is 50 notes long. The musical score can begin with any of these notes so that we have 88 possibilities for the first note played. For each of these 88 possibilities, there are 88 different possibilities for the second note, giving us a total of 88x88 = 7744 possibilities. Altogether, for a 50-note melody, we have 88^{50} possible melodies. Completely written out, this 98-digit number representing all possible melodies is:

167545823917329926683629711637865880974548517628774818744410515767715661531322845301892425438986524

To get a feel for the immensity of this number, it is greater than the *ice age number* (10^{30}), which is the number of snow crystals necessary to form the ice age, or the *Coney Island number* (10^{20}), which is the number of grains of sands on the Coney Island beach, or the *talking number* (10^{16}), which is the total number of words spoken by humans since the dawn of time. If Mutcer's melody machine were to produce a new 50-note melodic phrase every second since the beginning of the formation of the earth, it would not have produced every possible melody to this day. If you consider that the variable duration of each note adds an even greater number of melodic possibilities, it's virtually impossible that you will hear any 50-note musical piece you'll recognize. If you were to further consider a

Figure 37.7. *One frame from a musical score in a colorful video.* This is a musical representation produced by Malinowski's Music Animation Machine. The vertical and horizontal placement and the horizontal length of each bar indicates the pitch, timing, and duration of the note the bar represents. Some quickly played high notes are at the top of the score. Some bass notes are at the bottom.

machine which produced microtonal scales with other non-Western musical spacings not represented by the 88 piano keys, the number of potential human songs is too vast to contemplate.

37.3 Merry Christmas

> *"The full visual equivalent of music has yet to be discovered, but its existence can not be doubted – when it is discovered, it will prove to be a use of light and color so simple and yet so compelling that it will immediately be taken over into our everyday lives, on the same level as music but independent of it."*   Alex Gross, 1969, *East Village Other*

In the previous section, we saw how unlikely it was to generate any particular melody with the Professor's machine. But how well would the music machine do for simpler songs? For example, what if we were to consider children's songs or Christmas music which often utilize only the white notes near middle C on the piano. After all, why have the music machine select from 88 different possible notes when singers with even the greatest of human ranges use much less than a third of the piano keyboard's range (Figure 37.3). If we constrain the music machine to selecting from only 8 different white notes (which comprise an octave) and wait for it to generate a specific short sequence of notes which comprise a possible target melody (such as the 7 notes E, D, C, D, E, E, E, of the opening phrase in *Mary Had a Little Lamb*), could we expect to generate the target in a

Figure 37.8. *Transposing music into painting.* The first six bars of Chopin's "Valse, op. 69, no. 2.," are represented by Pierre Karinthi as paint on canvas. If you look carefully, you can see how the hills and valleys of the musical score correspond to the hills and valleys in the brush strokes. The rhythm of the left hand (bass cleff) is visualized as the periodic brush strokes toward the bottom of the figure. (For further information, see text.)

finite time? The answer is yes! The number of possibilities is 8^7, only about 2 million melodies. If you were to listen to one melody every second, you could hear all 2 million melodies in about a month. If you try to carry out this experiment, the task should probably be split between various listeners, so that no one person has to sit through all 2 million melodies. By doing this, you would hear snippets from numerous real nursery rhymes, lullabies, Christmas songs, etc. By having your music machine be a little more discriminating, you could have it avoid many redundant melodies. For example, it could  avoid melodies which have the same note repeated four or more times in a row. This would slightly decrease the month-long listening time. With this simpler music machine, you could easily produce many of the famous holiday songs you already know, and also Christmas songs you have never heard before. Merry Christmas.

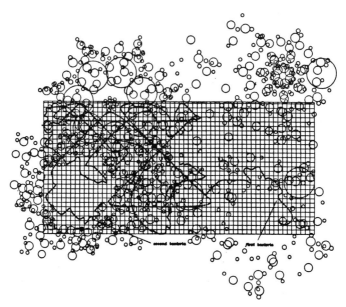

Figure 37.9. *Bacterial music.* Emanuel Dimas de Melo Pimenta is a composer of experimental music and has worked with graphical scores since 1978. In this score, moving *E. coli* "bacteria" were used to produce the music. Circles are food which, when eaten by a bacterium, produce a sound. Each time the a bacterium finds a food particle, its direction of motion changes. For more information, contact Emanuel at: Rua Tierno Galvan, Lote 5B-2. C, 1200 Lisboa Portugal.

37.4 Pink Machines

Good music, like a person's life or the pageant of history, is a wondrous mixture of expectation and unanticipated turns.   Martin Gardner, 1992

Those of you knowledgeable in noise theory will appreciate IBM researcher R. Voss's demonstration that melodies generated using special kinds of random number generators can produce quite appealing and realistic musical pieces. Professor Mutcer's random number generator is known as a *white noise* generator because it produced totally random numbers. Since no tone is related in any way to the sequence of notes that precedes it, the result is a totally uncorrelated sequence. Voss's *pink random number generators* produce pink random numbers which have correlations between them. For pink numbers, a number at one position in time is not independent of the value of a number at another position. These kinds of random number generators fall into the general class of random number generators called $1/f^\beta$ machines which produce progressions closest to "real" music when $\beta = 1$ (compared with $\beta = 0$ or $\beta = 2$). Here f refers to the frequency. The use of larger values of β in the $1/f^\beta$ equation produces a pattern of numbers with greater correlations than totally random white noise, where $\beta = 0$.

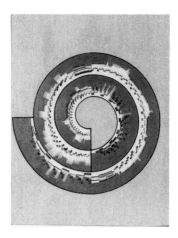 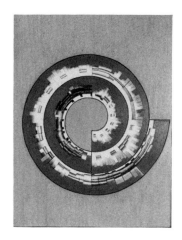

Figure 37.10. *A classical musical score represented by paint on canvas.* A musical bar is defined as a 45 degree angle from the center of the spiral. The first eight bars form a 360 degree angle. (Used with permission of the artist, Pierre Karinthi.)

Since one version of Mutcer's music machine used totally random numbers to select tones, so that all the notes were uncorrelated, it took a long time to find a particularly pleasing melody. The musical references at the end of the chapter should give more information on pink and other weird ways of generating human-like music.

37.5 A Simple Way to Produce Beautiful Music

"No one could remember all of Beethoven's Fifth Symphony from a single hearing, but neither could one ever again hear those first four notes as just four notes! Composers do not dare use this simple, four-note motive any more... because an accidental hint of it can wreck another piece by unintentionally distracting the listener."

Marvin Minsky, 1981, *Computer Music Journal*

The algorithm I like to use to produce correlated musical notes (Pseudocode 37.1) creates musically interesting pieces by avoiding Mutcer's purely random approach to select notes. Here I use a modified *random walk* algorithm to produce the tones. The "walk" starts at middle C on a piano keyboard (represented as a 0 value in the program variable *note*) and thereafter the walk meanders around the white notes on the keyboard. Each new note is either one or two steps above or below the previous one (Pseudocode 37.1). To produce even nicer sounding melodies, with very little added program complexity, also include a third condition that has the program randomly use a "step=4," in addition to the "step=2 and step = 1" already in the code. And have the computer reset *note* back to zero whenever *time* is a multiple of 15, that is, after every group of 15 notes is

```
ALGORITHM: How to Create Music
    note = 0
    DO time = 1 to 50;
        /* random numbers between 0 and 1: */
        GenRandomNumber(r1)
        GenRandomNumber(r2)
        if r1 > .5 then sig = -1; else sig = 1
        if r2 > .5 then step = 1; else step = 2
        note = note + sig*step
        PrintOut(time, note);
    END
```

Pseudocode 37.1. *How the computer can create music.*

played. This prevents the random walk from gradually drifting off the left or right side of the "keyboard." Try inventing algorithms for producing pleasing duration values for each note. Quite nice melodies often result from this ultra-simple method simply using random durations or introducing periodicities by giving every 4th note a duration longer than the other 3 notes. After your composition is completed, tap it out on a piano. You can compare my method in the pseudocode to (less musical) totally random music by multiplying the program variable *r1* by 88 and converting the resulting values to 88 tones on a keyboard. This will not sound too much different than the music your three-year-old might produce by hitting keys with a single finger. Almost every listener agrees that the modified random walk approach is more pleasing than the totally random music.

37.6 Fact File

37.6.1 Ink Splattered Scores

In the December 1959 *Scientific American* Lejaren Hiller describes how he produced random music and interesting looking musical scores by splattering ink on a blank musical staff and then converting the position of the random dots of ink to the placement of notes in a traditional musical score.

37.6.2 Pigeon Music

"A popular song has 100 measures, 1000 beats. What must the martians imagine we mean by those measures and beats, measures and beats! The words themselves reveal an awesome repetitiousness. Why isn't music boring? Is hearing so like seeing that we need a hundred glances to build each musical image?"   Marvin Minsky, 1981, *Computer Music Journal*

In 1984, Porter and Neuringer studied the ability of pigeons to discriminate between different melodic lines. Specifically, the researchers taught pigeons to discriminate between Bach flute music and Hindemith viola music. In another study they showed that with further training, some pigeons could extrapolate their recognition success to excerpts from pieces not previously heard. For this study, the researchers used excerpts from a Bach organ piece and Stravinsky's *Rite of Spring*. (Source: Porter, D. and Neuringer, A. (1984) Music discrimination by pigeons. *Journal of Experimental Psychology,* volume 10.)

37.6.3 New York Skyline Music

In 1946, Joeseph Schillinger translated the silhouette of the New York skyline to musical notation. The higher the building, the higher the note on the musical score. It has been reported that this system of translation was also used by other composers, notably George Gershwin in writing *Porgy and Bess*. (Source: Reichardt, J. (1975) *Cybernetic Serendipity*. Praeger: NY.)

37.6.4 Hailstone Music

Bill Richard from Commodore notes that the *hailstone number sequence* can produce interesting melodies. This number sequence, discussed in my first book *Computers, Pattern, Chaos and Beauty*, starts with any integer x, and produces the next integer in the sequence using the following rules:

if x is even
  then x = x / 2
  else x = 3 x + 1

The process is repeated. For example, the hailstone sequence for 3 is: $H(3) =$ {3, 10, 5, 16, 8, 4, 2, 1, 4, ... }. Like hailstones falling from the sky through storm clouds, this sequence drifts down and up, sometimes in seemingly haphazard patterns. Also like hailstones, hailstone numbers always seem eventually to fall back down to the ground (the integer "1"). Richard used x as a frequency and scaled it so that it would remain in the audio spectrum. For example, he mapped the number 1 to 40 Hz, because 1 Hz is simply too low to be musically useful. He notes that the hailstone numbers produces "a relatively pleasing sequence."

37.6.5 Chess Music

A one-time chess player, artist Ronald R. Brown from Pennsylvania composes music using the *chess Knight's tour*. The Knight's tour problem is one of the oldest known problems in the history of chess. In chess, the Knight can move only in a prescribed L-shaped pattern. The problem is to move a Knight on a chessboard so that all 64 squares of the board are traversed only once. The number of distinct solutions to the Knight's tour problem is immense – estimates range from 31 million to 168!/105!63!. The exclamation point is the factorial sign: $n! = 1 \times 2 \times 3 \times \cdots n$. To create chess music, Brown first writes a solution to the Knight's problem, such as the one below:

50	11	24	53	14	37	26	35	Up 4
23	62	51	12	25	34	15	38	Up 3
10	49	64	21	40	13	36	27	Up 2
61	22	9	52	33	28	39	16	Up 1
48	7	60	1	20	41	54	29	Middle C
59	4	45	8	53	32	17	42	Down 1
6	47	2	57	44	19	30	55	Down 2
3	58	5	46	31	56	43	18	Down 3

To understand this table of numbers, the Knight starts at the position marked "1"

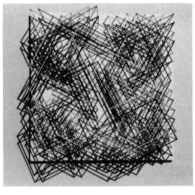

and then proceeds to the position marked "2" and so on, traversing all the squares on the chess board. This can be mapped to interesting music by considering each Knight's position as a note, the pitch of which is determined by the row it is in. Starting at middle C, the next note is two white notes lower, the third note three white notes lower (from middle C), etc. By tracing various paths that the Knight follows as it meanders around the board, Ronald Brown also produces interesting abstract art. A recent newspaper article quotes Brown describing his chess art, "Some people don't approve of this because they feel art must be spontaneous. My answer is that this is spontaneous because I don't know what it's going to look like until I've done it." Shown here is his 24"x24"x8.5" "Tour de Four I," an artwork showing four tours on a single grid.

37.6.6 Latvian Folk Music

The Folklore Institute of Latvia contains 1,011,482 folksong texts in its libraries. It also has 28,488 melodies in its archives. (Source: Hartson, 1988.)

37.6.7 Music Animation Machine

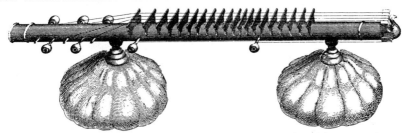

Novel computer-generated musical scores are being explored by several computer music experts. For example, the score produced by a device called the "Music Animation Machine" is a colorful, new-age musical representation. Developed by musician Stephen Malinowski, a video tape of this score is wonderful to watch while listening to the accompanying music. No musical background is required to appreciate and learn from the pretty patterns. Let me tell you a little about the method. In place of conventional musical notation, this method uses a bar-graph notation in which each note is represented by a colored horizontal bar. The vertical and horizontal placement, and the horizontal length, of each bar indicates the pitch, timing, and duration of the note the bar represents. In addition, color identifies the instrument that is playing the note. (See Figure 37.7.) As you watch the patterns unfold in a video tape available from Malinowski, you can see and hear features of music that you would have missed without the notation. For more information on the videotape of animated musical scores, contact: Music Animation Machine, c/o Stephen Malinowski, 1850 Arch Street # 5, Berkeley, CA 94709.

37.6.8 Music in Paintings

"The scale of frequencies perceived by our eyes (the colors) is 500 times smaller than that of sounds."   Pierre Karinthi, *Leonardo*

Dr. Pierre Karinthi is an artist, scientist, and inventor living in Jouy-en-Josas, France. He received his Ph.D. in chemical engineering and is Director of Innovation at the research center of a large international chemical company. Among his artistic works are classical musical scores represented as paintings on canvas

(Figure 37.8 and Figure 37.10). Every note frequency is visualized by a given length on the paining. For example, the higher the frequency, the longer the brush stroke. A color is assigned to each note, depending on its pitch. Karinthi finds that musical similarities of rhythm and phrasing are often clearly visualized in his paintings. For specific details on how Karinthi translates musical scores to paintings, see: Karinthi, P. (1991) A contribution to musicalism: an attempt to interpret music in painting. *Leonardo*. 24(4): 401-405.

37.6.9 Mozart Numbers

"Of course, we would like to study Mozart's music the way scientists analyze the spectrum of a distant star."

Marvin Minsky, 1981, *Computer Music Journal*

In order to compute any Mozart symphony number S from its Köchel number K you can use

$$S = 0.027465 + 0.157692K + 0.000159446K^2. \tag{37.1}$$

(The Köchel catalogue is a chronological list of all of Mozart's works, and any work of Mozart's may be referred to uniquely by its Köchel number. For example,

the "Symphony number 40 in G minor" is K.550.) The formula will give an answer not more than two off, 85% of the time. For further details, see Hartson (1988).

Mozart once wrote a waltz in which he specified 11 different possibilities for 14 of the 16 musical bars of the waltz, and 2 possibilities for one of the other bars. This gives 2×11^{14} variations of the waltz. What percentage of the number of these waltzes have humans heard? What percentage of the waltzes *could* a human hear in a lifetime?

37.6.10 Music Notation Modernization Association

The Music Notation Modernization Association holds regular conventions. For more information, contact: Thomas S. Reed, Executive Director, Music Notation Modernization Association, PO Box 241, Kirksville, MO 63501.

37.6.11 Strange Musical Notation Patents

U.S. Patent 2,232,264   - Diagram musical score
U.S. Patent 3,698,277   - Analog system of music notation
U.S. Patent 3,700,785   - Means for simplified rewriting of music
U.S. Patent 1,424,718   - Musical notation
U.S. Patent 1,515,403   - Device for teaching piano playing
U.S. Patent 1,603,296   - Chart for piano instruction
U.S. Patent 1,544,427   - Music in synchrony with moving pictures
(Patents are obtainable by sending $1.50 to United States Patent and Trademark Office, Commissioner of Patents and Trademarks, Washington DC 20231.)

37.6.12 Music of the Spheres

The ancient Greeks attempted to establish relationships between numbers, musical scales, and the orbits of planets. The Greek's *Music of the Spheres* linked music and astronomy, although today we know that there is no scientific significance to their proposed relationship between planetary orbits and musical scales.

37.6.13 Music of the Sumerian Tablets

Seven thousand years ago, when stone-age farmers lived in Egypt, no one lived in the southern plain between the Tigris and Euphrates Rivers. Around 4,500 B.C., some people settled there and soon found that the mud, when baked, turned hard like a stone – nice for making bricks, hammers, and even nails. Later the priests invented cuneiform writing which was scratched into clay tablets; these tablets have survived by the thousands to give modern humans a record of Sumerian life. In addition, Sumerian clay tablets have been found (in modern-day Iraq) which show an eight note music scale (circa 1800 B.C.), perhaps one of the earliest examples of written music.

37.7 For Further Reading

1.   Clynes, M. (1989) *Sentics: The Touch of Emotions*. Avery Press, 350 Thorens Ave., Garden City Park, New York, NY 11040. (This is a fascinating work on patterns in music and life by an esteemed neuroscientist, concert pianist, electronics engineer, inventor, poet, and philosopher. Prof. Clynes has developed a method and mathematical parameters for having a computer music program give maximum satisfaction to the brain. He has obtained patents on his computer program and set up a company called Microsound International Ltd., in Sonoma, California, to refine his methods.)

2.   Clynes, M. (1982) *Music, Mind, and Brain: The Neuropsychology of Music.* Plenum: NY.

3.   Paulos, J. (1988) *Innumeracy* Vintage: NY.

4.   Gardner, M. (1992) *Fractal Music, Hypercards, and More...* Freeman: NY.

5.   Dodge, C. (1988) Profile: a musical fractal *Computer Music J.* 12(3): 10-14.

6.   Hofstadter, D. (1982) *Metamagical Themas. Scientific American.* 246: 16-28.

7.   Voss, R., Clarke, J. (1978) $1/f$ noise in music: music from $1/f$ noise. *J. Acoustical Society of America.* 63: 258-263. Also: Clarke, J., Voss, R. (1975) $1/f$ noise in music and speech. *Nature.* 258: 317-318.

8.   Roades, C. (1985) Research in music and artificial intelligence. *ACM Computing Surveys.* 17:163-190.

9.   Chowning, J. (1973) The synthesis of complex audio spectra by means of frequency modulation. *J. Audio Engineering Society.* 21(7): 46-54.

10. Cogan, R. (1984) *New Images of Musical Sound.* Harvard University Press: Massachusetts.

11. Dillon, M., Hunter, M. (1982) Automated identification of melodic variants in folk music. *Computers and the Humanities.* 16: 107-117.

12. Koopmans, L. (1974) *The Spectral Analysis of Time Series.* New York: Academic Press, pp. 165-189, 279, 306-209.

13. Minsky, M. (1981) Music, mind and meaning. *Computer Music J.* 5:28-44.

14. Mitroo, J., Herman, N., and Badler, N. (1979) Movies from music: visualizing musical compositions. *Computer Graphics (Siggraph).* 13: 218-225.

15. Pierce, J. (1983) *The Science of Musical Sound.* Freeman: NY.

16. Starr, D. (1984) Computer chorus. *OMNI Magazine.* 6: 41.

17. Roades, C. (1985) Research in music and artificial intelligence. *ACM Computing Surveys.* 17:163-190.

18. Risset, J. (1986) Pitch and rhythm paradoxes: Comments on Auditory paradox based on fractal waveform. *Journal of the Acoustical Society of America.* 79: 186-189.

19. Dodge, C., Bahn, C.R. (1986) Musical fractals. *BYTE.* 11(6): 185-96.

20. Berkowitz, S. (1985) New aesthetics for musical variation. Proceedings of the 5th Symposium on Small Computers in the Arts (Cat. No.85CH2218-6) IEEE Comput. Soc. Press.

21. Pickover, C. (1986) Representation of melody patterns using topographic spectral distribution functions, *Computer Music Journal* 10(3): 72-78.

22. Pickover, C. (1988) Novel graphics allow computer synthesis of singing human voices. *Computer Technology Review* (Winter Issue) 7(16): 79-89.

23. Roads, Curtis, (1986) The Tsukuba Musical Robot. *Computer Music Journal.* 10(2): 39-43.

24. Hachimura, K, Ohno, Y. (1987) A system for the representation of human body movements from dance scores. *Pattern Recognition Letters.* January. 5: 1-9.

25. Hartson (1988) *Drunken Goldfish and Other Irrelevant Scientific Research.* Sterling Publishing: NY.

Chapter 38

Interlude: Computer Mouths

Rhoda Grossman of San Francisco, California has been using traditional media in her fine art and illustration for about 20 years. Lately, however, she has grown rather fond of the computer as a vehicle for artistic expression. My favorite artwork of hers are the humorous and expressive "face scapes" which use facial features as the building blocks of her design. Her first big exposure to computer art came at a computer show called Comdex '89. After the show, she brought home a mouse and a primitive paint program, which she practiced using on her neighbor' personal computer. Grossman writes:

> In the summer of 1990, I purchased a second-hand Mac II system, and subscribed to Macworld and MacUser. In short, having quickly overcome a lifetime of fearing machines and an attitude that computer couldn't really produce "Art" I was hooked.

Shown here is her computer artwork titled "Woodnan/Mouths." To create these kinds of images, Grossman scans a color photo using Adobe Photoshop (v. 1), and then she uses various image processing features to create the final work. For further information, contact: Rhoda Grossman, 25 Franconia Street, San Francisco, CA 94110.

A Mademoiselle J.W. Stirling

DEUX NOCTURNES

Op. 55 Nr 1

Chapter 39

There is Music in our Genes

Organisms which have evolved on this earth are governed by multitudes of periodicities. Individual genes have been duplicated often to the point of redundancy. This principal even appears to govern the manifestations of human intellect; musical compositions also rely on repetitious recurrence.

Susumu and Midori Ohno, *Immunogenetics*.

39.1 Ohno's DNA Music

Dr. Susumo Ohno is an extraordinary man. Born in 1928 in Seoul, Korea he became a naturalized U.S. citizen in 1957. His vast career includes a multitude of awards, honors and prestigious research positions.

Currently he holds the Ben Horowitz Chair of distinguished scientists in reproductive genetics in the Department of Theoretical Biology at The Beckman Research Institute of the City of Hope, Duarte, California. Some of his books and papers are listed at the end of this chapter.

Dr. Ohno's field of specialization is evolutionary molecular biology, and the aspect of his work that may be of most interest to general readers is the musical representation of genetic sequences. DNA contains the basic heredity information of living cells. Naturally occurring DNA sequences, symbolized by the letters G, C, A, and T, contains many patterns. (The G, C, A, and T symbols represent the building blocks of DNA and are also known as "bases" or "nucleotides.") One notable feature of DNA is the frequent repetition of various short sequences through an organism's genome. For example, genetic sequences which code for phosphoglycerate kinase (a sugar metabolizing enzyme), contains building blocks of AAGGCTGCTG and its truncated 6-base derivative AAGCTG. These basic segments are repeated, seemingly

Code Table Song

Figure 39.1. *Music from genetic and protein sequences.* Nobuo Munakata and Kenshi Hayash at the National Cancer Institute in Tokyo represent biological sequence data as musical scores in order to find repeating patterns and differences between sequences. This piece is called "Codon Song."

indiscriminately, through much of the gene. Ohno sees a striking similarity between this repetition of small DNA sequences and the musical songs of humans. He thinks of these kinds of DNA building blocks as principle melodies that are developed into endless variations by base substitution and truncation. Genes also contain tandemly recurring base sequences which are not related to these building blocks, and these introduce the desired complexity into musical compositions, which are described in the following paragraphs.

Many of Ohno's papers discuss the translation of the genetic information into musical scores. In order to fill the octave scale, two consecutive positions are assigned to each of the four bases in ascending order of A, G, T, and C. Some of the details and justification for this mapping can be found in his papers.

He finds that the phophoglcyerate kinase gene, if played on a violin, is "hauntingly melancholy, as though reflecting the Weltschmerz of the gene that persevered for hundreds of millions of years." Reverse conversion of music to DNA sequences produce equally startling results. For example, Ohno maps pieces such

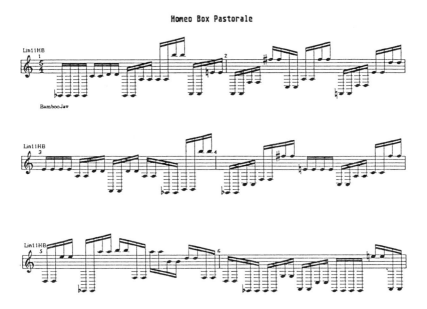

Figure 39.2. *Music from genetic sequences.* This is part of a song made from a piece of a protein in a nematode (worm), fruity fly, and human. The title is "Homeo Box Pastorale." Some of the sequences, when split into three simultaneously played melodies, produce "leisurely and peaceful" tunes.

as Frederic Chopin's *Nocturn, opus 55, no. 1*, to musical scores and shows that the Nocturn sequences have remarkable similarities with DNA sequences (see the frontispiece for this chapter). Some of these similarities arise from the fact that both DNA and gene sequences contain tandemly recurring segments. Therefore, one way of creating interesting synthetic music is to start with DNA sequences and listen to the beautiful results after conversion to music. Using Ohno's rules and by listening to the DNA, you can readily recognize various patterns and periodicities. Sometimes Ohno adds interesting chords to complement the single note meoldies.

For those of you with genetics background, Ohno finds that *primoridal* coding sequences are similar to musical compositions of the early Baroque periods, whereas "modern coding sequences that endured for a few billion years are like those of the late Romantic period." Ancient bacterial sequences, such as those that code for sugar metabolizing enzymes like glyceraldehyde 3-phosphate dehydrogenase, seem to have sets of patterns different than exhibited by more modern bacterial sequences. These differences are made obvious in the DNA music. Ohno believes that the first set of prebiotic coding sequences to be translated were repeats of base oligomers (small segments). On the other hand, during subsequent evolution, new genes always arose from redundant copies of preexisting genes (large DNA sequences). This gives rise to the Baroque and Romantic sounds of ancient and modern DNA, respectively.

Four Helix-Turn-Helix Degenerating

Figure 39.3. *Music from protein sequences.* This is generated from bacterial sequences played with a 16th note offset.

Below is a segment from a composition which Susumu Ohno sent me titled "Chicken lens αA crystallin." You can read more about it in his book chapter in *Modern Trends in Human Leukemia VIII* (Springer, 1989). The score below is reprinted with permission from Dr. Ohno.

39.2 Munakata/Hayashi Gene Music

"... Both genes and music are made of linear and quantized information which represent unfathomable diversity and mystery. However, we are not confident about how to disentangle the intricate logic of life's composition."
Naobuo Munakata and Kenshi Hayashi, 1991

Nobuo Munakata (right) and Kenshi Hayashi (left) are researchers at the Radio-biology Division and Oncology Division of the National Cancer Center Research

Institute in Tokyo.[19] Like Ohno, they have also experimented with gene music, but they use a simpler scheme to assign tones to DNA. They explain that some previous musical mapping schemes have used an octave or larger intervals, which are "not practical for laypeople to sing, hum, or whistle while reading or typing sequences." Instead, they set the music interval to a fifth and choose four tones (re, mi, sol, la) as shown below:

G   C   T   A

re mi sol la

Of the three possible mappings illustrated here, Munakata and Hayashi chose the middle one. The left mapping produces sounds which are "stable and optimistic – favored in Western and Chinese folk music," while the right one is "lamentable and pessimistic, favored in Indonesian and Okinawan music." The middle four notes are "simple-minded and unsophisticated, as favored in Mongolian, Korean, and Japanese music." Once having represented the DNA sequences as musical scores, they use the "DNA Inspector" program on the Macintosh computer to play back DNA sequences according to their assignment.

Munakata and Hayashi also have generated music from amino acid sequences (the basic building blocks of proteins) using the following mapping:

| MIDI Note | D1# | F1 | G1 | A1# | C2 | D2 | F2 | G2 | A2 | C3 | D3 | E3 | G3 | A3 | B3 | D4 | E4 | F4# | A4 | B4 |

| Amino Acid | Arg | Lys | His | Asp | Glu | Asn | Gln | Ser | Thr | Gly | Pro | Ala | Cys | Tyr | Trp | Phe | Met | Leu | Val | Ile |

Basic | Acidic | Polar | Nonpolar | Aromatic | Hydrophobic

They prefer the sound of music synthesizers to the Macintosh computer.[20] Therefore, Munakata and Hayashi also use state-of-the art MIDI (musical instrument digital interfaces) for playing their DNA music through synthesizers, and they often play more than one sequence at a time so that differences between sequences will be spotted easily. A one-beat offset may be used to stress unique repeating patterns like the leucine repeat in so-called *zipper proteins*. For example, in their piece named "Song of Courtship and Clocks" they play sequences of fruit-fly and fungus genes using two different instruments, harp and clarinet. To convert genetic sequence data in text-file format (which comes from various genetic data bases) to MIDI-note files, they use a commercial program *Hyper-MIDI 2.0* (EarLevel Engineering) working within *HyperCard* on a Macintosh computer.

---

[19] Nobuo Munakata is head of the Radiosensitization Section and his major research area in the radiation genetics of bacteria and nematodes (worms). Kenshi Hayashi is the head of the Oncogene Product Section and is interested in the structure of genes.

[20] Nobuo Munakata writes to me "With apology to purists using traditional music instruments, I must rely on Japanese gadgets (Yamaha's TX81Z, TX802, and SY77) controlled by German boxes (Atari ST with Notator and Synthworks) and American devices (Macintosh with HyperMIDI and Vison), a rare combination of diligence, stringency, and indulgence."

Figure 39.1, Figure 39.2 and Figure 39.3 are typical musical scores from their biological sequence data.

39.3 For Further Reading on Gene Music

"DNA was the miracle, the self-replicating molecule, the very stuff of life. Its intricate chemical cryptography contained all the information necessary to form another human being. If anything in life were sacred, he thought, this was it. Genetic material spanned time, approached eternity, bound past and present and future in an enormous evolutionary chain linking ancestry to posterity. To change it seemed sacrilege, an invitation to divine wrath."

Alan Engel, *Variant*

1. Engel, A. (1988) *Variant*, Donald Fine: NY. (An excellent fictional account of gene manipulation with startling consequences for several young Russian boys.)

2. Ohno, S. (1989) Modern coding sequences are in the periodic-to-chaotic transition. *Modern Trends in Human Leukemia VIII*. Springer: New York. pp. 512-519. (Includes a 2-page musical score for the musical transformation of a part of the chicken αA crystalline coding sequence.)

3. Ohno, S., Ohno, M. (1986) The all persuasive principle of repetitious recurrences governs not only coding sequence construction but also human endeavor in musical composition. *Immunogenetics*. 24:71-78. (Contains four pages of musical scores.)

4. Ohno, S. (1988) Codon preference is but an illusion created by the construction principle of coding sequences. *Proceeding of the National Academy of Science*. 85: 4378-4328.

5. Ohno, S. (1988) Of words, genes and music. In *NATO ISI Series, Vol H32, The Semiotics of Cellular Communication in the Immune System*. Sercarz, E., ed. Springer: NY. pp 131-147.

6. Ohno, S. (1991) The grammatical rule of DNA language: messages in palindromic verses. In *Evolution of Life, Fossils, Molecules and Culture*. Springer: NY.

7. Hayashi, K., Munakata, N. (1984) Basically musical. *Nature*. 310: 96.

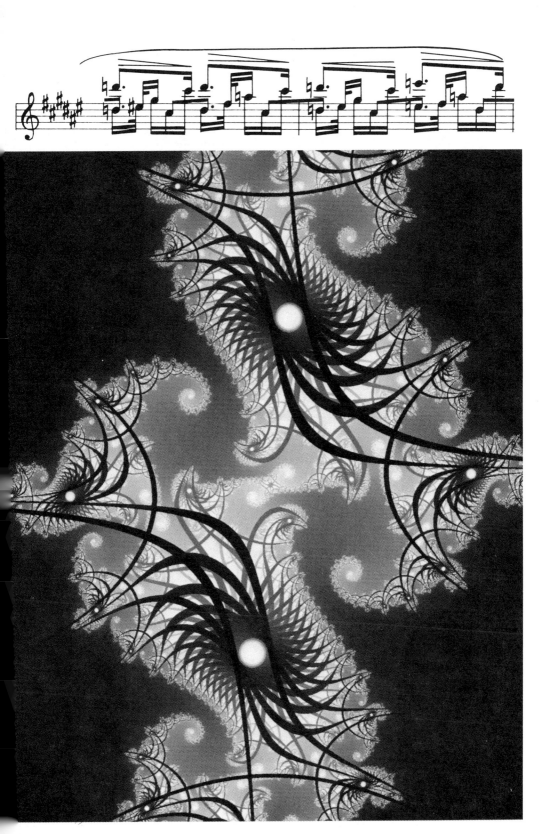

$Z \rightarrow Z^2 + (-0.74543 + 0.11301i)$

Chapter 40

Bach's Impossible Violin

Over the decades unconventional musicians have evoked strange sounds from conventional instruments. For example, American composer John Cage (pictured here), a pupil of such musical giants as Schoenberg and Edgard Varese, com-

posed: random music, silent music, and works for a "prepared piano" with such foreign objects attached to the strings as screws, bolts, rubber bands, bamboo slivers and pins. Perhaps one of the strangest sounds a violin ever produced occurred on a New York stage: the sound of a violin burning. This event was staged by Lamont Young and Charlotte Morrman. Charlotte also played an underwater cello piece called *The Intravenous Feeding of Charlotte Morrman.*

J. S. Bach also played some interesting tricks with violins, illustrated in his musical score (facing page). A violinist can play at most two simultaneous notes. However, the beginning of a ciac-cona by Bach (from his "Sonata IV" for *unaccompanied violin*), calls for several four-note chords! How is this possible? It turns out that these four-note chords can be approximated by playing the notes very quickly in sequence. Also note that starting at the 10th bar (towards the end of the second row of notes) three distinct voices are called for. This is like asking one singer to sing as three different people. A good violinist can simulate this by bowing each note differently in order to give each a different loudness and musical texture. The human ear seems to perceive three different violins because the melodic lines don't have big changes in pitch, and because the pitches don't overlap.[21]

---

[21] (The musical score is from John Pierce's *The Science of Musical Sound.* © 1983 by *Scientific American Books.* Reprinted with permission of W.H. Freeman and Co.)

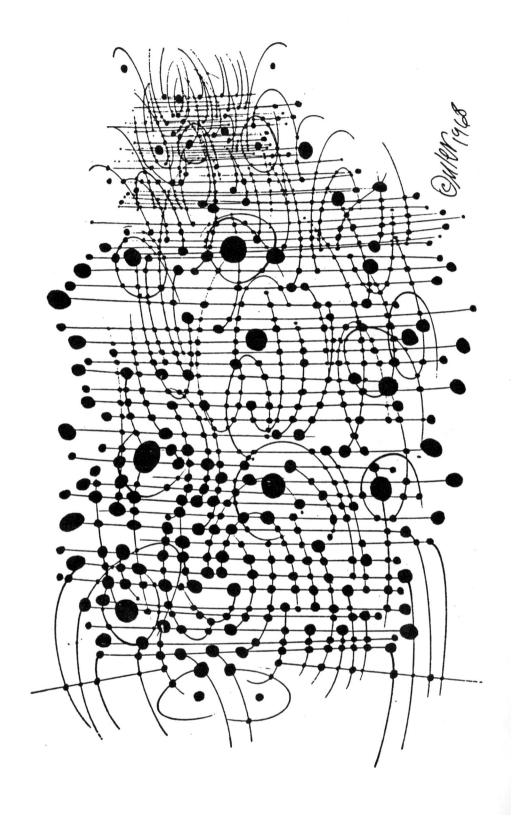

Chapter 41

Interlude: Alien Musical Scores

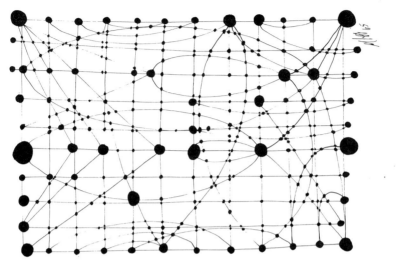

"I am making a plea for anyone truly interested in turning computer graphics into a more serious art form, to study art, history and theory, to go back to the simpler art forms and learn what makes them artistic. Why is a line drawing, made with a pencil, the most elemental of human media, capable of becoming art? This question is not easily answered, but in my opinion it requires considerable study and exposure to great works of art."

Robert Mueller, 1983, *Creative Computing*

Robert Mueller is a visual artist from Roosevelt, New Jersey who paints with oils, does traditional woodcuts and drawings, and sculpts in wood and clay. He also has theorized about electronic media and computer art for many years (see references). My favorite artworks of his are the extremely minimal art forms which he calls *schemas*. His conviction is that significant art can be made using the most elementary media – a conviction confirmed by the history of art. Working within a set of rules, Mueller draws crow-quill black and white images, inspired in part by Picasso illustrations and also by mathematical coordinate plots. The reason he calls these new art forms "schemas" is because they remind him of schematic circuit diagrams. To my eye, they are reminiscent of some beautiful, alien musical scores. Mueller himself says that, in addition to inspiration from the simplicity of Picasso's work, his schemas have musical underpinnings:

How, then, can a simple matrix of black and white lines and dots possibly match the perceptual richness of a flute or violin? If one is tuned into it, a line, by itself, can manifest nervousness, calmness, boldness, tentativeness, and sketchiness, or even humor or sadness.

Prior to studying art, Mueller studied electrical engineering at MIT. He also has a degree in philosophy from NYU. He remarks, "During boring or too abstruse lectures in a higher mathematics class, I found myself day-dreaming over the wonderful plotted curves in textbook tables of functions." To make the schemas, Mueller observes four major constraints:

1. Every junction must be joined with a beadlike dot.
2. All lines must be terminated with a dot or by feathering to a point.
3. Parallelism and repetition must be used frequently.
4. All images must be nonrecognizable.

So visually interesting are his simple schemas that I have scattered them about this book for readers to enjoy and ponder. An entire book could be devoted to the study and development of Mueller's schemas, so I can only touch the surface here. Those readers desiring to learn more should consult the first reference at the end of this chapter. See also Figure 37.5 and the "Preface" for additional schemas.

41.1 For Further Reading

1. Mueller, R. (1991) Schemas: the evolution of a minimal visual art form. *Leonardo*. 24(3): 273-280.
2. Mueller, R. (1983) When is computer art art? *Creative Computing*. January. 136-144.
3. Mueller, R. (1967) *The Science of Art: The Cybernetics of Creative Communication*. Day Publishers.
4. Mueller, R. (1972) Idols of computer art. *Art in America*. May-June: 68-73.

41.2 Cross References

The following sections are concerned with questions regarding whether or not computer-generated art is really good art: "Is Computer Art Really Art?" on page 169, "Are Fractal Graphics Art?" on page 95, and "Interlude: Marking Time" on page 289.

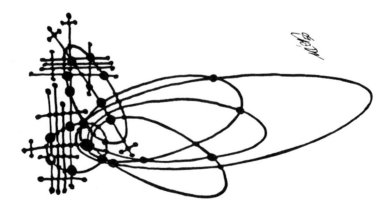

Part IV

SPACE

Chapter 42

How to Stuff An Elephant
Into a 24-Dimensional Sphere

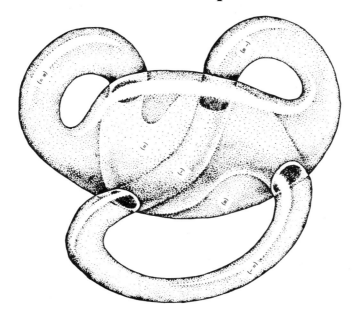

"Even the mathematician would like to nibble the forbidden fruit, to glimpse what it would be like if he could slip for a moment into a fourth dimension."
Kasner and Newman, *Mathematics and the Imagination*

"A man who devoted his life to it could perhaps succeed in picturing himself a fourth dimension."
Henri Poincare

I know of no subject in mathematics that has intrigued both the young and old as much as the idea of a *4th dimension*. For decades, there have been many popular science books and science-fiction novels on this subject. In the early 60's the TV show *The Outer Limits* impressed viewers with a creature from the galaxy Andromeda who lived in a higher dimension than ours. Although the creature is both wise and friendly, its visit to our world causes quite a pandemonium. My favorite short science-fiction story on the subject is Robert Heinlein's *And He Built A Crooked House*, first published in 1940. It tells the tale of a California architect who constructs a 4-dimensional house. He explains that a 4-dimensional house would have certain advantages:

"I'm thinking about a fourth spatial dimension, like length, breadth, and thickness. For economy of materials and convenience of arrangement you couldn't beat it. To say nothing of ground space – you could put an eight-room house on the land now occupied by a one-room house."

Figure 42.1. *African elephants waiting to be stuffed into a 24-dimensional sphere.*

Unfortunately, once the builder takes the new owners on a tour of the house, they can't find their way out. Windows and doors which normally face the outside of the house now face inside. Needless to say some very strange things happen to the poor people trapped in the house.

The fourth dimension need not remain confined to the realm of science-fiction, beyond the range of exciting experiment and careful thought. The following exercises should be accessible to high school students, and computer programmers of all ages. Let me begin by considering the concept of distance in various dimensions, and then gradually work my way up to more sophisticated concepts such as the possibility of stuffing huge African elephants into tiny 24-dimensional spheres (Figure 42.1). Many readers will be familiar with how to compute the distance d between two points (x, y) and (x', y') on a plane:

$$d = \sqrt{(x - x')^2 + (y - y')^2} \tag{42.1}$$

(You can derive this equation by drawing diagrams, and using the Pythogorean theorem which states that the length of the hypotenuse of a right triangle equals the square root of the sum of the squares of the other two sides.) This formula can be extended to compute distance between two points in three dimensions simply by adding another term

$$d = \sqrt{(x - x')^2 + (y - y')^2 + (z - z')^2} \tag{42.2}$$

Similarly, we may extend the previous formula to 4, 5, 6, ... or k dimensions! Various scholars have debated whether humans can truly grasp what a 4-dimensional line and 4-D distance are. Kasner and Neuman remarked in 1940 (the same year that Heinlein published his science-fiction tale about the 4-dimensional house):

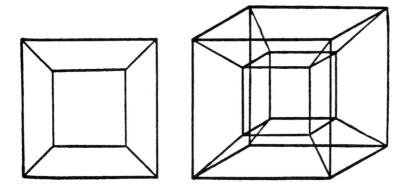

Figure 42.2. *A 4-D analogue of the 3-D cube, called a hypercube or tesseract.*

"Distance in four dimensions means nothing to the layman. Even four-dimensional space is wholly beyond ordinary imagination. But the mathematician is not called upon to struggle with the bounds of imagination, but only with the limitations of his logical faculties."

In order to help visualize the fourth dimension, various graphical representations of four-dimensional figures have been attempted throughout the ages. Figure 42.2 shows a 4-D analogue of the 3-D cube called a *hypercube* or *tesseract*. Figures such as this have been drawn for at least a half a century. Today, mathematicians use computer graphics to visually study the geometrical properties of hypercubes and related 4-D objects. One notable mathematician involved with visualizing the shadowy world of the 4th dimension is Tom Banchoff of Brown University. Banchoff has created several computer graphics movies illustrating the mind-boggling properties of hypercubes and other 4-D objects as they are rotated or enlarged.

42.1 Hyperspheres

"We sail within a vast sphere, ever drifting in uncertainty, driven from end to end."   Pascal

Let's start considering some of the exciting experiments which you can conduct using a pencil and paper or calculator. My favorite 4-dimensional object is not the hypercube but rather its close cousin, the *hypersphere*. Just as a circle of radius r can be define by the equation $x^2 + y^2 = r^2$, and a sphere can be defined by $x^2 + y^2 + z^2 = r^2$, a hypersphere in 4 dimensions can be defined simply by adding a 4th term: $x^2 + y^2 + z^2 + w^2 = r^2$, where w is the 4th dimension! I want to make it easy for you to experiment with the exotic properties of hyperspheres by giving you the equation for their volume. (You can find derivations for the formulas which follow in the Apostol reference.) The formulas will permit you to compute the volume of a sphere of *any* dimension, and you'll find that it's relatively easy to

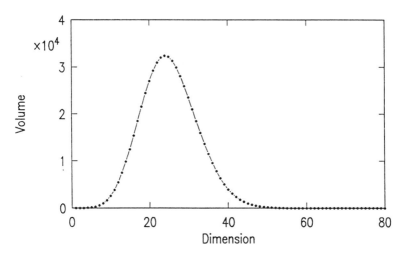

Figure 42.3. *Volume of a radius 2 sphere as a function of dimension.*

implement this formula using a computer or hand calculator. For *even* dimensions, k, the volume of a k-dimensional sphere is

$$V = \frac{\pi^{k/2} r^k}{(k/2)!} \qquad (42.3)$$

The exclamation point is the mathematical symbol for factorial. For example, the volume of a 6-dimensional sphere of radius 1 is $\pi^3/3! = 5.1$. For odd dimensions, the formula is just a bit more intricate:

$$V = \frac{\pi^{(k-1)/2} m! 2^{k+1} r^k}{(k+1)!} \qquad (42.4)$$

where $m = (k+1)/2$.

The formulas are really not too difficult to use. In fact, with these handy formulas, you can compute the volume for a 6-dimensional sphere just as easily as for a 4-dimensional one. Pseudocode 42.1 lists some of the necessary steps used in creating a computer program to evalutate this formula. Figure 42.3 is a plot of the volume of a sphere with radius 2 as a function of dimension. For radius 2 and dimension 2, the previous equations yield the value 12.56, which is the area of a circle. A sphere of radius 2 has a volume of 33.51. A 4-D hypersphere of radius 2 has a volume of 78.95. Intuitively one might think that the volume should continue to rise as the number of dimensions increase. The volume, or perhaps we should use the term "hypervolume," does grow larger and larger until it reaches a maximum – at which point the radius 2 sphere is in the 24th dimension. At dimensions higher than 24, the volume of this sphere begins to decrease gradually to 0 as the value for dimension increases. An 80-dimensional sphere has a volume of only 0.0001. This apparent turn-around point occurs at different dimensions

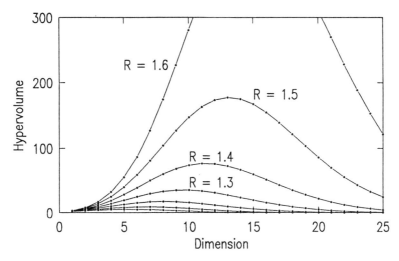

Figure **42.4.** *Volume of k-dimensional spheres for radii of 1, 1.1, 1.2, 1.3, 1.4,1.5, and 1.6.*

depending on the sphere's radius, r. Figure 42.4 illustrates this complicated feature by showing plots of the volume of a k-dimensional sphere for radius 1, 1.1, 1.2, 1.3, 1.4, 1.5, and 1.6 as a function of the dimension. For all the sphere radii

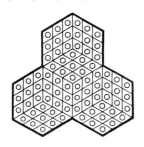

tested, the sphere begins to grown in volume to a point, and then it begins to decline. (Is this true for all radii?) For example, for $r = 1$, the maximum hypervolume occurs in the 5th dimension. For $r = 1.1$ the peak hypervolume occurs in the 7th dimension. For $r = 1.2$, it occurs in the 8th dimension. Here is a great example of how simple graphics, like the illustration in Figure 42.4, help us humans get a grasp of the very non-intuitive results of a hypergeometrical problem! If we examine the equations for volume more closely we notice that this funny behavior shouldn't surprise us too much. The denominator contains a factorial term which grows much more quickly than any power, so we get the curious result that an infinite dimensional sphere has no volume. (In fact, factorials ($n!$) grow faster than powers of 2, the Fibonacci numbers, n^2, and the prime numbers (P_n). They, however, don't grow as fast as coupled exponentials of the form n^n.)

Using the equations for volume given here, you'll find that an 11-dimensional sphere of radius 2 feet is 333,763. Considering that the volume of a brontosaurus is about 100,000 cubic feet, does this mean that the brontosaurus could be crammed into this small 11-dimensional sphere? This amusing thought is just a prelude to the questions which follow.

```
ALGORITHM: Compute the Volume of a 24-Dimensional Ball
pi = 3.1415926; r = 2; k = 24
/* If even dimension: */
IF ((k // 2) = 0) then do
    ans = ((pi ** (k/2.)) * r**k)/factorial(k/2)
END
/* If odd dimension: */
IF ((k // 2) = 1) then do
    m = (k+1)/2; fm = factorial(m); fk = factorial(k+1)
    ans =   (pi**((k-1)/2.)* fm * (2**(k+1))*r**k   ) / fk
END
say k ans
/* A recursive procedure to compute factorial */
factorial: Procedure
    Arg n
    If n=0 Then Return 1
    Return factorial(n-1)*n
```

Pseudocode 42.1. *How To compute the volume of a 24-dimensional ball.* (The program coded here is in the style of the **REXX** language.)

42.2 Stop and Think

> *"She reappeared, looking back at him from her fat flat suspicious face, and Kevin understood the reason why she had disappeared for a moment. It was because the concept of 'a side view' didn't exist in a world where everything was perfectly flat. This is Polaroidsville, he thought with a relief which was strangely mingled with horror."*   Stephen King, *Four Past Midnight*

Now the time has come for considering some really tough questions. If you are a teacher, why not give these to your students to answer.

1. By examining the graph in Figure 42.3 could a 24-dimensional sphere of radius 2 inches contain the volume of an African elephant?

2. Could a 1000-dimensional sphere of radius 2 inches contain the volume of an African elephant, considering that the sphere's hypervolume is very, very close to 0 (Figure 42.3)?

3. Could a circus animal trainer fit an African elephant into an 8-dimensional sphere (of radius 1 inch) as its aperture intersected with our 3-D world?

4. The number of atoms in a human's breath is about 10^{21}. If each atom in the breath were enlarged to the size of a marble, what percentage of a human's breath could fit into a 16-dimensional hypersphere of radius 1.1 inches?

5. What is the value of the 24-dimensional hypervolume of an elephant? To compute this, assume the height of a large African elephant, at the shoulder, is 11.5 feet.

6. What is the one-millionth dimensional hypervolume of the earth? Assume the earth to have a diameter of 4.18×10^7 feet. Also, very roughly approximate

the 4-dimensional hypervolume of Albert Einstein's brain. (The brain of an average adult male weighs 3 lbs 2.2 oz., decreasing gradually to 3 lbs 1.1 oz with advancing age.) The largest synagogue in the world is Temple Emanu-El on Fifth Avenue in New York City. Estimate its hypervolume. (This temple has a frontage of 150 feet on Fifth Avenue and 253 feet on 65th Street. When all its facilities are in use, more than 6000 people can be accommodated.)

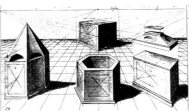

42.3 The Hypervolume of Temple Emanu-El and Related

"Particles that fall into a black hole may pass through a thin tube, or wormhole, and come out somewhere else in the universe. But wormholes occur only in imaginary time."   Stephen Hawking, 1990, *Playboy*

The answers to the previous six questions are: yes, yes, no, 100%, zero, and zero (for all parts of Question 6). To help understand these answers, consider the act of stuffing circular regions of a plane into a sphere. The circular discs are 2-dimensional, and hence have no thickness or volume. Therefore, in theory, you could fit an infinite number of these circles into a sphere – provided that the sphere's radius is slightly bigger than the circle's radius. If the sphere's radius were smaller, even one circle could not fit within the enclosed volume since it would poke out of the volume. Therefore, in answer to question one, the volume of an elephant *could* reside comfortably in a 24-dimensional sphere of radius 2 inches. In fact, an infinite number of elephant volumes could fit in a 24-dimensional sphere. Likewise, in answer to question 2, a 1000-dimensional sphere of radius 2 inches could contain a volume equivalent to that of an elephant. However, you could not physically stuff an elephant into either of these spheres because the elephant has a minimum length which will not permit it to fit. (Consider the example I gave of stuffing a large circle into a small sphere.) An elephant's volume equivalent could be *contained* within the sphere, but to do so would require the elephant to be first put through a meat-grinder which produces pieces no larger than the diameter of the sphere. This therefore answers question 3. Similarly, for question 4, you could fit an infinite number of 3-D marbles into the 16-dimensional sphere mentioned. Finally, just as a circular plate in 2 dimensions has zero thickness, and hence no volume, the elephant, the earth, Temple Emanu-El, and Einstein's brain have no "hypervolume" in higher dimensions.

42.4 Squeezing Einstein's Brain into a 4-Dimensional Sphere

"A sphere, which is as many spheres, solid as a crystal, yet through all its mass flow, as through empty space, music and light... Sphere within sphere; and every space between, peopled with unimaginable shapes, such as ghost dream, dwell in the lampless deep."

Percy Bysshe Shelley, *Prometheis Unbound*

As you will be able to understand from the last section, Einstein's brain should be able to fit into a 4-dimensional sphere with even the most tiny of radii because an infinite volume of 3-D objects can fit into a 4-D hypervolume. However, if the

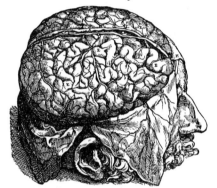

diameter of the sphere were smaller than the brain's maximum length, as with the African elephant, the brain would have to be put through a meat grinder first and fed gradually, sliver by sliver, into the sphere. While on the topic of brains, you may be curious to know that the mammalian brain is an example of an object which seeks to expand its dimension to fulfill its biological purpose. The huge 2-D surface of the brain is intri-

cately folded to fill a 3-D volume in order to increase its surface area. Science fiction writers may wish to ponder the idea of a human whose 3-D brain folds itself in the 4-th dimension to increase its capacity.

For your interest, the heaviest brain ever recorded was that of a 50-year-old man. It weighed 4 lbs. 8.29 oz., more than 1 lb. 7 ozs. heavier than average. Until 1991, serious scientists had believed that there was no correlation between intelligence and human brain size. Now there is evidence of some correlation.[22] Here is another interesting fact: Over the last 100 years, brains have been growing in size! If you examine postmortem records, you'll find that the average male brain weight has increased from 3 lbs. 0.4 oz. in 1860 to 3 lbs. 2.2 oz. today. Similarly with women, a growth from 2 lbs. 11.8 oz. to 2 lbs. 12.6 oz. has occurred, and in recent years women's brains have been growing almost as fast as men's. If brains continued to grow at this rate through the decades, in what year would a man's brain weigh more than 5 lbs?

---

[22] A recent study using magnetic resonance imaging has determined that there may be a size correlation between intelligence and brain size in humans. This first study to address this issue by examining the brains of normal, living subjects, was conducted in 1991. Previous answers have been ambiguous because researchers did postmortem studies of brains which shrink with age. Lee Willerman of the University of Texas at Austin has found that High-IQ college students have bigger brains. For more information, see the December 13, 1991 issue of *Science*, volume 254, page 1584, "Brains: Is Bigger Better?"

42.5 Marbles and Worms

This section lists some questions which only the most imaginative of readers will wish to consider. For example, if you were to slam and crack a 24-dimensional marble with your 3-D hammer, will the broken pieces all be 24-dimensional? Could you, in fact, break a 24-dimensional marble with a 3-D hammer?

A 3-D earthworm is burrowing thought the soil and encounters a 5-dimensional hypersphere, and sticks its head into it. Half its body is inside the sphere, and half its body is outside. Will this cause any disruption to the skin of the worm's body. Will the worm feel a difference?

You and your 3-D friend are in a 4-D sphere. Your friend's body is displaced from you along the 4th dimension. Is there any way you could see her or hear her speak? If you are a teacher, have your students dream up imaginative uses for a 4-D sphere, such as its use as an efficient waste disposal unit.

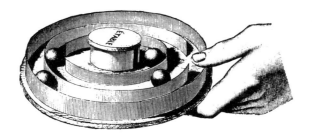

42.6 Student Exercises: Fractal Hyperspheres and More

Now that your mind has been stretched to its limit, I leave you with some more down-to-earth (yet interesting) graphics exercises.

1. A good student exercise is to draw a graph of $y = a^n/n!$ for a fixed a. You'll see the same kind of increase in y followed by a decrease as you do for hyperspheres.

2. Draw a 3-D plot showing the relationship between sphere hypervolume, dimension, and radius.

3. Plot the *ratio* of the volume of a k-dimensional hypersphere to the volume of a k-dimensional cube which encloses it, as a function of k. (Note that a box with an 2-inch long edge will contain a ball of radius 1 inch. Therefore, for this case, the box's hypervolume is simply 2^k.)

4. Plot the ratio of the volumes of the $(k+1)$-th dimensional sphere to the kth dimensional sphere for a given radius, r.

5. For more technical readers, compute the hypervolume of a fractal hypersphere of dimension 4.5. To compute factorials for non-integers, you'll have to use a mathematical function called the "gamma function." The even and odd formulas given in this chapter yield the same results by interpreting $k! = \Gamma(k + 1)$.

6. The surface area of an k-dimensional sphere is given by:

$$\frac{2\pi^{k/2}r^k}{(k/2)!} \tag{42.5}$$

(For odd values of k, you must use the gamma function as in the previous question.) How does surface area change as you increase the dimension k?

42.7 Other Dimensions and Superstrings

Scientists and philosophers still debate about the possibility that there really exists an observable 4th spatial dimension. In the same way that the two-dimen-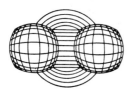sional surface of the Earth is finite but unbounded (because it is bent in 3-D into the shape of a sphere), many have imagined the 3-D space of our universe as being bent, in some 4-D space, into the shape of a hypersphere. In the past, however, there has been much skepticism on this subject. Martin Gardner, in his book *Mathematical Carnival*, stoically remarked:

> Is it possible for the human brain to visualize four-dimensional structures? The 19th-century German physicist Hermann von Helmotz argued that it is, provided the brain is given the proper input data. Unfortunately our experience is confined to three-space and there is not the slightest scientific evidence that four-space actually exists.

Since the time Gardner wrote this statement, there has been considerable research by Edward Witten, and others, in *superstring theory* which suggests that all physical phenomena arise from infinitesimal strings wriggling in no fewer than 10 dimensions.

As techically advanced as superstring theory sounds, superstring theory could have been developed a long time ago. This is according to Witten, a 40-year old theoretical physicist at the Institute for Advanced Study in Princeton. For example, he indicates that it is quite likely that other civilizations in the universe discovered superstring theory, and then later they derived Einstein-like formulations (which in our world predate string theory by more than half a century). Unfortunately for experimentalists, superstrings are so small that they are not likely be to be ever detectable by humans. If you consider the ratio of the size of a proton to the size of the solar system, this is the same ratio that describes the relative size of a superstring to a proton.

John Horgan, an editor at *Scientific American* wrote an article describing what other researchers have said of Witten and superstrings in 10 dimensions. For example, one researcher exclaimed that in sheer mathematical mind power, Witten exceeds Einstein and has no rival since Newton. When a Nobel Prizewining physicist was asked to comment on the importance of Witten's work, he said that he could not understand Witten's recent papers; therefore, he could not ascertain how brilliant Witten is.

42.8 Sparticles and 26-D Superstrings

"What we've learned in the 20th century is that the great ideas in physics have geometric foundations."   Edward Witten, 1991 *Scientific American*

I'll leave you with some other higher dimensional ideas which modern physicists have considered in the past, or are currently considering in the 1990s:

• Recent Kaluza-Klein theory (named after two European scientists) suggests the existence of additional dimensions that are rolled up or "compactified" in such a way that they are undetectable at macroscopic levels.

• Gabriele Veneziano, in the late 1960s, worked on string theories. However, interest in his particular version of the theory faded when other physicists showed they would only work in 26 dimensions!

• Some researchers believe that all known elementary particles have unseen symmetric twins called *sparticles*.

42.9 Fact File

42.9.1 Hyperbeings Look in Our Intestines

"What can hyperbeings do, and why do their acts initially seem so alien to us?"   Theoni Pappas, *More Joy of Mathematics*

Theoni Pappas in *More Joy of Mathematics* discusses *hyperbeings* who can demonstrate the kinds of phenomena that occur in hyperspace. For example, a  hyperbeing can effortlessly remove things before our very eyes, giving us the impression that the objects simply disappeared. This is like a 3-D creature's ability to remove a piece of dirt inside a circle drawn on a page without cutting the circle. The hyperbeing can also see inside any 3-D object or life form, and if necessary remove anything from inside. The being can look inside our intestines, or remove a tumor from our brain without ever cutting through the skin. A pair of gloves can be easily transformed into two left or two right gloves. And 3-D knots fall apart in the hands of a hyperbeing, much as a 2-D knot (a loop of string lying on a plane) can easily be undone by a 3-D being simply by lifting the end of the loop up into the third dimension.

42.9.2 Hyperdimensional Knights

Chess is essentially a 2-D game where pieces slide along the surface of the checkerboard plane. They usually can't jump up into the third dimension to get around one another. The Knight, however, is a hyperdimensional being (see previous paragraph) because it can leave the playing board plane to jump over other pieces in its way. Are there other hyperdimensional chess pieces? I once played a truly 2-D

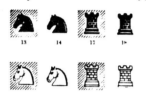

game where Knights could not leave the plane to get over other pieces. Try it. How does this affect the game? Could a world chess master constrained to using 2-D Knights defeat a good player using standard hyperdimenional Knights? What would have been the outcome for the game played between chess champions Herman Steiner and George Treysman in Chicago, 1937, if Steiner had a hyperdimensional *Rook* that could jump over other pieces? (See "Miraculous Chess Solutions" on page 311 and "Knights in Hell" on page 321 for more information on odd chess technologies and puzzles. See "Chess Music" on page 204 for music from chess.)

42.9.3 Where are Einstein's Children?

Have you ever wondered if Albert Einstein had children, and if so, what became of them? I was able to track down specific information regarding one of his sons from a book published in 1991. Hans Albert Einstein (1904-1973) was the first of Albert Eintstein's two sons. He was educated in Zurich, became a hydraulic engineer, and joined the faculty of the University of California at Berkeley in 1947. In 1959 he married his second wife, neurochemist Elizabeth Roboz. (Source: Roboz-Einstein, E. (1991) *Hans Albert Einstein: Reminiscences of His Life and Our Life Together*. Iowa Institute of Hydraulic Research: University of Iowa: Iowa City. 112 pp., $12.50.)

42.9.4 Rubik's Tesseract!

Many of you will be familiar with Ernö Rubik's ingenious cubical puzzle and its variations which include a 4x4x4x4 cube and puzzles shaped like tetrahedra. One natural variation that never appeared on toy store shelves is the 4-D version of Rubik's cube – Rubik's tesseract. Dan Velleman (Amherst College) discusses the 3x3x3x3 Rubik's tesseract in the February 1992 issue (v. 65(1): 27) of *Mathematics Magazine*. Many of his findings were discovered with the aid of a colorful simulation on a Macintosh computer. Velleman remarks, "Of course, the tesseract is somewhat harder to work with than the cube, since we can't build a physical model and experiment with it." Those of you interested in pursuing the details of this mind-shattering tesseract should consult his paper.

42.10 For Further Reading

1. Apostol, T. (1969) *Calculus, Volume II, 2nd. Edition* Wiley, New York.

2. Pappas, T. (1990) *More Joy of Mathematics.* Wide World Publishing/Tetra, P.O. Box 476, San Carlos, CA 94070.

3. Kasner, E., Newman, R. (1989) *Mathematics and the Imagination.* Tempus: New York. (A reprint of the 1940 edition.)

4. Gardner, M. (1965) *Mathematical Carnival.* Vintage: NY.

5. Heinlein, R. (1940) And he built a crooked house. In *Fantasia Mathematica*, Fadiman, C. ed. Simon & Schuster, NY (1958).

6. Cramer, J. (1989) *Twistor.* William Morrow: New York. (Cramer is a Professor of Physics at the University of Washington. The protagonists in the book, a male postdoc and a female graduate student working in the University of Washington Physics Department, are conducting an experiment which uses a rather peculiar configuration of electromagnetic fields that rotates normal matter into shadow matter (predicted by string theory), and vice versa, rather like rotating a stage where one set is replaced by another. The first time this happens, a spherical volume containing a lot of expensive equipment disappears. Subsequently, the postdoc and two small children are "rotated" to a shadow-matter Earth and trapped inside a huge tree, and an enormous sphere replaces them in the middle of their laboratory in Seattle.)

7. Lowry, E. (1963) The clock paradox. *American Journal of Physics.* 31: 59.

8. Banchoff, T. (1990) *Beyond the Third Dimension: Geometry and Computer Graphics and Higher Dimensions.* Freeman, NY (Answers questions such as: where is the fourth dimension? Does it exist? How do we get there? What does an object in the fourth dimension look like?)

9. Horgan, J. (1991) The Pied Piper of superstrings. *Scientific American.* Nov 265(5): 42-44.

10. Dewdney, A. (1984) *The Planiverse: Computer Contact with a Two-Dimensional World.* Poseidon: NY.

42.11 Credit

The twisted bottle at the beginning of this chapter is courtesy of artists/writer Paul Ryan of the Earth Environmental Group. For more details on this shape, see: Ryan, P. (1991) The earthscore notational system for orchestrating perceptual consensus about the natural world. *Leonardo.* 24(4): 457-465 (Pergamon Press). The drawing was done by Gary Allen. The bottle object is called a relational circuit.

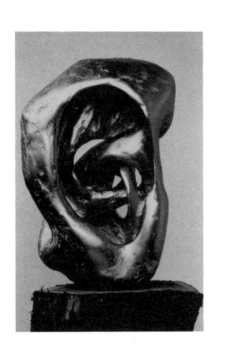

Chapter 43

Interlude: Tortured Surfaces

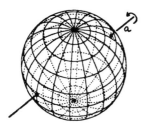 

In the 1990s, there are several internationally famous sculptors inspired by pure mathematics. One notable example is German mathematician Benno Artmann who creates mathematically inspired plaster sculptures as a way of conveying the beauty of intricate geometrical surfaces. The surfaces he chooses for his sculptures are not the simple saddles and parabaloids you may have seen in introductory geometry books, but rather the tortured, twisted (yet beautiful) surfaces lurking in the field of geometrical topology.

Artmann studied physics and mathematics at the universities of Tübingen, Göttingen, and Glessen where he received his Ph.D. in 1965. Today he is a Professor at the Technical University of Darmstadt. His interests include: "Hjelmslev's natural geometry, mathematical education, and the history of Greek mathematics." One of my favorite scholarly papers of Artmann's is his "Mathematical Motifs on Greek Coins," published in 1990. In this article Artmann attempts to fill in some of the gaps in our knowledge of the history of pre-Euclid Greek mathematics by presenting readers with discussions of mathematical images on ancient Greek coins.

Presented facing this page are photographs of three of Artmann's plaster models. His sculptures usually have rather long names, for example: "Heegaard-Zerlegung der 3-Sphäre in zwei Vollbrezeln." Artmann may be reached at: Prof. Dr. B. Artmann, Technische Hochschule Darmstadt, Fachbereich Mathematik, 6100 Darmstadt, Schlossgartenstr. 7, Germany.

43.1 For Further Reading

1. Artmann, B. (1990) Mathematical motifs on Greek coins. *The Mathematical Intelligencer.* 12(4): 43.

2. Pinkall, U., and Sterling, I. (1987) Willmore surfaces. *The Mathematical Intelligencer.* 9(2): 38. (Contains many unusual computer graphics diagrams of geometrical surfaces.)

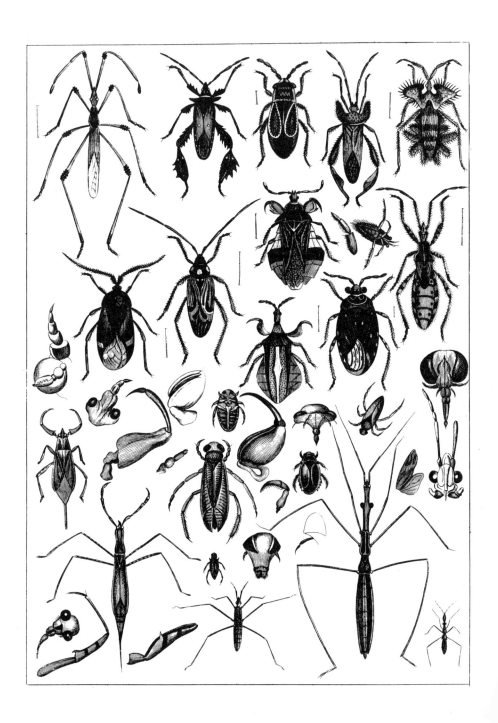

Chapter 44

Caged Siphonaptera (Fleas) in Hyperspace

"He showed me a little thing, the quantity of a hazelnut, in the palm of my hand, and it was round as a ball. I looked thereupon with the eye of my understanding and thought: What may this be? And it was answered generally thus: It is all that is made."   Julian of Norwich, 14th C

Many of you have probably seen simple-looking geometrical puzzles which require you to estimate the number of overlapping triangles within a diagram such as the one below:

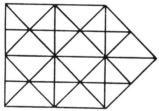

This figure contains 87 triangles. Can you count the number of triangles in the following, more difficult diagram?

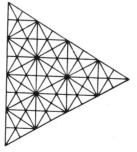

Actually, this second figure will consume too much of your time; let me give you the answer (653 triangles) so that you will be free to ponder the more interesting enigmas which follow. Why not give these two triangle puzzles to a friend to ponder?

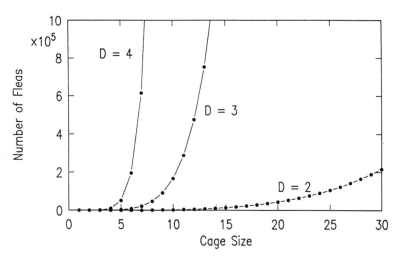

Figure 44.1. *Fleas.* Shown here is the number of fleas containable by a lattice cage assembly of "size" n in 2-D, 3-D, and 4-D.

My favorite puzzles are of a similar geometrical variety, and I call them "flea cages" or "insect cages" for reasons you will soon understand. I enjoy these flea cages because they are simpler to analyze than the triangle figures. Also, since the figures consist of a network of perpendicular lines, they are much easier for you (or your computer program) to draw. Consider a lattice of 4 squares which form one large square:

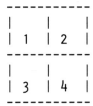

How many rectangles and squares are in this picture? Think about this for a minute. There are the 4 small squares marked "1," "2," "3," and "4," plus 2 horizontal rectangles containing "1 and 2" and "3 and 4," plus 2 vertical rectangles, plus the 1 large surrounding border square. Altogether, therefore, there are nine 4-sided overlapping areas. The lattice number for a 2x2 lattice is therefore 9, or $L(2) = 9$. What is $L(3)$, $L(4)$, $L(5)$, and $L(n)$? It turns out that these lattice numbers grow very quickly, but you might be surprised to realize just how quickly... The formula describing this growth is fairly simple for an $n \times n$ lattice: $L(n) = n^2(n + 1)^2/4$. The sequence goes 1, 9, 36, 100, 225, 441 ... For a long time, I've liked to think of the squares and rectangles (quadrilaterals) as little containers or cages in order to make interesting analogies about how the sequence grows. For example, if each quadrilateral were considered a cage which contained a tiny flea, how big a lattice would be needed to cage one representative for each

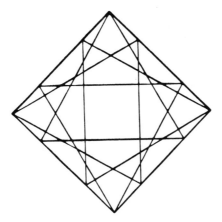

Figure 44.2. *Pattern of lines.* Is this a random jumble of lines? What patterns do you see? See text for details.

different variety of flea (Siphonaptera) on earth? To solve this, consider that

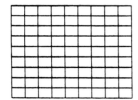

Siphonapterologists recognize 1,830 varieties of fleas. Using the equation I have just given you, you can compute that a small 9x9 lattice (at left) could contain 2025 different varieties, easily large enough to contain all varieties of fleas. (For Siphonaptera lovers, the largest known flea was found in the nest of a mountain beaver in Washington in 1913. Its scientific name is *Hystirchopsylla schefferi*, and it measures up to 0.31 inches in length, about the diameter of a pencil).

It is possible to compute the number of cage assemblies for 3-D cage assemblies as well. The formula is: $L(n) = ((n^3)(n + 1)^3)/8$. The first few cage numbers for this sequence are: 1, 27, 216, 1000, 3375. Tim Greer of Endicott New York has generalized the formula to hyperspace cages of any dimension, m, as $L(n) = ((n^m)(n + 1)^m)/(2^m)$. Let's spend some time examining 3-D cages before moving on to the cages in higher dimensions.

44.1 Various Zoos

How large a 3-D cage assembly would you need to contain all the species of insects on earth today? (To solve this, consider that there may be as many as 30 million species of insect, which is more than all other phyla and classes put together). Think of this as a zoo where one member of each insect species is placed in each 3-D quadrilateral. It turns out that all you need is a 25x25x25 ($n = 25$) lattice to create this insect zoo for 30 million species.

In order to contain the approximately 5 billion people on earth today, you would need a 59x59x59 cage zoo (see Figure 44.3). You would only need a

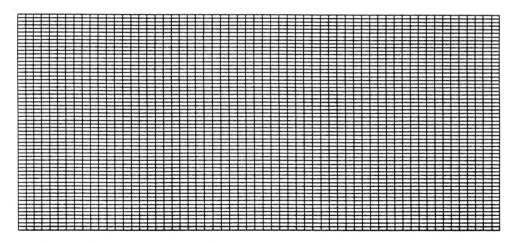

Figure 44.3. *A cage containing all humanity.* In order to contain the approximately 5 billion people on earth today, you would need a 59x59x59 cage zoo, the front face of which is shown here. You would only need a 40x40x40 (*n* = 40) zoo to contain the 460 million humans on earth in the year 1500.

40x40x40 (*n* = 40) zoo to contain the 460 million humans on earth in the year 1500.

Here is a table listing the size of the cages needed to contain various large numbers, assuming that each quadrilateral contains a single unit of whatever is listed (e.g pills, objects, stars, or colors):

1. Largest number of objects found in a person's stomach:
    2,533 (5x5x5 cage)[23]

2. Number of different colors distinguishable by the human eye:
    10 million (21x21x21 cage)

3. Number of Stars in the Milky Way galaxy:
    10^{12} (141x141x141 cage)

44.2 4-Dimensional Cages

Let's conclude by examining the cage assemblies for fleas in higher dimensions. I've all ready given you the formula for doing this, and it stretches the mind to consider just how many caged fleas a hypercage could contain, with one flea resident in each hypercube or hypertangle.

The following are the sizes of hypercages needed to house the 1,830 flea varieties I mentioned earlier in different dimensions:

---

[23] This number comes from a case involving an insane female who at the age of 42 swallowed 2,533 objects including 947 bent pins.

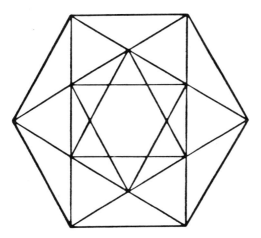

Figure 44.4. *Stars within stars.* How many triangles do you count? See text for details.

Dimension (m)	Size of Lattice (n)
2	9
3	5
4	4
5	3
6	3
7	2

This means that a small $n = 2$, 7-dimensional lattice (2x2x2x2x2x2x2) can hold the 1,830 varieties of fleas! An $n = 9$ hyperlattice in the 50th dimension can hold each electron, proton, and neutron in the universe (each particle in its own cage). Figure 44.1 shows the number of fleas containable by a lattice cage assembly of "size" n in 2-D, 3-D, and 4-D. For example, the lower right most point indicates a little more than 2×10^5 fleas can be contained in a 30x30 lattice.

44.3 Stop and Think: Coney Island, The Ice Age, Etc.

1. If each cage region were to contain a single snow crystal, what size lattice would you need to hold the number of snow crystals necessary to form the ice age, which has been estimated to be 10^{30} crystals? If you were to draw this lattice, how big a piece of paper would you need? Provide answers to this question for 2- and 3-dimensional figures.

2. If each cage region contained a single grain of sand, what size lattice would you need to hold the number of sand grains contained on the Coney Island beach, which has been estimated to be 10^{20} grains? If you were to draw this lattice, how big a piece of paper would you need? Also provide answers to this question for a hyperlattice in the 4th dimension.

3. A. Lakhtakia has noted that the lattice numbers $L(n)$ can be computed from triangular numbers $(T_n)^m$. Why should the number of cage assemblies be related to triangular numbers?[24]

4. The puzzle diagrammed in Figure 44.2 may first appear to be just a random jumble of lines, but if you look closely there are some interesting symmetries. I made this figure by placing 4 equilateral triangles of the largest possible size within the square with one point in each of the square's corners. (Can you have your computer draw this?) For the following two questions consider the lower left hand corner and upper right hand corner to be located at (0,0) and (1,1), respectively. What are the coordinates of the vertices where the triangles intersect the square? Can you draw the 3-D analog of this figure using triangular pyramids within a cube? Where would the coordinates of the triangular vertices in the 3-D model be located? (Can you have your computer draw this?)

5. In order to create the puzzle in Figure 44.4 I have divided a hexagon into nested stars. (Can you have your computer draw this?) This figure shows two nested stars. Therefore the nesting level, n, is 2. Hard as it may be to believe, there are 69 different overlapping triangles in this figure. Is it possible to develop a formula that gives the number of triangles as a function of the nesting level, n?

44.4 The Ways of Coprophiles

As mentioned earlier in this chapter, Siphonapterologists recognize 1,830 variety of fleas. How does this compare with other insects? Incredible as it may seem, there are around 300,000 species of beetles, making beetles one of the most diverse groups of organisms on earth. When biologist J.B.S. Haldane was asked by a religious person what message the Lord conveyed through His creations, he responded, "An inordinate fondness for beetles."

One of the most interesting books on beetles is *Dung Beetle Ecology* which was favorably reviewed in the November 8th issue of *Science Magazine*. Here are some intriguing facts about dung beetles from this review:

• A large number (about 7000 species) of the 300,000 species of beetles live off animal dung.

• Animal dung is often fiercely contested. On the African savanna up to 4000 beetles have been observed to converge on 500 grams of fresh elephant dung within 15 minutes after it is deposited.

• Some dung beetles fashion dung into balls and roll it away for burial. The dung-ball rollers (genus *Sisyphus*) were held sacred and immortalized by the

---

[24] The numbers 1, 3, 6, 10, ... are called triangular numbers because they are the number of dots employed in making successive triangular arrays of dots. The process is started with one dot, and successive rows of dots are placed beneath the first dot. Each row has one more dot than the preceding one.

ancient Egyptians. For these beetles, the completed dung ball is waved around as a sexual display and courtship attractor.

• *Kleptoparastic beetle* is the scientific term for a dung beetle which steals dung from others.

• African dung beetles bury one metric ton of dung per hectare per year.

• Dozens of species have been imported to Australia to handle the dung of cattle which could not be effectively handled by the native species.

• Insect dung communities involve hundreds of complex ecological interactions between coprophagous flies and their parasites, insects, mites, and nematodes.

• In South Africa, more than 100 species of dung beetle occur together in a single cow pat. One gigantic species, *Heliocopris dilloni*, resides exclusively in elephant dung. A few species of beetles are so specialized that they live close to the source of dung, in the hairs near an animal's anus.

44.5 For Further Reading

1. Heinrich, B. (1991) The ways of coprophiles. *Science*. 254(5033): 878-879.
2. Hanski, I., Cambefort, Y. (1991) *Dung Beetle Ecology*. Princeton University Press: NJ. 481 pp., illus. $60.00.

29.

Chapter 45

Squashed Worlds That Pack Infinity into a Cube

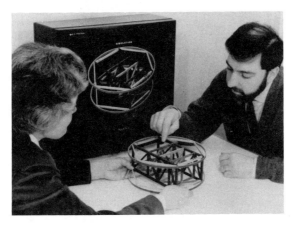

"Such as say that things infinite are past God's knowledge may just as well leap headlong into this pit of impiety, and say that God knows not all numbers. ... What are we man wretches that dare presume to limit His Knowledge."
St. Augustine

"There was from the very beginning no need for a struggle between the finite and infinite. The peace we are so eagerly seeking has been there all the time."
D. T. Suzuki

The concept of infinity has challenged humans for centuries. For example, Zeno (an Eleatic philosopher living in the 5th Century B.C.) posed a famous paradox involving infinity. The paradox seemed to imply that you can never leave the room you are in. As Zeno reasoned, in order to reach the door you must first travel half the distance there. Once you get to the half-way point, you must still traverse the remaining distance. You need to continue to half the remaining distance. The procedure can be repeated as diagrammed below:

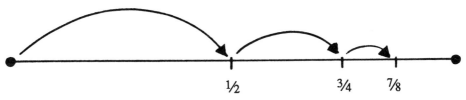

½   ¾   ⅞

If you were to jump 1/2 the distance, then 1/4 the distance, then an 1/8 of the distance, and so on, will you reach the door? Not in a finite number of jumps! In

1.41421356237309504880168872420969807856967187537694807317667973799073247846
1070388503875343276415727350138462309122970249248360558507372126441214970999
3583141322266592750559275579995050115278206057147010955997160597027453459686
2014728517418640889198609552329230484308714321450839762603627995251407989687
2533965463318088296406206152583523950547457502877599617298355752203375318570
1135437460340849884716038689997069900481503054402779031645424782306849293691
8621580578463111596668713013015618568987237235288509264861249497715421833420
4285686060146824720771435854874155657069677653720226485447015858801620758474
9226572260020855844665214583988939443709265918003113882464681570826301005948
5870400318648034219489727829064104507263688131373985525611732204024509122770
0226941125753627280495738108967504018369868368450725799364729060762996694138
0475654823728997180326802474420629269124859052181004459842150591120249441341
7285314781058036033710773091828693147101711116839165817268894197587165821521
2822951848847

Figure 45.1. *Why Hippasus died.*

fact, if you kept jumping forever at a rate of 1 jump per second until you are out the door, you will jump forever. Mathematically one can represent this limit of an infinite sequence of actions as the sum of the series $(1/2 + 1/4 + 1/8 + ...)$ The modern tendency is to resolve Zeno's paradox by insisting that the sum of this infinite series $1/2 + 1/4 + 1/8$ is *equal* to 1. Since each step is done in half as much time, the actual time to complete the infinite series is no different than the real time required to leave the room.[25] Many Greeks, however, could not accept the existence of infinity. In fact, when one of Pythagoras' disciples, Hippasus, found that $\sqrt{2}$ was irrational[26] (Figure 44.1), they killed him, for his colleagues could not accept this infinitely long, non-repeating number. However, other Greek

philosophers, when learning that the square root of 2 was not a rational number celebrated the discovery by sacrificing 100 oxen. (Weren't humans more passionate about mathematics in those days?)

In the October 1991 issue of *Omni*, Dave Jaffe wrote on Zeno's paradox, and I thought you would like to hear his amusing solution to the paradox, excerpted from his upcoming anthology of brainteasers titled *Mathematical Games That Could Not be Solved by People Who Claim They Have High IQs*:

---

[25] One easy way to compute the sum of this series is to use the formula $y = 1 - 2^{-n}$, which gives the sum of the first *n* terms. For $n = 10$, $y = 0.99902$.

[26] An irrational number cannot be expressed as a ratio of two integers. Transcendental numbers like $e = 2.718...$ and $\pi = 3.1415...$ and all *surds* (e.g. $\sqrt{2}$, cube roots, etc.) are irrational.

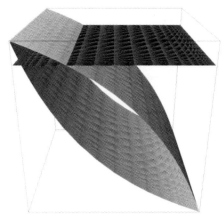

Figure 45.2. *In Zenograms, diagonal parallel planes warp and meet at infinity.* Horizontal planes remain flat.

Aristotle challenged Achilles to run a footrace with a tortoise. The tortoise would start the race at a point half the distance to the finish line. By the time Achilles reached that point the tortoise would have covered another half distance to the finish. And so it would go, Aristotle smirked, with Achilles forever closing on the tortoise but never catching it.

  Achilles thought long and hard, then asked the philosopher, "Uh, what if I stab it? ... I got a sharp spear. Cuts through turtle shell easy."

With this short introduction to infinity during the time of the Greeks, let's move on to an interesting graphical way of drawing infinitely growing mathematical formulas with the method outlined in the following. You can compress all of mathematical space from $-\infty$ to $+\infty$ into a cube bounded by -1 and +1. One way to do this makes use of the hyperbolic tangent function

$$\tanh x = \frac{e^x - e^{-x}}{e^x + e^{-x}} \tag{45.1}$$

At left is a diagram representing the behavior of this function. I call the resulting

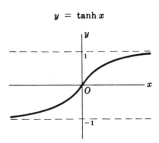

representation a Zenogram, after the ancient philosopher who studied various properties of infinity. My graphics program, called Zenospace, allows you to explore this strange squashed world using advanced computer graphics. No matter how large your numbers are, the tanh function can only return a maximum value of positive 1 (or a minimum value of minus 1). Here are some observations on this weird space. In the Zenogram, infinite diagonal parallel planes begin to curve, and meet at infinity (the sides of the box in Figure 45.2). Horizontal or vertical planes perpendicular to the x, y or z, axes will not curve. Paraboloids ($z = x^n + y^n$, $n = 2$) become squashed in interesting ways as they near the side of the box (Figure 45.3). (What happens as you

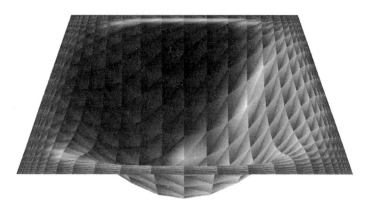

Figure 45.3. *In a Zenogram, a squashed paraboloid rises to infinity.*

increase *n*?) Spheres deform in interesting ways as they grow larger or are pushed towards the sides of the bounding box. As you push the sphere up, it flattens like a pancake. As you increase the radius of the sphere it begins to look cube-like. What would happen to a model of a human body as it walked around in zenospace? What would you see if you flew in an airplane in zenospace? If you are interested in other approaches to squashing coordinate systems for 2-D worlds, see Gibilisco's *Reaching for Infinity* (1990, Tab Books, PA).

"I looked round the trees. The thin net of reality. These trees, this sun. I was infinitely far from home. The profoundest distances are never geographical." – John Fowles, *The Magus*

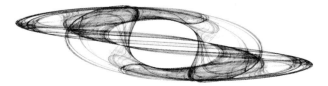

```
ALGORITHM: How to Compute Sqrt(2) to Many Decimal Places

/* accuracy is the number of digits */
accuracy = 100
x = 2
epsilon = x/10E'accuracy
guess = 1
do count=1 by 1 until(abs(old-guess) <= epsilon)
   old = guess
   guess = .5 * (x/guess + guess)
   end
Print "The square root of x is" guess.
```

Pseudocode 45.1. *How to compute sqrt(2) to many decimal places.* (The program coded here is in the style of the REXX language.)

Chapter 46

Bacon, the Mini-Oos

"The pi machine prints the digits of pi in a surreal typeface where every digit is half as wide as its predecessor. The complete printout fits on an index card, but not even the most powerful electron microscope will reveal the last digit." William Poundstone, 1988, *Labyrinths of Reason*

The following fictional story is included to stimulate your imagination regarding infinite geometric progressions and spaces. The story deals with rapidly multiplying creatures confined within a small glass dish. A few tables of numbers and program outlines will permit some of you to experiment with the behavior of these societies of organisms using a computer or pocket calculator, although you can just as easily appreciate the paradoxical and weird history of the tiny civilization that evolved in a laboratory dish without any computations.

Professor David Mutcer grinned as he gazed into the glass petri dish which rested on the wooden desk in his dimly lit bedroom. He had developed intelligent lifeforms, each about the size of a thumbnail, named *Oos*. (The term "Oos" is both the singular and plural form of the noun, and it rhymes with the word "moose.") These emerald-colored Oos exhibited a variety of shapes, and subsisted quite well on the limited amount of thick nutrient gel which lined the bottom of their glass enclosure. The two original Oos, named Dakota and Dextrose (at least that was as close as Dr. Mutcer could come to pronouncing their names) begat two smaller Oos named Dirigible and Dirk. Dirk and Dextrose begat Deli, Doornob, and Data. Data and Dirk begat Dante, Deer, Demeter, Diphenyl and Deliquesent. Dr. Mutcer faithfully recorded the genealogy of Oos in a large bound book he kept on the shelf in his private laboratory. Since the petri dish enclosed only a limited amount of space, each generation tended to become smaller and smaller in body size – an interesting example of the inheritance of acquired characteristics. On this particular day, the newest and tiniest Oos, son of Dante and Doobie, was born. His name was Bacon. Bacon was a cheerful chap, about the size of a dust speck.

Individual Length	Total Length
0.5	0.5
0.25	0.75
0.125	0.875
0.0625	0.9375
0.03125	0.96875
0.015625	0.984375
0.0078125	0.9921875
0.00390625	0.99609375
0.001953125	0.998046875
0.0009765625	0.999023438
0.00048828125	0.999511719
0.000244140625	0.999755860
0.0000305175783	0.999969483

Figure 46.1. *Oos miniaturization through time.* Assuming that a progenitor Oos were about 0.5 inches in length, and that a child's length were half of the parent's, this table gives a feel for the length of a child in each successive generation (Column 1), and the total (summed) length of Oos lined up in a row as a function of generation (Column 2). (For simplicity, Column 2 assumes that one child is produced in each generation.) What is the size of an Oos in the 5th generation if each child's length were three-fourths the parent's, rather than one-half?

46.1 Intergenerational Incest

Dr. Mutcer observed many characteristics of Oos society which were interesting to his visitors and friends. As one example, Dr. Mutcer frequently asked inquisitive guests to speculate on a society where *your great-great-great grandmother still lived but was about a hundred times your size.*

The Oos society was of necessity incestuous, particularly during the auspicious reign of the two thumbnail-sized progenitors, Dakota and Dextrose. As the number of Oos in each succeeding generation increased geometrically, mating between more distant cousins became possible, and, as in human cultures, was encouraged over brother-sister matings. Intergenerational incest, however, was rare because of size discrepancies. The only factor that limited a romantic rendezvous was in fact *body size*, since, as Dr. Mutcer was quick to point out, it was a little difficult to mate in a physically satisfying way with someone fifty times your size. Mutcer also often pondered: wouldn't there tend to develop some sort of hierarchy, either religious or governmental, based solely on size? Would society be responsible for the well being of its members which it could not see? Would such a question be meaningless since there might be no way to protect invisible members? And what about war? Could war exist in such a heterogeneous society?

Would different subsets of the population, because of size, develop their own separate societies, religion, and laws? Would little Bacon even believe that indi-

Individual Area	Total Area
0.25	0.25
0.015625	0.265625
0.00006103515625	0.26568603515625
0.00000000093132257461547851562 5	0.26568603608757257461547851 5
0.00000000000000000021684043449 7	0.26568603608757257483231895 0
1.1754943508222875079687365372 2E-38	0.2656860360875725748323189501 22
3.4544674220377778501545407451 1E-77	0.2656860360875725748323189501 22
2.9833362924800826973163861261 8E-154	0.2656860360875725748323189501 22
2.2250738585072013830902327173 2E-308	0.2656860360875725748323189501 22
1.2377384189530313101920733479 7E-616	0.2656860360875725748323189501 22
3.8299909843808741431786924048 0E-1233	0.2656860360875725748323189501 22
3.6672077351096943312428247838 8E-2466	0.2656860360875725748323189501 22
3.3621031431120935062626778169 2E-4932	0.2656860360875725748323189501 22
2.8259343862310545771109608744 7E-9864	0.2656860360875725748323189501 22
1.9964762888207717862636229907 5E-19728	0.2656860360875725748323189501 22

Figure 46.2. *Oos miniaturization through time.* This is the same as the previous table of numbers, except showing the *area* (Column 1) and total summed area (Column 2) of the Oos. Area is computed on the assumption that an Oos has a shape of a square. The "E" indicates scientific notation. Notice that in this simplified scenario, the area of all the Oos bodies in the petri dish reaches a constant, and therefore the Oos will not overflow their limited environment. What is the area of an Oos in the 5th generation if each child's length were three-fourths the parent's, rather than one-half?

viduals such as Dakota or Dextrose existed, or would they be relegated to the realm of mythological creatures, like the superhuman gods of ancient human societies?

46.2 Intergenerational Oos Communication

"We are told that the shortest line segment contains an infinity of points. Then even the shell of a walnut can embrace a spatial infinity as imponderable as intergalactic space."

William Poundstone, 1988, *Labyrinths of Reason*

The Oos world was a continuum. This means that even though individuals like Dakota and Dextrose could not see all their children, they could send them a message via a chain of Oos who would relay the message from one Oos to another in an ever-diminishing progression of messenger Oos. Of course, it was hard to be sure if someone too-small-to-be-seen really was there at all. When a message was received, it would probably be distorted, and it might be hard for a Mini-Oos to accept the fact that it had received a message from a creature it could not see but with whom it shared the same world. Any reply from the Mini-Oos, distorted in its turn by the reverse chain of ever larger messenger Oos, might seem to come from nowhere (and maybe, sometimes, it did).

```
ALGORITHM: How to Compute Oos size.
sum = 1
do i = 1 to 15  /* 15 generations */
  sum = sum * 0.5
  Print sum
end
```

Pseudocode 46.1. *How to compute Oos size.* Try size attenuations other than 0.5, for example, 0.75, or 0.9. Modify the program to compute the area of the dish covered by all the Oos bodies.

Yes, Dr. David Mutcer had many questions concerning Oos society, and he devoted a good deal of his waking hours to the study of Oos culture in an attempt to find the answers.

46.3 A Memory from Bacon's Early Childhood

"Scales and magnitudes are part of the stuff that scientists love. Cosmology and megascales on the one hand, and atoms (or subatomic particles) and microscales on the other, give us a sense of how grand nature is and how con-sistent our physical pictures are."   John I. Brauman, 1991, *Science*

Bacon, the dust speck sized Mini-Oos, lived in a small community of Oos about a half-inch from the glass side wall of the petri dish. Today his family was planning a trip to the great wall, something roughly equivalent to a resident of Atlanta going to the ocean.

"Mom, I can't wait until we see the wall!" Bacon squeaked with exponentially growing anticipation.

"Bacon, I know you will appreciate this vacation," Doobie, his mother, warmly replied. "After all, most of the Oos live so far away from the wall they can never even hope to touch its shiny surface."

Distance is a function of one's own size and one's ability to traverse it. What Dr. Mutcer could easily pick up with one hand and place in his lunch bag was as big as the British Isles to a microscopic Oos. There were many Oos, much smaller than Bacon, whose entire village could exist on a plain of nutrient gel no bigger than the size of Bacon's body. They could never hope to travel the distances required to see the great wall.

After about half an hour, Bacon and his family reached the wall.[27] Near the wall was a three-mile crescent of white nutrient gel called agar. Some moisture had collected, forming a miniature ocean. Bacon's mom parked her paramecium in the shade of a mound of gel that fringed the beach, and took out box lunches.

---

[27] Terms like "hour" and "mile" are used to give you a feel for time and distance as experienced in the Oos frame of reference.

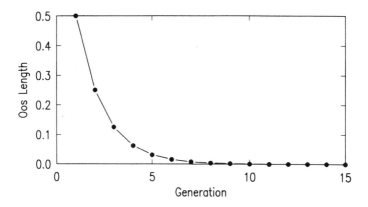

Figure 46.3. *The Oos World.* Length attenuation according to generation.

Bacon let out a squeal of joy and awe. The wall was immense, stretching for as far as his eye could see. Oos of all sizes, some smaller than Bacon by a factor of fifty, others three times his size, were gathered at the wall. Many Oos children were sliding down its surface, while adults could be seen surfing and sailing higher up on the glistening quartz ledges. Bacon ran until he was exhausted, and then he threw himself down on the gel and gleefully rolled to the water's edge.

During these early days of Oos evolution, the atmosphere in their enclosure was dense and rich in carbon dioxide. Various fungi grew along the shoreline. There were no fish in this waters, but there were various microscopic protozoa.

46.4 Love and War

> *"What am I, Life? A thing of watery salt, held in cohesion by unresting cells, which work they know not why, which never halt, myself unwitting where their Master dwells."*   John Masefield, *What am I, Life?*

During Bacon's life a quasi-religious government which reeked of oligarchic collectivism came to power. Dakota had come to be considered a god. (Most Oos couldn't see him anyway.) At this time in history all Oos were required to append to their name a numerical designation. For example, Bacon was now called Bacon 150 – the 150 designated that he was 150 times smaller than Dakota or Dextrose. The members of a village usually had designations which varied by plus or minus 5 size units; however, a size restriction for members of a village was not officially mandated by law. Unfortunately for Bacon 150, he fell in love with Diphone 200, an aquamarine beauty, but because of a new ruling, only Oos within 25 "points" of each others size could marry! This size restriction on marriage was enforced by the revolutionary guard of a new dictator, Death 50, who had come to power as a result of a popular uprising of the less educated classes against the license of the former regime.

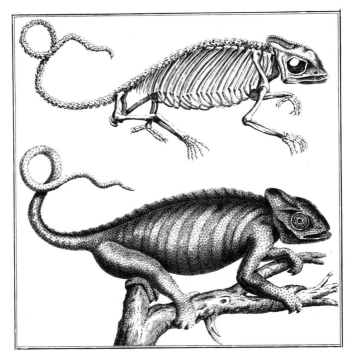

Figure 46.4. *A typical Oos-lizard construct formed from billions of microscopic Oos.* First the Oos construct the skeletal framework using roughly 1×10^8 Oos, and then add the various organ systems and pigment cells for external coloration. (See "Oos-Lizards Battle the World" on page 265 for details.)

These and other cruel mandates put forth by Death 50 precipitated an uprising from the more educated classes of Oos. Confined to their glass enclosure from which they could not emigrate, they were left only with the choice of submission or revolt. It was decided by the community at large that the Oos would try to oust Death 50, their vituperative king, and an open rebellion shortly ensued.

War raged on for generations. Death 50 still ruled the land, demanding absolute obedience from his subjects. Bacon 150 was one of the soldiers who began to march on the king's castle. This was a war for all Oos, and brave brethren fought together no matter what their size or religious persuasion. At Bacon's side was Dendrite 100 and a large number of "small folk," the 200 to 500 series. In addition to the small folk were some one hundred ultra-small folk upon their backs. One of them, Deeee 5000, would turn out to be the courageous Oos who won the war.

The heterogeneous group of Oos reached the castle wall and were quickly surrounded by the revolutionary guard. These were big fat brutes ranging from designations 55 through 75, and they were enough to drive Bacon's bivouac batty. With almost no effort the gregarious guards simply walked in circles in order to decimate Bacon's legions beneath their feet. At the revolutionary guards' sides

Figure 46.5. *Oos infiltration of an adult male human.* In order to commandeer a body, microscopic Oos travel the 31 pairs of nerves springing from the spinal chord, and then enter the nerves of the tongue and its vicinity. They were not always successful at this task. (See "Oos-Lizards Battle the World" on page 265 for details.)

stood the king's roving whores. And behind the revolutionary guard stood Death 50 in all his horror and glory. He gazed upon the battle scene and then suddenly cut loose with a hideous, stentorian roar (which to the small folk sounded like a dull pulse).

As already mentioned, some of the Oos were so small as to be nearly invisible to other Oos. Deee 5000 slipped by the guards, being so small that, even when stepped on, he found protection within the thin wrinkles in the guard's fleshy feet. Luckily for Bacon, Deeee 5000 had the mental perspicacity to leap into Death 50's throat. Deeee 5000 crawled to the esophagus where he began to release a potent neurotoxin. Deeee then penetrated Death's pyloric sphinctor where he secreted additional egregious exudate. Within minutes, the king was dead.

46.5   The End of an Era, and Horseradish

Dr. Mutcer had difficulty imagining Oos time. While an apple turned brown in just a few minutes in his world, many months might have elapsed in the Oos world. By now, decades had passed for the Oos culture. Exotic forms of government and religion died, as new forms quickly took their place. Cycles of war and peace continued (with peace the more common). Oos breathed and bled, crashed and died, smiled and cried, as the years rolled on. Bacon's glaucous grave stone stood on a lonely hill in the countryside near his village.

Through the months, Dr. David Mutcer grew weary of observing his energetic Oos. He needed something new to amuse himself. One day he plopped a teaspoon of purple beet horseradish in the center of the petri dish to see what would happen.

Horrible as it was, the Oos persevered. The horseradish redirected their evolution, and the Oos folk went through both physical and cultural changes. Their bodies had manifested a purple hue, and some of the generations had developed strange growths and diseases because of the putrid, nearly-liquid mass in the center of their world. Yet they did adapt. Whatever the suffering to individual Oos, as a species, Oos survived.

David Mutcer was fascinated. In his home laboratory notebook, he recorded the new forms of law and religion that evolved as a result of the horseradish. Many of the Oos had made use of the enzymes in the mucilaginous mess to create new industries. Dr. Mutcer grew concerned that they might find a way to dissolve regions of their glass enclosure with the potent chemicals.

46.6 Further Experimentation (with Purple Oos)

Even the cataclysmic events precipitated by the horseradish in the Oos enclosure failed to amuse Mutcer for long. As the days passed, he again became weary with the Oos. He needed even more excitement. One day he decided to place a beetle  inside the glass dish with the purple Oos to see what would transpire. The beetle destroyed a few villages but then, after a few seconds, it became rigid. The Oos began to infiltrate the beetle's circulatory system and nervous system, thereby keeping the insect in a state of dormancy where it could do no damage to their world. The purple Oos gradually colonized the beetle's body, and at times would use some of the new organic chemicals provided by the insect's body tissues for the benefit of their civilization. Tiny eburnian pieces of the chitinous material in the beetle's exoskeleton became a much-traded commodity.

Dagwood 10000, great-great-great-great-grand child of Bacon 150, spent his childhood years in a commune lodged near the tip of the beetle's right antenna. A religion similar to present day Judaism was practiced in most of the beetle's head and thorax. One day while Dagwood 10000 was at temple, he was told of the great land outside the Beetle. Dagwood could scarcely believe what he was hearing. He and his friends shivered in amazement and stupefaction. Dagwood and his celadon cenobites vowed that they would travel to this strange new land.

In the meantime, they would take a trip to a commune lodged in the beetle's pituitary gland.

Life outside the beetle progressed smoothly. A large industrial civilization grew at the site where the horseradish had been. In a real sense, Dr. Mutcer's cruel experiments had actually enriched the life of the Oos, due to the remarkable panoply of new raw materials which allowed their technology to progress at rates never dreamed of in the pre-purple days.

46.7 Destruction

A month later, Dr. Mutcer was in a bored, depressed mood. His wife had left him for a more handsome man and also because of the inordinate amount of time Dr. Mutcer spent observing his tiny fecund fellows.

Dr. Mutcer craved some new spicy action, and over the course of the next few days he tried several sadistic experiments. He spat into the petri dish. He sprayed a little hairspray in it. He held a match under it. A good 50% of the purple Oos civilization was destroyed, yet because of Oos resilience, the remainder adapted and survived. What new creatures had evolved? What was life like in the glass petri dish, in a world which had suffered so much anguish and sorrow, where life had become a travesty, and contentment a mere mockery of living in the shallow meaningless void?

46.8 Harsh Experiments with Beetle Oos and Purple Oos

Little did Dr. Mutcer realize that by subjecting his creatures to such harsh conditions he was causing them, as a result of natural selection, to become almost impervious to deadly stimuli.

Eventually, he became determined to put an end to all the Oos lifeforms. He sprayed insecticide on them. He put two copper leads into the thick nutrient agar, and then plugged the culture into a wall outlet. He poured nitric acid on them. But always there remained a few survivors to perpetuate the race. Finally he wrapped aluminum foil around the dish to exclude all light, and put them in the his kitchen freezer. He left them in the freezer for several weeks.

One Saturday night, while entertaining a young blonde named Tricia in his apartment, Dr. Mutcer heard a strange hissing noise coming from the freezer in his kitchen. He hesitantly walked to the kitchen, and then he screamed in the madness of extreme agony.

On the floor was what looked like a large, disembodied, purple dog's snout.

"Good evening," it croaked. "And who is the young lady?" the Snout-Oos leered, focussing its blood-shot eyes on Tricia.

"What do you want?! What are you?" gasped Mutcher.

"Dave, I am the result of eons of Oos labor. They have constructed me so that I may be their spokesman. Trillions of Oos line my nasal cavity." Dr. Mutcer was speechless, as was Tricia who nervously darted her eyes about the room. Only a few days ago Mutcer had met Tricia while shopping at the local grocery store, and her pleasant personality did much to lift his spirts since the acrimonious departure of his wife.

"Dave, I would like you to meet my two associates, Mr. Woo and Roxie." From one of the kitchen cabinets, oozed a slimy squid-like creature. This evidently was Mr. Woo. And Roxie, looking something like a ball of twine, fell from the ceiling. Dave Mutcer and Tricia let out a low moan.

"The only thing we request of you," continued the Snout-Oos, "is that you allow us live here in your apartment with you. We will try not to get in each other's ways."

"And if we refuse?" Mutcer yelled.

In response to Mutcer's question, Mr. Woo leaped into Tricia's mouth, lodged himself beneath her tongue, and began to secrete a green milky fluid. The pungent fluid smelled like absinthe and creosol. Tricia began to cough. Mr. Woo extended himself into her ear.

"For God's sake stop!" Dr. Mutcer cried. Mr. Woo withdrew from Tricia.

"That is what will happen if you refuse. This time the fluid was harmless; however, Mr. Woo has the capability of secreting millions of Mini-Oos with the fluid. Had he done that, a colony would have been seeded within her body, and within hours, they would be directing her body actions."

"So you see," Roxie's twine body quivered, "you have no choice in the matter."

"And what is your purpose?" asked Dr. Mutcer incredulously.

The Snout-Oos just grinned.

46.9 What Transpired in the Oos Civilization Prior to the Snout

As the Oos generations became smaller and smaller, there came a time when Oos bodies approached subatomic dimensions. Even though Oos did not die, except as a result of physical injuries, overpopulation was never really a problem because of Oos size attenuation. However, the Oos scientists became increasingly alarmed when they had surmised that the ordinary laws of physics would break down below atomic dimensions. In an attempt to avoid this potentially dangerous condition, a mating restriction was placed on the atomic folk. They alone in the entire Oos culture were forbidden to interbreed. Such a restriction on social behavior had not been instituted since the kakistocracy of Death 50.

As one would expect from any passionate society, the mating restriction did not last long, and soon a new generation of sub-atomic Oos, named Roobles, came into being. Roobles were a very strange folk. Most were very shy, unassertive creatures. Their memories were poor, and they were often uncertain of the simplest of things, such as their names or addresses. The more reliable of them were used primarily as messengers since they could traverse the petri dish in an instant due to peculiar quantum physical laws. In fact, it was rumored that some Roobles had currently attempted to tunnel through the glass wall of the petri dish and were exploring an exciting, totally new world unsupervised. When Oos scientists got wind of this, they nearly dropped their teeth. Within days the scientists began to use Roobles as probes. Some were sent out never to return. Others did finally make it back, and with them they brought tales of an enigmatic, wondrous land.

One of those who came back, a Rooble sometimes named db, would turn out to be instrumental in the Snout construction project and also would one day make indirect contact with Dr. David Mutcer. (This rooble proudly named himself db to indicate that he was a direct descendent of Beetle-Oos Dagwood 10000 and also had some of his ancestors in the Bacon line.) As could be imagined, family trees had become a big business.

46.10 Contact

"If you'll just follow me to the back of the kitchen, we have a surprise for you," said the Snout-Oos to Dr. Mutcer and Tricia.

As they arrived at the back of the kitchen, David Mutcer saw a sight that made him gasp. Covering the rectangular kitchen table was a thin coating of purple dust. The Oos had arranged themselves, in order of decreasing size along the table top. Through the dust poked flags of all sizes and colors designating various civilizations, kingdoms, governments, and guilds. Flags near the front of the table were often supported by one or two Oos, but Dr. Mutcer could imagine that flags further back along the table were supported by hundreds and thousands of microscopic Oos making concerted efforts to hold up their flag. Such an effort was probably far greater than the efforts made by the ancient Egyptians in their construction of the Great Pyramid at Giza.

The beetle of the Beetle-Oos was also present on the table, and protruding from its mouth was a green flag with a beetle insignia. Even though the farthest third of the

kitchen table appeared free of the purple dust, there were probably millions of Oos sitting there beneath the limit of human visual perception. Near the end of the table was marked an "x" about the size of a typewritten character. Dr. Mutcer stepped over to the table for a closer look. Nearest to him, on a stone throne and wrinkled by age, sat thumb-nail sized Dakota! For the next ten minutes, the Snout-Oos briefed Dr. Mutcer on the Roobles.

"This is the scenario," the Snout-Oos barked in a businesslike voice. "db, a Rooble, wishes to talk to you. He is stationed at the very center of the 'x' near the end of the table. He will send his messages via a preselected chain of Oos chosen for their reliability. When the message reaches Dakota, he will signal me. I will then relay the message to you. The process will take about one minute. Is what I said understood, Dr. Mutcer?" Dr. Mutcer looked at Tricia and then back at the Snout. He hesitated and then spoke.

"Understood."

46.11 More on Roobles

Roobles are hatched from tiny, mottled purple eggs. These eggs do not require warmth to develop, as do bird's eggs; however, singing is required to facilitate hatching.

All the Rooble eggs, no matter where they may be located in the petri dish, hatch in synchrony. Oos scientists postulated that an electromagnetic or optical-galvanic field would allow the eggs to somehow be in communication with one another. This hypothesis was soon abandoned when Oos scientists found evidence suggesting that all Roobles were actually just one Rooble individual delocalized in space. Since Roobles could move instantaneously to any part of the petri dish, it was possible for a Rooble to be at more than one place at once.   The "One Rooble Hypothesis" explained the synchronous hatching phenomenon, since in effect, only one egg was hatching. Months later, when db's family, at the request of Oos scientists, asked db about this possibility, db could give no conclusive answer.

After a few years, Oos scientists proved that db, and three dozen brothers and sisters, were in actuality all Roobles. For example, by displacing himself in time and space, db could form as many copies of himself as he desired. This made db a very important individual. Unscrupulous leaders often accosted db in an attempt to win him over to their particular political cause; however, db was a docile soul and also had no interest in the perils of politics.

In addition to moving through time, Roobles could partition time, which made them

particularly good workers, artists, and musicians. They could make one second become an hour for themselves, and therefore could accomplish tasks in seemingly very short times. Again, certain Oos began to take advantage of this talent and actually enslaved a portion of the Rooble population. Roobles were forced to work at the docks, in the mills, and at all forms of menial labor. This lasted for only a short time, because the Roobles revolted against their cruel task masters and obtained their freedom.

Not only could Roobles move through time and space but they could move through another dimension which other Oos could not understand. The Roobles called it E-space, and the closest thing to a coherent explanation of it was a dimension which had something to do with emotion.

It is interesting to point out, at the same time as the first Rooble hatching, scientists in Dr. Mutcer's world were first hypothesizing sub-atomic particles called quarks.

46.12 What db said to Dr. Mutcer

Through the chain of Oos starting with db and ending with Dakota, the message was relayed across the kitchen table. After Dakota received the message, he hobbled off his stone throne toward the Snout. The Snout then relayed the message to Dr. Mutcer.

"Since I am capable of traveling in space and reproducing myself ad infinitum, I am capable of forming any material object in your world. I am the be all, the end all, the power and the light, the judgement and the will. " The last line was thrown in by the Snout. db would never have been so arrogant.

"That's impossible! What about conservation of matter?" Dr. Mutcer exclaimed.

"What about it," the Snout-Oos mocked. Suddenly a huge, brown cigar appeared in the Snout's mouth. The Snout began puffing on it. Tricia gasped: her bright blue eyes twinkled with a mixture of fascination and revulsion. With the nepheligenous cigar dangling from the corner of its mouth, the Snout continued.

"And if that is not enough evidence for you Mutcer, perhaps Tricia has a thing or two to tell you." Tricia looked nervously around the room and remained silent. She placed one of her hands on Mutcer's hand. Mutcer gave it a reassuring squeeze and tried to comfort her with a smile.

"If she wont talk, I will," the Snout snorted. "Ever notice anything strange while you were with her late last night? Eh, Mr. Mutcer? Why don't you ask your dear Tricia?"

Tricia could not meet Dr. Mutcer's gaze. "Please Mr. Snout," she implored.

"What are you talking about, Snout? Tricia, what is going on?" Mutcer yelled. The three of them were motionless and silent for several seconds.

"Cat's got your tongue, Tricia?" said the Snout. With those words, Tricia's purple digestive tract evaginated from her oral cavity, and at the same time her hair turned purple, wriggled off her head, and quickly scurried under a nearby couch. Her esophagus danced.

"Yes Dr. Mutcer, Tricia was a Rooble aggregate," croaked the Snout. Mutcer screamed and dropped to the floor, as wave upon wave of sadness and shock overwhelmed him.

46.13 Dr. Mutcer's Apartment

"What do you want from me, Snout?" asked Dr. Mutcer, obviously shaken by the entire situation. His fists clenched in a confusing amalgam of fear, horror, and rage.

"All we want is to be able to use your apartment for the next few months without being disturbed. We need more space to live in, and the remainder of your apartment will do just fine." Dr. Mutcer had no choice. He agreed to the atrabilious Snout's request.

Within the next few days, a fine film of purple dust began to cover the walls and ceilings of the rooms in Dr. Mutcer's apartment. After a week, Dr. Mutcer's bedroom, and a thin path to the front door, were all that remained Oos-free. Meanwhile, Mr. Mutcer began dating a new woman named Melissa. He explained to her the situation with the Oos so that she would be prepared when he took her back to his apartment. As Dr. Mutcer and Melissa opened the front door to his apartment, they were inundated by polychromatic Oos which fell out by the shovel-full into the adjacent hallway. Mutcer cursed. There was no way they would or could enter the apartment now. The Oos continued to pour out into the hallway. Mutcer thought he smelled a meringue pie. The landlady for the apartment building, a Mrs. Carrington, stepped into the hallway and saw the colorful, sand-like material spilling out of the room and into a nearby elevator shaft. Mrs. Carrington cursed. She walked up to Dr. Mutcer and Melissa. "Mutcer, what is this mess? This is the last straw. I will now begin eviction proceedings against you!"

"Wait Mrs. Carrington. Maybe I can get it cleaned up," Mutcer begged. "May I borrow a vacuum cleaner?."

"No way Mutcer. You're out." Just then, the Snout snaked his way out of a conical mound of Oos which protruded from the plush hallway carpeting. He was still puffing on his brown, putrid cigar.

"Mutcer, let me handle this. Mrs. Carrington, your usefulness is over." With those words, Mrs. Carrington experienced ataxy, turned purple, and exploded. Dr. Mutcer said nervously, "Rooble-aggregates certainly come in handy, don't they Snout?"

"Yes they do," laughed the Snout. With those words, Mutcer's new girl friend, Melissa, shattered. For a few minutes her disconnected larynx and attached carotid arteries continued to emit a screeching noise, and then at last the ineffective appendages were silent.

46.14 Oos-Lizards Battle the World

"For a mammal like man, there was something indescribably alien about the way reptiles hunted their prey. No wonder men hated reptiles. The stillness, the coldness, the pace was all wrong."

Michael Crichton, 1990, *Jurassic Park*

Months passed, and the Oos began to implement their plan for eventual domination of the northeast United States of America, and perhaps later, of the entire world. Oh, there were many pacifists among the Oos, especially among descendants of the Bacon and Beetle-line, but the increasing number of bellicose politicians made the voice of the little-Oos-on-the-street difficult to hear. Eventually, dictators and despots again came to power, and the Oos civilization returned to a pre-dynastic situation similar to the time of the much-hated ruler Death 50. When will history teach lessons which societies will learn?

At first, the Oos began the process of world-domination with the construction of human Oos-aggregates. A line of Tricia-series, Melissa-series, and Mrs. Carrington-series

were popular for a while; however, this method seemed to have only limited effectiveness because of the difficulty in maintaining proper neural activity in parts of the newly-invaded brain. After several weeks, coordination of several voluntary muscle groups in the arm and neck became impossible, and the Oos-aggregate had to be abandoned. The same limitation applied to the bodies of most other higher species that Oos tried to control, particularly dirhinous mammals and birds. In fact, of all the organisms tested, they found that a variant of the lowly lizard proved best for their purposes. For one thing, the lizard had a simple nervous system with auxillary ganglia organized in a small nerve net. The lizard was easy to control and easy to hide. Also, lizards seemed to strike feelings of terror and loathing in the hearts of humans, and this induced fear provided a psychological advantage to the Oos in their war against humanity. The final Oos-lizard model, decided upon by the upper-echelon commanders, had a purple hue to its body, and contained two extra anterior nerve centers to control a venom created specially for the lizard by Oos scientists operating from a laboratory in the corner of Mutcer's living room, near his sofa. To further enhance the Oos-lizard's destructive arsenal, small amber "death-trumpets" protruded from their oral cavities. These sound-producing appendages allowed the Oos-lizards to communicate with one another, and if required, they could emit several formants, or vocal-tract resonances, at specific frequencies which would shatter building materials, much as a skilled soprano can shatter a wine glass. The Oos-lizards smelled like bacon and horseradish burned in a brick kiln.

We need not detail all the battles fought between the Oos hordes and the courageous humans. But as an aid to future historians, a description of the very first encounter between the horrible Oos-lizards and humanity will be described.

46.15 The Oos-Lizards Meet Tammy and Burt

It was 12:02 in the night, and Tammy, a 16-year-old blue-eyed Caucasian female, and Burt, an 18-year-old Jewish male, were behind the Grand Union Store in Peekskill, New York. They were discussing their future together in Burt's father's '79 Oldsmobile. A cool breeze blew through the moist summer air, and occasionally an owl cried a lonely call into the pale moon-lit night. Katydids and cicadas buzzed. For a while the young couple gazed up into the incredible lamp of stars. Tammy mouthed a few trite platitudes, and Burt responded in kind.

"I love you Burt," Tammy whispered as she huddled closer to Burt and gazed into his azure eyes. Just then Tammy began to smell burnt bacon.

"Burt, do you smell something strange?"

"Yeah, it smells awful." The lizards began to slither along the new radial tires and gradually made their way up to the partially open windows.

"Burt, the smell's getting stronger!" Several hundred acerebral lizards traveled on the hood toward the young, and now, not-too-passionate couple. The equivalent of a 4-Star General sat atop the car's antenna to direct the troops. Burt was first to see them.

"Tammy, close your window!" By now the car was surrounded. Burt reached for his car keys. The chameleon general gazed at Burt, as its leathery skin changed color from burgundy to brown to purple. The windows were crawling with the purplish lizard bodies. All at once, as if on cue, the Oos-lizards withdrew their death-trumpets, and began to emit sound. It took only 5 seconds for the safety glass to shatter, and in another 2 seconds the young couple met their maker. Within the next hour, the surrounding forest grew quiet and the owl was terminated mid-hoot. In the distance a fire engine siren screamed like a dying woman, but was cut off quickly. A sick odor filled the air.

46.16 A World Turns Purple

Now there are no sounds, no cicadas to sing their sad tunes in the barren forests on a dying planet. One by one cities crumbled. Large mammals and batrachophagous animals were the first to be destroyed. And then, smaller marsupials, followed swiftly by birds and reptiles. A few alliaceous arthropods lived out their meager lives for a while amidst the purple mists and growths. Last to go, of course, were the crustaceans in the ocean and various lower forms of phyto and zooplankton. A marshy sea, mother of life, now stands choked with fungoid growths and galactophagous goo. On the last untouched island far from the once-teaming wharves and the chaotic realm of men, a solitary sea organism slithers along purple, shiny surfaces of rock, and with a last spasm of terror, fades into fetid chasms of empty air. Please whisper to us in our graves.

46.17 The Oos-King Reigns

Imagine a world with no shadows, no bright twinkling stars, no sun. Across the bleak purple landscapes walks a terrible, huge purple man. An Oos-construct the size of a sky-scraper steps on violet extensions of rock, breaking them with each footfall. His breath is thunder. Overhead, vague perpetual clouds float. Tiny skeletons line the bleak hillsides. Through the dense air, violet twisted, winged creatures fly crying shrill sounds. The Violet King has wandered aimlessly across the earth several times. In a world filled with dust, he is alone. The Oos King sits heavily on a mountain, and at night looks upward through the scintillating purple mists at the stars.

High speed time-sequential photographs of a pig's motion (1887).

Part V

TIME

Chapter 47

Time in a Bottle

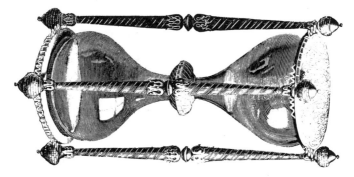

"I just can't seem to grasp the fact that time passes and the hands of the clock go round. Sometimes ... when the leaves whirl in the wind, I wish I could live again as before and run with them ... so that time would pass again. But there I stop and I do not care... I just bump into time."

Schizophrenic patient, *Time*

One day I placed a beautiful blue marble in a large glass bottle which had a small opening at its top. Later I began to shake the bottle to see if I could pop the marble out of the upper opening.

OPENING

MARBLE

BOTTLE

Even after violently shaking the bottle for 5 minutes, the marble did not leave the bottle through the tiny aperture. I grew curious. How long would it take for the marble to leave the bottle if I were to continue shaking? My arm grew weary with these experiments, and I finally decided to rig a machine to shake the bottle until the marble finally popped out of the opening. After about 1 hour of constant bouncing around in the bottle, the marble popped out!

What would happen if I were to place a series of bottles together so that only a small opening connected the bottles. Bottle 1 would have just one opening, just as my bottle did. Bottle 2, however, would have 2 openings, one which connected it to Bottle 1, and the other which connected it to Bottle 3, and so on.

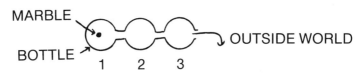

MARBLE

BOTTLE

OUTSIDE WORLD

1 2 3

Let's assume that it takes one hour for the marble to find an opening, as it did in my experiment. How long would it take for the marble to leave Bottle 2 and jump

Figure 47.1. *The winged hourglass and the scythe.* This symbolizes the flight of time and the certainty of death. (Rosicrucian emblem book, circa 1650)

into Bottle 3? How long would it take for the marble to find its way to Bottle 4? How long would it take for the marble to exit Bottle n? Remember that in each of the intermediate bottles, the marble has just as likely a chance of moving into a previous bottle as it does moving forward. (Assume this is an ideal system. It has no friction, gravity, etc.)

It turns out that the average time to get from Bottle 1 to the nth bottle's opening to the outside world is approximately $n(n + 1)/2$ times the average time to find an opening. (For a large number of bottles, you can approximate[28] this equation by n^2.) For example, it will take 55 hours for the marble to leave the 10th bottle pictured below:

How would you picture 5000 hours in a diagram which resembled the previous picture of bottles chained together? It turns out that 5000 hours is represented by a picture of 100 bottles. This means that it will take you a good part of a year to shake the marble out of a connected series of 100 bottles!

What happens if we now provide *two* openings between each bottle? One opening is free-flowing, and the other has a one-way valve allowing the marble only to travel in a *backward direction* – a direction away from the opening of final egress. The average time for the marble to get out of the nth bottle in the

---

[28] This formula can be derived using concepts relating to random walk and diffusion problems. Depending upon whether or not you assume a continuous space or discrete space the answers are slightly different when the assemblage contains just a few bottles. An additional complication is that the first bottle is different from the rest. However, as stated, if a large number of bottles are considered, the time is proportional to n^2.

case of one forward opening and M backward openings can be approximated by $2 \times (M + 1)^n/M^2$. This equation, which may be used for $M \geq 1$, was derived in 1991 by Dr. Shriram Biyani using statistical arguments.[29]

As you should expect, the addition of one-way backward valves between the connected bottles increases the time for the marble to exit the chain of bottles because the marble has a better chance of going backward than forward. In order to facilitate our discussion of the incredible characteristics of this bottle chain, I've invented some nomenclature. Rather than say, "3 bottles with two backward openings and one forward openings between them," I'll simply use the symbol $B(3,2)$. In all of the following discussions and examples there is always one forward connector and M backward connectors between the bottles. For example, here is a picture of a $B(9,2)$ system. Each connector is represented by a line:

Can you guess, or calculate, how long it will take a marble to leave the last bottle of $B(9,2)$? It turns out that it will take over a year of shaking to get the marble out of the bottle chain.

Here are some other "time-in-a-bottle" diagrams for you to ponder. The following $B(9,5)$ collection represents the life of a human being:

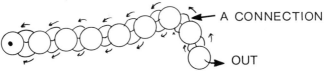

$B(15,5)$ represents roughly 1.6 million years, or the number of years ago that *Homo Erectus* was born:

Homo erectus (upright man) is thought to be the direct ancestor of humans (*Homo sapiens*), and a *Homo erectus* skeleton was discovered in Kenya in 1985 and dated to 1.6 million year ago. Thus, we may call $B(15,5)$ the "*Homo Erectus* number*." If this ancient human began shaking the 15 bottles and handed this

---

[29] A derivation of this formula is available from me upon request. It turns out that the *average* bottle number reached in a given time approaches a constant. The formulas here give the average time until the *first* time the *n*th bottle is exited.

arduous, although mindless, task down from generation to generation, only today would the marble finally pop out of the last bottle.

The earliest and most primitive known dinosaur is the *Herrerasaurus* discovered in 1989 at the foot of the Andes in Argentina. It is believed to be about 230 million years old. The $B(15,7)$ assemblage below can represent this span of time:

The $B(15,10)$ assemblage below represents more than twice the age of the Earth (4.5 billion years):

47.1 Stop and Think: Old Wine and Cocky the Cockatoo

"We still cannot say what time is; we cannot agree whether there is one time or many times, cannot even agree whether time is an essential ingredient of the universe or whether it is the grand illusion of the human intellect."

Davis and Hersh, 1986, *Descartes' Dream*

As we've just seen, various bottle collections can be used to represent different spans of time. Why not try to draw time-in-a-bottle diagrams for the following ages? If you are a teacher, have the students draw each time span in three different ways by varying the number of backward connectors or the total number of bottles. Look for various representations of time in historical texts, such as the illustration in Figure 47.1.

1. The oldest datable wine ever found was in two bottles in Xinyang, Hunan, China from a tomb dated to 1300 B.C. Given only five time-bottles, how many backward connections would you have to use to represent the age of the wine?

2. The age of the universe is thought by some astronomers to be about 143 eons or gigayears old (an eon or gigayear is 1 billion years). Represent this by time-in-a bottle diagrams.

3. The longest irrefutable age reported for any bird is 80 years, for a male cockatoo named Cocky who died in a London Zoo. Represent this by time-in-a bottle diagrams.

4. Which is larger, the number of possible chess games, which some have reported to be around

$$10^{10^{10^{70.5}}}$$
(47.1)

or $B(15,20)$?

5. Draw diagrams for the following (all times given in years from present):
    a) Beginning of life on earth (3.25×10^9),

b) Age of fishes (3×10^8),
c) Age of mammals (7.5×10^7),
d) Age of mammoths (10^6), and
e) Isaac Newton (3×10^2).

47.2 Hypertime and EternityGrams

"The dog hears some sound from the farmer's house and thinks of the shotgun with its wide black holes like a figure eight rolled onto its side. The dog knows nothing of figure eights, but even a dog may recognize the dim shape of eternity if its instincts are honed sharp enough."

Stephen King, *Four Past Midnight*

Thomas Aquinas believed God to be outside of time and thus capable of seeing all of the universe's objects past and future in one blinding instant. If an outside observer existed in hypertime, it could see the past and future all at once. To better understand this, draw a picture called an "EternityGram" of two (2-D) disks rolling toward each other, colliding, and rebounding. This diagram, adapted from Dewdney's *Planiverse*, shows 2 spatial dimensions along with the additional dimension of time. You can think of successive instants in time as stacks of movie frames which form a 3-D picture in hypertime in the EternityGram. EternityGrams are timeless. Hyperbeings would see past, present and future all at once.

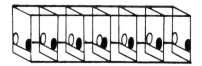

Below is another EternityGram, showing a ball moving through space and time. The fact that the ball comes back on itself indicates that it has traveled backward in time. (I computed this image on an IBM RISC System/6000.)

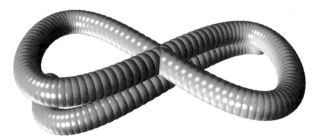

47.3 Fact File: Chronons, Mastodon Feces, Etc.

"It's as if time were a rubber band, and you were on an end stretched out tight. If you pull the medallion off, we snap back to the future."
Harlan Ellison, "Demon With a Glass Hand," *The Outer Limits*

• Nobel prize winning physicist Richard Feynman once suggested an approach to quantum mechanics in which antiparticles are viewed as particles momentarily traveling backward in time.

• The fundamental unit of quantized time is called the "chronon."

• Time is frequently the subject of science fiction movies, books, and TV shows. In an episode of *Star Trek – The Next Generation* called *Time Squared* the starship *Enterprise* enters a time zone shaped like a Möbius strip. The characters were doomed to repeat the same sequence of events over and over again.

• In 1990, the clock which maintained the primary time standard is callled the "cesium NBS-6." The machine is 6 meters long. When operated as a clock the device keeps time with an error of about 3 millionths of a second per year. In 1992, Hewlett-Packard Co. unveiled a new atomic clock that will remain reliable to the second for the next 1.6 million years. The $54,000 device is the size of a desktop computer.

• In 1991, the oldest living bacteria ever found were discovered beneath a golf course in Newark, Ohio. Their home for 11,999 years was a 23-inch-long, reddish brown tube-

shaped mass embedded in black peat moss. Its convoluted shape, and its pungent odor, led paleontologists to believe that they had found the remains of a mastodon's intestinal contents. Gerald Goldstein, a microbiologist at Ohio Wesleyan University, brought "five bags of the stuff" back to his laboratory where he determined that the bacteria in the fertile feces were alive. These are the oldest living organisms ever found. By comparing these ancient microbes with their contemporary counterparts, researchers may learn more about genetics and evolution. (Source: Folger, T. (1992) Oldest living bacterial tell all. *Discover*. January. 30-31.)

• In April, 1990, *Playboy* magazine printed an interview with world-famous physicist, Stephen Hawking. In the interview, Hawking speaks of another kind of "time" called "imaginary time." Here are some excerpts, to push your imagination beyond its breaking point:

> Imaginary time is another direction of time, one that is at right angles to ordinary, real time. We could get away from this one-dimensional, linelike behavior of time... Ordinary time would be a derived concept we invent for psychological reasons. We invent ordinary time so that we can describe the universe as a succession of events in time, rather than as a static picture, like a surface map of the earth... Time is just like another direction in space.

47.4 For Further Reading

"Mathematics is the one subject in which time is irrelevant."
Davis and Hersh, 1986, *Descartes' Dream*

1.   Grabiner, J. (1974) Is mathematical truth time-dependent? *American Mathematics Monthly*. 81: 354-365.
2.   Gardner, M. (1992) *Fractal Music, Hypercards, and More...* Freeman: NY.
3.   Dewdney, A. (1988) *The Planiverse*. Poseidon: NY.
4.   Goudsmit, S., Claiborne, R. (1978) *Time*. Time-Life Books: NY.

Chapter 48

Interlude: Art Beyond Space and Time

Paul Hartal is an artist whose ideas, like his artwork, seems to span space and time. Not only is he a painter and poet, and an inventor of "lyrical conceptualism" (a new element in the periodic table of art), but Dr. Hartal is also the director of the Center for Art, Science, and Technology, in Montreal. The Center facilitates the exchange of ideas between the various domains of human knowledge. Hartal notes:

> The present human condition calls for the rise of a new, inclusive form of culture in which art should play a most prominent role. We need the imagination, the intuition, the insight, the lateral reasoning faculty, as well as human values, that are excluded from the rigid methodology of science, but are intrinsic to art.

Hartal's interests are wide ranging: from space, to time, to perceptual ambiguities, to aeronautical and astronomical artworks. Here is a remark he once made about space:

> Artistic space was non-Euclidean long before Einstein... In ancient Egypt or in Byzantium, for example, artists created murals in which the subject matter was rendered without taking into account the empirical laws of visual perception.
>
> In the modern era the rise of non-Euclidean geometry and the concept of the fourth dimension affected the studio artist. They made a significant impact on the development of cubism, surrealism, and other movements of modern art.

On time, he notes:

> Existence is bound up with time. To contemplate the latter is to add to the enigma of the first. Is time the cosmic matrix of existence, or is generated by it? Does time stand still, or does it flow? If it is in a state of flux, what is its speed? And since we measure speed by the ratio of traveling distance to the periodic motion of the clock, how are we supposed to measure the velocity of time? By time itself?

I've scattered some of Hartal's diagrams throughout this chapter to give readers a flavor for his style. Shown facing this page is a picture from his series "The Eightfold Way." Below is his painting "How to Make a Torus Out of a Painting." It shows the topological transformation of a rectangular plane into an anchor ring with a self-repetitive image (oil on canvas, 18"x24"). Hartal can be reached at the Center for Art, Science, and Technology, P.O. Box 1012, St. Laurent, Montreal (Quebec) Canada H4L 4W3.

48.1 For Further Reading

1. Hartal, P. (1988) *The Brush and The Compass: The Interface Dynamics of Art and Science*. University Press of America: NY.

2. Hartal, P. (1990) Space art or space science? *Pulsar*. Nov-Dec, p 11.

3. Hartal, P. (1990) Perceptual ambiguity and metaphoric conceptualization. *Contemporary Philosophy*. 13(4): 1-4.

4. Henderson, L. (1983) *The Fourth Dimension and Non-Euclidean Geometry in Modern Art*. Princeton University Press: NJ.

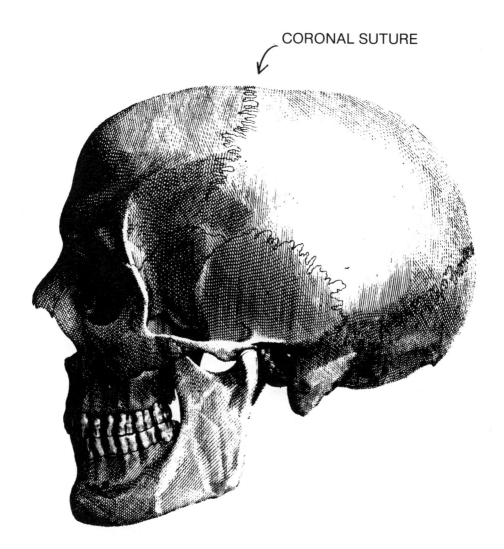
CORONAL SUTURE

Chapter 49

Time-Skulls, Bouncing Bones, And Building Your own Time Machine

"What then is time? If someone asks me, I know. If I wish to explain it to someone who asks, I know not."

Aurelius Augustinus, Bishop of Hippo in North Africa

"Many animals can react to time. A rat can learn to press a lever that will, after a delay of some 25 seconds, reward it with a bit of food. But if the delay stretches beyond 30 seconds, the animal is stumped."

Goudsmit and Claiborne, *Time*

The human skull has intrigued and frightened humans since the dawn of human kind (Figure 49.1). Skulls also have had monetary value. For example, in 1977, the skull of Swedish philosopher Emanuel Swedenborg (1688-1772) was bought by the Royal Swedish Academy of Sciences for 5,500 pounds, making it the most expensive skull in the world. (It now resides in the Session Room of the Academy.) The largest animal skull ever found belongs to the long-frilled ceratopsid dinosaurs whose skulls measure up to 9' 10" in length and weigh 2.2 tons.

Skulls have been used for many purposes throughout time. Figure 49.1 shows some of these. For example in the 1500s many skulls were used as monstrances (vessels in which the consecrated Host is displayed for adoration of the faithful). Below is skull-watch from the 1400s:

I was once told of a primitive tribe that used the cranial cavity of human skulls to store valuables, such as bits of gold. After hearing about such customs, it wasn't too hard for me to imagine an interesting scenario involving skulls, bones, and

Figure 49.1. *Skulls.* (Top) Symbol of death, with the motto "My glass runneth quickly." (Joost Hartgers, Amsterdam, 1651). (Bottom) Relic monstrance in the shape of a skull and thighbone. (A monstrance is a vessel in which the consecrated Host is displayed for adoration of the faithful.) (Amsterdam, 1648)

time. Consider the following. A native in the secluded rain forest takes a human skull and places 10 knucklebones inside it. He turns the skull so that the 10 bones sit on the front part of the skull near the frontal bone. Covering the opening to the spinal cord with his hand, the man then shakes the skull so that the 10 bones bounce around the skull in random directions. As they bounce off one another and off the sides of the skull, some will remain in the front part of the skull – but others will cross the cornonal suture (which roughly divides the skull cavity into 2 halves, front and back) and bounce into the back part of the crainal cavity (see frontispiece) In the course of time, the distribution of knucklebones in the two halves will inevitably become more uniform – that is, the entropy of the system will increase. After a few seconds the skull will approach a state of maximum entropy, with nearly equal numbers of knucklebones on each side of the coronal

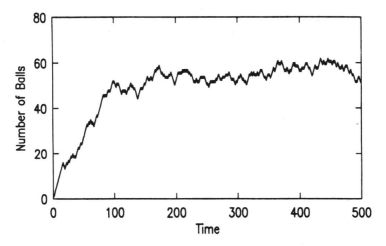

Figure 49.2. *Results of time machine experiments (500 minutes).*

suture. The process is not time-symmetrical because the reverse process, in which all the bones end up on one side of the suture, will never occur.

In actuality, I should not use the word "never" to describe the chances that the bones will at some point all again be on the same half of the skull cavity. There is a *small* probability that all the bones will end up on either one of the two sides of the skull. Let's imagine that you place the skull on a shaking machine and take an X-ray of the skull every minute to see where the knucklebones are located. With just one knucklebone, the odds on a state of low entropy are one in one. The knucklebone must be on one side or the other, so every observation you make will surely indicate that "all the bones" are on one side. With three bones, the odds that you will see all the bones on one side drops to 1 in 4. This means, on average, you will see this happen one time in every 4 times you examine the skull. If you look every minute, you'll have to wait, on average, 4 minutes until you see this happen. With 10 balls, you'll have to wait, on average, 512 minutes! You can calculate the odds of finding all the bones on one side of the skull using $P = 2^{n-1}$ where n is the number of bones. The following are some *time-skulls* showing you how long you will have to wait to see all the bones on one side of the skull for different numbers of bones.

Twenty knuckle bones in the skull represent a year. That is, if you look at the skull with an X-ray machine once a minute, you will have to wait a year before seeing all the bones in one half of the skull.

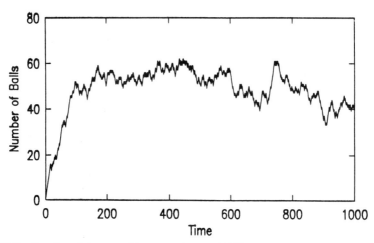

Figure 49.3. *Results of time machine experiments (1000 minutes).*

Below is a skull representing the life of a human. (27 bones gives 127 years.)

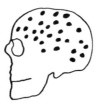

The oldest known mummy is dated to about 4,500 years ago. Here is a time-skull representing this period of time with 32 bones:

The longest measure of time is the *kalpa* in Hindu chronology. It is equivalent to 4,320 million years – roughly 52 knuckle bones:

CLOCKS OF ALL AGES

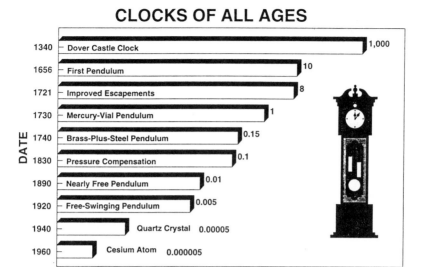

ERROR IN SECONDS PER DAY

Figure 49.4. *Clocks of all ages.* Clocks have become more accurate through the centuries. Early mechanical clocks, such as the Dover Castle, varied by several minutes each day. In the 1980's, cesium atom clocks lost less than a second in 3,000 years. In 1992, Hewlett-Packard Co. unveiled a new atomic clock that will remain reliable to the second for the next 1.6 million years. The $54,000 device is the size of a desktop computer.

Below is twice the age of the earth (4.5 billion years) (53 bones).

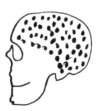

All this helps to prove that, while it is possible that entropy (and therefore, in a certain sense, time) will reverse itself by chance, it is highly unlikely so long as the system involved contains more than a few elements. Let me explain. Most scientists believe that the second law of thermodynamics expresses the one-way nature of time for large macroscopic systems. The entropy of a system, which is related to a gain or loss of organization, must always increase as a result of the second law of thermodynamics. You are an *entropy-losing machine*, since you maintain a complex organization of atoms in your body. However you achieve this entropy loss by disorganizing the atoms in food. (Much of the food energy is lost as body heat which dissipates into the air.) The entire *system* of you and your surroundings gains entropy. This one-way direction for entropy carries with it a

```
ALGORITHM: How to Create a Time Machine.
/* Place all balls in box 2          */
/* b(i) = 2 means ball is in box 2 */
/* b(i) = 3 means ball is in box 3 */
Do i = 1 to 100; /* 100 balls */
     b(i) = 2;
End;
DO j = 1 to 1000   /* 1000 minutes */
     GenRandom(r)
     r = r * 100 + 1
     if b(r) = 2 then b(r) = 3 ; else b(r)=2
  /* Print number of balls in box 2 */
     sum = 0;
     do i = 1 to 100;
         if b(i) = 2 then sum = sum + 1
     end;
     Print(j,sum)
END
```

Pseudocode 49.1. *How to create a time machine.*

one-way direction for time. Ice cubes melt, but do not spontaneously reform from liquid water. Even though elementary interactions can be symmetrical with respect to time, in our full-scale world, time, like an arrow, moves in only one direction.

A few scientists speculate that time will end. Austrian physicist Ludwig Boltzman long ago predicted the end of the universe as an attainment of maximum entropy. In this burned-out universe with no stars and no life, there will be no change by which time can be measured or observed. Some scientists have guessed that time will end on A.D. 10^{22} (10,000 billion years from now).

49.1 Build Your Own Time Machine

> *"We could imagine a world in which causality does not lead to a consistent order of earlier and later. In such a world the past and the future would not be irrevocably separated, but could come together in the same present, and we could meet our former selves of several years ago and talk to them. However, it is an empirical fact that our world is not of this type. Time order reflects the causal order of the universe."*
>
> Hans Reichenbach, 1951, *The Rise of Scientific Philosophy*

Here's a quick experiment which helps to demonstrate why time goes forward on a macroscopic scale. Take three small boxes. In Box 1 place 100 white slips of paper, numbered 1 through 100. In Box 2 place 100 slips of green paper, numbered 1 through 100. The third box, Box 3, is empty. Randomly choose white slips of paper from Box 1. The number you pick will indicate to you which slip of green paper to move. If you pick a white paper with the number 7 on it, then move the green slip of paper from Box 2 to Box 3. Replace the white paper in Box 1, and repeat the process.

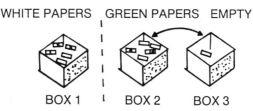

Each time, the number on a white piece of paper tells you that a particular green piece of paper is moved either from box 2 to box 3 or vice versa. (If it is in Box 2 move it to Box 3. If it is in Box 3, move it to Box 2). Can you guess what will happen after repeating this process 100 times? After some time has past, Box 2 and Box 3 will hold about equal quantities of green pieces of paper. You can think of the green pieces of paper as heat energy being homogenously distributed through space. On a macroscopic scale, energy flow and time flow proceed together – the direction of time. Entropy, which seems to give direction to time's arrow on a macroscopic scale, offers a *preferred* direction. While it's possible that the green slips of paper can all go back to Box 2, it is very unlikely.

You can build your own *entropy time machine* using your personal computer. The simulation with the white and green pieces of paper is outlined in the program code Pseudocode 49.1. I like to think of the process as a cosmic hand (representing the laws of chance) moving balls of energy around the universe. Imagine that the cosmic hand moves the balls of energy once a minute. Figure 49.2 and Figure 49.3 show you the number of these balls of energy (or green slips of paper) which reside in one of the boxes as a function of time. We soon achieve a maximum state of disorder where about 50 percent of the balls are in each box.

49.2 Stop and Think

> *"In relativity theory, in the subtle fusion of time and space known as Minkowskian space-time, the space dimensions seem to lord it over the time dimensions, and the whole structure exists as a frozen manifold outside of time."*   Davis and Hersh, 1986, *Descartes' Dream*

What effect would the use of different numbers of balls (or green slips of paper) have on the graphs in Figure 49.2 and Figure 49.3?

Figure 49.4 shows how timekeeping accuracy has changed through the centuries. What scientific and sociological effect would there be on our world today if clocks were no more accurate than the Dover Castle Clock (Figure 49.4)? You might be intrigued to know that the first clocks had no minute hands. In fact, the minute hand only gained importance during the Industrial Revolution. Imagine a modern world with clocks lacking minute hands.

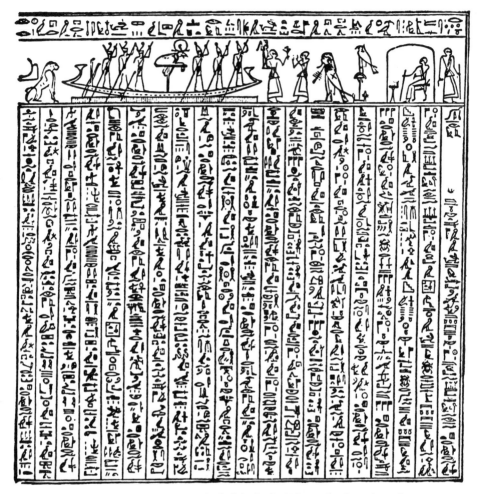

Page from an Egyptian papyrus *Book of the Dead,* which was placed into the tomb with the mummies as a guide for the souls of the departed.

Chapter 50

Interlude: Marking Time

"Space-time has no beginning and no end. It has no door where anything can enter. How break and enter what will only bend?"

Archibald MacLeish, *Reply to Mr. Wordsworth*

Karen Guzak is a Seattle, Washington artist whose computer art has been shown in the New Museum and the Brooklyn Museum in New York, in the San Francisco Museum of Modern Art, and in the Davidson Galleries in Seattle. She also has had work included in a touring show of twelve Northwest artists in France. She writes:

> It is only in the last few years that a few adventurous artists, surrounded by the smell of linseed oil and the dirty smudges of charcoal, have overcome their resistance to electronic media, and have taken on the computer as an art-making tool. Artists have been resistant to new tools before – for example, the printing press and the camera – as *machines* not fit to the expressive necessities of the human heart and human hand. However, there are some artists who welcome the vast varieties of line, shape, texture, space, value, and color available through computers.

To create her pieces of art, Karen uses a paint software program and a digitizing tablet with an electronic stylus, or light pen. She then makes choices about colors, shapes, and line quality. Her works require four to eight hours to complete. When ready, she keys instructions to an ink-jet printer that produces color by mixing four dyes of squirted ink: red, yellow, blue, and black. The technical process from ink-jet printout to lithograph plate involves programming the computer to print out a black and white version for each color of the image, eliminating all other colors, in effect creating printouts which correspond to color separations. Karen then manipulates the black and white printouts with an opaque white solution, pen and pencil. Her themes are big landscapes, relationships (particularly the relationship between two sorts of elementary shapes), quartz and jewels, the contrast between the macroscopic and microscopic, and the sense of time passing.

Shown at the beginning of this chapter is a photograph of her piece titled "Marking Time" (22x29 inches, 29 colors). The image at the end of the chapter is called "quartz dance" (22x29 inches, 25 colors). Karen remarks:

> There is still some belief out there, that if it's made by a machine, then it "ain't Art." However, there are some of us who combine the ancient and honorable picture making traditions with the new and powerful electronic technologies. For me, the computer has facilitated integration of the old with the new, and has allowed me to experiment, to explore, to play, and to speak my visual language in terms consistent with this time in history and with this place in the world.

Karen Guzak can be reached Studio 5A, 707 South Snoqualmie, Seattle, Washington 98108.

50.1 Cross References

The following sections are concerned with questions regarding whether or not computer-generated art is really good art: "Is Computer Art Really Art?" on page 169, "Interlude: Alien Musical Scores" on page 221, and "Are Fractal Graphics Art?" on page 95.

Part VI

STRANGE TECHNOLOGY

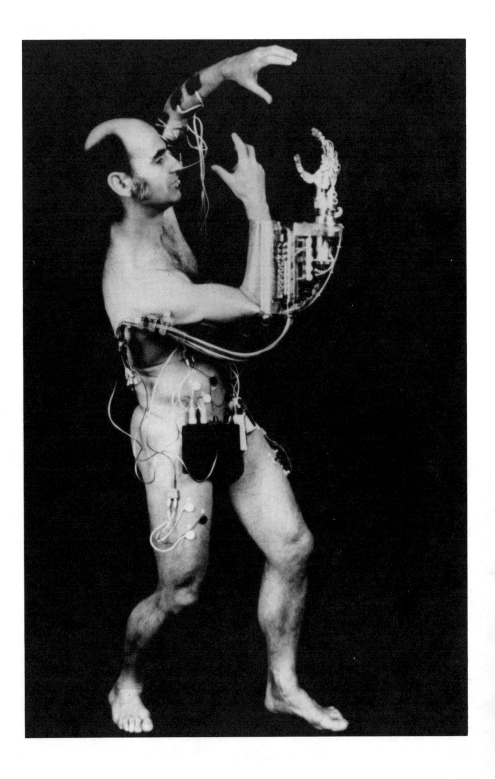

Chapter 51

Robot Checkers-Players, Surgeons, and Chefs

51.1 Checkers Enchiridion

"If automobile technology had advanced at the same rate as computer technology, a Rolls-Royce would travel at supersonic speeds and cost less than a dollar." William Poundstone, 1988, *Labyrinths of Reason*

"The computer, insofar as it solves the equations of mathematical physics, insofar as it is an instrument of oracularity and purports to tell us today what will happen tomorrow, collapses time by making the future appear now." Davis and Hersh, 1986, *Descartes' Dream*

About A.D. 1100 an unknown individual, probably living in the south of France, invented a war game played out on a board containing black and white squares. Each player had twelve pieces which could move one square diagonally in any direction. A piece made a capture by jumping diagonally over the enemy piece to land on an empty square immediately beyond. The game later became known as draughts in England, and the early American settlers took the English game to North America where it is known as checkers. Mathematicians today have determined that a checkers game has an incredible 10^{20} possible variations. (In chess, some estimate the number to be 10^{44}. The ancient Chinese game of Go has a walloping 10^{120} positions.)

Imagine a robot arm moving checkers pieces around a playing board as quickly as it can. Let's assume that it can grasp a checker, pick it up from one square, and move it to another at the rate of one move per second. For how long would the robot arm be working? Longer than the life of a man? Longer than the period of rotation of the Milky Way? The answer is "yes" to both questions. In fact there are more checkers positions than there are stars in the Milky Way galaxy. The total distance travelled by the robot arm in the mindless movement exercise would be greater than the distance from the earth to the moon. In fact

Figure 51.1. *Rochester checkers playing robot.* (Photo courtesy of James Montanus and the University of Rochester. Photo by Chris Brown.)

the distance travelled would be about the distance of the center of our galaxy from the sun.

While the idea of a robot moving checkers around a board to demonstrate every possible move may seem futuristic or even a little silly, checker-playing robots are already in operation today. In the past, several computers have been programmed to calculate checkers moves; however, *Rochester Robot* at the University of Rochester, New York is the first computer-driven robot to not only think through the strategy but to actually see the pieces and move them (Figure 51.1). The robot looks a little funny with its four-inch yellow foam nose. It uses its "nose" to move the checkers, taking jumps when necessary and sliding checkers off the board. The Rochester robot uses 12 processors for vision, reasoning, and motion tasks. The robot computes each of its moves in about a second. If you try to cheat it, or make an illegal move, the robot's voice synthesizer admonishes you with the words, "You cannot do that!" The robot integrates several different styles of parallel computing in one operating system.[30]

---

[30] Some readers may be interested in more technical details of the robot's operation. The vision systems consist of a binocular head containing movable cameras for visual input, a robot arm that supports and moves the head, a checker pushing tool (referred to as the robot's nose), a special-purpose parallel processor for high-bandwidth low-level vision processing, and a general-purpose MIMD parallel processor for high-level vision and planning. This Butterfly Plus Parallel Processor has 24 nodes, each consisting of an MC68020 processor with hardware floating point and memory managing units, and 4 MBytes of memory. Various different board representations are used to help the processors play checkers, including a digitized image of the board from the TV camera

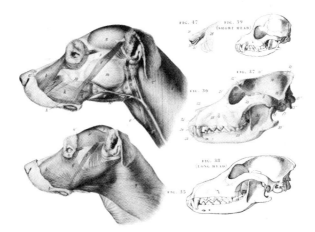

Figure 51.2. *Robot dog surgeons.* A 250-pound robot named *Robodoc* is the first robot to perform surgery on a human. Currently Robodoc routinely operates on arthritic dogs. Robodoc carves out the cavity in the bone where an implant will be inserted. Perhaps by the end of the decade Robodoc will aid orthopedic surgeons who already do 160,000 hip replacements in the United States each year. (See text for details.)

51.1.1 Fact File

• One fairly difficult checkers puzzle to solve is called *The 8 Checkers Puzzle*. Place eight checkers on a checkerboard so that no two checkers lie in the same column, row, or diagonal.

• There are over 4,000,000 ways that 8 pieces can be placed on a 64-square checkerboard.

51.2 Pizzabot

"Huge enterprises like IBM, Bell Telephone, and General Electric maintain grassy research centers – called 'funny farms' by the disrespectful – where whole platoons of mathematicians are paid to do little else but think."

David Bergammini, 1963 *Mathematics*

(512x512x8 bits), and a quantitative description of the (X,Y,Z) locations of the centroids of the pieces on the board and their color. The strategy portion of the robot's brain was written, in part, by Michael Scott. Brian Marsh and his colleagues are using checkers play to investigate ways of integrating computer programs written in different languages. For more information, consult: Marsh, B., Brown, C. LeBlanc, T., Scott, M., Becker, T., Das, P., Karlsson, J. and Quiroz, C. (1991) The Rochester Checkers Player: multi-model parallel programming for animate vision. *Technical Report 347*, University of Rochester, Computer Science Dept., Rochester, NY 14627.

"The test is not going to be whether we do good science or not. The test is: Is the company [AT&T][31] *going to be healthy or not. To say that we'll ever be totally happy, that I'm going to bring the 1950s back – sorry I can't."*
Arnold Penzias, 1991 *Scientific American*

Robots of the future will not only play checkers but also serve us food. *Pizzabot*, the world's first pizza-making robot, was developed by engineers at Carnegie-

Mellon to help disabled people become more independent and even manage pizza restaurants. The robot arm is placed in front of a semicircular counter, with ingredients such as cheese, mushrooms, and sauce within easy reach. A voice-recognition system permits one to select one of two possible pizza sizes and 12 condiments. PizzaBot spreads the sauces with an S-shaped swirl, and then applies the mozzarella by shaking a scoop. When first tested, PizzaBot made 50 delicious pizzas in a row without any errors.

51.3 Robot Surgeons

"The name of Leonardo da Vinci will be invoked by artists to prove that only a great artist can be a great technician. The name of Leonardo da Vinci will be invoked by technicians to prove that only a great technician can be a great artist."
Alex Gross, 1968, *East Village Other*

Robot surgeons are also already operating in the 1990's. A 250-pound robot named *Robodoc* is the first robot to perform surgery on a human. Currently Robodoc routinely operates on arthritic dogs at the veterinary clinic of Hap Paul, head of Robodoc development at Integrated Surgical Systems in Sacramento, California. Robodoc carves out the cavity in the bone where an implant will be inserted. Robodoc is about 10 times as accurate as a human holding a drill. Sensors monitoring pressure on the drill bit will stop Robodoc if it were to start cutting into soft tissue! Perhaps Robodoc will aid orthopedic surgeons by the end of the decade who already do 160,000 hip replacements in the United States each year.

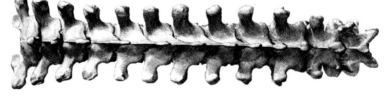

---

[31] Arno Penzias is the Vice President of research at AT&T Bell Labs. He is also a Nobel Laureate. His quotes are from: Corcoran, E. (1991) Rethinking Research: Bell Labs seeks a new model for industrial research. December, *Scientific American*, pp. 136-139.

Chapter 52

Bar Codes in the 21st Century

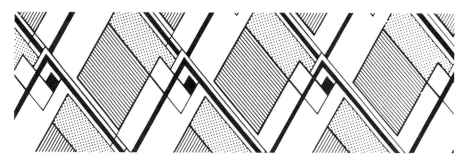

Most Americans have become familiar with printed bar codes on the cans, packages, and covers of all kinds of consumer goods – from sardines, to Steven King novels, to Ninja Turtle toys. Introduced almost twenty years ago, bar code information is encoded in the varied widths of the spaces and bars printed on the paper. A cashier scans across the row of bars with a laser. This row of bars represents a number which can be associated with specific information, such as the price of the object, in the cash register's computer or in a central database. One reason these bar codes work so well is that there is a redundancy of information over the height of the bar code symbol.

The current bar codes can be thought of as one-dimensional codes since they only carry information in one direction. Bar codes of the future, however, will be two and three dimensional. At left is an example of a 2-D bar code which contains

Lincoln's Gettysburg Address in a two inch square!

This kind of bar code (called PDF417) was developed by Symbol Technologies (Bohemia, NY) and is scannable by linear scans, such as produced when using a laser scanner. PDF stands for "portable data file," because these postage stamp sized patterns really can contain an entire file of information. To enable the scanner to detect any kind of barcode problems (for example, mud, hair, or dandruff on the bar code), each row of a PDF417 symbol contains what is called a "row checksum." In addition, each tiny individual symbol contains two error detection code words to ensure that all data has been recovered accurately. In fact, PDF417 allows users to choose one of nine security levels which allows users to sacrifice barcode space for better error recovery, as needed. Curious readers, who want to learn more about PDF technology, should see the April 1990 issue of the *IEEE Computer Magazine*.

Figure 52.1. *Bar codes are used to track the activities of honeybees.* Pollination is estimated to be worth $20 billion per year to American agriculture. (Photo courtesy of INTERMEC.)

Another kind of 2-D barcode stacks several rows of 17 spaces and 18 bars on top of one another, with start and stop codes at each end. Shown below is such a bar code from the INTERMEC Corporation in Everett, Washington.

158600

CALCIUM

Aside from these futuristic bar codes, more standard bar codes are being increasingly used in novel situations. For example, in the last few years, bar codes have been used to track live honeybees for pollination research (Figure 52.1). Tiny bar codes are placed on the backs of bees. The labels, which don't interfere with normal bee activity, code for bee identification numbers which are automatically scanned each time a bee enters or leaves a hive.

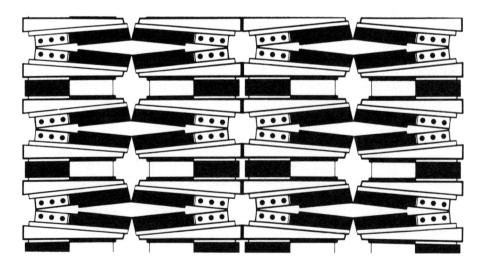

Chapter 53

Cyberspace and Nomadology

53.1 Sentient Trees in Multiperson Spaces

Computers of the future will allows us to enter lifelike, computer-generated realities. Strap on a pair of goggles and you can gaze into a three-dimensional world limited only by the speed with which your computer can change the images in response to your eye and head motions. Some call this sense of actually being present within a new reality a "virtual reality" or cyberspace (Figure 53.1 and Figure 53.2). The degree to which cyberspace becomes undifferentiated from reality depends partly on the development of new ways for humans to physically interact with the computer's reality (such as 3-D goggles and gloves). New 6-dimensional trackers which monitor a physical object's spatial position and orientation, along with speech recognition devices, will help the process. Randal Walser, a cyberspace researcher at Autodesk Incorporated, notes that "multiperson" spaces, where several people interact, are especially important because they promise to be far more lively than spaces in which you interact only with a computer. He further comments:

> In a multiperson space, there will always be a possibility that the virtual objects you encounter are directed by human intelligence... Sometimes you will be surprised to find that objects, like trees and refrigerators, that you assumed were unintelligent, are in fact full of sophisticated abilities. This will bring cyberspace alive, giving it a magical and delightful (if spooky) quality.

53.2 Nomadic Research Labs

A field of technology related to virtual reality and cyberspace is *nomadology*. Nomads are human/bicycle hybrids that travel around the country, and which allow the human user to be immersed in the ebb and flow of global information. The most famous of nomads is Steven K. Roberts of the Nomadic Research Labs at Sun Microsystems in California. His bicycle accommodates a computer, a citi-

Figure 53.1. *Virtual racquet-ball.* Interactivity in cyperspace includes such actions as moving, grasping, releasing, and throwing. (Photo courtesy of Autodesk, Inc.)

zens band radio, a ham radio, solar panels for power, and much more. He installed four buttons on each handlebar and built in a computer over the front wheel. Amazingly, he can ride while at the same time entering information into  the computer using the handlebar buttons. To prepare for the future, Roberts is currently working on a more sophisticated nomad bike with 105 gears. In low gear Roberts has to pedal at 60 revolutions a minute to go 1.2 miles an hour. The solar cells dump 72 watts of solar energy into the batteries which supply the computers, refrigerators, and other devices. The console contains three screens run by separate computers. He can link to other computers using the on-board phone, use the speech recognition device for providing input, and use the satellite navigation system for guidance. For more information, you might consult his *Journal of High-Tech Nomadness*, available from Nomadic Research Labs, PO Box 2185, El Segundo, CA 90245.

53.3 Time Traveler

A recent video game called *Time Traveler* (Sega Enterprises, San Jose) subjects a viewer to a three-dimensional illusion without resorting to fancy goggles or holograms. The unit has a video monitor which actually points away from the player and towards a spherical concave mirror. Images from the monitor reflect off the

Figure 53.2. *Virtual bicycle ride.* (Photo courtesy of Autodesk, Inc.)

mirror and project onto a darkened area.

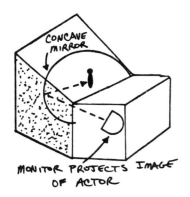

If you like, you can thrust your hand into these lifelike miniaturized characters (actors, not animated cartoon figures) which appear to be in free space. At left is a diagram of the video and concave mirror set up. The game begins with an appeal from a scantily clad princess who begs the player to help her. A 16-bit Intel 80188 dedicated controller processes the player's selections which control a videodisc.

53.4 Virtual Reality, Al Gore, and Jerry Garcia

Figure 53.3, Figure 53.4. and Figure 53.5 show additional examples of futuristic technology which enable humans to interact with computers in innovative ways. You may be interested to know that the term "virtual reality" was coined by Jaron Lanier, Founder and CEO of VPL Inc., to describe interactive 3-D imaging. Today, you can put on a "DataGlove" (Figure 53.4) and a stereoscopic headset (Figure 53.3 and Figure 53.5) to transport yourself in to virtual worlds that are used by physicians for simulated surgery or by NASA for space exploration. Lanier has demonstrated virtual reality methods to such interested people as Steven Spielberg, Jerry Garcia of the Grateful Dead, and Presidential Candidate

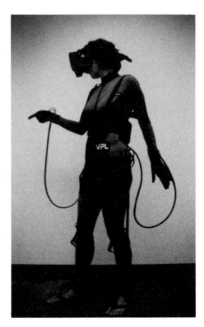

Figure 53.3. *A DataSuit and EyePhone.* These allow the user to fly through and interact with a virtual world generated by computer. (Courtesy of VPL Research, Inc, Redwood City, CA.)

Al Gore. Lanier has also noted that "virtual reality has the potential to create a bridge between people who heretofore have been separated due to disabilities."

53.5 Fact File

• The following advanced computer laboratories, among others, are pursuing active research projects in virtual reality: NASA Ames, NASA Goddard, the National Center for Supercomputing Applications, the Electronic Visualization Laboratory at the University of Illinois at Chicago, the MIT Media Lab, and the University of North Carolina. These labs are currently using virtual reality hardware to study biomolecules, engineering designs, mathematical functions, plasma physics, cosmology, and general reactivity. (Source: Smarr, L. (1991) Visualization captures the imagination of physics. *Computers in Physics.* Nov/Dec 5(6): 564.)

• Steve Bryson and Creon Levit have developed a *Virtual Windtunnel* at NASA Ames. This virtual reality hardware immerses a researcher in a computer simulation of air flow around airplanes and space shuttles. Users of the virtual tunnel see computer graphics in "3-D head-tracked wide-field stereo," using a device called a Fake Space boom, and they control the position of streamlines (indicating airflow) using a VPL Dataglove. (Source: Smarr, L. (1991) Visualization captures the imagination of physics. *Computers in Physics.* Nov/Dec 5(6): 564.)

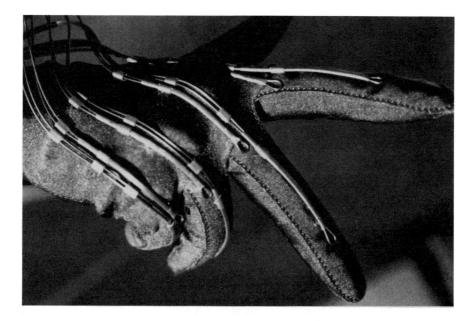

Figure 53.4. *A DataGlove which conveys finger positions to the computer.* Devices such as these can control robot hands. Within the next few years, musicians, dancers, artists, film-makers, sports enthusiasts, surgeons, and masseuses will have access to these devices. (Courtesy of VPL Research, Inc, Redwood City, CA.)

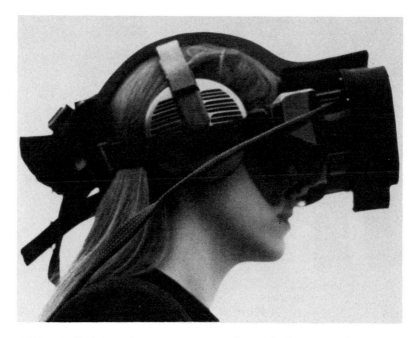

Figure 53.5. *An EyePhone for seeing into virtual worlds.* (Courtesy of VPL Research, Inc, Redwood City, CA.)

Chapter 54

Practical Fractals

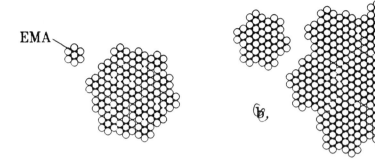

A *fiberoptic faceplate* is an array of millions of optical-fiber tubes packed into a thin cylindrical pipe. The composite tube acts as an *image-plane transfer device*. This means that an image entering one surface exits the other surface as an undistorted digitized image, regardless of the shape of the optical tube. You can use these tubes as a kind of periscope by bending them in order to see around a corner.

Recently, one fiberoptic researcher, Lee Cook at the Gallileo Electro-Optics Corporation in Sturbridge, Massachusetts, was interested in preparing arrays of optical waveguides which were perfect as possible. Analysis of certain recursive tilings led Cook and his colleagues to conclude that the edges of optically useful tilings were fractal in nature. This led to the development of assembly techniques and fractal array structures which allowed the Gallileo researchers to prepare highly ordered fiber arrays. One patent has already been granted on these techniques.

Many believe that *fractal fiberoptics* (a trademarked term) are the first engi-

neered fractal materials with optically useful properties. A fractal fiber-array, which consists of fibers of fibers (called *multi-multifibers*) results in an extremely high degree of internal order and an optically useful packing in the fiberoptic, evidenced in Figure 54.1. This increased order produces a markedly improved image contrast. The perimeters of these new multi-multifibers are exactly analogous to the fractal object, called a Gosper snowflake, shown here. (To create a Gosper snowflake, recursively transform each face of an equilateral hexagon into three segments of equal length so as to preserve the original area of the solid.) In the image at the end of this chapter, three "pipes" sitting atop a Gosper snowflake fractal, which itself illustrates the interlocking structure of

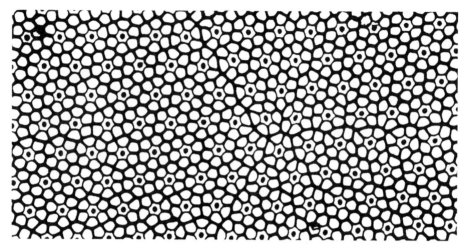

Figure 54.1. *A practical fractal.* This is a photograph of the first fractally organized fiberoptic face plate for practical applications. You can see repeated clusters of the seven-element multifiber if you look closely. This leads to a very highly ordered array with useful optical properties. (Photo courtesy of Lee Cook/Galileo Electro-Optics Corp.)

fractal fiberoptics. If you look closely, you can see how the pipe effectively transmits the image on the bottom plane to the top. For more information, consult: Cook, L., Patterson, S. (1991) Fiberoptics for displays. *Information Display.* June 7(6): 14-17.

The frontispiece for this chapter shows a Gopalsamy function which I computed using an IBM RISC System/6000. See "Descriptions of Color Plates" on page 412 for formulas.

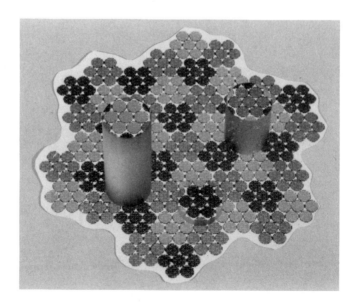

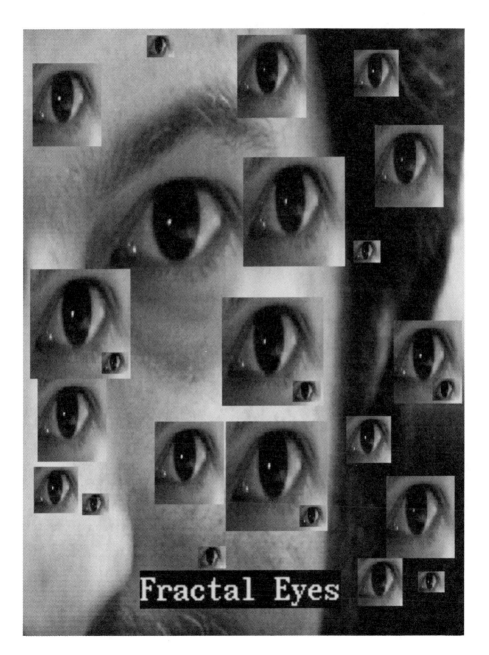

Fractal Eyes

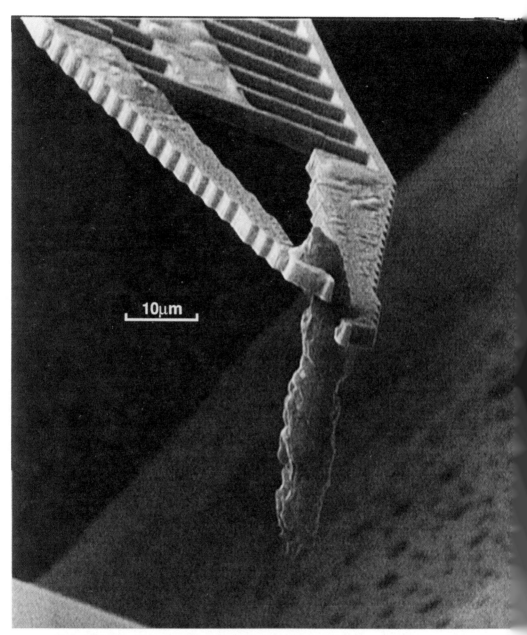

This microgripper, made by C.-J. Kim, A. P. Pisano and R. S. Muller of Berkeley Sensor & Actuator Center, holds an Euglena (a single cell protozoa, 7x40 μm), preserved by K. D. Lee. The SEM picture has been taken with the help of V. Gutnik.

Chapter 55

Interlude: Embracing Euglenas
With Invisible Pliers

Facing this page is what appears to be a pair of massive tweezers gripping a huge sausage-shaped creature. However, this is an image taken through a scanning electron microscope. The tweezer arms are bits of silicon about 400 microns long, smaller than a flea. In fact the "microgripper" – as it is called by Chang-Jin Kim (below), Richard Muller, and Albert Pisano of the University of California, Berkeley – is not visible to the naked eye. And the sausage shape is really a singe-celled protozoan called a euglena!

Microgrippers may have applications in biomedical and *micro-telerobotics*. This means that they could serve as miniature robot hands which position a cell under a microscope or could simplify the most delicate of surgeries. Will micro-surgeons of the future use microgrippers to enter minute vessels, and to explore the intricate caverns of the brain?

So potentially important is this technology that, in 1991, the Japanese government approved $160 million for a multiyear national effort in micromachine technology. Kensall Wise of the University of Michigan notes that "The potential impact will exceed anything that has come along since microprocessors."

For further reading, see: Amoto, I. (1991) The small wonders of microengineering. *Science* July 26, 253: 387-388. Also see: Kim, C.-J., Pisano, A., Muller, R., Lim, M. (1990) Polysilcone microgripper. *Technical Digest, IEEE Solid-State Sensor and Actuator Workshop*, Hilton Head Island, South Carolina. June, pp. 48-51. The SEM photo was taken with the help of V. Gutnik.

Too Many Bishops

Chapter 56

Miraculous Chess Solutions

"Many have become chess masters — no one has become the master of chess."

Tarrasch

Although Gary Kasparov, chess champion of the world, has vowed that no machine shall ever defeat him, many researchers suggest that chess playing computers will soon defeat the best human players in the world. Chess playing hardware has become progressively faster over the last few years. As an example, Figure 56.1 shows the hardware heart of one of my favorite recent inventions in the field of computer chess. The fully configured 24-processor machine can search around 10 million chess positions per second!

Over the last few centuries, chess masters have claimed that a win cannot be forced in certain pawnless endgames, such as the one shown here in this schematic representation of a chess board.[32]

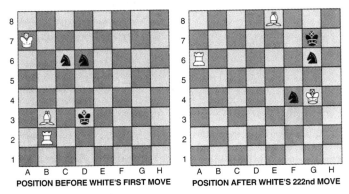

POSITION BEFORE WHITE'S FIRST MOVE   POSITION AFTER WHITE'S 222nd MOVE

Chess experts previously thought that the best play must lead to a draw in an endgame such as this. However, a recently designed chess program which ran for more than four hours on a massively parallel computer (Thinking Machines

---

[32] The chess diagram is from: "Endless Engames" by Phillip E. Ross. © 1991 by *Scientific American, Inc.* Picture by J. Johnson. All rights reserved.

Figure 56.1. *Hardware heart of a chess computer.* When fully configured this computer is capable of searching 10 million positions per second. As a comparison, Cray Blitz searches at 1/40th the speed, or 250,000 positions per second, when running on a "top of the line" 8-processor Cray YMP general-purpose supercomputer. (Cray Blitz is the name of the program that won the 4th and 5th World Computer Chess Championship in the early to middle 1980s.) Figure courtesy of Feng-Hsiung Hsu, a developer of this hardware, IBM Watson Research Center.

Corp.), has found a way to win. The program was written by Lewis Stiller (a 25-year-old graduate student at Johns Hopkins University), and the winning sequence consists of a walloping 223 moves, by far the longest chess sequence in the centuries' long history of chess. Stiller has opened the door for analysis of a problem considered too tough for even the fastest computers. By performing one of the largest computer searches ever conducted, Stiller proved for the first time that a king, a rook, and a bishop can defeat a King and two Knights.[33]

Philip Ross, an editor for *Scientific American*, notes that for the first 200 moves of the endgame "the pieces seem to dance about aimlessly, conforming to no rules that a human master might recognize and follow. Matters become clear only near the end, when the Black King's back is against the wall and its attendant Knights can no longer protect one another." After 222 moves, the white King moves into square f5, forcing the win of a Knight.

---

[33] The computer program is 10,000 lines long, and it solved the chess problem in five hours after considering 100 billion moves by retrograde analysis working backward from a winning position. The program can solve a five-piece endgame in about a minute and a six-piece endgame in four to six hours.

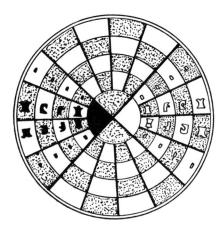

Figure 56.2. *Byzantine circular chess.* This medieval form of chess is played on a circular board with 64 spaces and 4 "citadels." There is no pawn promotion, and if two players' pawns are played around the board and meet face to face blocking each other, the opponent removes them both and then make his own move. If a player's King is forced to enter his opponent's citadel, he is considered to have reached a sanctuary and the game ends in a draw. (Figure from R.C. Bell's *Board and Table Games from Many Civilizations*, Dover: NY.)

Other researchers have proved that King and Queen win against a King and two bishops. This is an endgame that previous chess manuals had concluded would end in a draw! As a result of computer solutions such as these, the International Chess Federation had to amend its rule on how long a game can go on before it must be declared a draw. (Previously, players had to force a win within 50 moves after the last capture of a piece or move of a pawn.)

56.1 Fact File

"In the opening of a game, the master should play like a book, in the midgame he should play like a magician, in the ending he should play like a machine."   Speilmann

• In 1991, the world's strongest commercially available chess computer is the *Mephisto Lyon 32 Bit*.[34] This computer relies on expert programming rather than

---

[34] In the early 1990's there were many commercially available chess software packages for personal computers. They include great graphics and run on a variety of machines. Here are just a few: *Checkmate* (Interplay Productions, 3710 S. Susan, Suite 100, Santa Ana, CA 92704; 714-549-2411), *Chessmaster 2000* (The Software Toolworks, 19808 Nordhoff Pl., Chatsworth, CA 91311; 818 885-9000), *Chessmaster 3000* (The Software Toolworks, 60 Leveroni Court, Novata, CA 94949; 415 883-5157, 415 883-3000), and

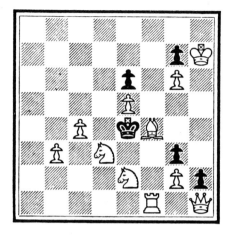
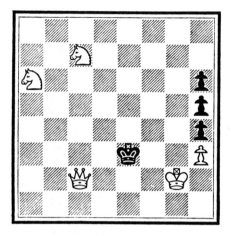

Figure 56.3. *Very difficult endgames.* Can you solve these endgame puzzles? In each puzzle, white mates in three moves. Can your chess computer solve these baffling beauties?

processing power, and it is the winner of the 1991 World Microcomptuer Chess Championship held in Vancouver, B.C. Its cost is around 2,000 dollars. For more information: Fidelity Electronics International Inc., 13900 N.W. 58th Ct., Miami, FL 33014.

• There are 1,840 different moves which can be made on a chessboard. Each move is represented as a line segment in the graph below (adapted from Gardner, 1992):

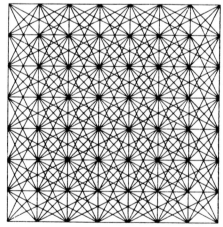

World Class Chess, (Valueware, Melody Hall Publishing Corp., Northbrook, IL 69965).

56.2 Superqueens, Amazons, and Pegasus Pieces

"Of chess it has been said that life is not long enough for it – but that is the fault of life, not chess. "   Napier

Some of you may be interested in the fascinating and powerful chess piece formally known as a *Superqueen* or *Amazon*. This is a special chess piece that com- bines the moves of a Queen and a Knight. Gardner (1992) notes that it is not possible to place *n* superqueens on an *n* by *n* board so that they do not attack one another when *n* is less than 10. Try this. You may also wish to play a game of traditional chess, replacing your Queens and your opponent's Queens with Superqueens. Finally, you should try playing a chess game with all four Knights replaced with (what I call) *Pegasus* pieces. These pieces combine the moves of a Knight with that of a bishop. If your two Knights are replaced by two Pegasus pieces, and your opponent's Queen is replaced by a superQueen, who will win?

56.3 International Computer-Chess Championships

"A win by an unsound combination, however showy, fills me with artistic horror."   Steinitz

Each year there is a world computer-chess tournament sponsored by the Association for Computing Machinery. In November 1991, IBM's computer-chess system called Deep Thought II won the 22nd International Computer-Chess Championship at the Supercomputing '91 conference in Albuquerque, New Mexico. There were a number of tough competitors. Deep Thought II (running on an IBM RISC computer equipped with 24 custom processors) competed against and defeated Zarkov (HP workstation), M Chess (80486), HiTech (Sun, special hardware), Cray Blitz (Cray, 8 processors), and The Chess Machine (RISC PC adapter). M Chess came in second. Also competing were Mephisto (68030), LaChex (CRAY uniprocessor), Bebe (custom processor), Socrates (80486), BP (80486), and Delicate Brute (Sun).

56.4 Relativistic Chess

Kevin Whyte of the Department of Mathematics at the University of Chicago has described a chess variant called "relativistic chess." He invented this form with Lee Corbin. In brief, squares which are attacked by your opponent do not exist for you. This means that you pass "through" them as if they were not there. A few examples will help clarify this. If a rook were to face a pawn, all the squares between the pawn and the rook do not exist for the pawn – it's as if the rook were sitting on the square directly in front of the pawn; thus the pawn cannot move. Similarly, if a bishop attacks a pawn, then the bishop is considered one square away diagonally and can be taken by the pawn. All intermediate squares do not exist, as far as the pawn is concerned. Kings are non-relativistic, and move normally. The reason for this exclusionary rule is that the Kings would be virtually impossible to checkmate if relativistic, since they could skip over any attacked squares – as if the squares did not exist.

56.5 Infinite Chess

Tim Converse from the University of Chicago has studied a chess variant where the game is played on an extremely large board or on one that extends arbitrarily in all directions. Queens, rooks, and bishops are permitted unlimited movement in the directions they are allowed to move. The arbitrary-extent version of the game would be well suited for play using a computer. Converse notes that this game would be very different from standard chess. For one, pawns would become extremely unimportant, and probably a lot of the initial moves would be long moves by the major pieces. Of course, if there were no borders at all, the game could get very sparse as the pieces quickly dispersed through the board. Infinite Chess is an interesting problem for game-playing computer programs, since the programs would not only have to limit the number of moves they look ahead (as usual), but they would also have to limit their "spatial" horizon as well.

56.6 Black Hole Chess

A year ago, I developed a variant of chess called "Black Hole Chess" where two "black holes" are placed on the board, as indicated in the following diagram. Any pieces forced across these holes are removed from the board. Needless to say, if a King is forced into a hole the game is over.

56.7 Gun Chess, Ghost Chess, Fairy Chess, and Other Variants

"Fairy Chess offers an infinite field for the expression of Man's scientific and artistic imagination, and adds new glory to his intellectual achievement."   T. R. Dawson, *Rex Multiplex*

Philippe Schnoebelen of Grenoble, France, has brought several other variants of chess to my attention. In "Gun Chess," the capture of pieces is different from standard chess in that the capturing piece does not move. It's as if the capturing piece shoots the opponent's piece from a distance (and the enemy piece is then removed, as in standard chess). This makes it almost obligatory to respond to checks by moving the King.

Another strange chess variant was played by Schnoebelen in high school. The game is the same as standard chess except that the first player to "check" (not to checkmate) the other King wins. Schnoebelen writes:

> On the surface, this minor change in chess rules may not seem very strange, but White has a very quick forced win by playing: 1. Nc3 (threatening 2. Nd5 or 2. Nb5, and 3. Nf6+ or Nc7+). A complete winning strategy can be described with a few nested if-then-else statements; therefore, I was able to write a pocket-calculator program to play it perfectly.

Fairy chess utilizes "fairy" pieces and was invented and popularized by T.R. Dawson. These games often use freak pieces such as the "Princess," combining the powers of a Knight and Bishop. A well-known problem magazine called *Feenschach*[35] is exclusively devoted to "fairy/heterodox" chess problems. These problems also include the use of multiple kings which must be checkmated all at once and ghost men that can be passed through by other pieces. Another version uses a partition which is placed on the board, and the players put down their pieces (secretly) on whatever squares they wish.

56.8 Madhouse Chess, and Martian Chess

Madhouse chess has the following simple rule: instead of capturing the opponent's piece, the piece is simply moved to a square of the "captor's" choice. In this game, pieces are conserved in the same way that there is conservation of mass in chemical reactions. Yet another variant called Martian Chess uses a 10x10 board.

56.9 Hexagonal Chess

Marc R. Roussel of the University of Toronto has studied hexagonal chess. The game is similar to standard chess, except that the squares are hexagons, and the moves of the different pieces are appropriately modified. Roussel writes:

> There are three colors of squares instead of the usual two; this is to satisfy the constraint that no two nearest-neighbor squares can be the same color. The Bishops are confined to a single color as in ordinary chess so each side gets three Bishops to start with. The Rooks move along straight lines (of which there are now three instead of two emanating from any given square) and the Queen's move is still a combination of a Rook's and a Bishop's; this makes the Queen unusually mobile.

[35] For information on the fairy chess magazine *Feenschach* (Zeitschrift für Märchenschach), contact: Bernd Ellinghoven, Königstr. 3, D-5100 Aachen, Germany. For information on another strange, fairy chess magazine called *Rex Multiplex (Revue Trimestrielle Consacree Aux Echecs Feeriques)*: 150 Francs par an (5 numeros) a l'ordre de D. Blondel-Rex Multiplex, No de Compte Cheque Postal: 20 567-47 A Paris. Directeur: Denis Blondel, 22 Allee des Bouleaux, 94510 La Queue en Brie, France.

56.10 5x5 Chess

Martin Gardner in his book *Further Mathematical Diversions* describes a game called Mini-Chess which is played on a 5x5 board. Each player has 5 pawns and only one each of the remaining pieces. The playing strategy is interesting since the opening move is guaranteed to be attacking.

56.11 Crushed Chess

Here's a game I loved to play. Every 10 moves, the board becomes smaller. You start with the standard 8x8 board. 10 moves later, the board becomes 6x6, thus eliminating all the squares which form the square border frame of the original board. Think of this as an ever-diminishing square board centered within a square board within a square board, and so on. If a piece is caught on a row or column which is eliminated, the piece itself is eliminated. The player who retains the King the longest is the winner.

56.12 Evolution Chess, Carnivore Chess, and Others

Here are some other mind-bending variations which will be of interest to some of you. I would be interested in hearing from any who have tried these games.

1. *Carnivore Chess* - A roving (additional) piece devours any chess piece it encounters as the game proceeds. Before each move in a standard chess game, the carnivore piece is moved one square in any direction on the board, executing a random walk on the playing board. The piece is initially positioned near the center of the board, as diagrammed below. The game is played as standard chess except for the addition of this dangerous carnivore piece. Whenever the carnivore piece moves onto a square already occupied by a chess piece, the piece on the square is eliminated.

2. *Evolution Chess* - In this version, pieces evolve into more powerful pieces as the game proceeds, or as a piece moves onto certain designated positions on the board.

3. *Fossil Chess* - After a Pawn's first move it becomes a fossil, and can no longer move for the rest of the game. An attacking piece may capture a fossil, but the attacking piece is immobilized as a result.

4. *Too Many Bishops* - In this version, each player acquires an additional Bishop before each turn. The Bishop is placed on a position determined by the opponent. The game ends when a King is captured, or a player cannot move due to the mob of Bishops on the board, or when a player cannot add a Bishop at the start of a turn because all squares are occupied. For clarification, here is how each turn starts: 1) Your new

Bishop is placed on the board at a position determined by your opponent. 2) Next, you are free to move the new Bishop or any other of your pieces as usual.

5. *Double Chess* - Two boards are placed along side one another. Pieces travel freely between boards as diagrammed below.

6. *Crowded Chess* - This is a real fun one. In front of the usual row of Pawns, each player has an extra row of Pawns. Since each player has two rows of Pawns, the playing board becomes very crowded.

7. *No Pawn Chess* - This is the same as the standard game, except that fewer (or no) pawns are used.

56.13 Fibonacci Chess

This game involves the use of the Fibonacci sequence to determine the number of moves a player is permitted during his or her turn. (See "Apocalypse Numbers" on page 337 for background to the Fibonacci sequence: 1, 1, 2, 3, 5, 8, ...) To play Fibonacci chess, you make one move, and then your opponent makes a move. You make 2 moves. Your opponent makes 3 moves. You make 5 moves, and so on. David Bradley, one of the inventors of this chess variant, remarks, "The fun part is the fact that you must inflict a lot of damage while you can, because the next player gets so many more moves than you had."

56.14 For Further Reading

1. Gardner, M. (1992) *Fractal Music, Hypercards, and More...* Freeman: NY.

2. Fraekel, A., Lichentestein, D. (1981) Computing a perfect strategy for NxN chess requires   time exponential in N. *Journal of Combinatorial Theory, Series A* 31: 199-214.

56.15 Cross References

See "Hyperdimensional Knights" on page 236 for a description of 1-D Knights and hyper-dimensional rooks. See "Knights in Hell" on page 321 for a puzzle involving Knights. See "Chess Music" on page 204 for music from chess. See "Magic Squares, Emperor Yu, Chess Knights, Etc." on page 66 for a chess Knight magic square.

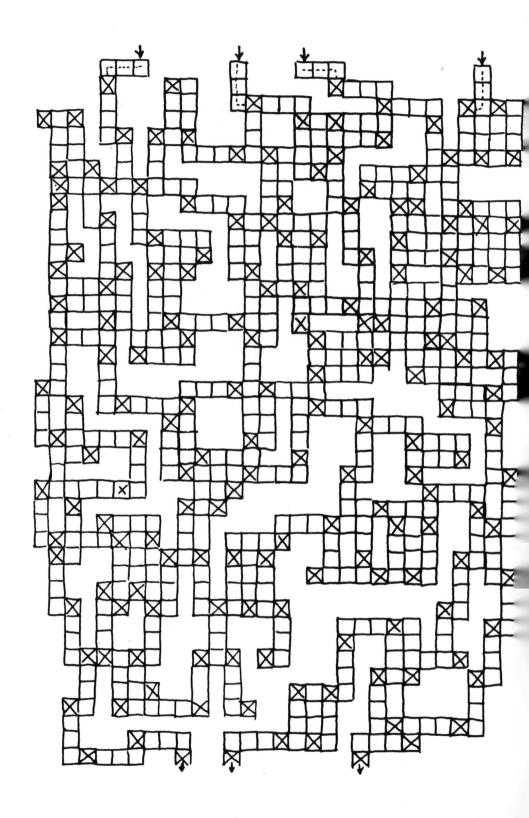

Chapter 57

Knights in Hell,
And Other Chess Charivari

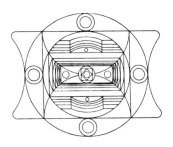

57.1 Knights in Hell

"Some Knights don't leap – they limp. "   Chessmaster Tartakover

"Get a Knight firmly posted at King 6 and you may go to sleep. Your game will then play itself."   Chessmaster Tartakover

Having just finished a chapter on unusual chess technology, you may be interested in my favorite chess puzzle called the Knight's Gambit (facing this page). Your move is that of a chess Knight, except that instead of moving two squares ahead and one to the right or left, you should move three squares ahead and one to the right or left. The four beginning points (arrows at top) have dotted lines to get you started! You may only pause to rest on a square marked with an "X." Your goal is to get a Knight to an exit at one of the bottom arrows. How would you design a computer program to solve this puzzle? (Note: this problem is extremely difficult.)

57.2 Fiendishly Difficult Eight Pawn Problem

"There have been times in my life when I came very near thinking that I could not lose even a single game. Then I would be beaten, and the lost game would bring me back from dreamland to earth. Nothing is so healthy as a thrashing at the proper time, and from few won games have I learned as much as I have from most of my defeats. "   Chessmaster Capablanca

While growing up near Asbury Park, New Jersey, I would often be presented by my father with strange chess problems to ponder. I suppose today, children (and adults) will resort to commercially available chess machines to help solve problems, much like calculators are used instead of slide rules and pencil and paper.

One of my favorite problems is diagramed at the end of this chapter, and I recall it most vividly because of the strange diagonal row of six black pawns. I believe the problem was actually formulated in the late 1800's. It is white's turn to play and force a win. Can you solve this fiendishly difficult problem? Can most commercially available chess machines solve this? If you own a chess computer, try this on it.

57.3 Cross References

See "Hyperdimensional Knights" on page 236 for a description of 1-D Knights and hyperdimensional rooks. See "Miraculous Chess Solutions" on page 311 for chess technology and other curiosities. See "Chess Music" on page 204 for music from chess.

57.4 For Further Reading

Quinn, L. D. (1975) *Challenging Mazes*. Dover: New York. (Lee Daniel Quinn designed this Knight maze.)

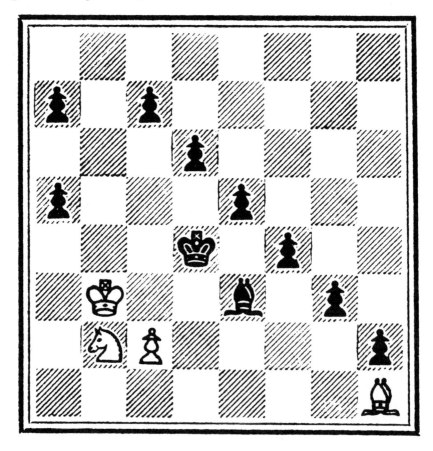

Chapter 58

Interlude: Prehistoric Insect Sculptures

Like some gargantuan prehistoric insect, Bruce Beasley's sculpture "Dorion" has come to rest on three legs outside a well known American building. The sculpture consists of steel polyhedra and soars 20 feet into the air. The stainless steel body scintillates in the sunlight. Transporting his two-ton insect sculptures is possible because they consist of four elements which can be bolted together. These works are extremely stable because the pointed legs are located far apart at the vertices of a triangle.

Beasley's past work includes huge acrylic pieces, other large insect sculptures, prehistoric birdlike sculptures displayed in airports, and sculptures molded from scraps taken from the Cypress section of freeway that crushed 42 people when it collapsed during the October 17th Loma Preita earthquake. After the tragedy, he asked the construction workers tearing apart the freeway for a small piece of the metal. About his sculpture created from the metal part of the freeway, Beasley notes, "I wanted to express the sense of recovery and rebirth – the idea that something comes out of the ruins."

Beasley has pieces in the permanent collections at the Oakland Museum, the Museum of Modern Art in New York, the Guggenheim Museum, and the *Musee d'Arte Moderne* in Paris. He can be reached at: 322 Lewis Street, Oakland, CA 94607.

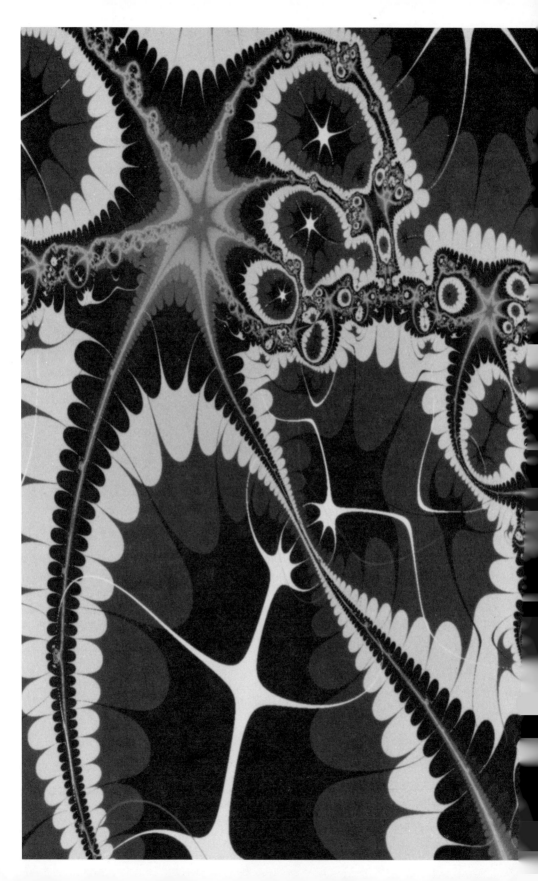

Part VII

WEIRD NUMBERS

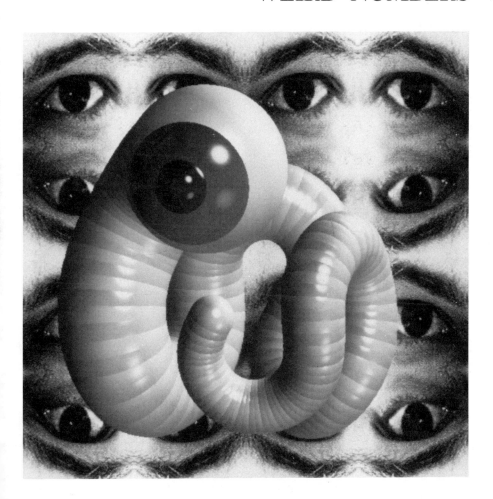

PON·TEN

Chapter 59

Bicycles from Hell

"I'm one of those people who believe that life is a series of cycles – wheels within wheels, some meshing with others, some spinning alone, but all of them performing some finite, repeating function."

Stephen King, *Four Past Midnight*

A few years ago, while attempting to stimulate some young math students, I recounted a mythological tale about a demon bicyclist riding through the burning depths of hell. My story was as follows. In the crimson caves of Hell rides a bicyclist. He rides by the lost human souls, and allows them to view his bicycle wheels for one minute. Surprisingly, each of his wheels has a mathematical formula that can be written out by starting at the correct number and following around the wheel's circular tire in a clockwise or counterclockwise direction until the formula is determined. For example, the following bicycle wheel contains the formula $5 \times 3 = 15$. (You start at the "5" and proceed clockwise, inserting the appropriate mathematical symbols as needed.)

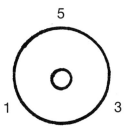

If the you are not able to determine the correct formula within one minute, you are relegated to the Stygian depths for all eternity. However, if you can correctly identify the formula before the bicyclist rides on, then you enter the empyrean realm of paradise.

The following are three other bicycle wheels from hell. Can you identify the formulas they contain? Only the symbols $+$, $-$, $\times$, $/$, $=$, and exponentiation are permitted. You may use each of these symbols, at most, two times in your

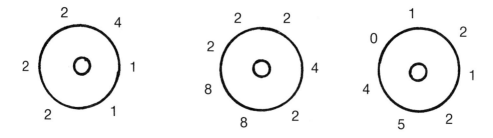

Figure 59.1. *The eternal bicyclist.* Can you solve these wheels?

formulation. For example, 1 × 2 × 3 × 4 would not be permitted because the multiplication symbol is used three times. Concatenation of digits to form multi-digit numbers is allowed as often as needed. (You must proceed around the wheel back to the starting point, or beyond the starting point as in the 5 × 3 = 15 example). Can you solve my wheels in Figure 59.1?

Note that if I did not constrain the number of times you could use the opera-tion symbols, it would be possible to formulate various cycles with 1 in them (but not zeros) simply using a repeated exponential such as $1^{i^{j \cdots}} = 1$. The first wheel falls into this category. Similarly, any cycle with one and only one "0" in it can likewise be solved by using all exponentials: $0^{i^{j \cdots}} = 0$. The third wheel falls into this category. Jim McLean of Boca Raton, Florida was the first person to notice this and solve these puzzles without the constraint of the number of operation symbols permitted.

59.1 Solutions and Future Experiments

My solution for the left-most hell wheel in Figure 59.1 is 22 × 2/4 = 11. The other two wheels are left as exercises for you. When I presented these wheels to other researchers, I was stunned by just how many solutions my wheels have. Here are some other possible solutions to the first wheel: $2^{11} - 4 + 2 + 2 = 2$, or 1 × 2 + 2 + 2 × 4/1 = 12, or 2 × 2 = 4 = 1 + 1 + 2, or 1 + 1 × 2/2 + 2 = 4, or $(((1^1)^2) \times 2) \times 2 = 4$, or 2 + 2 − 4 + 1 + 1 = 2, or 4 − 1 = 1 + 2 × 2/2, or 1 × 12 × 2 = 24, or 224112 = 224112. A few respondents challenged me with wheels of their own devising (Figure 59.2).

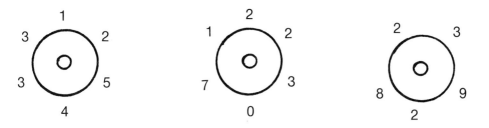

Figure 59.2. *More wheels.* Can you solve these wheels? After seeing my wheels, a few colleagues sent me their own. These were submitted to me by Davode Crippa, Stephen Kay, and Geoff Bailey.

59.2 Bicycles Wheels From Purgatory

Since there are often many solutions for a single wheel, a much tougher problem is to devise wheels for which there are no solutions. Can you do it? Of course, as Bill Mayne (Florida State University) has pointed out to me, for any string of digits around the wheel $a \ldots z$ there are always solutions involving multiple revolutions of the wheel: $a \ldots z = a \ldots z$, $a \ldots za \ldots z = a \ldots za \ldots z$, etc. (For example, $12345 = 12345$ is a case of a trivial wheel revolution solution.) At a minimum we must either limit the number of cycles to less than two or rule out such solutions as a special case.

59.3 Fact File

• More than 90 million Americans ride bicycles.
• The longest tandem bicycle ever made is approximately 67 feet long (for 35 riders) and was built by Pedalstompers Westmalle of Belgium.

Chapter 60

Shruludidi Spheres Between Uranus and Pluto

The thing looked like a grotesque beachball with a trunk, a beachball covered with fine hair which wavered like tendrils of seaweed in a running tide. Its proboscis swelled like a firehose which had been tied in a knot. Sam watched, frozen in horror and fascination, as the thing which called itself Ardelia Lortz strangled on its own fuming guts.

Stephen King, *Four Past Midnight*

During my years in graduate school I wrote a number of science fiction tales dealing with strange creatures who were fascinated by mathematics. The story I recall most vividly described a sentient race of nearly spherical creatures named the Shruludidi, who lived far out in interplanetary space, somewhere between Uranus and Pluto.

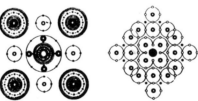

A few of the Shruludidi bore vestigial fins and flippers, evolutionary remnants of their aquatic days centuries ago, prior to their migration into interplanetary space. From the body of many creatures protruded several retractable stalks, each bearing a single, unwinking eye. The number of eyes varied from individual to individual. Interestingly, the number of eyes on an individual Shruludidi occurred in direct proportion to its status in the Shruludidi society.

The density of creatures in space had remained nearly constant for the last century – around 1000 Shruludidi per cubic mile of space. Except for the president and science advisor, who were sterile, the other Shruludidi had no means with which they could direct their motions; these 1-foot balls flew through space in random directions, and sometimes bounced off one another. (The oleaginous Shruludidi could change their appearance somewhat to suit their aesthetic tastes by altering their body shapes, but they always had to maintain a nearly spherical appearance in order to maintain structural integrity.) When one Shruludidi bounced off another, a mating process was consummated and a child was born. An invisible force field confined the Shruludidi to the area of space near Pluto and Uranus, so their density was fairly constant.

On one frigid day, the science advisor to the Shruludidi president was asked by the president to solve a particularly vexing problem. Due to the fading sunlight this area of space was receiving, the Shruludidi lived shorter lives. In fact, they could only travel about 1000 miles before dying of old age. The science advisor was asked if this 1000-mile limitation was too short to enable sufficient chance encounters between the Shruludidi to allow mating and continuation of the species. The president looked into the 101 eyes of his science advisor, and with a deep, stentorian voice, asked:

"What is the average distance moved by Shruludidi spheres between collisions with one another?"

Obviously, if the distance moved by the creatures was not great enough, too few children would be born. The science advisor worked long and hard and, when finished with the computation, he presented the solution to the president on a tattered piece of paper. The president looked at the paper with his 1,597 quivering eye stalks, took out a knife, and killed the science advisor.

It turned out that the species would not survive because the average distance the spheres would have had to travel before having a chance encounter was 1,575 miles – far too long to allow enough breeding before a Shruludidi died of old age.

How difficult was the Shruludidi science advisor's computation to make con-

sidering that no computer was available to him in interplanetary space? How would the average distance travelled between chance encounters have changed as a function of the density of Shruludidi organisms or the size of the Shruludidi? It's possible to compute this average distance (known as *the mean free path* to physicists) using the following formula: $L = 1/(4\pi\sqrt{2}\ \alpha b^2)$. Here, L is the average distance travelled before hitting another sphere, α is the density of sphere-creatures, and b is the radius of a sphere. From the equation, you can see that as the radius of the spheres increase, or the density of the spheres increase, the distance travelled before hitting another sphere (as you might expect) decreases.

The Shruludidi science advisor simply used $\alpha = 1000$ spheres / cubic mile, and $b = 0.000189$ miles (1 foot).

60.1 Stop and Think

It's possible to explore some amazing problems simply by using the equation for *mean free path* and trying different values for the sphere radius and sphere density in space.

1. For example, what is the distance a Shruludidi would have to travel before bouncing off another Shruludidi if their radii were only an inch? (When you apply the equation, make sure you use the two input variables in the same units of measurement. One inch is 0.0000157 miles.)

2. If you had placed two blow-fish in a 30-gallon fish tank, what is the average distance they would have to travel before bouncing off one another, assuming their movements were random?

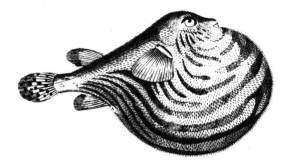

3. Draw a 3-D graph of L versus α versus b to better understand the relationship between these three variables.

4. If you were given a box the size of a house with 10 marbles shaking inside it randomly, what is the average distance travelled by a marble before hitting into another marble? Is the distance close to 1 mile? Or 100 miles? Or is it closer to the distance Magellan ships' travelled as they circumnavigated the globe? Or the distance from the earth to the moon?

5. Given a box with bacteria of standard size (radius = 0.00001 feet) with a density of 1000 per cubic foot, the average distance a bacterium will have to travel before bouncing into another bacterium is about five times the height of the Empire State building in New York City. What density of bacteria would be required to produce a mean free path equivalent to the length of the Suez Canal (5.44×10^5 feet)? What density of bacteria would be required to produce a mean free path equivalent to the average distance of the earth to the sun (4.9×10^{11} feet)?

6. The frequency of collisions of Shruludidi citizens per second is given by $f = 4\pi\sqrt{2}\ \alpha b^2 v$. Here, v is the velocity of the spheres. How many collisions would occur per second, in the president's original depressing scenario, for different velocities?

> *"The universe is mostly vacuum. In the remote regions between galaxies, you would be lucky to find a single atom in a space the size of the Louisiana Superdome."*   Hans Christian von Baeyer, 1992, *Discover*

Chapter 61

Interlude: Explosion Art (Detonography)

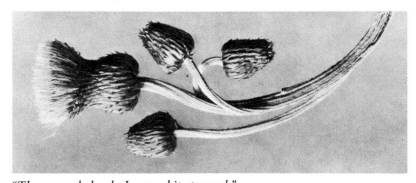

"The ground shook; I was a bit stunned."
Richard Wolkmir, 1987, *Smithsonian Magazine*

"Our first explosions produced just rubble and shrapnel. My husband thought this was crazy."   Evelyn Rosenberg, 1987, *Smithsonain Magazine*

For several years artist Evelyn Rosenberg has been visiting a firing range strewn with blown-apart jet fighters in the arid hills above Socorro, New Mexico. Rosenberg has pioneered a novel art form, which she and her husband have dubbed "detonography." To produce her art, she detonates "detasheets" to create beautiful and intricate metal sculptures expressing the immenseness of geological time, and the universality of myth. The blast of an explosion forces metal into a mold and leaves the metal imprinted with the mold's image in bas-relief. To clean the soot away from the metal, she use acetone and a wire brush. Next she brushes the metal with exotic chemicals such as liver of sulfur which produce beautiful patches of color on the surface. Copper nitrate and a blowtorch are used to put on the finishing touches.

Rosenberg's studio is behind her house in Albuquerque, New Mexico, which she shares with her husband Gary, chairman of the neurology department at the University of New Mexico School of Medicine. Her work has been featured in numerous international exhibitions, and on many television shows. More than fifty newspaper articles and reviews have appeared on her work since her first one-person show in 1970.

Rosenberg mentioned to me that detonography is a way to make large scale work at a fraction of the cost of bronze casting and with a look which can be achieved in no other way. On the next page is a photograph of a detail of "Evolutionary Geoscape II" (4 feet x 21 feet, from the New Mexico Museum of Natural History). It is made of copper, brass, and aluminum. The entire award-winning piece traces a time-line from ferns and insects progressing through fish, reptiles, birds, mammals, and humans. Each panel has a preshistoric animal and its modern day counterpart. In this section, you can see a prehistoric bird and a modern day eagle.

Those of you interested in reading more about Rosenberg may consult: Wol-komir, R. (1987) She's an artist whose explosives make a lasting impression. *Smithsonian Magazine*. December. pp. 167-171. Rosenberg can be reached at 4812 Madison Court, NE, Albuquerque, NM 87110.

Chapter 62

Apocalypse Numbers

"Never dismiss the intuition of the ancients, who believed that number is the essence of all things. Number is the secret source of entire cultures, and men have been killed for their heresies and seductive credos. The whole history of mathematics is subterranean, taking place beneath history itself, a shadow-world scarcely perceived even by the learned."   Don DeLillo, *Ratner's Star*

The book called the Revelation (or Apocalypse) of John is the last book of the New Testament (with the exception of the Syriac-speaking church, which has never accepted it). Various mystics have devoted much energy to deciphering the number 666, said by John the Apostle to designate the Number of the Beast, the Antichrist.[36] About a year ago, I began a computer search for apocalypse numbers. These are Fibonacci numbers with precisely 666 digits. As described in other chapters, the sequence of numbers (1, 1, 2, 3, 5, 8, ...), is called the *Fibonacci sequence* after the wealthy Italian merchant Leonardo Fibonacci of Pisa, and it plays important roles in mathematics and nature. These numbers are such that, after the first two, every number in the sequence equals the sum of the two previous numbers $F_n = F_{n-1} + F_{n-2}$. (See Pseudocode 64.2 for hints on how to program Fibonacci numbers.) It turns out that the 3,184th Fibonacci number is apocalyptic, having 666 digits. For numerologist readers, the apocalyptic number is:

11672437408149554123343576457921418406897471744343943723633128273
62620824523853129606823272103122788807682449798760734559719751986
31224699392309001139062569109651074019651076081705393206023798479
39189700037747512447134402546795076870699055032297133437094009365
44424118152068579040410434005685680811943795030019676693566337923
47218656896136583990327918167352721163581650359577686552293102708
82722424710947638211542756826882004025850498611340877333322087361
64591167264971986989157913558834313855569580021219281470520871752

---

[36] More recently, mystical individuals of the extreme fundamentalist right have noted that each word in the name Ronald Wilson Reagan has six letters.

0674893636617125338042205880265529140335814561951460427946535764 6729028117115407601267725615728671557460702606785922979179042488 5 3892358861771163

62.1 Stop and Think

"There is but one master [painter] who has taken notice of the neglected upper sky. He has followed its passions, and its changes, and he has brought down and laid open to the world another apocalypse of Heaven."

Ruskin, *Modern Painters (1843-1860)*

1. Is the number shown here the only apocalyptic Fibonacci number?

2. Does there exist an apocalyptic prime number?

3. Is there any significance to the fact that the first four digits and last four digits (1167 and 1163) of the apocalypse number are both dates during the reign of Frederick I of Germany who intervened extensively in papal politics?

4. Is it just a coincidence that the keys of a piano appear to exhibit a segment of the Fibonacci sequence 1, 2, 3, 5, 8, ... ? There are 2 black notes, followed by 3 black notes. There are 5 black keys in an octave and 8 white keys in an octave!

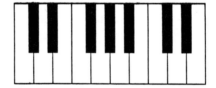

62.2 Fact File: 666 in Beards and in Britain

• On July 10, 1991, Procter & Gamble announced that it was redesigning its moon-and-stars company logo. The company said it is eliminating the curly hairs in the man-in-the-moon's beard that to some looked like 6s. The Fall 1991 issue of the *Skeptical Inquirer* notes that "the number 666 is linked to Satan in the Book of Revelations, and this helped fuel the false rumors fostered by fundamentalists." A federal judge in Topeka, Kansas, has approved settlements in the last of a dozen lawsuits filed by Procter & Gamble Co. to halt rumors associating the company with Satanism.

• On May 1, 1991, the British vehicle licensing office stopped issuing license plates bearing the numbers "666." The Winter 1992 issue of the *Skeptical Inquirer* reports two reasons given for the decision: cars with 666 plates were involved in too many accidents, and there were "complaints from the public."

Chapter 63

Interlude: Large-Scale Holosculptures

"The world of mathematics and physics, like the world of imagination, is far removed from the tangible and visible; and yet, to the mathematician, as to the poet, this world of pure form has an enduring reality."
Helen Poltz, 1955, *Imagination's Other Place*

Holosculptures are hybrid artworks integrating holograms and fiberoptics with both sculptures and electroacoustic music. In his huge outdoor holosculpture called *Homage to the Vital Forces of Quebec*, Georges Dyens (a sculptor, holographer, and educator in Quebec, Canada) provides viewers with a masterpiece of form and shape as they stroll along the St. Lawrence river in Montreal. The illustration here is just a small detail of the entire piece which represents a cube at the instant right after an explosion. In fact, this is just one piece of the shattered cube! A large "20x40 inch rainbow transmission" hologram is built into a column in the work (not visible in this view). The hologram displays an image of the cube at the exact moment of explosion.

You can read more about Dyens' work in: Dyens, G. (1989) Holoscuptures: holography and sculpture, spirit and matter. *Leonardo*. 22(3/4): 383-388.

Chapter 64

1597 Problem

There can be no dull numbers, because if there were, the first of them would be interesting on account of its dullness.　　　　Martin Gardner, 1992

1,597 is an interesting number. It is both a prime number[37] and a Fibonacci number,[38] and it is also the year in which the Edict of Nantes was drafted, which gave French Protestants (Huguenots) a degree of freedom, opening public offices to them and permitting them to hold public worship in certain cities. (Pseudocode 64.1 will show you how to search for all prime numbers that are also Fibonacci numbers.)

Moreover, 1597 is fascinating because it is an "emirp," a prime number that turns into a different prime number when its digits are reversed (7951).

"1597" is also the basis for a number problem I posed in 1991 for which a solution seemed unlikely. Consider the formula $x = \sqrt{(1597y^2 + 1)}$.

Is x ever an integer for any integer y greater than 0? You may wish to first compute a few values of x in order to get the feel for the formula:

y	x
1	39.97
2	79.93
3	119.89

You can see that for $y = 1$, 2, or 3, x is not an integer. Is it ever an integer? The first method you might use to answer this question is to write a short computer

---

[37] A prime is a positive integer that cannot be written as the product of two smaller integers. The number 6 is equal to 2 times 3, but 7 cannot be written as a product of factors; therefore, 7 is called a prime number or prime. Here are the first few prime numbers: 2, 3, 5, 7, 11, 13, 17, 19, 23, 29, 31, 37, 41, 43, 47, 53, 59.

[38] See "Apocalypse Numbers" on page 337 for background to this sequence of numbers (1, 1, 2, 3, 5, 8, ...), called the *Fibonacci sequence*. See "Fibonacci Chess" on page 319 for Fibonacci chess games. How much money would you be willing to gamble that the number of people in the frontispiece's photo is neither a prime number nor a Fibonacci number?

```
ALGORITHM: How to Compute Prime Fibonacci Numbers
n = 100; g = 1; h = 1;
/* First generate a Fibonacci Number */
DO i = 3 to n;
    f = g + h;   b=1;
    /* now check if it is prime */
    ff = f * 0.5;
    DO j = 2 to ff;
        IF (f//j) = 0 then DO;
            /* if f is not evenly divisible
               by j then it is not prime */
            b = 0;
        LEAVE;
        END;
    END; /*j*/
    /* Print f if it is a Prime Fibonacci Number */
    IF (b = 1) then Print f
    h = g; g = f;
END; /* i */
```

Pseudocode 64.1. *How to compute prime Fibonacci numbers.* (The program coded here is in the style of the REXX language.)

program that would simply try thousands of values of y, starting at $y = 1$. The program would continually increment y while testing x – for as long as your patience and machine time allowed. The program could check each x value to see if it were an integer. Unfortunately, your program would run for weeks, and probably months, and you would finally toss up your hands and exclaim that there is no solution. However, it turns out there is an *infinite* number of solutions, and the first individual to solve the 1597 problem was Noam D. Elkies of the Mathematics Department of Harvard University. The reason it would take your computer so long to find these infinite number of solutions is the fact that the smallest integer value for x is:

$$x = 519711527755463096224266385375638449943026746249 \qquad (64.1)$$

for a y value of

$$y = 13004986088790772250309504643908671520836229100. \qquad (64.2)$$

Dr. Elkies, however, did not solve this through the super CPU-intensive search method for finding integer solutions that I just outlined. In fact, it has been known at least since the time of French mathematician Fermat (1601-1665) that for any positive integer D which is not a square, there are infinitely many integers x, y such that $x^2 = Dy^2 + 1$. Since I gave you the number 1597, which is a prime number and hence cannot be a square, one knows immediately that there is a solution. Furthermore there is a known algorithm which can be used to solve problems such as these. These methods involve the use of a continued fraction representation for $\sqrt{D}$ in order to find the smallest solution. These algorithms

```
ALGORITHM: Print 30 Fibonacci Numbers
Dimension Fib(30)
Fib(1)=1
Fib(2)=1
For n = 1 to 28
    Fib(n+2) = Fib(n+1) + Fib(n)
Next n
For x = 1 to 30
    Print Fib(x)
end
```

Pseudocode 64.2. *How to compute Fibonacci numbers.*

are now implemented on several commercially available symbolic computation software packages, which is what Elkies used to solve the 1597 problem.

64.1 Stop and Think

1. 1597 is an "emirp," a prime number that turns into a different prime number when its digits are reversed. Can you find any other emirps? How rare are emirps? What is the largest emirp ever computed? Can you find any *Iccanobif* numbers? These are Fibonacci numbers that turn into different Fibonacci numbers when their digits are reversed. Is it possible that Iccanobif numbers do not exist?

2. Here are some variations to the equation I gave, some of which may be more easy than others to find integer solutions. Can you find an integer solution to any of the following:

$$x = \sqrt{1597y^2 + 2} ,$$ (64.3)

$$x = \sqrt{1597y^2} ,$$ (64.4)

$$x = \sqrt{1597 + y^2} ,$$ (64.5)

$$x = \sqrt{1597y^2 + \sqrt{2}} ,$$ (64.6)

or

$$x = \sqrt{1597y^2 - 1} ?$$ (64.7)

Hint: only two of these five equations have integer solutions.

3. Here are the first few prime Fibonacci numbers: 2, 3, 5, 13, 89, 233, 1597, 28657. How large a prime Fibonacci number can you compute?

Chapter 65

Terrible Brahmagupta Numbers
In the Seventh Century

"A person who can within a year solve $x^2 - 92y^2 = 1$ is a mathematician."
Brahmagupta

"As in our Middle Ages, the scientists of India, for better and for worse, were her priests." Will Durant, 1954 *Our Oriental Heritage*

Brahmagupta, a great Indian mathematician of the 7th century, was interested in huge numbers. Problems, such as the one he posed in the quotation above, have always made me wonder about the history of large number problems. How long ago were the first huge number problems posed, solved, or even considered solvable by humans? As an example of a large number problem here we will consider an interesting question recently posed by Chris Long of Rutgers University. I call these kinds of numbers *Brahmagupta numbers* after this Hindu mathematician and astronomer who was so intrigued by huge number solutions to simple-looking problems.

Brahmagupta (558 - 660 A.D.) (not to be confused with *Brahmaputra*,[39] a great river of Tibet, India, and Bangladesh, or *Brahmacharia*)[40] wrote a book in verse form called the *Brahma-sphuta-siddhanta*,[41] two chapters of which were devoted to mathematics. The chapters include arithmetical progression, quadratic

---

[39] Many have said that the Brahmaputra ranks among the most important rivers of the world. It is 250 miles longer than the Ganges and is a highway of commerce through the fertile valley of Assam. The nature of its upper course was long an unsolved mystery to explorers due to the fact that exploration was barred by the hostility of mountain tribes.

[40] *Brahmacharia* is a vow of chastity taken by the ascetic student — a vow of absolute abstention from all sexual desire.

[41] The only translations I could find of his mathematical work were Colebrooke's book *Algebra, with Arithmetic and Mensuration, from the Sanskrit of Brahmagupta and Bhascara, Preceded by a Dissertation on the State of Science as Known to the Hindus* (1817) and another book, Sengupta's *The Khandakhadyaka, an Astronomical Treatise by Brahmagupta* (1934).

equations, and proofs of various geometrical theorems on the right-angled tri-angle, on surfaces and volumes, and on areas of triangles. Brahmagupta, among other ancient mathematicians, was responsible for the following major operations with zero:

$$a - a = 0 \tag{65.1}$$

$$a \pm 0 = a \tag{65.2}$$

$$\pm a \times 0 = 0 \tag{65.3}$$

$$0 \times 0 = 0 \tag{65.4}$$

and

$$\pm a/0 = \text{Kha-cheda } \infty. \tag{65.5}$$

(The last operation is also attributed to Bhaskara II.)[42] Brahmagupta also pro-posed interesting ways of solving equations of the form: $nx^2 \pm c = y^2$.

Let's turn our attention to Brahmagupta numbers. Please don't expect to solve the following problem with pencil and paper! The solutions involve the ratio of numbers so large that if you were to place a dot on a paper every second until you had a number of dots equal to the Brahmagupta numbers, our Milky Way galaxy will have rotated many times.[43]

The problem deals with rational numbers. A *rational number* is a number that can be expressed as a ratio of two integers. Here are some fine examples: $1/2$, $4/3$, $7/1$, 8. All common fractions and all terminating (or repeating) decimal fractions are rational. Certain trigonometric ratios of certain angles are even rational, for example $\cos 60° = 1/2$. (This is in contrast to irrational numbers like e and π, – called transcendental numbers – and all surds such as $\sqrt{27}$.)

The problem can be stated as follows. Find the smallest rational number x (smallest in the sense of smallest numerator and denominator) such that there exist rational numbers y and z and

$$x^2 - 157 = y^2, \quad x^2 + 157 = z^2 \tag{65.6}$$

Jim Buddenhagen of Southwestern Bell Advanced Technology Laboratory gave a behemoth solution:

$x = a/b$ where $a =$

50240182995338036981137754312294030993135017466889667584728816492946182669894640083390462472702407772686242505697440870727011829516260394275244183508553341864729654604103996100686780343137 61

---

and

$b =$

55207127859076258183875569461342697367786240398108265147202579226331920116659466022175218717871386078381699548684974799036529476971927068616591606845144977158476992422410434693821197457720

$y = a/b$

where

$a =$

49761683090826152894597764890084942156110771985477729386907419538978932445636040315578821358685390299974609232140115116898760462425776366369130298600523042926133030229451654705083119687366 39

and

$b =$

55207127859076258183875569461342697367786240398108265147202579226331920116659466022175218717871386078381699548684974799036529476971927068616591606845144977158476992422410434693821197457720

$z = a/b$

where

$a =$

50714168343553589561367834820259004354677190166380717272112514688668416204079391389484427548409998628396610688499937346660544850726462041214489884598731864517189496456476576826531843826804161

and

$b =$

55207127859076258183875569461342697367786240398108265147202579226331920116659466022175218717871386078381699548684974799036529476971927068616591606845144977158476992422410434693821197457720

Buddenhagen solved this using theory provided by Don Zagier in a book titled *Introduction to Elliptic Curves and Modular Forms* (page 5) by Neal Koblitz – and by using a large-integer computer software program called "Maple" (University of Waterloo).

If you substitute these huge numbers into the previous equations, you'd find that $x^2 - y^2 = 157$ and also that $x^2 - z^2 = -157$, which are good solutions to the problem. But are these the *smallest* solutions? Not quite! But even the smallest solution contains unimaginably large numbers. For example, it turns out that the absolute smallest value for x, is

$$\frac{224403517704336969924557513090674863160948472041}{17824664537857719176051070357934327140032961660} \qquad (65.7)$$

For more information on these type of problems you can consult Mazur's paper titled "Arithmetic on Curves" which appeared in the *Bulletin of the AMS* (14(2): 255, 1986).

65.1 Stop and Think

1. Considering that the Brahmagupta numbers ($x^2 - 157 = y^2$, $x^2 + 157 = z^2$) contain so many digits, what would have mathematicians in earlier centuries thought about a problem such of this?

2. Historically speaking, how long ago was a solution to this problem even possible to arrive at?

3. Could someone have solved the Brahmagupta problem, for example, in 1940 or 1950? What problems considered unsolvable today will be solvable in 50 years?

4. Can you find any 7th-century Brahmagupta numbers for the original integer problem: $x^2 - 92y^2 = 1$ given in the quotation at the beginning of this chapter? Hint: some solutions to this should be easy to discover using a personal computer.

5. One can generalize the 7th-century formula to $x^2 - Ny^2 = 1$. Are there any numbers, N, for which there is no solution to this problem? For example, Lew Mammel, Jr. of AT&T Bell laboratories could not find a solution for $N = 53$ when doing a computer search for all integers y less than 6365.

65.2 Wild India

Those of you interested in the natural history of the Indian subcontinent should not miss Gerald Cubitt and Guy Mountfort's photographic celebration *Wild India: The Wildlife and Scenery of India and Nepal* (MIT Press, 1991, 208 p, color, $39.95). The text describes the area's natural resources as well as the pressures imposed by population growth. More than 400 color photographs capture the exquisite natural environment.

Chapter 66

Incredibly Difficult Number Sequences

"*The ratio of the height of the Sears Building in Chicago to the height of the Woolworth Building in New York is the same to four significant digits (1.816 vs. 1816) as the ratio of the mass of a proton to the mass of an electron.*"   John Paulos, *Innumeracy*

Can you supply the missing number in the following sequence?

    10, 11, 12, 13, 20, ?, 1000   (66.1)

If not, don't be disappointed. Roughly 90 percent of my colleagues with Ph.D.'s could not solve this, even after considering the sequence for a long time.
    Perhaps looking at another sequence generated by the same rules might help:

    10, 11, 12, 13, 14, 20, 22, ?, 1010   (66.2)

Not yet? Perhaps an even longer sequence, generated using the same rules, will finally clue you in:

    10, 11, 12, 13, 14, 15, 16, 17, 18, 21, 23, 25, 32, 101, ?, 10001   (66.3)

For the first two sequences, the missing numbers are 22, and 101 respectively. To create the first sequence, I represented the number "8" in different bases, from base 8 to base 2. For those of you not familiar with numbers represented in bases other than 10 (which is the standard way of representing numbers) consider how to represent any number in base 2. Numbers in base 2 are called binary numbers. The presence of a "1" in a digit position of a number base 2 indicates that a corresponding power of 2 is used in determine the value of the binary number. A 0 in the number indicates that a corresponding power of 2 is absent from the binary number. The binary number 1111 represents $(1 \times 2^3) + (1 \times 2^2) + (1 \times 2^1) + (1 \times 2^0) = 15$. The binary number 1000 represents $1 \times 2^3 = 8$. Can you now solve the third sequence?
    Here are some other difficult sequences. Can you supply the missing number in the following sequences?

10, ?, 1111110010, 10000100011101000110001011110100, ?   (66.4)

or

11, 1011, 1111110011, 10000100011101000110001011110111, ?   (66.5)

101, 1100101, 10000110010010101000101, ?   (66.6)

These sequences seem to be growing very large rather quickly. How many digits would the 20th entry in these sequences contain?

66.1 Crazy Sequences

The following are fascinating number sequence problems sent to me by readers. Those who submitted sequences were asked to rate the difficulty of solving their sequences on a 4-point difficulty scale: 1) Easy, 2) Difficult, 3) Extremely Difficult, and 4) Nearly impossible to solve by mere mortals. Keep in mind that these ratings are determined by mathematicians and therefore may not reflect the difficulty of the problem for non-mathematically trained individuals!

66.1.1 Schoenleber Number Sequence Problem

Can you supply this missing number?
77, 49, 36, 18, ?
Difficulty rating: 2. (Contributed by Claus Schoenleber, Germany)

66.1.2 Diep Number Sequence

Can you supply this missing number?
2, 71, 828, ?, ...
Difficulty rating: 2. (Contributed by Thanh Diep, Stanford University)

66.1.2.1 Silverman Number Sequence

3, 4, 5, 7, 11, 13, 17, 23, 29, 43, 47, 83, 131, 137, 359, 431, 433, 449, 509, 569, 571, 2971, 4723, 5387, ? ...
Difficulty rating: 4. (Contributed by Bob Silverman, The MITRE Corp.)

66.1.3 Somos Number Sequence Problem

1, 1, 1, 1, 1, 1, 3, 5, 9, 23, 75, 421, 1103, 5047, 41783, ? ...
Difficulty rating: 4. (Contributed by Michael Somos)

66.1.4 Chernoff Number Sequence

360 is the 3rd term of the mystical sequence:
2, 12, 360, ?, 174636000, ...
What is the 4th term? Difficulty rating: 4. (Contributed by Paul Chernoff, California)

66.1.5 Trice Number Sequence

21, 36, 55, 60, 67, 68, 92, ?, 125
Difficulty rating: 4. (Contributed by Greg Trice, Ontario. He learned about this sequence 25 years ago and claims that few people ever can solve it. It was once posed as a question on the "University Challenge" TV program.)

66.1.6 Balden Number Sequence

11, 121, 1001, 11011, 121121, ...
or
1, 10.01, 100.01, 101.01, 1000.1001, 1010.0001, 10000.0001, 10001.0001, ...
What is the next number in these sequences? Difficulty rating: 4. (Contributed by Bruce Balden, British Columbia.)

66.1.7 Some Solutions

To solve the class of sequences exemplified by Equation (66.5), continue to convert between decimal and binary representations. For example, 11 (decimal) is 1011 (binary). 1011 (decimal) is 1111110011 (binary). And so on.

The solution to the Schoenleber sequence is 8. To solve this, place a multiply operator between two digits: $7 \times 7 = 49$, $4 \times 9 = 36$, $3 \times 6 = 18$, $1 \times 8 = 8$. (There is no following number).

The solution to the Diep sequence is 1828. The ith term of the sequence is the next i digits of e ($e = 2.7182818284...$).

The Silverman sequence lists the indices of the prime Fibonacci numbers. For example, the third, fourth, and fifth Fibonacci numbers ($F3, F4, F5$) are primes. (See "1597 Problem" on page 341 for background on prime Fibonacci numbers.) He notes that one could also construct extremely difficult problems using the Lucas primes: 0, 2, 4, 5, 7, 8, 11, 13, 16, 17, 19, 31, 37, 41, 47, 53, 61, 71, 79, 113, 313, 353, 503, 613, 617, 863, ... For example, L863 is prime. (The Lucas sequence is 2, 1, 3, 4, 7, 11, 18, 29, 47, ...).

The solution to the Somos sequence involves the formula: $a(n) = (a(n-1)a(n-5) + a(n-2)a(n-4) + a(n-3)a(n-3))/a(n-6)$. This has been published in the journal *Mathematical Intelligencer* vol. 13, no. 1, page 40.

A few other solutions are found in "Solution Saraband" on page 419.

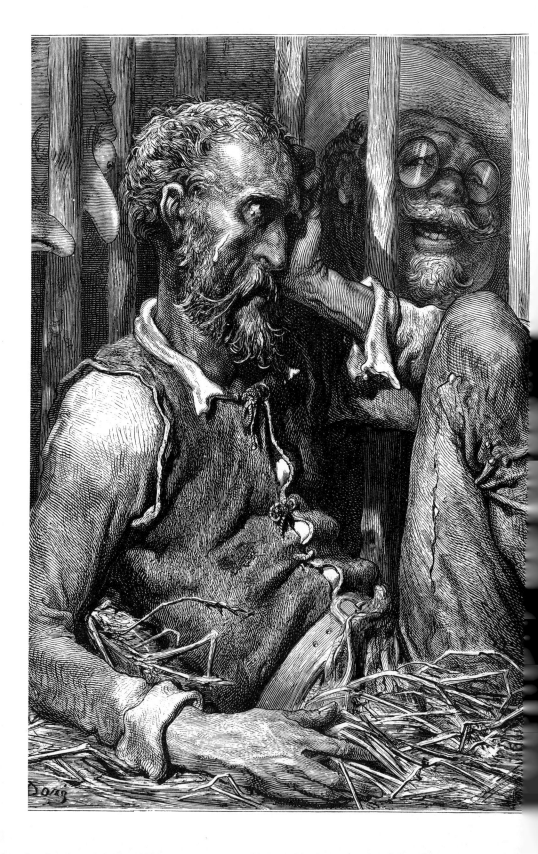

Chapter 67

Interlude: Catching Criminals

Imagine that it is midnight in New York City. The night is damp and dark, and your daughter has just been assaulted. At the police station, she is asked to help draw the face of the criminal. Normally this is a somewhat difficult task, even with the aid of a police sketch artist. However, in the 1990's, a computer program may help her render a more dependable likeness of criminal than ever before thought possible.

The new program called "FacePrints" assembles twenty faces selected at random from over 34 billion possible combinations. A victim simply rates each face on its similarity to the criminal's face. How the victim numerically rates each face on its similarity with the criminal will determine which 20 *new* candidate mug shots the computer next displays. After several iterations of the program, the victim has "bred" a composite likeness of the criminal, with no artistic skill or talent required on the victim's part. According to Craig Caldwell, a New Mexico State University graduate student developing the software, the final drawing can be striking similar to the image of the criminal. The illustration shown here shows the target criminal (left) and the composite image (right) produced after 10 generations.

FacePrints' algorithm is based on Darwin's theory of natural selection and the principles of genetic evolution. The ratings of witnesses determine which faces are the "fittest" and which will be reproduced when creating the next generation of 20 faces.

Victor Johnson of the Psychology Department of New Mexico State University (Las Cruces, New Mexico) created the prototype for FacePrints program in 1988. The development of FacePrints was financed by the Department of Justice, although it may have many other applications. For example, it may help psychologists characterize facial beauty by having subjects breed their ideal face using the program. One may wonder if the program could be used by science-fiction film directors to breed fantastic looking alien faces which will be the most frightening to the majority of people. The possibilities are endless.

For further reading, see: Travis, J. (1991) Gotcha! *Science News*. Aug 17, 140(7): 109.

Chapter 68

The Arabian Nights Factorial

"I love to count. Counting has given me special pleasure down through the years. I can think of innumerable occasions when I stopped what I was doing and did a little counting for the sheer intellectual pleasure of it."

Don DeLillo, *Ratner's Star*

With the exception of the Koran, no other work of Arabic literature has been better-known and more influential in the west than the *Thousand and One Arabian Nights*. This collection of stories is grouped around a central story involving a Sultan and his lovers. Upon discovering that his wife has been unfaithful to him, the Sultan vows to take a bride every day and have her executed at dawn. When Scheherazade was chosen to be his new wife, each evening she told a story to the Sultan but did not finish it, promising to do so the following night if she survived. This continued for a thousand and one nights, until the Sultan grew deeply in love with Scheherazade and gave up his cruel plan altogether.

With this introduction, we turn now to a special number called the *Arabian Nights factorial*. This number is defined as the number *x* such that *x!* has 1001 digits. (The exclamation point is the factorial sign: $n! = 1 \times 2 \times 3 \times 4 \times \cdots n$). Factorials grow rather quickly: 5! = 120, 10!=3,628,800, and 15! = 1,307,674,368,000.

The question "What is the Arabian Nights factorial?" is just one question in a collection of thousands compiled by Chris Cole, the editor of "Rec.Puzzles Frequently Asked Questions List."[44] "Rec.Puzzles" is an electronic bulletin board which is part of a large worldwide network of interconnected computers called Usenet. The computers exchange news articles with each other on a voluntary

---

[44] The puzzle collection editor, Chris Cole, can be reached at chris @ peregrine.com, or at P. O. Box 9545 Newport Beach, CA 92658. Cole is a founder, and Vice President and Chief Technical Officer of Peregrine Systems, and he holds a master's degree in physics from Harvard University.

basis.[45] Some define "Usenet" as the set of people (not computers) who exchange puzzles, tips, and news articles tagged with one or more universally-recognized labels, called "newsgroups." Group topics range from bicycles, to physics, to music. Usenet started out at Duke University around 1980 as a small network of UNIX machines. Today there is no UNIX limitation; there are versions of the news-exchange programs which run on computers ranging from DOS PCs to mainframes. Most Usenet sites are at universities, research labs, and other academic and commercial institutions. The largest concentrations of Usenet sites outside the U.S. seem to be in Canada, Europe, Australia and Japan.

With this digression, let's return to the original question: what is the Arabian Nights factorial? The answer is 450! (450 factorial). In his puzzle collection, Cole notes that determining the number of zeroes at the end of x! is not too difficult once you realize that each such zero comes from a factor of 10 in the product $1 \times 2 \times 3 \times ... \times x$. Each factor of 10, in turn, comes from a factor of 5 and a factor of 2. Since there are many more factors of 2 than factors of 5, the number of 5's determines the number of zeroes at the end of the factorial. The number of 5's in the set of numbers $\{1...x\}$ (and therefore the number of zeroes at the end of x!) is: $z(x) = \text{int}(x/5) + \text{int}(x/25) + \text{int}(x/125) + \text{int}(x/625) + ...$ This series terminates when the powers of 5 in the denominator exceed x. Can you program this?

To get a feel for the number of articles and different Usenet bulletin boards, consider that: 137,682 articles, totaling 274.400175 Mbytes (336.293781 including headers), were submitted from 14389 different Usenet sites by 36719 different users to 1740 different newsgroups for an average of 19.600012 Mbytes (24.020984 including headers) per day!

Chapter 69

U-Numbers and MU-Numbers

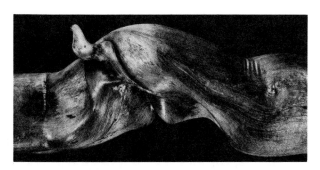

"[As a teenager] I thought that if it's at all possible, or practical, to become a mathematician, I would want to be one. Of course, from a practical point of view, it was very difficult to decide on studying mathematics ... at the university because ... to make a living in mathematics was very, very difficult."

Stanislaw Ulam, *Mathematical People*

Mathematician Stanislaw Ulam is probably best known for his theoretical calculations which were useful for building the Hydrogen bomb. However he also worked on a range of fascinating topics in his lifetime including iteration, strange attractors, Monte Carlo methods, the human brain, random number generators, number theory, and genetics. One of my favorite number sequences, called "U-Numbers" by mathematicians in his honor, is computed as follows. Start with any two positive integers, for example 1 and 2. Next continue with those numbers (taken from the positive integers in increasing order) which can be expressed in just one way as the sum of two distinct earlier members of the sequence. Here are the first few U-numbers starting with 1 and 2. I'll designate this sequence as $U_{1,2}$:

1 2 3 4 6 8 11 13 16 18 26 28 36 38 47 48 53 57 62 69 72 77 82 87 97 99 102 106 114 126 131 138 145 148 155 175 177 180 182 189 197 206 209 219

For example, 5 is not a U-number because there is more than one way to form 5 from summing previous sequence members, for example, 5=3+2 and 5=4+1. On the other hand, 6 is a U-number because it can only be formed by 6=4+2.

I've made some interesting-looking plots by doing

```
DO For all Ulam Numbers, U
    MovePenTo(U,0); DrawTo(U,U);
END
```

This looks like a series of unequally spaced vertical lines which gradually rise (Figure 69.1). The spacing is what I like the best. It's very erratic, displaying miscellaneous gaps where no Ulam numbers exist. Many times there are visually

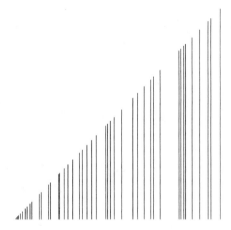

Figure 69.1. *Visualization of U-numbers.*

interesting clumps and pairs. If you prefer, in your computer program, just DrawTo(U,C), where C is the vertical most (*y*) coordinate of your graphics screen. This will give the plot a bar-code appearance. Looking at these kinds of graphs, can one determine if there are arbitrarily large gaps in the sequence of U-numbers?

Notice that on the U-number graph there are pairs of consecutive U-numbers corresponding to (1,2) (2,3) (3,4) and (47,48). Are there infinitely many consecutive pairs? P. Muller, in his masters' thesis at the University of Buffalo in 1966, calculated 20,000 terms and found no further examples! On the other hand, more than 60% of these U-number terms differed from another by exactly 2.

What are U-numbers like for other starting integers? Here are a few terms I calculated with starting numbers 1 and 9:

1 9 10 11 12 13 14 15 16 17 18 20 36 38 39 40 41 42 43 44 46 66 67 68 69 70 71 72 73 92 101 121 122 123 124 125 126 127 146 155 174 182 201 211 229 230 237 256 284 285 286 287 288 289 290 291 311 348 365 368 369 370

Here are a few terms with starting numbers 1 and 3:

1 3 4 5 6 8 10 12 17 21 23 28 32 34 39 43 48 52 54 59 63 68 72 74 79 83 98 99 101 110 114 121 125 132 136 139 143 145 152 161 165 172 176 187 192 196 201 205 212 216 223 227 232 234 236 243 247 252 256 258 274 278

Notice how these $U_{1,3}$ numbers have many terms separated by 2. Finally, the following is a long U-number sequence computed for the starting numbers 100 and 101. (I computed this massive sequence using a computer program designed for me by Michael Clarke of the United Kingdom).

100 101 201 301 302 401 403 501 504 601 603 605 701 706 801 803 805 807 901 908
1001 1003 1005 1007 1009 1101 1110 1201 1203 1205 1207 1209 1211 1301 1312 1401
1403 1405 1407 1409 1411 1413 1501 1514 1601 1603 1605 1607 1609 1611 1613 1615
1701 1716 1801 1803 1805 1807 1809 1811 1813 1815 1817 1901 1918 2001 2003 2005
2007 2009 2011 2013 2015 2017 2019 2101 2120 2201 2203 2205 2207 2209 2211 2213
2215 2217 2219 2221 2301 2322 2401 2403 2405 2407 2409 2411 2413 2415 2417 2419
2421 2423 2501 2524 2601 2603 2605 2607 2609 2611 2613 2615 2617 2619 2621 2623
2625 2701 2726 2801 2803 2805 2807 2809 2811 2813 2815 2817 2819 2821 2823 2825
2827 2901 2928 3001 3003 3005 3007 3009 3011 3013 3015 3017 3019 3021 3023 3025
3027 3029 3101 3130 3201 3203 3205 3207 3209 3211 3213 3215 3217 3219 3221 3223
3225 3227 3229 3231 3301 3332 3401 3403 3405 3407 3409 3411 3413 3415 3417 3419
3421 3423 3425 3427 3429 3431 3433 3501 3534 3601 3603 3605 3607 3609 3611 3613
3615 3617 3619 3621 3623 3625

L. Kerry Mitchell, an aerospace engineer at the NASA Langley Research Center in Hampton, Virginia suggested to me the concept of modified U-numbers, or "MU-numbers." For these cases, addition is replaced by multiplication in the definition of U-numbers. Starting with 2 numbers greater than 1, continue the sequence with those numbers that can be written only in one way as the product of 2 previous elements. For initiators of 2 and 3, here are the first 20 MU-numbers:

2 3 6 12 18 24 48 54 96 162 192 216 384 486 768 864 1458 1536 1944 3072

24 is on the list since it can be written only as 2×12, but 36 is not since it can be written as 2×18 or 3×12. Notice that $MU_{2,3}$ are all even after "3." Why? Are all MU numbers even?

69.1 For Further Reading

1. Cooper, N. (1989) *From Cardinals to Chaos.* Cambridge University Press: New York. (Topics: Stan Ulam, iteration, strange attractors, Monte Carlo methods, the human brain, random number generators, number theory, and genetics.)

2. Guy, R. (1981) *Unsolved Problems in Number Theory.* Springer: New York.

3. Recamoan, B. (1973) Questions on a sequence of Ulam. *American Mathematics Monthly.* 80: 919-920.

Chapter 70

Phi in Four 4's

"Mathematics is the wrong discipline for people doomed to nongreatness."
Don DeLillo, *Ratner's Star*

The number 1.61803..., called the golden ratio, appears in the most surprising places, and because it has unique properties, mathematicians have given it a special name, ϕ. This symbol is the Greek letter Phi, the first letter in the name Phidias, the classical Greek sculptor who used the golden ratio extensively in his work. A *golden rectangle* has a ratio of the length of its sides equal to 1: ϕ. Many have reported that the golden rectangle is the most visually pleasing of all rectangles, being neither too squat nor too thin. Various artistic works are said to contain examples of golden ratios, for example: the Greek Parthenon, Leonardo da Vinci's *Mona Lisa*, Salvador Dali's *The Sacrament of the Last Supper*, and much of M.C. Escher's work. The smaller bricks in the wall (shown in the frontispiece photo) have a width/heigth ratio equal to ϕ.

Since $\phi = (1 + \sqrt{5})/2$, it has some rather amazing mathematical properties. For example,

$$\phi - 1 = \frac{1}{\phi}; \quad \phi\phi' = -1; \quad \phi + \phi' = 1; \quad \phi^n + \phi^{n+1} = \phi^{n+2} \qquad (70.1)$$

where $\phi' = (1 - \sqrt{5})/2$. Both ϕ and ϕ' are the roots of $x^2 - x - 1 = 0$.

In September of 1991 I conducted the following contest regarding ϕ:

> Arrange four 4's, and any of the ordinary mathematical symbols, to give as good an approximation to the famous mathematical constant known as the golden ratio, phi ($\phi = 1.61803$), as you can find. Allow yourself the symbols:), (, +, -, x, /, the usual notations for roots, powers, factorials, and the decimal point. Factorials are to be of integers only. Concatenation of 4's is allowed (e.g. 44).

> 1. Contest 1. Use as many mathematical symbols as you wish.
> 2. Contest 2. Limit yourself to using, at most, 4 of each mathematical symbol. For example, you can only use the multiply symbol 4 times.

Phil Hanna from New York had some excellent approximations, including:

$$\sqrt{\sqrt{\sqrt{44/(4/4)}}} = 1.6048394 \tag{70.2}$$

and

$$\frac{4}{(\sqrt{4} + \sqrt{4}/4)} = 1.6 \tag{70.3}$$

For Contest 2, he found:

$$\sqrt{\sqrt{4 + \sqrt{\sqrt{4 \times 4 \times 4}}}} \sim 1.61651660, \tag{70.4}$$

which differs from ϕ by 1.517×10^{-3}.

Leopold Travis from Brandeis University wrote to me: "Let $s(x)$ denote the square root of x, and let

$$l = s(s(s(44))) \times s(s(s(s(s(s(s(s(s(s(s(s(4^{**}(4!))))))))))))) \tag{70.5}$$

where ** denotes exponentiation." Then $l = 1.61792833086266 \ldots$ and $\phi - l = 0.00010565788722 \ldots$

70.1 Closer and Closer

Ken Shirriff, from California, noted that for Contest 1, one can obtain results arbitrarily close to ϕ, since infinitely repeated square roots yield numbers approaching 1:

$$\sqrt{\sqrt{\sqrt{\ldots (4) \ldots}}} \rightarrow 1. \tag{70.6}$$

Therefore $\phi = (1 + \sqrt{4 + 1})/\sqrt{(4)}$ exactly, where 1 can be approximated as closely as desired with a single 4 and many square roots. For contest 2, the best he could do was:

$$1.618644 = \frac{4}{(.4 \times 4!)^{.4}} \tag{70.7}$$

with an error of .000611

Similarly, the following, from Paul Leyland of the UK can be used to compute ϕ to arbitrarily close precision:

$$\phi = \frac{\sqrt{\sqrt{4}/.4} + \sqrt{\sqrt{\sqrt{\ldots(4)\ldots}}}}{\sqrt{4}} \tag{70.8}$$

To see this, note that

$$\sqrt{\frac{\sqrt{4}}{.4}} = \sqrt{\frac{2}{2/5}} = \sqrt{5} \tag{70.9}$$

and the limit of $4^{1/2^n} = 1$ as n goes to infinity. David G. Caraballo of Princeton discovered: $(0.4 + 4^{-4}) \times 4$. This equals $1.615625...$, and so it differs from the golden ratio by around 0.00240.

The ultimate winner of the contest, however, is Brian Boutel, of the Victoria University of Wellington, New Zealand, who was the first person to find an *exact* solution:

$$\phi = \frac{\sqrt{(4)} + \sqrt{4! - 4}}{4} \tag{70.10}$$

since ϕ, as noted previously, is defined as $1 + \sqrt{5}/2$.

When I extended the contest to computing ϕ using five 5's, six 6's, etc., David G. Caraballo from Princeton, New Jersey noticed that exact solutions can be computed using five 5's and *seven* 6's:

$$\frac{5 + 5 \times \sqrt{(5)}}{5 + 5} \tag{70.11}$$

and

$$\frac{6 + 6 \times \sqrt{6 - 6/6}}{6 + 6} \tag{70.12}$$

He proposes a general solution involving the integer k. We need at most $(2k - 5)$ k's to give an exact value using only k's and the operations previously described. Can you prove this?

Other very imaginative answers for 5 five's are:

$$\phi = (5/5 + \sqrt{5}) \times \sqrt{0.5 \times .5} \tag{70.13}$$

from Jaroslaw Tomasz Wroblewski, and

$$\frac{(5/5) + \sqrt{5}}{\log_{\sqrt{5}}(5)} \tag{70.14}$$

from Seth Breidbart of Morgan Stanley & Co., New York.

Phil Hanna gave the following exact solutions for ϕ in eight 8's and nine 9's:

$$\phi = \frac{8 + 8 \times \sqrt{\sqrt{\sqrt{8 + 8}} + 8/8}}{8 + 8} \tag{70.15}$$

$$\phi = \frac{9 + 9 \times \sqrt{\sqrt{\sqrt{9}} + 9/9} + 9/9}{9 + 9} \tag{70.16}$$

Peter Ta-chen Chang asked the following: 1) What is the smallest positive integer that can't be expressed using only 4 fours? 2) What is the smallest number of fours (or some other integer) that will generate all positive numbers? 3) What is the smallest collection of operations that will work with question 2)?

My ϕ contest described in this short chapter was stimulated by another short paper published in 1962 where Conway and Guy asked a similar question for constructing π. (Conway, J., Guy, M. (1962) Pi in four 4's. *Eureka*. 25: 18-19.)

Chapter 71

Interlude: Microscapes

Michael Davidson, a research scientist at the Institute of Molecular Biophysics at the Florida State University in Tallahassee, creates photomicrographs resembling unusual alien landscapes. He calls these photomicrographs "microscapes," and he has created a collection of a thousand beautiful and surreal scenes based on microscopic chemical compounds.

Photomicrography has been used for years for recording scientific data in a spectrum of disciplines. Davidson notes that the introduction of new films with improved emulsions, coupled to the progress made in optical coatings technology and computer-assisted exposure monitors, has enabled researchers to acquire high quality photomicrographs which are deeply color-saturated and high in contrast. The growing interest in photomicrography as an art form is evidenced by numerous photomicrography contest sponsored by companies such as Nikon, Polaroid, Olympus, and the Bethesda Research Lab.

Davidson's work often focuses on the use of multiple exposure color photomicrography using crystals grown from chemicals and biological macromolecules. Two to nine exposures are realized on 35-mm transparency film. The basic construction involves the use of brightfield and darkfield illumination, cross polarization, differential interference contrast, and Rheinberg illumination assisted by color filters.

Shown facing this page is "Wheatland," a multiple (4) exposure of ascorbic acid (the "wheat" in the foreground), stretched polyethylene (the morning sky), polybenzyl-l-glutumate (the stars), and the field diagram defocused (the morning sun).

71.1 For Further Reading

1. Strzelecka, T., Davidson, M., Rill, R. (1988) Multiple ligquid crystal phases of DNA at high concentrations. *Nature*. 331: 457-460.

2. Davidson, M., Page, M., French, M. (1991) Drugs for bugs. *American Laboratory*. August. pp. 34-38.

3. Davidson, M. (1990) Fabrication of unusual art forms with multiple exposure color photomicrography. *The Microscope*. 38(4): 357-365.

Chapter 72

On Mountain Climbing and a Strange Series

"To live for some future goal is shallow. It's the sides of the mountain which sustain life, not the top. Here's where things grow."
Robert Pirsig, *Zen and the Art of Motorcycle Maintainance*

The word "series" in mathematics usually refers to the sum of a finite or infinite sequence of terms. I like to think of a series from a mountain climber's perspective. Like a mathematical series, some mountains may eventually level off to a grassy plateau, while others shoot up into the clouds beyond our vision. This analogy should become clearer as you read further. An infinite series, for example, can be written in the form

$$a_1 + a_2 + a_3 + \cdots a_n + \cdots \tag{72.1}$$

or more compactly as Σa_n. Here are some examples of infinite series:

$$1 - 1/2 + 1/3 - 1/4 + 1/5 \ldots \tag{72.2}$$

and

$$1 - 2 + 3 - 4 + \cdots \tag{72.3}$$

Equation (72.2) is an example of an *oscillating convergent series* since the terms are alternately greater and less than the limiting value 0.6914. The fact that this series has this limiting value, towards which it tends, implies *convergence* (Pseudocode 72.2 shows you how to create the graph of this series which is shown in Figure 72.1.) Many convergent series are less wobbly; that is, they converge in a non-oscillating fashion where the values simply rise (or fall) monotonically to a limit. Think of this limit as the mountain climber's plateau or valley. In contrast to these convergent series, Equation (72.3) is an example of a *divergent* series since it does not tend to some finite value.

Often a graph can be used to show the value to which a series converges. Figure 72.1 shows this for Equation (72.2). The values gradually converge to 0.6914. However one must be wary of this graphical approach as evidenced by the

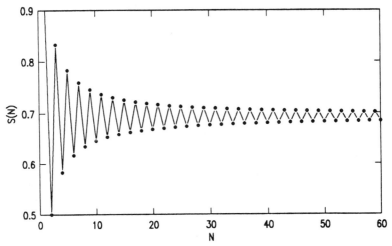

Figure 72.1. *An oscillating convergent series.*

fascinating series brought to my attention by Ross McPhedran of the Department of Theoretical Physics at Australia's University of Sydney. Consider the infinite series

$$S(N) = \sum_{n=1}^{N} \frac{1}{n^3 \sin^2 n} \qquad (72.4)$$

The Σ indicates summation, for example

$$\sum_{n=1}^{4} n = 1 + 2 + 3 + 4 \qquad (72.5)$$

If you plot the sum $S(N)$ as a function of n, it appears to converge nicely for the first 354 terms. Figure 72.3 shows a small table of values, starting at $N = 22$, so that you can see the rise, and smooth leveling off, to a value near 4.8. (I computed this using Pseudocode 72.1). Seems pretty tame at this point. In fact, I would have guessed that the series was converging to 4.8. However, at $N = 355$, the series' values suddenly jump up to 29.4! This is fine example for students on the danger of looking at graphs and tables of numbers in order to assess convergence. Why does the seemingly well-mannered behavior suddenly skyrocket at $N = 355$? The reason is simple when viewed in hindsight. First, recall that $\sin(N \times \pi) = 0$. Since 355 is almost a multiple of π, the values for $S(N)$ jump at this point! In fact, because $355/113 = 3.14159$ is such a good approximation to a multiple of π the series jumps very abruptly. Further jumps might occur later, whenever an excellent rational approximation to π is encountered. Can you find other jumps? I have examined the first hundred thousand terms and do not find a large jump other than at $N = 355$. What would an infinitely patient mountain climber find as

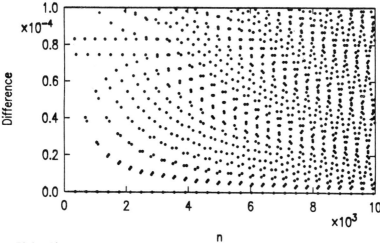

Figure 72.2. *Close approximations to Pi.*

he "walked" along this series for an infinite number of miles? Mathematicians have worked on the frequency of rational approximations to π, but their knowledge is not yet sufficient to answer whether this series converges or not. Figure 72.2 shows a plot of those values of N between 0 and 10,000 which are *almost* multiples of π. Stated more mathematically, Figure 72.2 is a plot of N for

$$| \frac{N}{k} - \pi | < \varepsilon \tag{72.6}$$

where ε is 0.0001. The points at $\varepsilon \sim 0$ are located at multiples of 355. (They appear to be on the zero axis due to the resolution of the graph.) Pseudocode 72.2 shows you how to compute this graph.

72.1 Credit

I thank Ross McPhedran, Department of Theoretical Physics, The University of Sydney, Sydney NSW 2006 Australia, for useful comments and for bringing the series in Equation (72.4) to my attention. Ross attributes this equation to the French physicist Professor Roger Petit, Laboratoire d'Optique Electromagnetique, Faculte des Sciences et techniques de St. Jerome, Marseille 13397, France.

Apparent convergence for the first few hundred terms.

N	S
22.00000	4.75410
23.00000	4.75422
24.00000	4.75430
25.00000	4.75796
26.00000	4.75806
27.00000	4.75811
28.00000	4.75873
. . .	. . .
307.00000	4.80686
308.00000	4.80686
309.00000	4.80686
310.00000	4.80686
311.00000	4.80697
312.00000	4.80697
313.00000	4.80697
314.00000	4.80697

Figure 72.3. *Apparent convergence of the first few hundred terms for the strange series.* (It seems that the series converges to a value close to 4.80697.)

```
ALGORITHM: How to Compute Strange Series

s=0
DO n = 1 to 400
   olds=s
   s = s + 1./(n**3 * (sin(n))**2)
   PrintValueFor(n, s)
   if ((s-olds) > 3) then Print("I have found a jump")
END
```

Pseudocode 72.1. *How to compute the strange series.*

```
ALGORITHM: How to Compute Oscillating Sign Series
s=0
DO i = 1 to 60
    if ((i mod 2) = 0) then t = -1; else t = 1
    v = (t / i)
    s = s + v
    PrintValueFor(i,s)
END
```

Pseudocode 72.2. *How to compute oscillating sign series.* (See Equation (72.2).)

```
ALGORITHM: How to Create the pi dot map.
pi = 3.1415926
DO k = 1 to   10000
 DO n = k to 10000
    ratio = n/k
    diff = abs( ratio - pi )
    if (diff < .0001) then PlotPointAt(n,diff)
 END
END
```

Pseudocode 72.3. *How to create the pi dot map figure.* (See Figure 72.2.)

Chapter 73

The Terrible Twos Problem

"No definition of science is complete without a reference to terror."

Don DeLillo, *Ratner's Star*

On one cool April day a few years ago in New York City, I approached a street vendor in order to purchase a pretzel. While waiting, I observed the following enigmatic encryption written in chalk on the dirty street: $5 = 2^2 + 1$. We will probably never know who wrote this and why it was written, but the equation stimulated me to conduct the "Terrible Twos" contest in August of 1991. In this contest, participants were to construct numbers using just ones and twos, and any number of $+$, $-$, and $\times$ signs. People were also allowed exponentiation. As an example, let's first consider the problem where only the digit one is allowed. The number 80 could be written:

$$80 = (1 + 1 + 1 + 1 + 1) \times (1 + 1 + 1 + 1) \times (1 + 1 + 1 + 1) \qquad (73.1)$$

If we let $f(n)$ be the least number of digits that can be used to represent n, then we see that $f(80) \leq 13$. A contest which allows only ones for forming small numbers turns out not to be very interesting. However, once the digit 2 is also allowed, the problem becomes fascinating. Here is an example:

$$81 = \left(2^{2 + 1} + 1\right)^2 \qquad (73.2)$$

Here $f(81) \leq 5$. Is this the best you can do?

The explicit goal of The Terrible Twos Contest was to represent the numbers 20, 120, and 567 with as few digits as possible. I received hundreds of responses, and wish that I could report all of the observations and entries in this chapter. Here are some examples. The first triplet of answers came from R. Lankinen of Helsinki, Finland:

$$f(20) \leq 5, \text{ for } 20 = 2^{2 + 2} + 2 + 2 \qquad (73.3)$$

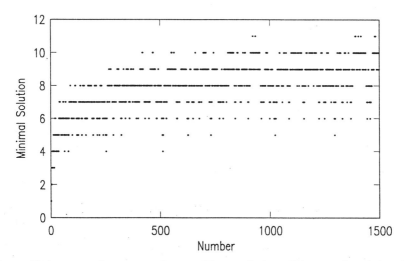

Figure 73.1. *Minimal integer solutions.* These solutions $f(n)$ were found for the first 1500 numbers. Concatenation of integers is not allowed.

$$f(120) \leq 6, \text{ for } 120 = ((2 + 1)^2 + 2)^2 - 1 \qquad (73.4)$$

$$f(567) \leq 9, \text{ for } 567 = 2 \times 2 \times ((2 \times (2 \times 2 + 2))^2 - 2) - 1 \qquad (73.5)$$

But is this the best one can do for the three numbers? It turns out that 567 can be constructed with just 8 digits. In fact, the contest winner, who first computed the minimum values for all three numbers, is Dan Hoey of Washington DC. Here are his minimal answers (which, I believe, use the smallest possible number of digits):

$$f(20) \leq 5 \text{ for } 20 = (1 + 2 + 2) \times (2 + 2) \qquad (73.6)$$

$$f(120) \leq 6 \text{ for } (2 + (1 + 2)^2)^2 - 1 \qquad (73.7)$$

$$f(567) \leq 8 \text{ for } (2^{2 + 2 + 2} - 1) \times (2 + 1)^2 \qquad (73.8)$$

The contest becomes more interesting if we allow concatenation of digits (thus permitting multidigit numbers such as 11, 12, 121, etc.) For this case, the winning entries come from Mark McKinzie of the University of Wisconsin's Mathematics Department. Here are Mark's answers:

$$f(20) \leq 3 \text{ for } 20 = 22 - 2 \qquad (73.9)$$

$$f(120) \leq 4 \text{ for } 120 = 11^2 - 1 \qquad (73.10)$$

$$f(567) \leq 6 \text{ for } 567 = (2 + 1)^{2 + 1} \times 21 \qquad (73.11)$$

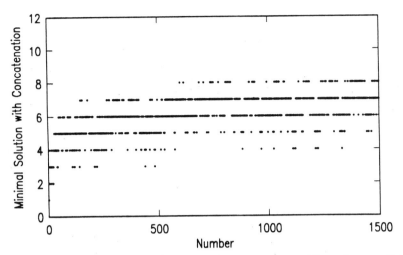

Figure 73.2. *Minimal integer solutions with concatenation.* The solutions $f(n)$ were found for the first 1500 numbers. Concatenation of integers is allowed (that is, multidigit numbers such as 12 and 121 are permitted).

Another equally successful set of answers comes from Ya-xiang, Beijing, China:

$$f(20) \le 3 \text{ for } 20 = 21 - 1 \tag{73.12}$$

$$f(120) \le 4 \text{ for } 120 = 121 - 1 \tag{73.13}$$

$$f(567) \le 6 \text{ for } 21 \times (2 + 1)^{2 + 1} \tag{73.14}$$

Other minimal answers were submitted, and I must confess that the winners of the contest were sometimes determined as much by the speeds of our electronic communication networks as by intellectual prowess.

I collaborated with Ken Shirriff of the University of California for much of the analysis of this problem. Ken wrote a computer program in C which not only searches for the minimal solution for the first 1500 integers but also searches for the number of minimal ways to construct a number. For example, without allowing concatenation (multidigit numbers), he finds that there are 208 different ways to write the number 20, and 1128 different ways to write the number 21! Even more exciting is the fact that these 208 and 1128 different ways to write minimal solutions change to just 2 ways and 1 way if concatenation is allowed. (After all, there is just one way to minimally write 21 by concatenating 2 and 1.)

The program finds solutions by using dynamic programming techniques. It starts with the one digit base cases, and combines these numbers to generate all numbers that have shortest solution of two digits. The one and two digit results are combined to yield all numbers with three digit shortest solutions. This process continues until all the desired numbers have been found. In order to keep the computations from growing too quickly, Ken Shirriff prunes the results by dis-

Without Multidigit Expressions:		With multidigit expressions:	
Digits	Hard Number	Digits	Hard Number
2	3	2	3
3	2	3	5
4	7	4	7
5	13	5	29
6	21	6	51
7	41	7	151
8	91	8	601
9	269	9	1631
10	419	10	7159
11	921	11	19145
12	2983	12	71515
13	8519	13	378701
14	18859		
15	53611		
16	136631		
17	436341		

Figure 73.3. *Hard numbers.*

carding any results over 10000. He also limits results to integers by only using positive exponents. While the first limit probably has no effect on the results, there are a handful of shorter solutions that are only obtained by using negative exponents.

Figure 73.1 and Figure 73.2 show plots of our computed values of $f(n)$ vs. n for both non-concatenation and concatenation contests. Interestingly, minimal solutions comprised of less than 12 digits can be found for all numbers tested (on average, one needs about 7 digits to minimally construct n, $1 \leq n \leq 1500$).

73.1 Hard Numbers

"He could find how numbers behaved, but he could not explain why. It was his pleasure to hack his way through the arithmetical jungle, and sometimes he discovered wonders that more skillful explorers had missed."

Arthur C. Clarke, 1956, *The City and The Stars*

Let us also define the concept of "hard numbers" $f_h(n)$ which are the smallest numbers requiring $f(n)$ digits. For example, 921 is the smallest number which requires a walloping 11 digits for its expression. Running his program on the integers up to one million, Shirriff found the hard numbers listed in Figure 73.3. Plots of n vs. $f_h(n)$ seem to increase exponentially.

73.2 Unusual Solutions

The contest winner, Dan Hoey, also wrote a Lisp program to confirm his hand calculations, and as with Shirriff's C program, he did not initially check for negative exponents. However, he later extended his program to negative exponents, and discovered they sometimes result in shorter solutions. For instance, Hoey notes that if negative exponents are not checked, one might conclude that $f(640) = 8$. However, look at Hoey's amazing solution $f(640) = 7$ found when using negative exponents:

$$640 = (2^{((2 + 1)^2)}) \times (1 + 2^{-2}). \tag{73.15}$$

Nevertheless, he believes that 20, 120, and 567 do not benefit from the use of negative exponents unless some subexpression has a denominator or numerator exceeding 10^{12}. He found an interesting solution with negative exponents for 567:

$$567 = (2^{2^2} + 2)^2 \times (2 - 2^{-2}) \tag{73.16}$$

He further wonders whether future searches should consider using irrational numbers. Hoey writes, "In the same way that negative exponents imply fractions, fractional exponents imply irrational numbers, and then irrational exponents imply transcendental numbers. In fact, one could obtain complex numbers, too, but I don't think that is any help, and you have problems with branch cuts there." One question is whether there are any "integers" that benefit (in the sense of requiring fewer ones and twos) by considering and using irrational numbers, or rational numbers formed with fractional exponents. Is there any integer that benefits from using irrational exponents? I think this is a fertile ground for significant future research.

In closing, I do not know for certain whether all of the $f(n)$ values listed here are truly the minimal values. In most cases, they were arrived at through computation and not through any mathematical theory. I look forward to hearing from readers who may be able to find even smaller values than the ones listed here. Finally, you may be interested in another contest conducted in 1989 called the "Very-large-number Contest," where participants were asked to construct an expression for a very large number using only the digits 1, 2, 3, and 4, and the symbols: "(," "),", decimal point, and the minus sign. Each digit could be used only once. The names of people who sent the 10 largest numbers were published in (Pickover, 1990, 1991).

Much of the participation and discussions for my *Terrible Twos Problem* occurred in the mathematics discussion group "sci.math" on the Usenet computer network, where this contest took place.

73.3 References

1. Pickover, C. (1990) Results of the very-large-number contest, *J. Recreational Math.* 22(4): 249-252. Also: Pickover, C. (1991) *Computers and the Imagination.* St. Martin's Press, New York

2. Guy, R. (1981) *Unsolved Problems in Number Theory.* Springer: New York.

Chapter 74

AIDS

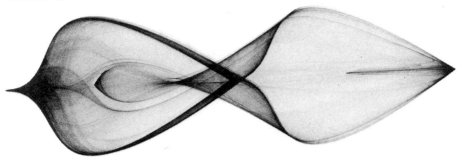

This short chapter contains a contemporary lesson demonstrating the power of simple computer programs and graphics in understanding the spread of diseases. If you are a teacher, why not compute and graph the numbers discussed here and show them to your students as an illustration of the likelihood of contracting AIDS (Acquired Immune Deficiency Syndrome) in various situations? The AIDS virus[46] was first reported in 1981. By April 1990 the total number of U.S. deaths due to the virus was 78,341.

In 1988, John Paulos[47] noted that the chance of contracting AIDS in a single unprotected heterosexual episode from a partner *known* to have the disease is about one in five hundred. (Paulos reported that this is the average value from a number of studies.) Therefore, the probability of *not* getting AIDS from a single such encounter is $499/500$. Let's assume that an individual has one encounter every day. The chances of not contracting AIDS after two days is $(499/500)^2$. The probability of not contracting AIDS after n days is $P = (499/500)^n$. Using the program code in Pseudocode 74.1 it's easy to compute and graph the chances of acquiring AIDS after a year. It turns out that an individual has about a 50 percent chance of not contracting AIDS after a year in the scenario just described. After two years (near the rightmost point in the graph of Figure 74.1) the chance of not getting AIDS is 23%. Paulos noted that using a condom, the risk of being infected with someone who has the disease is $1/5000$. If the partner's disease status is not known, but he or she is not a member of any known

---

[46] The frontispiece figure for this chapter is by Michael Davidson (see "Interlude: Microscapes" on page 365). It shows a photomicrograph of AZT (3'-azidothymidine) which is one of the most effective anti-AIDS medication developed to date.

[47] The specific AIDS statistics and analysis comes from the national bestseller: Paulos, J. (1988) *Innumeracy*, Vintage: NY. These figures are average estimates which are likely to change with geographic location, with further research, and with time. They are also highly dependent on the gender of the infected individual. I do not suggest any behavioral actions on the part of readers, but simply wish to illustrate the use of simple computer graphics for dealing with a perplexing contemporary dilemma.

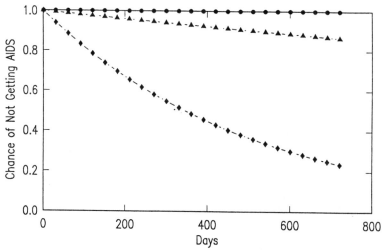

Figure 74.1. *The spread of AIDS.* Using the program code in this chapter, the chance of *not* getting AIDS is shown for an individual having unsafe heterosexual intercourse every day with someone who has the disease (diamonds). The triangles indicate the chances when using a condom. Symbols are spaced at 30-day intervals. The circles indicate the chances with unprotected sex, with someone whose disease status is unknown (but he or she is not a member of any known risk group). A curve was also plotted which indicates the chances with protected sex, with someone who's disease status is unknown (but he or she is not a member of any known risk group); however, the curve could not be visually distinguished from the curves (with circles), at the graph's resolution.

high risk group, the chances per episode of contracting AIDS is 1/5,000,000 (unprotected) and 1/50,000,000 (protected).

I was surprised at the difficulty I had in confirming the "1/500" and related values that Paulos suggested for contracting AIDS. In fact, various other probabilities for contracting AIDS have been reported which differ significantly from those suggested by Paulos. For example, some biologists in 1991 have reported to me that men have 1 in 10 odds of contracting AIDS from heterosexual contact with an infected partner, and women have 1 in 5 odds of contracting AIDS from an infected male partner. Using these figures, we can draw charts similar to Figure 74.1. Figure 74.3 shows graphs using these more ominous odds. The obvious discrepancies between the two figures suggest that this chapter be considered more as a general lesson in how to compute the chances of avoiding a disease as a function of the number of contacts with a carrier. In fact, you can embellish the program in this chapter to create your own science-fiction *Andromeda Strain* simulation in order to model the spread of a disease through a population.

Figure 74.2. *A computer graphics representation of HIV protease.* More specifically, this is a graphic of the Human Immunodeficiency Virus (HIV) Type 1 Protease (Fitzgerald et al., 1990), which I computed using graphics software running on an IBM RISC System/6000. The coordinates come from the Protein Data Bank at Brookhaven National Laboratory. This enzyme is responsible for making the AIDS virus functional.

74.1 Comments from Colleagues

The following are comments from researchers who became aware of my interest in computing these AIDS probabilities. I think you will find some of their opinions of interest. For example, one researcher remarked:

> What's surprising to me is how little one hears about the odds of infection. Maybe this is because medical/education experts feel the numbers would appear to be reassuring to the largely innumerate public.
>
> The 1/500 figure reported by Paulos sounds way too high. If you use this in your simulation I'd wager the overall infection rate will be much higher than in real life. But if you consider the high degree of promiscuity in the teenage population, 1/500 odds should have led to the infection of a large percentage of teenagers.

Another researcher noted:

> The problem with using probabilities of getting AIDS is that they result from what here in Switzerland would be called a Milchmaedchenrechnung – a calculation made by a dairy maid. Epidemilogical models do not fit well with a constant probability of transmission per unprotected (or protected) intercourse. There are differences in transmissibility between individuals, maybe because of the presence or absence of other venereal diseases, maybe because of large differences in the concentration of viruses in bodily fluids.

A researcher from the University of New Mexico:

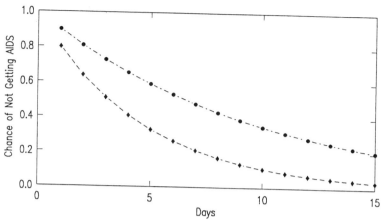

Figure 74.3. *The spread of AIDS.* This chart differs from the previous in that different probability factors are used, which are discussed in the text. Circles indicate the chances for a man not contracting AIDS after having daily heterosexual contact with an infected partner. Diamonds indicate the chances for a woman not contracting AIDS from an infected male partner.

There is an assumption here of linear risk per exposure that is very likely to be incorrect. Studies of transmission have shown that there is no relationship between length of a relationship and likelihood of transmission. This argues that factors specific to a particular couple (genital ulcers, viral load?) are more important than number of sexual episodes. Thus, if you're going to get it, you get it right at the start.

A final sobering statement from a biologist:

The odds of contracting AIDS from an accidental jab with a needle having infected blood has been reported in the scientific literature: one in four hundred. Anyone who can give you statistics on the probability of contracting AIDS from any random sexual encounter is doing it off the top of his head, and has no scientific basis for it. There is an excellent article in *Nature* (volume 352, 15 Aug. 91) regarding the heterosexual epidemic in Africa. Among the really scary stats quoted there (such as that pregnant women are now considered a risk group, in some cities having an infection rate of 30%) is the comment that it is impossible to accurately determine the probability of contracting AIDS from any given encounter, because people neither accurately remember nor willingly recount how many times they had sex with any given partner. Men have 1 in 10 odds of contracting AIDS from heterosexual contact with an infected partner, and women have 1 in 5 odds of contracting AIDS from an infected male partner. The second statistic is believed to be due to the high frequency of untreated minor yeast and bacterial infections in women, which is true world-wide. If either partner has an additional sexually transmitted disease such as herpes, gonnorhea, chlamydia or syphilis, the probability increases drastically, due to the presence of immune cells at the site (ready targets.)

```
ALGORITHM: How to compute chances of not contracting AIDS.
/* */
a = 499/500        /* heterosexsual */
b = 4999/5000      /* condom */
c = 49999999/50000000
d = 4/5
e = 9/10

odds = a
DO days = 1 to 730 by 30
        chance = odds**days
        PrintValue(days,chance)
END
```

Pseudocode 74.1. *How to compute your chances of not contracting AIDS.* (The variables a, b, c, d, e are different probabilities, which are discussed in the text. Simply try different values for the variable "odds.")

74.2 Fact File

• In 1991, in the world as a whole, at least 70% of the people infected with the AIDS virus are believed to have caught it from heterosexual encounters.[48]

• In 1990, 4,890 teenage and adult women were diagnosed with AIDS, and at least 100,000 more are feared to be carrying the virus.

• Heterosexual sex surpassed gay sex for the last two years as a way of spreading the infection. Among adult men and women, cases of heterosexually transmitted AIDS rose from 1,631 in 1989 to 2,289 in 1990.

74.3 Mystery Dance

For readers interested in our sexual heritage, see Lynn Margulis and Dorion Sagan's *Mystery Dance: On the Evolution of Human Sexuality* (Summit Books, 1991, 224 p., $19.95). The book argues that virtually all our ancestors have left their mark on contemporary sexual behavior. The authors track sexuality through a long line of nonhuman ancestors, from monkeys to promiscuous bacteria.

---

[48] The source for the AIDS "Fact File" is: Radetsky, P. (1991) Straight sex and AIDS vaccines. *Discover.* January. 52-53.

74.4 For Further Reading

1. Anderson, R. May, R. (1991) *Infectious Diseases of Humans: Dynamics and Control*. Oxford University Press: New York. 757 pp. $115.00.

2. James, G., Steele, N. (1991) Epidemics and the spread of disease. In *Mathematical Modelling*. Oxford University Press: NY. (Teachers and students of mathematical modeling will find this book a rich source of examples ranging from insulating houses to basketball, and from modelling epidemics to studying the generation of windmill power.)

3. Fitzgerlad, P., McKeever, B., van Middlesworth, J., Springer, J., Heimbach, J., Leu, C.-T., Herber, W., Dixon, R., Darke, P. (1990) Crystallographic analysis of a complex between Human Immunodeficiency Virus Type 1 Protease and acetyl-pepstatin at 2.0-angstroms resolution. *Journal of Biologial Chemistry*. 265: 14209.

4. For information on the Protein Data Bank which contained the atomic coordinates of the molecular model in this chapter, see: Bernstein, F. C., T. F. Koetzle, G. J. B. Williams, E. F. Meyer, Jr., M. D. Brice, J. R. Rodgers, O. Kennard, T. Shimanouchi, M. Tasumi (1977) The Protein Data Bank: A computer-based archival file for macromolecular structures. *Journal of Molecular Biology*. 112: 535-542;

Below is another view of the HIV protease molecule.

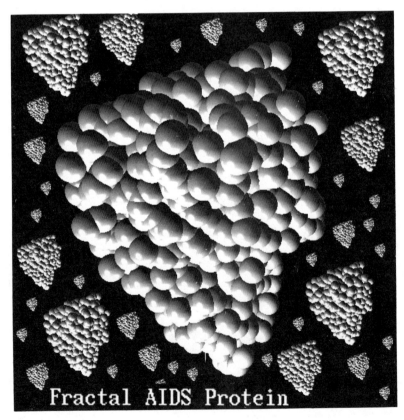

Fractal AIDS Protein

Chapter 75

Musings on Large Robbins Numbers
And Friden Calculators

"Jesearc sat motionless within a whirlpool of numbers. He was fascinated by the way in which the numbers he was studying were scattered, apparently according to no laws, across the spectrum of integers."

Arthur C. Clarke, 1956, *The City and The Stars*

In 1991, David P. Robbins published an article in *The Mathematical Intelligencer* with the unusual title "The Story of 1, 2, 7, 42, 429, 7436, ..." The paper deals with an interesting sequence of integers starting with 1 – but very quickly its members include behemoth numbers with 100's of digits. The sequence can be represented by $R_1, R_2, R_3, \ldots$, and it can be computed using the following formula:

$$R_n = \prod_{i=0}^{n-1} \frac{(3i+1)!}{(n+i)!} \tag{75.1}$$

The Π symbol indicates a repeated product. For example,

$$\prod_{i=1}^{3} i = 1 \times 2 \times 3 = 6. \tag{75.2}$$

The exclamation point is the factorial sign: $n! = 1 \times 2 \times 3 \times \cdots n$. Using Equation (75.1) it is not too difficult to determine the seventh and eighth terms of the series:

218347, 10850216

and I've included a list of the first 25 numbers in Figure 75.1. The 31st number (the largest I've computed) is:

7457901645375312545846943364460201024500933619811717193425944
4873965806173020494546519036225529743875880806424576

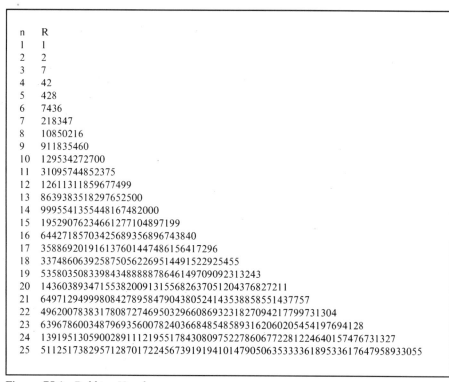

```
n    R
1    1
2    2
3    7
4    42
5    428
6    7436
7    218347
8    10850216
9    911835460
10   129534272700
11   31095744852375
12   12611311859677499
13   8639383518297652500
14   9995541355448167482000
15   195290762346612771048897199
16   6442718570342568935689674384 0
17   3588692019161376014474861564172 96
18   3374860639258750562269514491522925455
19   535803508339843488888786646149709092313243
20   14360389347155382009131556826370512043768272 11
21   649712949999808427895847904380524143538858551437757
22   4962007838317808727469503296608693231827094217799731304
23   639678600348796935600782403668485485893162060205454197694128
24   139195130590028911121955178430809752278606772281224640157476731327
25   5112517382957128701722456739191941014790506353333618953361764795893305 5
```

Figure 75.1. *Robbins Numbers.*

Before going further and offering a challenge, let me tell you a bit about Dr. Robbins himself (picture at left) and the problem he was working on. Robbins is a

mathematician at the Communications Research Division of the Institute for Defense Analysis in Princeton, New Jersey. He received his formal mathematics education at Harvard and MIT. Robbins refuses to state any mathematical speciality, insisting that he is "interested in any mathematical problem as long as its statement is easily understood and surprising." I was interested to learn that he has enjoyed computers since childhood, beginning with a peculiar fascination with his father's Friden calculator. (I had never heard of a "Friden calculator," but quickly found out after consulting colleagues. More about Friden calculators later in this chapter....)

Robbins exclaims that the sequence in Equation (75.1) has the mathematical community all in a quandary. In the last few years the sequence has arisen in three separate and distinct problems dealing with the analysis of combinations, and no one on earth has been able to explain why. The details of the branch of

```
ALGORITHM: How to Compute Robbins Numbers.
/* The user types in the value of n when the program starts. */
ARG n
R = 1;
DO i = 0 to n-1
    numer = factorial(3*i+1);
    denom = factorial(n+i)
    R = R * (numer/denom)
END;
/* Now write out the value */
SAY R
EXIT
/* Below is a recursive procedure for computing factorial */
factorial: PROCEDURE
      Arg n
      IF n=0 Then Return 1
      Return factorial(n-1)*n
```

Pseudocode 75.1. *How to Compute Robbins Numbers.* (The program coded here is in the style of the REXX language.) This computes values for the first equation in this chapter.

mathematics called *combinatorics* are beyond the scope of this book but the next section should whet your appetite by discussing one application.

75.1 Alternating Sign Matrices

Where does R_n have significance? For one thing, it seems to have relevance to the number of ways numbers in special kinds of matrices can be arranged. As most of you probably know, a matrix is an array of numbers organized in rows and columns. Here is an example of a matrix with 5 rows and 5 columns:

$$\begin{bmatrix} 0 & 1 & 0 & 0 & 0 \\ 1 & -1 & 0 & 1 & 0 \\ 0 & 1 & 0 & -1 & 1 \\ 0 & 0 & 0 & 1 & 0 \\ 0 & 0 & 1 & 0 & 0 \end{bmatrix} \qquad (75.3)$$

This is a *square NxN* matrix where $N = 5$. Its entries are all 0's, 1's, and -1's, and its rows and columns have sum 1. Also notice that, upon omitting the zeros, the 1's and -1's alternate in every row and column. Such matrices are called *alternating sign matrices*. For $N = 1$ there is one alternating sign matrix, and for $N = 2$ there exist 2 alternating sign matrices. For $N = 3$, there are 7 matrices including

$$\begin{bmatrix} 0 & 1 & 0 \\ 1 & -1 & 1 \\ 0 & 1 & 0 \end{bmatrix} \qquad (75.4)$$

Notice that the number of different NxN alternating sign matrices appears to be following the sequence in Equation 1: 1, 2, 7, ... We might be tempted to conjecture that R_N gives the number of alternating sign matrices with N rows and N columns. In fact Robbins has checked, by computer, that this conjecture holds for all N up to $N = 16$. However, it's never been proved that this conjecture holds in general.

75.2 Some Challenges

Let us return our attention to Equation (75.1). It is not obvious from Equation (75.1) that the values of R_n are even integers! Might there not be a value for n such that the denominator doesn't divide the numerator evenly? You need not wonder about this too long. Robbins says that all values of R_n are indeed integers. Why not test this for yourself by listing out a few numerator and denominator terms? Even if you do not have access to a computer, a pocket calculator should suffice for the first few terms.

Can you compute more than the six terms in the title of Robbins' article? Could the 31st term given in this chapter be the largest Robbins number ever computed. Can you break this record? I wrote a short program in IBM's programming language REXX which allows one to work with super-large integers (Pseudocode 75.1). Perhaps this will give you a hint as to how to program the formula (Equation (75.1)) in the programming language available to you. Alternatively, there are many simple software packages used to compute large integers, such as Mathematica (Wolfram Research). Other notable examples are the large-integer programs of Harry Smith. Harry J. Smith, best known for his massive 45,391-digit, record-breaking "Juggler" number (Pickover, 1991) uses his own software package to perform multiple precision integer arithmetic. He tells me that his package is written in the object-oriented programming language Turbo Pascal 5.5 by Borland International, Inc. Smith's super-precision calculator software also computes transcendental functions to thousands of decimal places. You may want to write to him to ask how you can program your own large-integer program. His address is Harry J. Smith, 19628 Via Monte Drive, Saratoga, CA 95070. Another alternative, for example, is the large-integer program Matlab (Mathworks, South Natick, MA).

75.3 Stop and Think

I call a Robbins number R_n *Robbinmorphic* if it terminates with n. For example, some one-digit Robbinmorphic numbers are $R_6 = 7436$ and $R_7 = 218347$. (For more on other *morphic* numbers, including: undulating undecamorphic and undulating pseudofarey-morphic integers, centered hexamorphic numbers, and cakemorphic numbers, see (Pickover, 1991).) If n were a 2-digit number, the last 2 digits of the Robbins number would be considered when checking morphicity. And so on.

In this chapter, the reader is invited to ponder the question: Does there exist a Robbinmorphic number for $n > 7$? I have searched for such an integer for all decimal integers

n ($1 \leq n \leq 31$) and have found no such integer, and one might conjecture that no such number exists. Of course, sparse numerical evidence such as this provides no real answer to the question, and it would be interesting if it were possible to prove the conjecture that there is no Robbinmorphic integer, or to find such a number. It is also interesting to speculate whether there is anything special about the arrangement of digits within any of the Robbins numbers. Certain Robbins numbers, such as the 14th Robbins number which starts with 999 and ends with 000, do not seem perfectly random. Are the arrangement of digits random?

75.4   What is a Friden Calculator?

In the beginning of this chapter I told you about David Robbin's childhood fascination with Friden calculators. Not knowing what these machines were myself, I asked a few friends to tell me about this calculator relic of the past. It seems my query elicited quite a few childhood memories of these late 1950s electromechanical machines. Coincidentally, C. Hassell of Tucson, Arizona, like Robbins, had very emotional memories of his father's Friden calculator. The text of his letter to me is as follows:

"The Friden calculator conjures up some of the strongest images I can recall from my childhood. My dad was a mechanical engineer and occasionally on Saturdays he would bring me to his office in downtown Chicago where he would assign me to some vitally important drafting task while he was busy at his desk. The highlight of my day came when he allowed me to enter some problems into his Friden calculator.

It was a desktop electromechanical calculator about the size of a PC, and it was a true marvel to watch in action. The keyboard consisted of probably 15 - 20 columns of ten digits each with an area off to the right for entering math operators after loading the numeric operand field. There was a huge carriage (similar to a typewriter's) at the top of the machine containing tiny windows, one for each column, each containing a small mechanical number wheel which served as the calculator's display.

I used to ponder the complexity of the cams, levers, shafts and reduction gears that powered the beast as I sat and watched it gyrate through a computation. The carriage would slide back and forth several times while the mechanics issued all kinds of incredible whirring and clattering sounds. Finally it would screech to a halt and lo and behold, the answer would be awaiting in the little windows atop the carriage.

Well, if you've endured my trip down memory lane up to this point, thanks. My dad passed away six years ago and it still just takes a small stimulus to induce a flood of nostalgia on my part."

Finally, W. Huyck of Raleigh, North Carolina, notes, "As I recall, they once cost about the same as a new car. With the square root function it would have been a nice new car."

75.5 Xi Xi Xi Xi

As indicated earlier in this chapter, Π is the symbol for product in mathematics. For example,

$$\prod_{i=1}^{4} i = 1 \times 2 \times 3 \times 4. \tag{75.5}$$

The symbol for summation in mathematics is Σ, for example:

$$\sum_{i=1}^{4} i = 1 + 2 + 3 + 4. \tag{75.6}$$

Is there a math symbol for repeated exponentiation? I haven't come across any in the mathematical literature, so suggest you make your own symbol for exponentiation. One colleague suggested the Greek capital xi (for Xponentiation).

$$\Xi_{i=1}^{3} i = 1^{2^{3}} \tag{75.7}$$

Since exponentiation is neither commutative nor associative, you should be very careful about how you define this operation – no matter what symbol you choose to represent it. For example, you should interpret a^{bc} to mean $a^{(b^{c})}$. The Ξ operator produces very large numbers very quickly. (Can you make a graph showing the rate at which these numbers grow?) The operator also makes for some very attractive and impressive looking notations:

$$\frac{\Xi_{i=1}^{3} \Xi_{j=1}^{4} \Xi_{k=1}^{5} \dfrac{i}{jk}}{\Xi_{i=1}^{3} \Xi_{j=1}^{4} \Xi_{k=1}^{5} \dfrac{i}{j+k}} \tag{75.8}$$

75.6 For Further Reading

1. Robbins, D. (1991) The story of 1, 2, 7, 42, 429, 7436, ... *The Mathematical Intelligencer*. 13(2): 12-18.
2. Pickover, C. (1991) Juggler Geometry, In *Computers and the Imagination*. St. Martin's Press, New York.

Facing this page is a *Callistemma brachiatum* (scabious) seed said to have been found in the gears of a Friden calculator. The seed is enlarged 27 times. (Photo by K. Blossfeldt.)

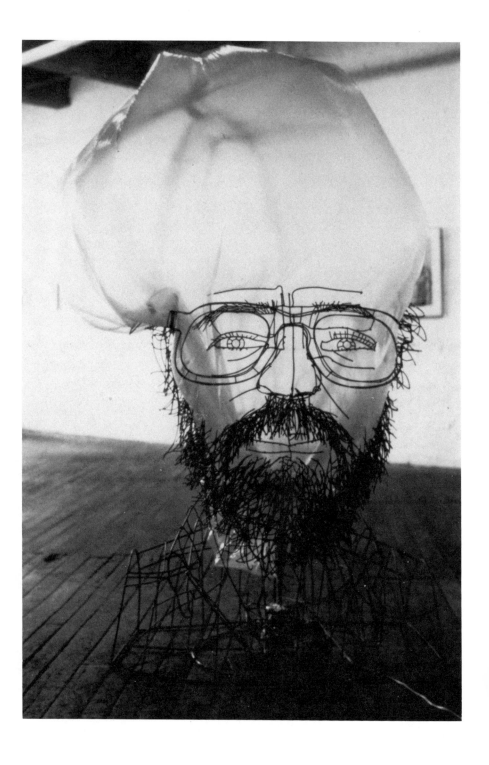

Chapter 76

Interlude: Electric Sculptures
With Swelled Heads

For years I've been admiring the work of Jim Pallas, an artist from Grosse Pointe Park, Michigan, who creates zany and inventive mechanized sculptures which are sometimes computer-controlled. His works embody an interesting mix of humor and the profound, and always represent a fusion of art and technology. They beep, they move, they shiver and shake. Shown at left is his "Portrait of the Artist...." When applauded to, a sensor, at the base of the piece, blows hot air into the plastic bag, causing the head to swell.

Another sculpture for which Pallas has grown famous is the *Nose Wazoo*, a five-foot-tall electronic creature which responds to the environment (above). The sculpture consists of several parts: the tripod base which holds the compressor and electronics, the vertical gimbal which pivots on the base, and the torso and head which contain two pneumatic cylinders for nose thrusts and neck flexes. There's also an airtank, and a sensory apparatus. The neck flexes, and the nose extends. The Nose Wazoo see his surroundings through four lenses with photocells. These eyes are very sensitive to changes in light levels. Its infra-red motion detector senses human body heat from as far away as thirty feet. It senses his own orientation with five internal mercury switches. Information from these sensors is gathered in a 6502 microprocessor located in his foot. The creature responds in life-like, intelligent ways to visitors in the room.

Below is one of Pallas' custom-designed printed circuit board patterns to control all the functions of a work that responds to viewers. The border is a 2^{36} binary counter.

WATCH
THIS
SPACE

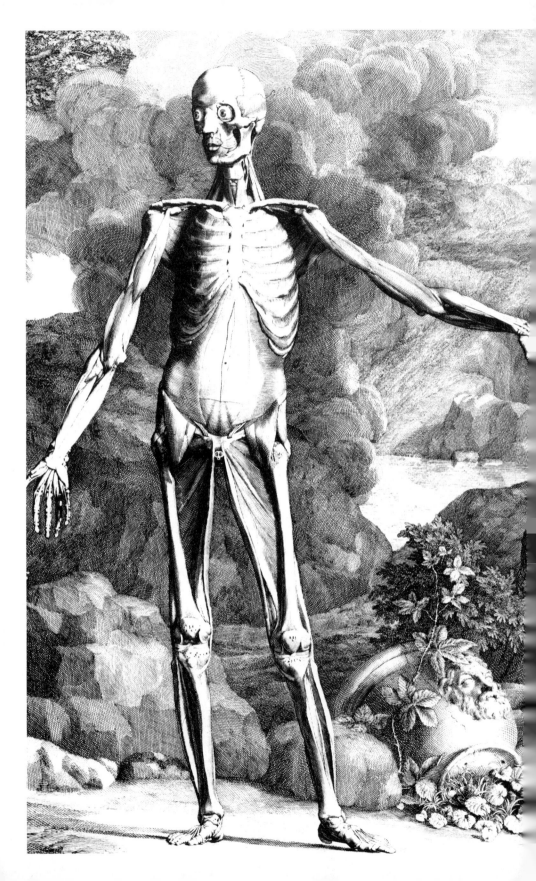

Chapter 77

Parasites on Parade

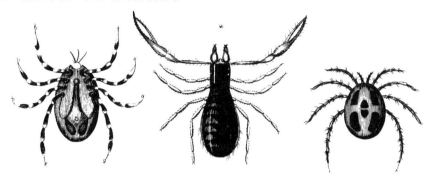

> *"He dove his thumb into the soft glob of red licorice he held, making it a little bigger than the parasite which lay on Sarah's neck... He bent forward toward the blistery growth. It was covered in a spiderweb skein of cris-scrossing white threads, but he could see it beneath, a lump of pinkish jelly that throbbed and pulsed with the beat of her heart."*
>
> Stephen King, *Four Past Midnight*

Parasites have plagued and weakened humans since the dawn of time. Parasites are organisms which live on or in another organism, and they derive their nutrients from that organism. Often parasites are small, but the hagfish, which sucks out the flesh of other fish, might either be classified as a predator or as a parasite. The tapeworm, often yards long, is indisputably a parasite. In the 1990's, parasitic infestations affect a great number of people. For example, infestation of pinworm (*Enterobius vermicularis*) approaches 100 percent in some tropical areas of the world. Parasites often exhibit peculiar biological behaviors. For example, ribbon worms absorb themselves when food is scarce. One specimen, in captivity, was known to have digested 95 percent of its own body in a few months without suffering any ill effects. Its weight returned to normal after food was offered.

With this admittedly unwholesome introduction, I'm sure I have turned a number of readers away. However, for those strong few who have remained, the following kinds of parasites can be studied without resorting to macabre biological experiments; instead we use the clean, dry, and sterile computer or pocket calculator to probe for numerical parasites.

The number 102,564 is a remarkable number I discovered one day during my late evening computer explorations. I call this number a "parasite number," for reasons which will soon become clear. In order to multiply 102,564 by 4 simply take the 4 off the right end and move it to the front to get the answer. In other words, the solution is the same as the multiplicand except that the number 4 on the right side is moved to the left end:

$102,564 \times 4 = 410,256.$

Isn't this an incredible number? How many numbers with this quality exist within the fabric of our universe of numbers? These kinds of numbers remind me 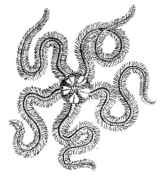 of a biological organism which contains a parasite (digit) which roams around the body of the host organism (the multidigit number in which the parasite resides) as it gains energy by feeding (the multiplication operation). I've written several programs which run a long time on an IBM mainframe in order to search for parasite-containing numbers, such as 102,564. (From here on I'll call parasite-containing numbers *parasite numbers* for brevity.) If you search for all potential parasite numbers generated by different 1-digit multipliers, you'll find that they are exceedingly rare. It seems that the only parasite number less than one million is the 4-parasite 102,564. (The term "4-parasite" indicates that the number 4 is the multiplier.)

Do the other digits give rise to any parasite numbers? Are there multipliers for which no parasite number exists? How much computer time will be spent on this, now that I have asked this question?

There do exist occasional "pseudoparasites" lurking within the integers less than a million. These are numbers like 128,205 which when multiplied by 4 also move the last digits to the first:

$128,205 \times 4 = 512,820$

(I call these "pseudoparasites" only because the last migrating digit is not the same as the multiplier.) Here are some other 4-pseudoparasites:

$153846 \times 4 = 615384$

$179487 \times 4 = 717948$

$205128 \times 4 = 820512$

$230769 \times 4 = 923076$

Here is a 5-pseudoparasite: $142857 \times 5 = 714285$

Both parasites and pseudoparasites are exceedingly rare. As I search during the late night hours, with my computer programs, for more examples, I challenge you to beat me in my search using the computer of your choice.

77.1 Behemoth Parasites

After showing my single 4-parasite number to several colleagues, Keith Ramsay of the University of British Columbia came up with an amazing formula to gen-

erate parasite numbers. It turns out that my brute-force computational searches would have taken far too long to find larger parasite numbers. Suppose we start with a multiplier digit d and wish to find some d-parasite. All we have to do is use the formula $d/(10d - 1)$, and use the unique segment of digits before the cluster repeats.[49] Let me explain with an example.

Suppose I'd like to find a large parasite for 2. Let's divide 2 by 19 to get $2/19 = 0.105263157894736842$. The "105263157894736842" portion repeats over and over, and is a 2-parasite because

$$2 \times 105,263,157,894,736,842 = 210,526,315,789,473,684. \qquad (77.1)$$

This number, by the way, is larger than the number of stars in the Milky Way galaxy. Here's an incredible-sized 6-parasite:

$6/59=.10169491525423728813559322033898305084745762711 86440677966...$

$10169491525423728813559322033898305084745762711 86440677966 \times 6 =$
$6101694915254237288135593220338983050847457627 118644067796$

See how the 6 migrates from the right end to the front after multiplication? Knowing Ramsay's formula, you can amaze your friends with multidigit parasites containing hundreds of digits.

Mike Dederian of Harvey Mudd College in California found something unusual about a 5-parasite

$$1020408163265306122448979591 83655 \qquad (77.2)$$

which can be written as: 1 (02) (04) (08) (16) ... to emphasize the doubling of digits. The reason for this initial pattern is not obvious to us.

---

[49] Every fraction, when expressed as a decimal, either "comes out even" as in $1/8=0.125$, or it repeats as in $1/3=0.33333$ where a single digits occurs over and over again, or it has group-repeats as in $1/7 = 0.142857\ 142857\ ....$

77.2 Fact File

After seeing my parasite numbers, Joseph S. Madachy, editor of the *Journal of Recreational Mathematics* sent me a paper he wrote in 1968 which appeared in *The Fibonacci Quarterly* (6(6): 385-389). In the paper are recipes for "instant division" which resembles what we might call (using my terminology) "reverse pseudoparasites." If you wish to divide 717,948 by 4 merely move the initial 7 to the right, obtaining 179,487. Madachy also gives another example:

$$9,130,434,782,608,695,652,173 \tag{77.3}$$

can be divided by 7 by transposing the initial 9 to the end, obtaining

$$1,304,347,826,086,956,521,739 \tag{77.4}$$

Interestingly, all of Madachy's computations were done on a Friden calculator (see "Musings on Large Robbins Numbers and Friden Calculators" on page 385).

Stop and Think

1. What is special about the fraction 137174210/1111111111? Try computing this to find out. You'll be amazed when you gaze upon its decimal representation.

2. Make a list of all pseudoparasites less than one million.

3. Do there exist "ultraparasites" which multiply by swapping both the left- and right-most digits?

Males with No Digestive Tracts

During the height of my interest in biology, I became fascinated by exotic examples of parasitism in animal species. My favorite examples are those which show the effect of environment on sex determinism. The sea worm *Bonnelia* is an intriguing example. If the free-swimming *Bonnelia* larvae settle on the sea bottom, they develop into females, each with a long proboscis (flexible tube). On the other hand, larvae that land on the female proboscis develop into tiny males that lack digestive organs and exist in parasitic fashion in the genital ducts of the female. (When I once lectured about this creature, one male chauvinist in the audience remarked that this was the ultimate example of women's liberation in the animal kingdom.) Why not try to model population growth of *Bonnelia* using your computer? Use an array to represent 50 unoccupied sites on the ocean floor. Each time a larvae lands on an empty site, the array element changes from 0 to "F" (for female). Each time a larvae lands on a site containing an F, the array element changes from F to "M" (for male/female combination). How many parasitic males exist after 100 larvae have dropped? (If you like, you can have an organism die after a certain number of iterations, in which case the array element returns to the value of "0").

Chapter 78

Pyramids of Blood

What is the volume of human blood on earth today? In other words, if all approximately 5.4 billion people from every country on earth were drained of their blood by some terrible vampire machine, what size container would the machine require to store the blood? The answer to this is quite surprising. Think about it before reading further.

The average adult male has about six quarts of blood. Considering that a large part of the earth's human population are women and children, let's assume that each person has an average of one gallon of blood. This gives 5.4 billion gallons of blood in the world. Considering that there are 7.4805185 gallons per cubic foot, this gives us 7.22×10^8 cubic feet of human blood in the world. The cube root of this value indicates that all the blood in the world will fit in a cube about 897 feet on a side. To give you a feel for this figure, the length of one of the sides of the Great Pyramid in Egypt is 755 feet. The length of the S.S. Queen Mary is 1000 feet. The height of the Empire State Building is 1,400 feet. This means that a box with a side as long as the S.S. Queen Mary could contain the blood of every man, woman, and child living on earth today.

John Paulos in his remarkable book *Innumeracy* discusses blood volumes as well as other interesting liquid volumes, such as the volume of water rained down upon the earth during the Flood in the book of Genesis. Considering the biblical statement "All the high hills that were under the whole heaven were covered," Paulos computes that half a billion cubic miles of liquid had to have covered the earth. Since it rained for forty days and forty nights (960 hours), the rain must have fallen at a rate of at least fifteen feet per hour. Paulos remarks that this is "certainly enough to sink any aircraft carrier, much less an ark with thousands of animals on board."

Stop and Think

1. Compute the volume of body fluid for an average fish. What size container would be needed to contain all the blood of all the fishes in the world? Today, is there more monkey blood in the world or more human blood? One thousand years ago was there more monkey blood in the world or more human blood?

2. Today, is there more insect blood in the world or more human blood? What size container is required to store all the insect blood in the world?

Fact File: Schizophrenic Spider Blood

In 1959, N. A. Bercel fed the blood of schizophrenic patients to spiders. In order

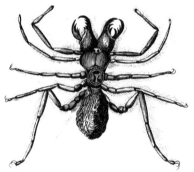

to accomplish this feeding, Bercel first squirted the blood into an amputated fly abdomen, which was then placed on the spider web. The spider ate the fly, and, as a result, increased its frequency of creating simple webs with just a few strands. Such webs are often seen from spiders prior to molting. (Source: Bercel, N. (1959) The effect of schizophrenic blood on the behavior of spiders. In *Neruo-psychopharmacology*. Bradley, Deniker, and Raduouco-Thomas, eds. Elsevier.)

Pictured below is a battle between a scorpion and a common barrel spider.

*"A man is a small thing,
and the night is very large
and full of wonders."*

Lord Dunsany
The Laughter of the Gods

Part VIII

APPENDICES

Appendix A

Philobiblic Potpourri

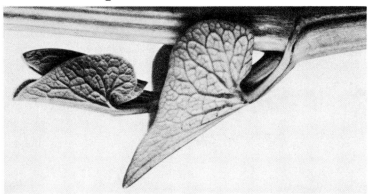

A.1 Literature for Lacubration

– a listing of unusual references.

1. Barwise, J., Moss, L. (1991) Hypersets. *The Mathematical Intelligencer*. 13(4): 31. (Answers the question, "What are hypersets?" One author remarks, "Confronted by such an expression years earlier, I experienced the same sense of vertigo experienced on my first encounter with continued fractions, but without the corresponding uplifting feeling given by the solution of the continued fraction.")

2. Sizer, W. (1991) Mathematical notions in preliterate societies. *The Mathematical Intelligencer*. 13(4): 53-41. (Answers questions such as, "What level of mathematical development was obtained before societies developed written languages? How much of early recorded mathematics is a recording of what was known long previously?")

3. Frazier, K. (1991) *The Hundredth Monkey: And Other Paradigms of the Paranormal*. Prometheus Books, 400 p, $17.95. (In 1976, the Committee for the Scientific Investigation of Claims of the Paranormal (CSICOP) was established. They're goal is to provide accurate, scientific information about bizarre paranormal claims. This collection gives scientific explanations for alien-abduction experiences and spontaneous human combustion deaths, among other phenomena.)

4. Meyer, A. (1991) Dangerous curves ahead. *MicroCad News*. November, 58-63. (Describes the mathematics of various strange curves, particularly those used in designing triple overpass roads for highways.)

5. Plotz, H. (1988) *Imagination's Other Place: Poems of Science and Mathematics*. Thomas Crowell: NY. (Poems about chemistry, biology, medicine, astronomy, geography, and physics. Poems about scientists like Einstein, Euclid, and others.)

6. Gelertner, D. (1991) *Mirror Worlds: Or the Day Software Puts the Universe in a Shoebox ... How it Will Happen and What it Will Mean.*. Oxford University Press, 237 p., $24.95. (Describes the future of computer technology.)

7. Keenan, D. (1991) To dissect a mockingbird: a graphical notation for the lambda calculus with animated reduction. (A paper on unusual representations of birds' songs

available from: David Keenan, 116 Bowman Parade, Bardon QLD 4065 Australia. Here is a quote from his erudite paper:

"It is a wonderfully bizarre fact that each song of a combinatory bird is not merely the name of another bird but is actually a complete description of the internal plumbing of that other bird. That is, each song is actually a brain map of some bird. Since a song is a complete description of how some bird will respond when it hears another bird, and the only important thing about a combinatory bird is how it responds when it hears another bird, we see that songs and singers are interchangeable. So we can say that the birds sing birds to each other, or we can equally say that what we have is a bunch of songs that sing songs to each other. Their language has no distinction between verbs and nouns. A description of action can equally well be a name. To emphasize this, in the future we call our diagrams *song maps*."

Below is a typical diagram from Keenan's paper:

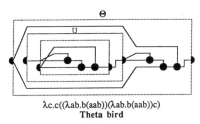

$\lambda c.c((\lambda ab.b(aab))(\lambda ab.b(aab))c)$
Theta bird

8. Pappas, T. (1990) *More Joy of Mathematics.* Wide World Publishing/Tetra, P.O. Box 476, San Carlos, CA 94070.

9. Philip, A.G.D., Frame, M., Philip, K. (1991) *Volume 1, Midgets on the Spike.* L. Davis Press: NY. (Contains a number of images of the Mandelbrot set with extreme magnifications of midgets and spikes, up to 1.4×10^{359}. Contact: L. A Davis Press, 1125 Oxford Place, Schenectady, NY 12308 for ordering information.)

10. *Symmetry: Culture and Science,* a quarterly journal on all aspects of symmetry in art, science, and culture. Contact: ISIS-Symmetry, PO Box 4, Budapest H-1361 Hungary.

11. Chernev, I. (1960) *Chessboard Magic!* Dover: NY.

12. Chernev, I. (1965) *The Bright Side of Chess.* Dover: NY.

13. Toole, B. (1992) *Ada, the Enchantress of Numbers: A Selection from the Letters of Lord Byron's Daughter and Her Description of the First Computer.* Strawberry Press: CA. (For further information, contact: Critical Connection, PO Box 452, Sausalito, CA 94966. This book answers questions such as: Was the software language Ada properly named? Was she mad or a visionary? Did she predict the impact of today's computer revolution?)

14. Zagier, D. (1989) The dilogarithm function in geometry and number theory. In *Number Theory and Related Topics.* Oxford University Press, NY. (This paper, presented at the Ramanujan Colloquium in Bombay in 1988, discusses the behavior of the "dilogarithm function" defined by

$$Li_2(z) = \sum_{n=1}^{\infty} \frac{z^n}{n^2} \qquad (A.1)$$

15. Barbeau, E. (1979) Euler subdues a very obstreperous series. *American Mathematics Monthly*. 86: 356-371.

16. Cherfas, J. (1991) Disappearing mushrooms: another mass extinction? *Science* 254: 1458. (As fungi vanish from Europe, scientists search for causes – and possible effects on forest ecology.)

17. O'Brien, S.J. et al. (1991) Molecular biology and evolutionary theory: The giant panda's closest relatives. In *New Perspectives in Evolution*. Warren and Koprowski, eds. Wiley-Liss.

18. Bowcock, A.M. et al. (1991) Drift, admixture, and selection in human evolution: a study with DNA polymorphisms. *Proceedings of the National Academy of Science*. 88: 839-843.

19. Ohno, S., Yomo, T. (1991) The grammatical rule for all DNA: junk and coding sequences. *Electrophoreses*. 12: 103-108.

20. Davis, P., Hersh, R. (1986) *Descartes' Dream*. Harcourt Brace Jovanovich: NY.

21. Costello, M. (1988) *The Greatest Puzzles of All Time*. Prentice-Hall: New York.

22. Albert, E. (1992) Crosswords by computer, or 1,000 nine-letter words for fun and profit. *Games* Febr. 16(1): 10-14.

23. Williams, A. (1992) *Jigsaw Puzzles: An Illustrated History*. Wallace-Homestead Book Co. 362 pp., paper, $24.95. (Anne Williams is one of the world's foremost experts on jigsaw puzzles, and is a Professor of economics at Bates College in Lewsiton, Maine.)

24. Roach, J., Tatum, J. (1988) Using domain knowledge in low-level visual processing to interpret handwritten music: an experiment. *Pattern Recognition* 21(1): 333-344.

25. Chess, D., Peevers, A., Pickover, C., Reed, A. (1989) Car radio scanner differentiating music from speech. *IBM Technical Disclosure Bulletin*. October 32(5B): 12-13.

26. Fagarazzi, B. (1988) Self-similar hierarchical processes for formal and timbral control in composition. *Interface* (Netherlands) 17(1): 45-61.

27. Pickover books. *Spiral Symmetry, Visions of the Future, The Pattern Book, The Visual Display of Biological Information, Computers and the Imagination*, and more. For information: PO Box 549, Millwood, NY 10546-0549 USA.

28. Markovsky, G. (1992) Misconceptions about the Golden Ratio. *College Mathematics Journal*. 23(1). (A fascinating paper debunking various myths associated with the golden ratio and its place in art and nature. Highly recommended. Reprints available from: Prof. George Markovsky, Computer Science Dept., University of Maine, Orono, ME 04469.)

A.2 Product Pavan

– A short section on innovative software, artwork, and related curiosities to simulate your imagination.

1. Imagicians Artware Inc., Box 1005, Manotick, Ontario, Canada K4M 1E9. (Innovative and beautiful art derived from mathematics. Postcards.)

2. The Newtonian Sandbox, an MS-DOS program by Judah Schwartz of MIT. Educational software for demonstrating: velocity-dependent frictional forces, oscillatory motion, etc. Contact: Prof. Judah Schwartz, School of Engineering, 20C-215, Massachusetts Institute of Technology, Cambridge, MA 02139; judah @hugse1.bitnet.

3. Electronic checkers machine. Contact: Saitek Ltd., 12/F Chung Nam Center, 414 Kwun Tong Road, Hong Kong.

4. Vexahedron. A puzzle made of 8 blocks of wood, each with a magnet embedded in the center of one side. Contact: Tensegrity Systems Corp., 1632 Rte 9, Tivoli, NY 12538.

5. Chaotic Dynamics Workbench, by Roger Rollins of Ohio University. Nonlinear systems, pendulums, oscillators. Contact: Prof. Roger Rollins, Dept. of Physics and Astronomy, Clippinger Labs, Ohio University, Athens, OH 45701-2979; rollins @ cgruni.phy.ohiou.edu.

6. Civilizaiton. Strategy game where 2-4 players build a civilization through trade, agriculture, technology, and law. Avalon Hill, 4517 Hartford Road, Baltimore MD 21214.

7. Mapper, for IBM-compatible computers, developed by James Harold. Fractals, Lyapunov exponents, Poincare sections. Clear manual. Contact: James Harold, Dept. of Physics, University of Maryland, College Park, MD 20742; harold@ lpe.umd.edu.

8. Variance. Strategy game. Get your pawns from your home base to your opponent's. Certain sections of the board slide. Dash, Box 13344, San Antonio, TX 78213.

9. WaveMaker (a Macintosh program by Freeman Deutsch of the Harvard-Smithsonian Center for Astrophysics), an interactive computer simulation depicting the oscillation of beads connected by elastic strings. Contact: Prof. Freeman Deutsch, Project Insight, Harvard College Observatory, 60 Garden St. MS 71, Cambridge, MA. 02138; fsd@ cfa.harvard.edu.bitnet.

10. EM Field, a program that runs on both Macintosh and MS-DOS computers, by David Trowbridge of Microsoft Corporation. The program shows students the effect of electric fields associated with a small number of charged particles. Contact: David Trowbridge, Multimedia Publications, One Microsoft Way, Microsoft Corporation, Redmond, WA 98052-6399; microslft!davidtro @ uunet.uu.net.

11. New World. Strategy game. 2-6 players colonize Europe during the 15th and 16th centuries. Avalon Hill, 4517 Hartford Road, Baltimore MD 21214.

12. Spreadsheet Physics Worksheets (an MS-DOS program by Charles Misner of the University of Maryland), a spreadsheet program allowing students to use numerical analysis to solve physical problems. Contact: Prof. Charles Misner, Dept. of Physics, University of Maryland, College Park, MD 20742-4111; misner@ umdhep.bitnet.

13. Fractal Postcards. The Mathematical Association, 259 L Leichester, LE2 3BE UK.

14. Mathematical calendars, t-shirts, and optical illusion slide shows. T. Pappas, c/o Wide World Publishing/Tetra, P.O. Box 476, San Carlos, CA 94070.

15. Set. A puzzle game invented by mathematician and computer programmer Marsha J. Falco. A game of logic and perception for one or more players. Set, 301 Cowley, E. Lansing, MI 48823. Fax (517) 351-4341.

16. *Dragons 4*, an IBM PC compatible computer program for fractals. Contact: Larry Cobb, By House, Dean Down Drove, Littleton, Winchester, Hants, S022 6PP England.

17. *Fractal Report*, a newsletter on fractals. Published by J. de Rivaz, Reeves Telecommunications Lab. West Towan House, Porthtowan, Cornwall TR4 8AX, United Kingdom.

18. *AMYGDALA*, a fascinating newsletter on fractals. Write to AMYGDALA, Box 219, San Cristobal, New Mexico 87564 for more information.

19. Crossword puzzle software. Mel Rosen, 11718 Nicklaus Circle, Tampa, FL 33624. Also: Crossword Construction Set, for the Macintosh. Uses a 250,000 entry database to fill grid selections of up to 25 words. Contact: Alan Richter, 340 Riverside Drive, Apt 3-D, New York, NY 10025.

20. *Algorithm - Recreational Programming Magazine*. P.O. Box 29237, Westmount Postal Outlet, 785 Wonderland Road S., London, Ontario, Canada, N6K, 1M6. ($19.95). Topics include: fractals, artificial life, iterative system, computer art, cellular automata, special games, screen-saver programs, robotics and artificial intelligence, neural and genetic computing, music, viruses, programming advice, and much more.

21. *Fractal Calendar*. Address inquiries to J. Loyless, 5185 Ashford Court, Lilburn, Georgia 30247.

22. *The Best of Journal of Chaos and Graphics*, Three volumes in one wild and informal paperback book. Topics: fractals, computer art, devil's curves, music, and much more. Published by: Media Magic, PO Box 507, Nicasio, CA 94946 USA (Toll free: 1-800-882-8284. $10.00, plus $2.00 postage and handling, US orders; $4.00 postage and handling non-US orders.)

23. *YLEM – Artists using science and technology*. This newsletter is published by an organization of artists who work with video, ionized gases, computers, lasers, holograms, robotics, and other nontraditional media. It also includes artists who use traditional media but who are inspired by images of electromagnetic phenomena, biological self-replication, and fractals. Contact: YLEM, Box 749, Orinda, CA 94563.

24. *Recreational and Educational Computing Newsletter*. Dr. Michael Ecker, 909 Violet Terrace, Clarks Summit, PA 18411.

25. *Strange Attractions*. A store devoted to chaos and fractals (fractal art work, cards, shirts, puzzles, and books). For more information, contact: *Strange Attractions*, 204 Kensington Park Road, London W11 1NR England.

26. *Pickover Software Sampler*, Bourbaki, PO. Box 2867, Boise, Idaho 83701. (Software for drawing and exploring many of the images in *Computers, Pattern, Chaos and Beauty*, St. Martin's Press: NY).

27. *Illuminations*, visible music by Ken Jenkins. The images are complex, graceful, and mesmerizing. The soundtrack includes three new pieces of New Age/Space music. Contact: Willow Tree, PO Box 1439, San Rafael, CA 94915.

28. *MEDIA MAGIC: The Fractal Universe Catalog*, PO Box 507, Nicasio, California 94946. This fine company distributes books, videos, prints, and calendars.

29. *ART MATRIX*, creator of beautiful postcards and videotapes of exciting mathematical shapes. Write to ART MATRIX, PO Box 880, Ithaca, New York 14851 for more information.

30. *Sculpture* magazine is published bimonthly by the International Sculpture Center, 1050 Potomac Street, N.W., Washington D.C. 20007. The ISC is an organization devoted to the advancement of contemporary sculpture. Actives include the Sculpture Source, a computerized artists' registry and referral service. Typical topics covered by the magazine: interactive art, sky art, holographic installations, art and technology.

31. Hargittai, I., Pickover, C. (1992) *Spiral Symmetry* World Scientific Publishing, 687 Hartwell Street, Teaneck, New Jersey 07666-5309. Phone: 201 837-8858 Hardcover, $48.00, 650 pages. ISBN 981-02-0615-1. Spirals in nature, art, and mathematics. Fractal spirals, plant spirals, artists' spirals, the spiral in myth and literature...

32. Booklet and newsletter on various topics in recreational math, fractals, number theory, and the golden ratio. Send self-addressed envelope with two stamps to Gary Adamson, PO Box 16329, San Diego, CA 92176-0329.

33. *Millenium Magazine 2000*. Topics: fractals, nanotechnology, the big bang, time spirals, peace. Peter Sorensen, 1431 Ocean Ave., Suite 516, Santa Monica, CA 90401.

34. *Children's Math Calendar*. Charles Babbage and early computers. Fibonacci and unexpected squares. QED Books, 1 Straylands Grove, York YO3 0EB England.

A.3 Curiosity Cavalcade

– a section for curious readers on unusual applications of computers and technology.

• Perhaps one of the most unusual applications of computers has been to the study of

spider amputees. Reed, Witt and Jones, in 1965, used a computer to analyze the effect of leg removal on spider web formation. Legless spiders were found to produce webs with fewer radii, and with fewer spiral turns, than normal spiders. No differences were found between chopping off the left or right leg. (Source: Reed, C., Witt, P, Jones, R. (1965) The measuring function of the first legs of *Araneus diadematus Cl. Behavior*. 25: 98-119.)

• In 1934, Rowley showed that goldfish can distinguish between circles whose diameters differ by as little as 3 millimeters. Can you distinguish such circles? Have your computer draw a series of circles and compare your visual acuity to that of a goldfish. (Source: Rowley, J. (1934) Discrimination limens of pattern and size in the goldfish. *Carassius auratus. Genet. Psychol Monogr*. 15: 245-302.)

• In 1991, Walter Stewart and Ned Feder of the National Institute of Health used a computer program called a *Plagiarism Detector* to determine if a book can legally be called a plagiarism of another book. They are planning a court appearance of the technique, if they are permitted to testify as expert witnesses in a trial over disputed rights to a textbook on plastic surgery. Using his computer program, Stewart calculated the percentage of 30-letter strings that are identical between the two books in question. In two introductory chapters, he found a 57% match between books.

• *The Numerical Arrow Puzzle.* Place the digits 0 through 9 in each of the circles of the arrow pictured below according to the following rule: Each pair of digits connected by a line must make a two-digit number that is evenly divisible by either 13 or 7. For example, 8 and 7 connected by a line would be appropriate because the number 78 is divisible by 13. (You can consider the two digits in one order or the other.) Do not use a digit more than once. I've placed the number 5 in the tail of the arrow to get you started. Is there a solution? Try this simple-looking (although difficult) problem on a few friends.

• "Robot Checkers-Players, Surgeons, and Chefs" on page 293 discussed several unusual examples of robotics technology. In 1992, an automated cow-milking system, the "Robo Milkmaid," was under study at the Maryland Agricultural Experiment Station. The device is novel in that it hooks itself up to the cow. The system opens a gate, scrubs the cow's udder, and attaches the milker. It also feeds the cow.

• "There is Music in our Genes" on page 211 discussed musical scores from genetic sequences. In 1992, an electronic sheet-music system became available which allows sheet-music purchasers to customize a musical score before purchasing it. For example, users may use the electronic touch screen to change the music's key. This interactive "NoteStation" then allows the buyer to print the final selection when satisfied. NoteStation is available in nine California music stores. For further information, contact: MusicWriter, 170 Knowles Dr., Suite 203, Los Gatos, CA 95030.

• "Bertrand Russell's Twenty Favorite Words" on page 183 discussed unusual words. One odd word frequently used by biologists in 1992 is "extremeophile." Extremeophiles are microorganisms living in extreme environments, such as bacteria that flourish in concentrated organic solvents, at pH 12, or in boiling water, or at extreme pressures. One notable extremeophile explorer is Japanese scientist Koki Horikoshi who recently completed a 5-year, $15-million study of these strange creatures.

• Here's an interesting question which appeared in the February 1992 issue of *Games* magazine. "What is the number of countries bordering the country whose name differs by only one letter from the name of a U.S. capital whose name differs only in its two final letters from the name of another U.S. state capital?"

• "Is Computer Art Really Art?" on page 169 discussed various issues in computer art. Cas Strachelberg, gallery assistant at the Paula Cooper Gallery in New York's SoHo district has commented: "Pieces that look as if they are computer generated are having a hard time." One of the tricks for having computer art accepted to galleries, and even to computer graphics art shows, is to produce art that does not look as if it were created on a computer. This excludes most fractals derived from mathematics. (Source: *Computer Pictures*, Jan/Feb 1992, pg 24.)

• "The Drums of Ulupu" on page 71 described unusual rhythms produced by the Morse-Thue sequence. Harry J. Smith, after reading this chapter, produced several IBM PC programs allowing you to hear the rhythms on a personal computer. He remarks, "The rhythms are memorable, recognizable, definitely not random, and all the versions remind you of the others." His programs are in MS-DOS 5.0 QBasic. For information, contact: H. Smith, 19628 Via Monte Dr., Saratoga, CA 95070.

A.4 Descriptions of Color Plates

To produce the color plates for 2-D patterns, I used an IBM 3090 mainframe computer. To produce the 3-D representations, I used an IBM RISC System/6000. Resolution varied between 600x600 and 1500x1500 pixels per picture. The programming language was either PL/I or C.

Cover image: The "brain" was simulated by tracing the trajectory of an irregularly oscillating conical pendulum. For each instant in time, the pendulum leaves behind a sphere at its current position. Over time, the collection of sphere traces out the irregular, bumpy, brain-like pattern. The sphere collection is turned upside down for artistic effect. (You can also achieve similar effects by executing a random walk on a hemisphere.) The background is constructed using randomly positioned spheres superimposed on an image of the moon, taken through a Celestron telescope, centering on the moon's Mare Crisium. The moon photo is image-processed so that it resembles a gaseous cloud. The graphics computation was executed on an IBM RISC System/6000. I find that images such as these, which combine physics, astronomy, and mathematics in a fanciful setting, do much to stimulate young peoples' interest in studying physics and astronomy!

1. Lava-like form produced by the 3-D algorithm described in "Lava Lamps in the 21st Century" on page 109.

2. Lava-like form produced by the 3-D algorithm described in "Lava Lamps in the 21st Century" on page 109.

3. Lava-like form produced by the 3-D algorithm described in "Lava Lamps in the 21st Century" on page 109.

4. Bachnoff Klein Bottle surface. (See "Mandalas, Screws, Pears, and Klein Bottles" on page 97.)

5. Mandala surface. (See "Mandalas, Screws, Pears, and Klein Bottles" on page 97.)

6. Pear surface. (See "Mandalas, Screws, Pears, and Klein Bottles" on page 97.)

7. Screw surface. (See "Mandalas, Screws, Pears, and Klein Bottles" on page 97.)

8. Gopalsamy mapping for $x \to -2xy + c_1$, $y \to -(x^2 - y^2) + c_2$. ($c_1 = c_2 = -0.19$).

9. Lundin 2-D map. (See "Labyrinthine Lundin Curves" on page 103)

10. Worm sculpture produced by mathematical equations. Backround eyes are described in "Interlude: I See Your Eyes at Night in Dreams" on page 31.

11. Eyescape, described in "Interlude: I See Your Eyes at Night in Dreams" on page 31.

12. Lava-like form produced by the 3-D algorithm described in "Lava Lamps in the 21st Century" on page 109.

13. Halley fractal map. The recipe for this form is given in my book *Computers, Pattern, Chaos, and Beauty* (St. Martin's Press, NY, 1990). See "Fractal Spiders and Frame-Robertson Bushes" on page 87 for similar patterns.

14. Kaleidoscope design produced using methods described in "Electronic Kaleidoscopes for the Mind" on page 23.

15. Kaleidoscope design produced using methods described in "Electronic Kaleidoscopes for the Mind" on page 23.

16. Kaleidoscope design produced using methods described in "Electronic Kaleidoscopes for the Mind" on page 23.

17. Colored froth and bubbles characterizing the behavior of the iteration of the complex-valued function:

$$f(z): z \to \lambda \left[(\lambda z - \lambda/z) - \frac{1}{(\lambda z - \lambda/z)^2} \right] \qquad (A.2)$$

(λ plane map, with $z_0 = 0.5$.)

18. Image processed froth. (See previous.)

19. Modified Pokorny function computed for the iteration of $z' = 1/(z^2 + (0.5, 0.1))$ (See "Pokorny Fractals" on page 92).

20. Glynn function computed for the iteration of $z \to z^{1.5} - 0.2$ where z is complex.

21. Glynn function (see previous).

22. Computer-simulated leaf vein pattern (see Credits for more information).

A.5 Acknowledgments and Credits

All mathematically related computer graphics, and all of the color plates, were created by the author.

The copyright for artwork produced by artists featured in the "Interlude" sections, remains with the artists, and I thank them for permission to reproduce their works in this book. I owe a special debt of gratitude to Akhlesh Lakhtakia, Robert Stong, Dawn Friedman, Mike Frame, and Martin Gardner for various helpful suggestions regarding the book. The computer-generated kaleidoscope images represent collaborative research with Prof. Larry Rudolph, Department of Computer Science, Givat Ram Campus, Hebrew University, Jerusalem 91904 Israel. The Terrible Twos analysis is a collaboration with

Ken Shirriff (University of California). Holly Roth drew the bar and pie charts for three figures in this book using Freelance 3.01 running on a PS/2 Model 70. She also imported two clip art diagrams from CorelDraw 2.0 for use in these figures. Stephen Malinowski provided the list of interesting musical patents. Much of the innovating software specifically for physics education (included in "Product Pavan") was listed in: Donnelly, D. (1991) CIP announces winners of second annual software contest. *Computers in Physics*. Nov/Dec 5(6): 636. Quotations at the beginning of several chapters come from Don DeLillo's *Ratner's Star* (Vintage Books: NY, 1980). The several "schema" diagrams are © 1992 by Robert E. Mueller (see "Interlude: Alien Musical Scores" on page 221). I thank Dr. Bruce Boghosian (Thinking Machines Corporation) for encouragement and helpful observations regarding some of the structures seen in the lava. John McIntyre (Physics/Astronomy Dept., Michigan State University) reported the comic book M-set information to me. Philippe Schnoebelen of Grenoble, France, brought the various fairy chess magazines to my attention.

The photograph of two people looking at a stick figure in "Squashed Worlds That Pack Infinity into a Cube" on page 249 is from Norman Kinzie. Art Appel photographed the moon which I used, after image processing, for the background in the cover.

The Farsi script at the beginning of the book (for the ancient Persian proverb, "The seeker is a finder") was written by Jalil A. Taghizadeh of Sherman Oaks, CA. There are various beautiful and exotic styles of writing this same phrase with Farsi characters. Mr. Taghizadeh also sent me an additional representations for the same phrase:

Below is an ornate Arabic script for the seal and signature of Abdul-Medjid Ibn

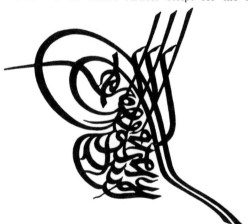

Mahamud, Sultan of Turkey (1822-1861). The chaotic pattern at the end of this section was sent to me by Arthur C. Clarke. To produce the pattern, Cherene (12 years old) and Tamara (6 years old) used a "secret" ingredient: wax crayons. They have given me permission to reveal the entire recipe here. Place a pan into an oven (300 degrees F). After 30 minutes, remove the pan, using a glove. Turn the pan upside down. Place a foil on it. Draw a shape on the foil with a crayon. Place a paper onto the wax and smooth it. Remove the paper. The photograph of the computer and broken television screen in the technology chapter is © 1990 by artist Wayne Draznin, Cleveland, Ohio. His artwork generally takes the form of multi-media installations and is concerned with issues of communication and representation.

Chopin's musical score (Nocturne) is from *Nocturnes and Polonaises* (Dover, NY). Many of the antique artworks in this book come from the Dover Pictorial Archive. Authors for archive books include: R. Huber, E. Gillon, J. Harter, W. Rowe, E. Lehrner,

S. Appelbaum, W. Harlow, and S. Horemis. The various old machinery pictures come from: Rowe, W. (1980) *Machinery and Mechanical Devices*. Dover: NY. The crowd scene photos are from Jim Kalett/Photo Researchers. Others old digrams and maps are from a reprint of an 1851 book: Heck, J. (1979) The Complete Encyclopedia of Illustration. Park Lane: NY. The photograph of the children playing the Chinese game Sz'kwa comes from: Bell, R., and Cornelius, M. (1988) *Board Games Round the World*. Cambridge University Press: NY. Gopalsamy numbers are courtesy of G. Gopalsamy, India.

The maze on page 1 is from: Quinn, W. (1975) *Challenging Mazes*. Dover: NY. The frontispiece for "Interlude: Animal Machines" on page 85 is titled "Moped Verwandlung" ("Moped Metamorphosis") © Michael Schulze (from the collection of Ed and Nancy Kienholz, Idaho; photo by Martin Specht). The endpiece photo for the Schulze chapter is titled "Copulation." The Stelarc images are © Stelarc, and the photographers include P. Fernuik and S. Hunter. The piano keyboard in Appendix A.3 is from Nicholas Mucherino. I computed the leaf vein pattern using Ken Shirriff's theory and data on generating fractals from Voronoi diagrams. Given a set of points, the Voronoi polygon around each point is the region of the plane closer to the selected point than to any other.

The "Voyager III" score at the beginning of the music part of the book is from David McCutchen and Jeff Greenwald. Here they have translated the art in the top figure into a score. The drawing is animated with the music. Contact McCutchen, 931 N. Gardner St., W. Hollywood, CA 90046.

The frontispiece for "Mutcer's Marvelous Music Machines" on page 191 shows Swiss-American composer Ernest Bloch (1880 - 1959) with his eminent pupil Roger Sessions (born 1896) in 1923. American composer Sessions' Symphony in E Minor was premiered by the Boston Symphony in 1927. Bloch wrote a notable opera *Macbeth* (1910) and several works based on Jewish culture.

A.6 Additional Mental Machicolation

– included in this section are additional books, videos, and related to stimulate your imagination.[50]

Virtual Reality Books

1. *Virtual Reality*, by J. Rheingold. 384 pgs, Hb, 1991.

2. *Virtual Reality: Adventures in Cyberspace*, by F. Hamit and W. Thomas, 256 pgs, color, 1991.

3. *Artificial Reality*, by M. Krueger. 300 pgs, color, Hb, 1991.

---

[50] As a special service for readers of this book who may find difficulty in locating some of these mind-stimulators, Media Magic has agreed to distribute all items in this section. Write to Media Magic, PO Box 507, Nicasio, CA 94946 for price and order information.

Visualization Books

1. *Visualization in Teaching and Learning Mathematics*, by W. Zimmermann and S. Cunningham, eds.. 223 pgs, color, Pb, 1991.

2. *Envisioning Information*, by E. R. Tufte. 126 pgs, 400 illus., color, Hb, 1990.

3. *Visualization: The Second Computer Revolution*, by R. Friedhoff and W. Benzon. 216 pgs, 200 illus, color, Pb, 1991.

Fractal Books

1. *From Newton to Mandelbrot: A Primer in Theoretical Physics*, by D. Stauffer and H. E. Stanley. 188 pgs, color, Pb, 1990.

2. *Fractals in Your Future*, by R. Lewis. 265 pgs, 250 illus, 1991.

3. *Fractal Forms*, by E. Guyon and H. E. Stanley. 60 pgs, color, Pb, 1991.

Chaos Books

1. *Chaos and Order in the Capital Markets: A New View of Cycles, Prices & Market Volatility*, by E. Peters, 228 pgs, 50 illus, Hb, 1991.

2. *From Clocks to Chaos: The Rhythms of Life*, by L. Glass and M. Mackey. 256 pgs, 99 illus, Pb, 1988.

3. *An Albumn of Fluid Motion*, by M. Van Dyke. 176 pgs, 200 photos, Pb, 1982.

Artificial Life Books

1. *The Recursive Universe: Cosmic Complexity and the Limits of Scientific Knowldege*, by W. Poundstone. 245 pgs, illus, Pb, 1985.

2. *Artificial Life II*, by D. Farmer, C. Langton, S. Rasumussen, and C. Taylor. 840 pgs, color, Pb, 1991.

3. *Cellular Automata: Theory and Experiment*, by H. Gutowitz. 250 pgs, illus, Hb, 1991.

Mathematical Thought Books

1. *Exploring the Geometry of Nature*, by E. Rietman. 194 pgs, illus Pb, 1989.

2. *Islands of Truth: A Mathematical Mystery Crusie*, by I. Peterson. 314 pgs, color, Pb, 1990.

3. *Alternate Realities: Mathematical Modles of Nature and Man*, by J. Casti. 485 pgs, illus, Hb, 1989.

Dimension, Form, and Geometry Books

1. *To Infinity and Beyond: A Cultural History of the Infinite*, by E. Maor. 294 pgs, color, Pb, 1991.

2. *The Fourth Dimension: Toward a Geometry of Higher Reality*, by R. Rucker. 200 pgs, illus, Pb, 1984.

Pattern Books

1. *Universal Patterns – The Golden Relationship: Art, Math, and Nature*, by M. Boles and R. Newman. 272 pgs, illus, Pb, 1991.

2. *Visions of Symmetry: Notebooks, Drawings, and Related Works of M.C. Escher,* by D. Schattschneider. 345 pgs, color, Hb, 1990.

Computer Artist Videos

1. *The Conquest of Form*, by W. Latham. 60 min, 1990.

2. *Moon Drum: Dream Songs Colored by Memories of Prehistory*, by J. Whitney. 60 min, 1991.

Fractal Animation Videos

1. *Mandelbrot and Julia Sets*, by Art Matrix. 2 hours, 1990.

2. *Chaos Made to Order*, by Bourbaki. 30 min, 1991.

Fractal Educational Videos

1. *The Beauty and Complexity of the Mandelbrot Set*, by J. Hubbard. 73 min, 1989.

2. *Simulation/Stimulation: Over the Edge*, by the Students, Faculty and Staff of the Electronic Visualization Lab, Univ. of Illinois, Chicago. 90 min, 1991.

Chaos Educational Videos

1. *Chaos: A Video Demonstration*, by R. Rucker. 30 min., 1990.

2. *Chaos and Randomness*, by C. Sprott. 60 min, 1991.

Virtual Reality Videos

1. *Senate Hearings on Virtual Reality*. 50 min, 1991.

2. *Cyberspace, Power, and Culture*, from Media Magic. 120 min, 1991.

Mathematical Thought Videos

1. *Not Knot*, from the Geometry Center of the University of Minnesota. 20 min, 1991.

2. *Geometrical Metaphors of Life*, by S. Tenen. 108 min, 1989. (Topics: meditation, Hebrew alphabet, self-organization.)

3. *Natural Minimal Surfaces via Theory and Computation*, by D. Hoffman. 80 min, 1990.

Journals

1. *Leonardo: The Journal of the International Society for the Arts, Science, and Technology*

2. *Cyberedge Journal: The World's Premier Newsletter of Virtual Reality.*

Appendix B

Solution Saraband

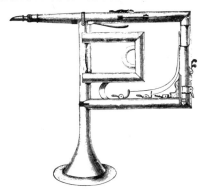

— how to solve a selection of puzzles posed in the book.

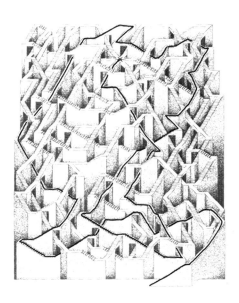

The solution to the computer-generated maze in Figure 1.6 spells out the name "Pickover." The solution for the text maze described in "An Impossible Maze?" on page 13 starts at the "T" in the lower left section and spells out "This is impossible."

The animal eye in "Interlude: I See Your Eyes at Night in Dreams" on page 31 is from a monkey.

All remaining ghost patterns in "Ghost Patterns and Puzzles" on page 49 are non-random.

In Figure 33.1 the ants are most likely to be in the region with the greatest area. In general, the number of ants in a chamber is proportional to the area. Does the interconnectivity of tunnels affect this?

The solution to the chess puzzle in Figure 56.3 is as follows. For the left diagram, 1 R-KKt1!, KxKt, 2 R-R1, K-K5, 3 Q-QKt1 mate. Other possible first moves can also to lead to mate. For the right diagram, 1 Kt-K8!, K-Q5, 2 K-B3, K-K4 (or Q4), 3 Q-K4 mate. Other first moves can also lead to mate.

The solution to the chess puzzle in "Fiendishly Difficult Eight Pawn Problem" on page 321 is:

1	P - B3ch	K - B4
2	Kt - R4ch	K - Kt4
3	P - B4ch	K - R3
4	B - B6	B - Kt8
5	K - B2	B - B7
6	K - Q1	B - Kt8
7	K - K2	B - B7
8	K - B1!	B - Kt8
9	K - Kt2	B - B7
10	K - R3	

The King proceeds (Kt4, B5, K6, Q7) to QB8, and then plays B-Kt7 mate!

The solution to the Knight maze in "Knights in Hell" on page 321 is diagrammed below (rotated 90 degress to save space):

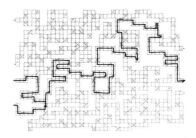

The solution to the Chernoff sequence ("Incredibly Difficult Number Sequences" on page 349) can be understood by examining the following table designed by Stuart Finkelstein (Pennsylvania):

$$2 = 2^1$$

$$12 = 2^2 \times 3^1$$

$$360 = 2^3 \times 3^2 \times 5^1$$

$$75600 = 2^4 \times 3^3 \times 5^2 \times 7^1$$

$$174636000 = 2^5 \times 3^4 \times 5^3 \times 7^2 \times 11^1$$

The 4th term is 75600. The solution for the Balden sequences can be arrived at as follows, according to Bruce Balden. To create the first sequence, you must consider powers of the polynomial $x + 1$ with coefficients modulo 3. Let me clarify. You can compute this with the binomial theorem: just consider the ordinary coefficients modulo 3. Therefore, $x + 1$ is represented as 11. $(x + 1)^2 = x^2 + 2x + 1$ is represented as 121. $(x + 1)^3 = x^3 + 3x^2 + 3x + 1$ is represented as 1331 which is reduced to 1001 since the coefficients are expressed modulo 3. $(x + 1)^4 = x^4 + 4x^3 + 6x^2 + 4x + 1$ is represented as 14641 which is reduced to 11011 when expressed modulo 3. For the second sequence, Balden says "use arithmetic base the golden ratio."

Index

Achilles   250
Africa   133, 138, 247
After Dark   17
AGAR   107
AIDS   379
Albinus, B.   121
Aliens, genes   162
Aliens, pi   151
Alternating sign matrices   387
Ana sequences   35
Anabiosis   35
Anatomy   121
Animal machines   85
Ant farms   173
Apolcalpyse numbers   337
Arabian Nights factorial   355
Archeology   138
Aristotle   250
Art
    Are fractals art?   95
    Genes   161
    Interstellar   107
    Is computer art art?   169, 222
Art and science   ix
Artmann, B.   239
Asimov, I.   ix
Astrahan, I.   149
Attractors   33

Bach's violin   219
Bacon   253
Bacteria, oldest   276
Banchoff Klein bottles   97
Banchoff, T.   227
Bar Codes
    Morse Thue   71

Product   297
    U-numbers   357
Batrachomyomachia   184
Beasley, B.   323
Beauty and the Bits   79
Beetles   246
Bicycles from hell   327
Bijan   71, 155
Bikes   299
Bits   79
Blood, pyramids   399
Blood, spider   400
Book of children   142
Bottle, time   271
Brahmagupta numbers   345
Brain pancakes   130
Brewster, D.   23
Brief History of Time   ix
Bush men   137

Caged Fleas   241
Cage, J.   219
Caldwell, C.   353
Cancer   128
Cantor cheese   38
Cantor set   37
Carey, E.   43
Carlson, S.   ix
Cavali-Sforza, L.   135
Cellular automata   109
Cemeteries of the future   107
Checkers   293
Chernikov patterns   55
Chess
    Black hole   316
    Carnivore   318

Circular   313
Computers   312
Crowded   318
Crushed   318
Eight Pawn Problem   321
Endgames   311
Evolution   318
Fairy   317
Fibonacci   319
Fossil   318
Games   313
Hexagonal   317
Hyperdimensional Knights   236
Infinite   316
Knight art   204
Knight magic square   66
Knights in Hell   321
Madhouse   317
Martian   317
Music   204
Relativistic   315
Too many bishops   318
5x5   318
Chi-shang, Y.   6
Children   141
China   153
Chinese games   143, 155
Chinese lattice designs   6, 7, 8
Chinese lattice mazes   9
Circular chess   313
Civilization   135
Clarke, A.   ix, 12, 385, 414
Clocks   276, 285
Clynes, M.   207
Cole, C.   355
Color plates   412
Comic strip   94
Computer Esophagus   121
Convergence   367
Conway, J.   36
Cook, L.   305
Coprophiles   246
Cornfields   93
Criminals   353
Cro-Magnon game   133
Crop circles   93
Cyberspace   299

da Vinci, L.   14, 169
Davidson, M.   365
Death tunnels   167
DeLillo, D.   414
Detonography   335
Differential equations   33
Dimensions   227
DNA, aboriginals   137
DNA, music   212
Dot patterns   49
Draznin, W.   414
Drum heads   95
Drums of Ulupu   71
Dung beetles   246
Dung, bacteria   276
Dyens, G.   339
Dye, D.   6, 9
Dynamical systems   33

Earthquakes   323
Earthscore notation   237
Eight Pawn Problem   321
Einstein's brain   232
Einstein's children   236
Einstein, A.   vii
Eisley, L.   86
Elephants in spheres   230
Elkies, N.   148, 195, 342
Emirp numbers   343
Emperor's New Mind   ix
Endgames   311
Esophagus, Computer   121
EternityGrams   275
Euglenas   309
Explosion   339
Explosives   335
Exponential notation   390
Extraterrestrial messages   161
Eye   149
Eyescapes   31

Faces   353
Facescapes   209
Factorial, Arabian Nights   355
Family trees   135
Fantastic Archeology   138
Farsi script   414
Feather fractals   33
Feminism   43

Fermat's theorem   148
Fiberoptics   305
Fibonacci chess   319
Fibonacci numbers   337, 341, 343
Fighting fish   63
Flea Cages   241
Fourth dimension   225
Fowles, J.   252
Fractal dimension   12, 38, 94
Fractal fiberoptics   305
Fractals   10
    Ana sequence   35
    Ant farms   174
    Are fractals art?   95
    Bits   79
    Cantor cheese   38
    Cantor set   37
    Comic strip   94
    Cornfields   93
    Dimension   12, 38
    Drum heads   95
    Feather   33
    Feminism   43
    Fiberoptics   305
    Frame-Robertson bushes   87
    Hilbert curves   12
    Likeness sequence   35
    Lundin curves   103
    Mandelbrot set   11, 87
    Mandelbrot set dimension   94
    Mandelbrot, B.   10, 87, 103
    Mazes   10, 12
    Multifractals   175
    Music scores   195
    Pokorny   87
    Self-similarity   103
    Shishikura, M.   94
    Sierpinski gasket   80, 174
    Snowflakes   12
    Spider   87
Frame-Robertson bushes   87
Friden calculators   389

Games
    China   155
    Civilization   137
    Cro-Magnon game   133
    My Computer Esophagus   121
    Pong Hau K'i   143
    Sim Ant   176
    Sim Earth   137
    Sz'wa   155
    Time travel   300
Gardner, M.   ix, 195, 234
Genes
    Art   161
    Children   141
    Human cultures   135
    Human genome project   166
    Messages   161
    Music   211
Genesis   399
Ghost children   141
Ghost patterns   49
Goals, lists   157
Goddard lists   157
Golden ratio   361
Goldfish   410
Gosper snowflakes   305
Greek coins   239
Greeks   361
Greenland Mummies   139
Grossman. R.   209
Gross, A.   198
Guzak, K.   289

Hailstone music   203
Haldane, J.   246
Hand, artificial   187
Hard numbers   376
Hartal, P.   277
Hawking, S.   ix, 276
Hayashi, K.   214
Heads, swelled   393
Heart, circuit   393
Heinlein, R.   225
Hesse, J.   152
Hilbert curves   12
Hilbert mazes   12
Hilgemeir, M.   36
Hippasus   250
Holosculptures   339
Human body   121
Human genome project   166
Hyperbeings   235
Hyperspheres   228

Il Labirinto   7
Immense Journey   86
India   345, 348
Infinity   346
Infinte spaces   249
Ink-splattered scores   202
Insect sculpture   323
Interstellar art   107
Invention, lists   157
IQ   viii
Irrational numbers   250

Jaffee, D.   151
Jaffe, D.   viii, 250
James, R.   95
Japanese   309
Jordan curves   45

Kaleidoscopes   23, 31
Karelitz, J.   26
Karinthi, P.   199, 205
Kim, C.-J.   309
King, S.   185
Klein bottle   237
Knight magic square   66
Knights in Hell   321
Koch curve   12

Laburnum   21
Labyrinth fish   17
Labyrinth parasites   17
Labyrinthistis   21
Labyrinthodontia   17
Labyrinths   17
   See also Mazes
Labyrinthula   21
Languages   137
Latin squares   63
Lattice cages   242
Lattice designs   6, 7, 8
Latvian music   205
Lava Lamps   109
Light pipes   305
Likeness sequence   35
Limit cycle   33
Lists, Goddard   157
Louis XIV   16
Lundin curves   103

Magic square   66
Malinowski, S.   205
Mandalas   97
Mandelbrot set   11
   Cornfields   93
   Dimension   94
   Mazes   11
   Spider fractals   87
Mandelbrot, B.   10, 87, 103
Marbles   233
Markovsky, G.   361
Mathematical formulas   145
Mathematical knowledge   148
Matrices, alternating sign   387
Mazes   3-22
   After Dark   17
   British   8
   Butterfly   19
   Chinese lattice   9
   Church   4, 13
   Computer   7, 9
   da Vinci   14
   Diagonal   15
   Discus Thrower   20
   Egyptian   6
   Fractal   10
   Hampton Court   16
   Henry VIII   16
   Hilbert curve   12
   Italian   7
   Jordan curves   45
   Koch curve   12
   Laburnum   21
   Labyrinth fish   17
   Labyrinth parasites   17
   Labyrinthistis   21
   Labyrinthula   21
   Largest   6
   Louis XIV   16
   Mandelbrot set   11
   Minoan   4
   Möbius   3, 21
   Movies   5
   New Harmony   16
   Octagonal   4
   Stairway   3, 21
   Tamil women   16
   Text   13
   The Ultimate Maze Book   13
   Truchet   14, 17

McCarty, K.   126
McMillan, T.   96
Mean free path   332
Merck   166
Messages in genes   161
Microgrippers   309
Microscapes   365
Minotaur   4
Minsky, M.   201, 203
Möbius maze   21
Moore neighborhood   113
Morse-Thue sequence   71
Mountain climbing   367
Mouths   209
Mozart numbers   206
Mueller, R.   ix, 145, 221
Multifractals   175
Mummies, Greenland   139
Munakata, N.   214
Music   191-222
    Animation machine   205
    Bach's violin   219
    Chess   204
    Christmas   199
    Genes   211
    Hailstone   203
    Ink-splattered   202
    Instrument range   194
    Latvian   205
    Mozart numbers   206
    Painting   199, 205
    Patents   207
    Pigeon   203
    Pink   200
    Random   202
    Score representation   198
    Skyline   203
    Spheres   207
    Sumerian tablets   207
    3n + 1   203
Music Notation Association   206
Musical Americans   197
Musical instruments   197
Mutcer, D.   191, 253

NASA   152
Near-Death Experiences   167
Nicaragua stamps   145
Noah's Ark   399
Nomads   299
Number sequences   349

Ohno, S.   191, 211
OMNI   viii
Oos   253
Organ waiting lists   125

Painting, music   199, 205
Pallas, J.   393
Panama Canal   178
Pappas, T.   235
Parasite numbers   395
Parasites   398
Patents, music   207
Paulos, J.   161, 349, 379, 399
Pears   97
Penrose, R.   ix
Persian proverb   x
Persian script   414
Peterson, I.   94
Peterson, M.   90
Phi   361
Phidias   361
Photography   44
Photomicrographs   365
Pi magic square   67
Picasso, P.   169
Pigeon music   203
Pink random music   200
Pipes   305
Pizza, robots   296
Pi, aliens   151
Pi, genes   161
Plagarism   411
Pokorny fractals   87
Polaroid Corporation   43
Poltz, H.   177
Pong Hau K'i   143
Procter & Gamble   338
Product listing   408
Pullen, W.   7
Pulsating Pumpkins   69
Pyramids of blood   399

Randi, J.   ix
Random Music   202
Random walks   134, 173
Rational numbers   346
Robbins numbers   385
Robot checkers player   293
Robot surgeons   296
Robots, pizza   296

Rosenberg, E.   335
Rudd, J.   69
Rudolph, L.   413
Russell, B.   183
Russo, D.   13, 15, 16

Sagan, C.   166, 185
Sams, G.   93
Schemas   221
Schulze, M.   85
Science-fiction   253
Screen saver   17
Sculpture   69, 85, 97, 323, 339, 393
Sculpture Magazine   410
Scultpure   239
Self-similarity   10, 103
Seventy-five words   56
Sexuality   383
Shadow-matter   237
Shepard, R.   40
Shirriff, K.   375
Shishikura, M.   94
Shruludidi spheres   331
Siamese fighting fish   63
Sierpinski gasket   80, 174
Sim Ant   176
sin(x)/x   103
Skulls   281
Skyline music   203
Slugs   45
Smithson, M.   35
Snowflake curve   12
Snowflakes   95, 305
Solutions   419
s'Soreff, S.   107
Space   225-267
Sparticles   235
Sperm   142
Spider blood   400
Spider fractals   87
Spiders   410
Spirals   177, 180
Square-roots   250
Stairway maze   21
Stamps, Nicaragua   145
Stelarc   187
Stomach, objects in   244
Store, chaos   93

Strange Attractions store   93
Strange attractors   33
Strange series   367
Sumerian tablets   207
Superstrings   234
Swelled heads   393
Symmetry   26, 31
Sz'wa   155

Taghizadeh, J.   414
Tamil women   16
Tarsier   161
Technology   293-319
Teleidoscopes   26
Temple Emanu-El   231
Terrible Twos problem   375
Time   271-290
Time in a bottle   271
Time machines   287
Toilet paper   177, 179
Topology   45
Triangle puzzles   241
Truchet mazes   14
Truchet tiles   14
Tunnels at death   167
Tunnels for drugs   130

U-numbers   357
Ulam, S.   357
Usenet   355

Virtual reality   299
Visible Human Project   129
Voss, R.   200

Wafers   130
Wegner, T.   90
Witten, E.   234
Woolworth building   349
Word lists   183

Xi notation   390

Zeno   249
Zenograms   249

1597 problem   341
666   338

About the Author

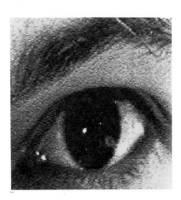

Clifford A. Pickover received his Ph.D. from Yale University's Department of Molecular Biophysics and Biochemistry. He graduated first in his class from Franklin and Marshall College, after completing the four-year undergraduate program in three years. He is author of the popular books *Computers and the Imagination* (1991) and *Computers, Pattern, Chaos, and Beauty* (1990), both published by St. Martin's Press. He is also author of over 200 articles concerning topics in science, art, and mathematics. Pickover is currently an associate editor for the international journal *Computers and Graphics* and is a member of the editorial board for *Computers in Physics* and *Speculations in Science and Technology*. He is a guest editor for *Computers in Physics* for a special issue on chaos, a guest editor for *Speculations in Science and Technology* for a special issue on the future of computing, and a member of the Book Review panel for *Leonardo*, an international journal on topics in art and science. Editor of *The Pattern Book: Recipes for Beauty* (World Scientific, 1993), *Visions of the Future: Art, Technology, and Computing in the Next Century* (St. Martin's Press, 1993), and *The Visual Display of Biological Information* (World Scientific, 1993), and coeditor of the books *Spiral Symmetry* (World Scientific, 1992) and *Frontiers in Scientific Visualization* (Plenum, 1993), Dr. Pickover's primary interest is in scientific visualization.

In 1990, he received first prize in the Institute of Physics' "Beauty of Physics Photographic Competition." His computer graphics have been featured on the cover of several popular magazines, and his research has recently received considerable attention by the press – including *CNN*'s "Science and Technology Week," *Science News*, and *The Washington Post* – and also in international exhibitions and museums. *OMNI* magazine recently described him as "Van Leeuwenhoek's twentieth century equivalent." The July 1989 issue of *Scientific American* featured his graphic work, calling it "strange and beautiful, stunningly realistic." Pickover has received several patents for novel computer input devices and display methodologies, including U.S. Patent 5,095,302 for a 3-D computer mouse. He can be reached at P.O. Box 549, Millwood, New York 10546-0549 USA.